THE LIBRARY OF 1

UNDER THE GENERAL E

JOHN HENRY RALEIGH A... ... WATT

JOHN STUART MILL

Literary Essays

THE LIBRARY OF LITERATURE

5

JOHN STUART MILL

Literary Essays

EDITED, WITH AN INTRODUCTION
AND NOTES, BY EDWARD ALEXANDER
UNIVERSITY OF WASHINGTON

The Bobbs-Merrill Company, Inc.
A SUBSIDIARY OF HOWARD W. SAMS & CO., INC.
PUBLISHERS • INDIANAPOLIS • NEW YORK • KANSAS CITY

John Stuart Mill, 1806–1873

Printed in the United States of America
Library of Congress Catalog Card Number 67–19655
First Printing

To the memory of

SOL FOX

PREFACE

The present volume brings together for the first time, from his published writings, speeches, and letters, John Stuart Mill's views on literature and its place in education and general culture. It is hoped that the book will serve the needs of scholars who have found Mill's literary criticism extraordinarily stimulating and extraordinarily difficult to come by, and that it will excite the interest of students who have not yet discovered the special power and relevance of Mill as critic of literature and culture.

This collection comprises essays on essentially literary subjects and excerpts of literary interest from works primarily concerned with cultural, educational, and sociological questions. Selections in the first group have been presented in their entirety, except in cases (such as "The French Revolution" and "Poems and Romances of Alfred de Vigny") where long passages of straight quotation and plot summary have been deleted.

"Attack on Literature," which originally appeared anonymously, is here printed for the first time under Mill's name. His 1829 debating speech on Wordsworth, which is here printed for the first time, has been placed in an appendix because, although much of the speech is written out for delivery, part of it is in the form of notes.

For their help in shaping this book, I wish to thank Professor Walter E. Houghton of Wellesley College and Professor G. Robert Stange of the University of Minnesota. For useful suggestions and help of various kinds, I am indebted to Professor Irvin Ehrenpreis, University of Virginia; Professor Fredrick M. Garber, State University of New York, Binghamton; Professor John M. Robson, University of Toronto; Professor Samuel N. Rosenberg, Indiana University; and Professor Robert D. Stevick, University of Washington. For typing a considerable part of the manuscript, I wish to thank Mrs.

Arlene F. Olwell. For help which amounted to collaboration, I am grateful to my wife, Leah Alexander.

The following publishers kindly extended permission to quote from works for which they hold copyright: The University of Chicago Press, for F. A. Hayek, *John Stuart Mill and Harriet Taylor: Their Friendship and Subsequent Marriage;* Columbia University Press, for the *Autobiography of John Stuart Mill;* University of Toronto Press, for *The Earlier Letters of John Stuart Mill: 1812–1848*, edited by F. E. Mineka.

Part of my introduction originally appeared in an article entitled "Mill's Theory of Culture" in the *University of Toronto Quarterly*, XXXV (October 1965), 75–88. I am grateful to the University of Toronto Press for permission to include it here.

E.A.

Seattle, Washington
November 1965

CONTENTS

Introduction
THE LIFE OF MILL xiii
CULTURE AND DEMOCRACY xviii
THE FUNCTION OF LITERATURE xxiii
John Stuart Mill—A Chronology xxx
Selected Bibliography xxxii
Note on the Text xxxix

LITERARY ESSAYS

On the Present State of Literature (1827 or 1828) 3
Attack on Literature (1831) 16
On Genius (1832) 30
Browning's *Pauline* (1833) 47
What Is Poetry? (1833) 49
The Two Kinds of Poetry (1833) 64
Tennyson's Poems (1835) 79
FROM Civilization—Signs of the Times (1836) 109
FROM The French Revolution (1837) 131
FROM A Prophecy (1838) 152
FROM Poems and Romances of Alfred de Vigny (1838) 155
FROM Bentham (1838) 188

FROM Coleridge (1840) 206
FROM Inaugural Address to St. Andrews (1867) 221
FROM Autobiography (1873) 255
Selected Letters (1831–1869) 292
Mill's Diary—Excerpts (1854) 333

APPENDIX—Wordsworth and Byron (1829) 343

INTRODUCTION

THE LIFE OF MILL

The emphasis that biographies of John Stuart Mill invariably place upon his education is especially appropriate to the present volume. In the account of his life given in the *Autobiography*, Mill himself says that in the poetry of Wordsworth he found the cure for the mental crisis induced by an overly analytic habit of mind, and that in literature generally he discovered the importance of that cultivation of feeling and imagination which had been absent from his own education.

From the time of his birth in 1806 John Stuart Mill was the subject of an educational experiment carried out by his father, the philosopher and historian James Mill. The elder Mill sought to raise his son to be a political reformer dedicated to the transformation of society along lines laid down by the Utilitarian philosophy of Jeremy Bentham. According to this creed, the exclusive test of all actions and institutions is whether they tend to produce pleasure or pain. In practice, this test meant a radical questioning of all existing customs and institutions that were not conducive to the greatest happiness of the greatest number of people; for Bentham and for James Mill all prospects of practical improvement in human affairs seemed to depend upon the inculcation of the principle that moral and legal usages must justify their existence on rational, rather than customary or traditional grounds.

In order to ensure that all his son's mental associations were rational and Utilitarian rather than customary or traditional, James Mill took complete charge of his education, denied him the company of other children, and kept him out of the reach of adults who were not Utilitarians. All the circumstances that might form his character were carefully controlled. When the young man was allowed to travel to France in 1820, he was put in the charge of Samuel Bentham, Jeremy's brother.

Mill's education was thorough, rigorous, and rational. He began to learn Greek at the age of three, and by the time he was eight, he had read, among other things, all of Herodotus, some of Diogenes Laertius' lives of the philosophers, and the first six dialogues of Plato—at which point he began Latin. "Of children's books, any more than of playthings, I had scarcely any, except an occasional gift from a relation or acquaintance. . . ." When, at thirteen, Mill began the intensive study of the "modern" subject of political economy, he had read widely and deeply in classical literature and ancient and modern history and been thoroughly instructed by his father in arithmetic, algebra, and science. Perhaps more important than the content of this regimen was its character: it was anything but mechanical. "My father never permitted anything which I learnt to degenerate into a mere exercise of memory. He strove to make the understanding not only go along with every step of the teaching, but, if possible, precede it." [1]

What, then, was there to object to in this curriculum? In his autobiography, Mill voices no criticism of his father for having introduced him, as a mere child, into the higher branches of knowledge; in fact, he calls it an exemplary practice. The major criticism which Mill was to make of his father's curriculum was not that it required too much too soon, but that it left something out altogether.

What this something was, Mill did not discover until the autumn of 1826. At this time it suddenly occurred to him that the achievement of the Utilitarian reforms to which his education had dedicated him, and the pursuit of the greatest happiness of the greatest number, would not necessarily make *him* happy. He seemed to have lost his reason for living. He now saw that his education had failed because his father had neglected to cultivate the emotional and imaginative side of his son's nature. James Mill had instilled in his son the revolutionary principles of the Utilitarian creed and had inculcated the

[1] *Autobiography of John Stuart Mill* (New York: Columbia University Press, 1924), pp. 6, 22.

habit of intellectual analysis as a weapon for the dissolution of false beliefs and harmful institutions; now this dissolvent was working upon the revolutionary doctrines themselves. Mill had received the "greatest happiness" philosophy as a set of rational principles; but they had failed to engage his emotions sufficiently to enable them to withstand "the dissolving force of analysis." In fact, lacking even the support that custom and inertia lend to the inherited prejudices of the community, these heterodox Utilitarian principles were even easier to dissolve than the orthodox principles they denied.

Mill's dilemma was solved not by the abandonment of his Utilitarian principles and of his dedication to democratic reform, but by the discovery of the means whereby his social and political principles could be intimately connected with the human instinct for joy. His reading of Wordsworth awakened him to the importance of the emotional side of life and led him to investigate the nature of literature. He began to define his views in 1827 and 1828 in discussions at the London Debating Society, where he found himself pitted against such unleavened Utilitarians as the politician John Arthur Roebuck. In the 1830's he wrote essays that criticized the Utilitarian view of literature as a mere substitute for more harmful forms of social pleasure and sought to demonstrate that literature was only of value to society insofar as it helped the individual to cultivate the powers of his heart and mind.

Mill's apprenticeship to literary criticism in the aftermath of his mental crisis may be thought of as the completion of his education. By 1840 his mind had turned once again to its old preoccupation with social and political questions. But it was a different mind, more aware than before of the need for a dual vision of society as a piece of machinery demanding to be improved, yet always dependent for its effective functioning on the quality and cultivation of unmechanical things called human beings.

In the period of his reaction against orthodox Benthamism, Mill made two new acquaintances who were to have a considerable influence on his life and work. In 1831 the Scottish writer Thomas Carlyle, ever ready to welcome disciples, saw "a new mystic" in the author of *The Spirit of the Age*, a series of articles in which Mill had pointed out many of the evils attendant upon an age of transition in beliefs and institutions. Despite Carlyle's virulent hatred of all that James Mill had preached—Utilitarianism, religious skepticism, democracy, logic, political economy—John Mill was attracted by what he supposed to be the Scotsman's artistic intuition of truths concealed from the logician's consecutive reasoning. Carlyle, for his part, made use of Mill's money and editorial favor to further his own literary career, and of Mill's books and specialized knowledge in the writing of *The French Revolution*. Inevitably, however, it dawned on Carlyle that Mill was not destined to be his disciple. By the time Carlyle came openly to worship force and to preach race hatred, he was fully aware that Mill was not merely his faithless disciple but his formidable enemy.

In Carlyle's view, one of the main reasons for Mill's intellectual waywardness and growing coolness toward himself was the influence of Harriet Taylor. Mill met her in 1830, when she was already married and the mother of two children. She was an attractive woman whose considerable intellectual pretensions were encouraged by the circle of Unitarian Radicals to which she belonged. Under their tutelage she began to write on a variety of subjects, prominent among them the subjection of women in marriage and in society generally. To Mill, Harriet seemed to have an emotional intensity of conviction that was a silent criticism of the more intellectual quality of his own beliefs. Carlyle, of course, had appeared to him in the same light, but Carlyle was not a woman; Mill fell in love with Harriet, and she came to exercise a strong influence over his thought.

Just how strong an influence Harriet exerted is a question still debated, as is the precise nature of their relationship between 1830, when they met, and 1851, when (Harriet's husband, John Taylor, having died in 1849) they married. We can be reasonably sure, however, that the relation between Mill and Harriet was technically Platonic during these two decades, although she lived apart from her husband and Mill spent much time in her company. As for influence, that is always difficult to define, but it is easier to deplore Harriet's influence over Mill's thought (many have done so) than to deny it completely. The seeds of his *On Liberty* (1859) and *The Subjection of Women* (1869), for example, may be found in Harriet's early writings on these subjects; the gradual softening of his objections to socialism in succeeding editions of the *Principles of Political Economy* (originally published in 1848) is directly attributable to her; and the reader of Mill's chronological bibliography of his published works cannot but notice the frequency with which works published after 1846 are described as "a joint production with my wife." Yet we must remember that Mill assimilated a great many influences in the course of his life and synthesized them into a comprehensive philosophy that was greater than the sum of its parts.

The years following Harriet's death in 1858 were a time of intense productivity for Mill. *On Liberty*, which has since become, with the possible exception of Milton's *Areopagitica*, the most famous defense of individual freedom ever written, was published in 1859; in 1861 Mill made his definitive statement on the mixture of promise and danger in democracy in *Considerations on Representative Government;* in 1863, in *Utilitarianism*, he came to terms with the philosophy in which he had been educated as a boy by leavening it with the humanism he had learned as a man. In *An Examination of Sir William Hamilton's Philosophy* (1865), his most ambitious work of the 1860's, Mill returned to the attack, begun long before in *A System of Logic* (1843), against intuitional metaphysics, as being not only false in itself but also harmful in its practical consequences. Here Mill wrote as a philosophical reformer concerned with proving that deep-seated feelings and beliefs are the products of circumstance and association, not ultimate elements of human nature. But in *Auguste Comte and Positivism*, published in the same year, Mill, by sifting the good from the bad in the philosophy of the French founder of sociology, sought to warn overzealous reformers that many of their schemes endangered liberty.

Mill ended an extraordinarily full, varied, and productive life at Avignon on May 7, 1873. His last words, reportedly spoken to his stepdaughter, have been amply confirmed by posterity: "You know that I have done my work."

CULTURE AND DEMOCRACY

After 1840, as we have seen, Mill returned to the nonliterary matters that had preoccupied him prior to his mental crisis. But he returned to them a new man, determined to apply the insights that his mental crisis and recovery from it had given him to the solution of the great social and political questions of his time. Having learned from his own experience that the fulfillment of the objects of Benthamite reform would not ensure individual happiness, he set out to show that the triumph of democracy would not guarantee a high culture. One of the major results of the mental crisis from which Mill had recovered with the help of poetry was a change of political outlook:

> I now looked upon the choice of political institutions as a moral and educational question more than one of material interests, thinking that it ought to be decided mainly by the consideration, what great improvement in life and culture stands next in order for the people concerned, as the condition of their further progress, and what institutions are most likely to promote that. . . .[2]

Mill's greatness lay in his ability to define and espouse the ideals of individual culture without forsaking the goals of Benthamite reform and of democracy itself. For him, the reconciliation of the ancient humanistic ideal of individual cultivation with the liberal and egalitarian ideal of democratic society was the great problem and also the great opportunity of modern civilization.

"Civilization—Signs of the Times" (1836) is an early expression of Mill's lifelong concern with finding the best way to

---

[2] *Ibid.*, p. 120.

reconcile democracy with the humanistic ideals of Greek civilization. Unlike most of his contemporaries, Mill sees that inevitably power must pass from a few individuals to the masses. Already, he points out, the middle and lower classes are almost on a level with their social superiors in knowledge and intelligence. Mill does not deplore this silent revolution; neither does he celebrate it. He tries only to discover the best way of preparing for democracy.

The essay asserts furthermore, that the moral effects of modern civilization, like the political effects, are a mixture of good and bad. In comparison with the masses the individual has lost some of his importance, and what individual energy remains is largely devoted to the pursuit of wealth. Yet manners have grown milder, and there is a greater sensibility to human suffering. The wealthy classes have become more humane but less heroic. The individual depends more than ever on opinion, but less than formerly on well-grounded opinion. There are more books and newspapers and more readers, but the consequence is that people read too much and too quickly to read well. In the absence of established standards, literature becomes merely an expression of current opinion and feeling and gives up trying to elevate them.

But the solution to the special problems of the present, Mill warns, is not a return to the past. There are many desirable elements of human life that are not the natural accompaniments of the growing democratization of society, but this does not mean that they cannot coexist with democracy. Mill argues not only that those advantages which were once enjoyed by a social elite may coexist with democracy but also that they only reach their full flowering in a democratic society:

> All that we are in danger of losing we may preserve, all that we have lost we may regain, and bring to a perfection hitherto unknown; but not by slumbering, and leaving things to themselves, no more than by ridiculously trying our strength against their irresistible tendencies: only by establishing counter-tendencies, which may combine with those tendencies, and modify them.[3]

[3] *Dissertations and Discussions*, 4 vols. (London: Longmans, Green, Reader, and Dyer, 1859–75), I, 188.

Mill hoped to prepare England to receive democracy in such a way that it would become the friend rather than the enemy of culture. He refused to compromise either his high ideal of individual culture or his belief in democratic government. Culture, in his estimation, was not to be saved by the preservation of aristocracy; neither was democracy to be comforted with a mediocre cultural ideal that rose no higher than its popular source. The idea of a cultural elite flourishing in the midst of a hopelessly imperfect society was repellent to Mill. When his friend Alexander Bain got the impression, from reading *On Liberty*, that Mill did not believe reformers should try to convert the world, Mill vehemently corrected him:

I meant nothing of the kind, and hold that we ought to convert all we can. We must be satisfied with keeping alive the sacred fire in a few minds when we are unable to do more—but the notion of an intellectual aristocracy of lumières, while the rest of the world remains in darkness fulfills none of my aspirations—and the effort I aim at by the book is, on the contrary, to make the many more accessible to all truth by making them more open-minded.[4]

Mill's definition of culture was aristocratic only in that he believed all men potential aristocrats. He did not believe that it was either desirable or possible for a man to perfect himself in isolation from his fellow men. He always looked upon knowledge as the means to a social as well as an intellectual end. In his St. Andrews lecture he said that knowledge serves both to exalt and to dignify the nature of the individual, and to make "each of us practically useful to his fellow-creatures." [5]

Mill's own brief career as an active politician illustrates as clearly as any of his activities the way in which he hoped to bring his own high cultural ideals to the great mass of people without in any way debasing those ideals. In politics he was a figure of almost quixotic integrity. In his candidacy for the

---

[4] *Letters of John Stuart Mill*, ed. H. S. R. Elliot, 2 vols. (London: Longmans, Green and Co., 1910), I, 223.

[5] *Inaugural Address Delivered to the University of St. Andrews* (London: Longmans, Green, Reader, and Dyer, 1867), p. 37.

House of Commons in 1865 he minced no words in criticizing his countrymen, and flattered no prejudices. He would not "campaign" but only state his views. When asked by a rally of workingmen whether he had written that workingmen were generally liars, he promptly replied, "I did." [6] A writer promoting Mill's candidacy had the temerity to present him to the voters as not so much a political as a cultural figure, and a rather awesome one at that:

> It is well that the electors of Westminster have undertaken the task of carrying to the House of Commons one whose eminent philosophy embraces all letters, art, and imagination, combines the ancient and the new, reform and tradition, the principle of permanence and the principle of progression, the practical spirit of Bentham and the reverent ideal politics of Coleridge—is catholic, practical, genial, sympathetic. . . .[7]

Although the Tories put forward their man as "the representative of the intelligent classes" and contrasted him with Mill as the embodiment of "popular ignorance," [8] the voters knew better: Mill was elected.

Mill found his model of a democratic culture in ancient Greece. Although he admired American democracy, he thought it an inadequate model for England to imitate. In a letter of 1860 to his disciple, Henry Fawcett, Mill warned that "it is an uphill race, and a race against time, for if the American form of democracy overtakes us first, the majority will no more relax their despotism than a single despot would. But our only chance is to come forward as Liberals, carrying out the democratic idea, not as Conservatives, resisting it." [9] Mill had learned from Alexis de Tocqueville, the French writer and student of American democracy, to fear the tyranny of a

[6] *Autobiography*, p. 199.

[7] W. D. Christie, "Mr. John Stuart Mill for Westminster," *Macmillan's Magazine*, XII (May–October 1865), 96.

[8] *Letters of Mill*, II, 32–33.

[9] MS letter from Mill to Henry Fawcett, February 5, 1860. Mill–Taylor Collection in the British Library of Political and Economic Science, Vol. III.

majority which might impose the imperfect culture of the average man as the ideal of all men.

Only in ancient Athens did Mill find a union of culture with democracy; and he wished to show his countrymen why, as he once wrote to Harriet Taylor, "an average Athenian was a far finer specimen of humanity on the whole than an average Englishman." [10] In 1846 Mill wrote that the ancient Greeks were "the most remarkable people who have yet existed" and that their history was more relevant to Englishmen of the mid-nineteenth century than even the history of their own country.[11] In 1859, in *On Liberty*, he found the Christian ideal of self-government inadequate when measured against the "Greek ideal of self-development." [12] In his discussion of "the ideally best polity" in *Considerations on Representative Government*, he supported his argument for giving ordinary citizens the chance to participate in the work of government by recalling that "the practice of the dicastery and the ecclesia raised the intellectual standard of an average Athenian citizen far beyond anything of which there is yet an example in any other mass of men, ancient or modern." [13]

Unlike other Victorians, Mill did not use the past primarily as a contrast with, and a standard by which to judge, the present. He sought, rather, to realize a synthesis between those parts of the truth that had been grasped in the past but were being overlooked in the present, and those that, merely because they had been ignored in the past, were monopolizing the attention of the present. He believed the achievement of democracy to be the great political object of his time; but he knew that human perfection required more than political jus-

---

[10] *John Stuart Mill and Harriet Taylor*, ed. F. A. Hayek (Chicago: University of Chicago Press, 1951), p. 144.

[11] "Early Grecian History and Legend," *Dissertations and Discussions*, II, 283.

[12] *On Liberty*, ed. Currin V. Shields (New York: The Liberal Arts Press, Inc., 1956), p. 76.

[13] *Considerations on Representative Government*, ed. Currin V. Shields (New York: The Liberal Arts Press, Inc., 1958), pp. 53–54.

tice, and that onto the modern political ideal it was necessary to graft an ancient cultural ideal. Mill never thought of democracy and liberty as self-justifying ends but as the political means of enabling all men to improve themselves in accordance with the highest ideals of Western culture.

THE FUNCTION OF LITERATURE

How does Mill's view of literature serve his belief in a democratic culture? How does his definition of the nature and function of literature give it a vital role in providing democratic societies with a high and noble ideal of individual perfection?

In his attempts to define poetry, and in most of his discussions of individual poets, Mill scrupulously separates poetry from rhetoric and oratory. In the essay "What is Poetry?" and in his review of Carlyle's *The French Revolution,* he refuses the title of poet to any writer who has designs upon his audience, who wishes to inculcate certain doctrines or urge certain actions. The poet's primary task, Mill in effect says, is to be sincere, to give a truthful picture of his own feelings and state of mind.

Such a view of poetry hardly seems the prelude to an exposition of the view that poetry serves a particular social and even political function. If the poet must do nothing more than be true to himself, of what possible use can his poetry be to others? Had not the great critics of the previous century given to the practice of poetry a moral justification which assumed that the poet addressed himself to the social world and used the tools of rhetoric to persuade his audience of moral truths?

Mill was aware of the moral objections that might be made to so "inner-directed" a view of art. But he was aware too that the conditions of the nineteenth century made it impossible for poetry to perform its moral function in the old way. The eighteenth-century poet, if he urged certain moral or political or philosophical doctrines upon his audience, could take it for granted that most of his audience would readily assent to these doctrines (even if it never acted on them). His audience was relatively small and homogeneous, and held many beliefs in common. The nineteenth-century writer, as Mill noted with dismay in his speech "On the Present State of Literature," had a potentially larger, but also more heterogeneous and less cultivated, audience. He had to address a society fiercely sectarian in religion and politics, and divided into factions on most other issues. In such an atmosphere the prudent author with high moral intentions must seek to gain influence by means other than didacticism. George Eliot, Mill's great contemporary who referred to herself as an aesthetic rather than a doctrinal teacher, wrote:

> If Art does not enlarge men's sympathies, it does nothing morally. I have had heart-cutting experience that opinions are a poor cement between human souls; and the only effect I ardently long to produce by my writings, is that those who read them should be better able to *imagine* and to *feel* the pains and the joys of those who differ from themselves in everything but the broad fact of being struggling erring human creatures.[14]

George Eliot's ideal of imaginative sympathy was also espoused by Mill. For Mill believed as firmly as Dr. Johnson that literature should perform a moral function. In his review of Tennyson, which appeared in 1835, just two years after his essays in definition, he declared that the highest end of poetry is "that of acting upon the desires and characters of mankind through their emotions, to raise them towards the perfection of their nature." [15] Poetry, that is, performs its moral function directly, not by urging men to think or to act differently, but by purifying and elevating their emotions so that they will become more receptive to true doctrines and more inclined to good conduct. Poetry is able to work upon the emotions precisely because it does not *try* to do so, but instead retains its artistic integrity.

---

[14] *The Letters of George Eliot*, ed. G. S. Haight, 7 vols. (New Haven: Yale University Press, 1954–55), III, 111.

[15] "Tennyson's Poems," *London and Westminster Review*, XXX (July 1835), 419.

Mill's aesthetic theory always stresses the need for imagination and sympathetic identification. In the essay on Bentham he calls imagination "the power by which one human being enters into the mind and circumstances of another."[16] It is a power characteristic of the poet and one that he cultivates in his reader, who is in effect asked temporarily to suspend his own rhythm of existence and to experience that rhythm which is the essence of a particular poem.[17] Without such imaginative identification, Mill insists, a human being can have no knowledge of the inner life of his fellow men.

Poetry, then, provides a kind of emotional knowledge; and Mill believed that only such knowledge could lead to genuine morality. In one of his articles on Plato, he said that arguments in favor of virtue, never persuaded anyone to *be* virtuous. Knowledge becomes virtue, he argued, only when it takes hold of the feelings–only, that is, when it is the kind of knowledge supplied by poetry.[18]

In 1840 Mill published the second of two laudatory reviews of Tocqueville's *Democracy in America* (1835); and in the second volume of the Frenchman's great work he found a peculiarly democratic justification for the belief that literature performs its moral function by cultivating imaginative sympathy. Tocqueville, as Mill noted in his review,[19] had used a letter written by the seventeenth-century French noblewoman Mme de Sévigné, in which the generally humane and cultivated lady jokes heartlessly about the murder and enslavement of peasants, in order to illustrate the want of fellow-feeling, in aristocratic societies, between the members of different classes. Democratic societies, on the other hand, argued Tocqueville, extended sympathies by breaking down class barriers and creating equality. The ordinary member of a democracy, because

---

16 *Dissertations and Discussions*, I, 354.

17 Mill discusses the supreme importance of rhythm in poetry in the essay on Vigny, *Dissertations and Discussions*, I, 326.

18 "Notes on Some of the More Popular Dialogues of Plato: The *Gorgias*," *Monthly Repository*, VIII (December 1834), 841–842.

19 *Dissertations and Discussions*, II, 45.

he feels himself to be, and often is, equal to all his fellow men, is able to imagine and thus to sympathize with even the worst hardships that his fellows may suffer.

Tocqueville thus provided Mill with a democratic sanction for his theory of the moral function of poetry. For after he had begun to absorb the influence of Tocqueville, Mill's theory of poetry always had a social dimension. It may be seen in the "Vigny" and "Bentham" articles of 1838, in the *Autobiography* which Mill was composing in 1853 and 1854, and in the Inaugural Address at St. Andrews of 1867.

The role that his conception of poetry plays in Mill's social and political philosophy may be understood by considering his argument for the feasibility of a Utilitarian morality in *Utiltarianism*, a work originally published in *Fraser's Magazine* in 1861. In the course of this argument, contained in Chapter Three of *Utilitarianism*, Mill transfers the pattern of his mental crisis and recovery to the solution of a general problem of moral philosophy. He first argues that the moral faculty of man may be developed, without doing violence to human nature, in any one of a number of different ways. Nearly any system of morality, or set of principles, may be inculcated in such a way as to make it speak to the individual with what appears to be the voice of conscience. Yet moral associations of an artificial kind will not take permanent hold unless they appeal to some essential principle of human nature: "Moral associations which are wholly of artificial creation, when intellectual culture goes on, yield by degrees to the dissolving force of analysis." The force of analysis had, as has been shown, nearly dissolved the young Mill's Utilitarian principles. On the basis of his own experience, Mill now warns that if the Utilitarian morality continues to make a purely intellectual appeal, it will indeed be doomed, even if the whole educational system of a country were used to enforce it. Fortunately, however, Mill continues, there exists a foundation for the Utilitarian social philosophy in the "social feelings of mankind." The task of the Utilitarian reformer was no longer simply to articulate and to teach the Utilitarian social philosophy, as Bentham and

James Mill had done; the task was to educate those emotions and sympathies that could make men take pleasure in doing good as defined by Utilitarianism:

Not only does all strengthening of social ties, and all healthy growth of society, give to each individual a stronger personal interest in practically consulting the welfare of others; it also leads him to identify his *feelings* more and more with their good. . . .[20]

Throughout *Utilitarianism* Mill is warning that a social philosophy which does not take into account all that part of life which is unconnected with action or morality will be incomplete and therefore incapable of commanding the full conviction of its supposed adherents. Such incompleteness and such ineffectuality are the penalties meted out to "Utilitarians who have cultivated their moral feelings, but not their sympathies nor their artistic perceptions." [21]

Six years after *Utilitarianism* appeared, Mill recommended poetry as the best means for cultivating the sympathetic and social feelings upon which the Utilitarian ethos was founded. Poetry, he says in the Inaugural Address of 1867, not only makes men love virtue and eschew selfishness, but it also—

brings home to us all those aspects of life which take hold of our nature on its unselfish side, and lead us to identify our joy and grief with the good or ill of the system of which we form a part; and all those solemn or pensive feelings, which, without having any direct application to conduct, incline us to take life seriously, and predispose us to the reception of anything which comes before us in the shape of duty.[22]

Thus poetry transforms our duty into our pleasure and makes possible the "disinterested love of virtue" that is recommended, surprising as it may seem to readers unacquainted with that work, in *Utilitarianism*.[23] The unleavened Utili-

---

20 *Utilitarianism*, ed. Oskar Piest (New York: The Liberal Arts Press, Inc., 1957), pp. 39–42.

21 *Ibid.*, p. 27.

22 *Inaugural Address*, p. 45.

23 *Utilitarianism*, p. 48.

tarian pursues virtue because it is conducive to pleasure; the Utilitarian leavened by poetry and its habitual enforcement of the association between virtue and pleasure comes to regard virtue as a good in itself. Poetry, as defined in the Inaugural Address, thus provides the motive power for the Utilitarian morality set forth in the earlier work.

Yet, in the same Inaugural Address that judges poetry by its social utility, Mill has much to say about the power of poetry to elevate the individual. For Mill believed that poetry performs its moral function not only democratically, by extending sympathies, but also aristocratically, by elevating them. Because he was aware that democracy could not supply the distinctively aristocratic virtues of heroism, nobility, and style, he hoped that literature would. In a review article of 1838 he deplored the way in which the modern system of education had removed the literature of chivalry and romance from the curriculum:

> The chivalrous spirit has almost disappeared from books of education; the popular novels of the day teach nothing but (what is already too soon learnt from actual life) lessons of worldliness, with at most the huckstering virtues which conduce to getting on in the world; and for the first time perhaps in history, the youth of both sexes of the educated classes are universally growing up unromantic.

Mill went on to praise the book he was reviewing because it presented to the imagination pictures of heroic men and women, "and greatly is any book to be valued, which in this age, and in a form suited to it, does its part towards keeping alive the chivalrous spirit." [24]

Thus, although he was aware of the failures of sympathy that characterized works such as the *Chronicles* of the fourteenth-century French poet Jean Froissart (and the society they depicted), Mill did not forget that the heroic impulse that inspired such works was much needed in democratic ages. He therefore criticized modern writers who, in their dogmatic

[24] "A Prophecy," *Dissertations and Discussions*, I, 285.

"realism" and worship of the ordinary, forgot that from the heroic characters of ancient literature "not only the noblest minds in modern Europe derived much of what made them noble, but even the commoner spirits what made them understand and respond to nobleness." [25]

In the Inaugural Address Mill combines his two definitions of poetry's power of moral inspiration. Only poetry, he argues, can cause us to sympathize with elevated ideals, but it is not only loftiness or heroic feelings that poetry cultivates. "Its power is as great in calming the soul as in elevating it—in fostering the milder emotions, as the more exalted." [26]

Mill's definition of poetry's moral function as its power to arouse imaginative sympathy is the link between his theory of literature and his idea of a democratic culture. By widening the sympathies of men and extending them to more objects, poetry re-enforces the peculiar power of democratic society; by elevating the sympathies of men, poetry brings to democratic society precisely those aristocratic qualities that it lacks. For these reasons Mill came to believe that "upon the existence of the capacity for sympathy rests the possibility of any cultivation of goodness and nobleness and the hope of their ultimate entire ascendancy." [27]

---

[25] *Ibid.*, I, 284.

[26] *Inaugural Address*, p. 45.

[27] *Three Essays on Religion* (London: Longmans, Green, Reader, and Dyer, 1874), p. 49.

JOHN STUART MILL

A CHRONOLOGY

1806 Born May 20, at Pentonville, London, the son of James Mill and Harriet Burrow Mill.

1809 Begins to learn Greek as part of the rigorous education given him by his father.

1819 Having already been instructed by his father in Greek, Latin, arithmetic, algebra, science, and classical literature, he begins the intensive study of political economy.

1820–21 With Sir Samuel Bentham (brother of Jeremy Bentham) in France. The visit helps to develop Mill's deep interest in the thought and society of continental Europe.

1822 The reading of Jeremy Bentham's *Traité de Législation* gives Mill a philosophy and even "a religion." He also founds the Utilitarian Society.

1823 Gains financial security by assuming a post in the East India Company's Examiner's Office, where his father was a high official.

1824 James Mill founds the *Westminster Review*, and John publishes his first articles in it.

1825 Helps to found the London Debating Society. Edits Bentham's *Rationale of Judicial Evidence*.

1826 Suffers a mental crisis, and recovers.

1831 Publishes seven articles called *The Spirit of the Age* in *The Examiner*.

1835 Edits *London Review*.

1836–40 Edits *London and Westminster Review*; is its sole proprietor from 1838 to 1840.

1843 Publishes *A System of Logic*, which he had been writing since 1830.

1844 Publishes *Essays Upon Some Unsettled Questions of Political Economy*.

1848 Publishes *Principles of Political Economy*.

1851 Marries Mrs. Harriet Hardy Taylor after a friendship of twenty-one years.

1853–54 Writes first draft of *Autobiography.*
1854–55 Tours France, Italy, Sicily, Corfu, and Greece.
1858 Retires from East India Company and goes with Harriet to the Continent. She dies at Avignon in November.
1859 Publishes *On Liberty*, first two volumes of *Dissertations and Discussions*, *Thoughts on Parliamentary Reform.*
1861 Publishes *Considerations on Representative Government.*
1863 Publishes *Utilitarianism* (reprinted from *Fraser's Magazine*, October–December 1861).
1865 Elected to Parliament from Westminster. Publishes *An Examination of Sir William Hamilton's Philosophy* and *Auguste Comte and Positivism.*
1866–67 Passionately involved in prosecution of Governor Eyre.
1867 Publishes third volume of *Dissertations and Discussions.* Gives Inaugural Address as Rector of the University of St. Andrews.
1868 Defeated in attempt for second term in Parliament; rejoins his stepdaughter, Helen Taylor, in Avignon.
1869 Edits and publishes his father's *Analysis of the Phenomena of the Human Mind.* Publishes *The Subjection of Women*, written in 1861.
1870 Works at bringing *Autobiography* up to date.
1871 Publishes seventh edition of *Principles of Political Economy.*
1872 Publishes definitive eighth edition of *System of Logic.*
1873 Dies of erysipelas at Avignon on May 7. His last words, reportedly spoken to his stepdaughter, were, "You know that I have done my work." The *Autobiography*, edited by Helen Taylor, was posthumously published.
1874 *Three Essays on Religion* posthumously published.

SELECTED BIBLIOGRAPHY

WORKS BY MILL

I. *Writings of Literary Interest*

"Attack on Literature," *The Examiner*, No. 1219 (June 12, 1831), pp. 369–371.

Autobiography. Edited by Helen Taylor. London: Longmans, Green, Reader, and Dyer, 1873. The closest to a "definitive" version presently in print is the edition by John Jacob Coss (New York: Columbia University Press, 1924).

"Bentham," *London and Westminster Review*, XXIX (August 1838), 467–506. Reprinted in *Dissertations and Discussions*, I, 330–392.

"Civilization—Signs of the Times," *London and Westminster Review*, XXV (April 1836), 1–28. Reprinted in *Dissertations and Discussions*, I, 160–205.

"Coleridge," *London and Westminster Review*, XXXIII (March 1840), 257–302. Reprinted in *Dissertations and Discussions*, I, 393–466.

"Comparison of the Tendencies of French and English Intellect," *Monthly Repository*, VII (November 1833), 800–804.

"The French Revolution," *London and Westminster Review*, XXVII (July 1837), 17–53.

Inaugural Address Delivered to the University of St. Andrews, 1 February 1867. London: Longmans, Green, Reader, and Dyer, 1867.

"Letters from Palmyra," *London and Westminster Review*, XXVIII (January 1838), 436–470. Reprinted, in small part, in *Dissertations and Discussions*, I, 284–286.

"Macaulay's *Lays of Ancient Rome*," *Westminster Review*, XXXIX (February 1843), 105–113.

"Notes on Some of the More Popular Dialogues of Plato," *Monthly Repository*, VIII (February–December 1834), 89–99, 203–211, 404–420, 633–646, 691–710, 802–815, 829–842; IX (February–March 1835), 112–121, 169–178.

"On Genius," *Monthly Repository*, VI (October 1832), 649–659.

"On the Present State of Literature," *The Adelphi*, I (January 1924), 681–693. A speech delivered in 1827 or 1828.

"Periodical Literature—Edinburgh Review," *Westminster Review*, I (April 1824), 505–541.

"Poems and Romances of Alfred de Vigny," *London and Westminster Review*, XXIX (April 1838), 1–44. Reprinted in *Dissertations and Discussions*, I, 287–329.

"Tennyson's Poems," *London and Westminster Review*, XXX (July 1835), 402–424.

"Theatrical Examiner," *The Examiner*, No. 1270 (June 3, 1832), p. 358.

"The Two Kinds of Poetry," *Monthly Repository*, VII (October 1833), 714–724. Reprinted in *Dissertations and Discussions*, I, 77–94.

"What is Poetry?" *Monthly Repository*, VII (January 1833), 60–70. Reprinted, in revised form, in *Dissertations and Discussions*, I, 63–77.

"Writings of Junius Redivivus," *Monthly Repository*, VII (April 1833), 262–270.

II. *Other Writings*

Auguste Comte and Positivism. London: Longman, Green, Longman, Roberts & Green, 1865.

Consideration on Representative Government. London: Parker, Son, and Bourn, 1861.

Dissertations and Discussions, Political, Philosophical, and Historical. Reprinted Chiefly from the Edinburgh and Westminster Reviews. 2 vols. London: John W. Parker and Son, 1859. 3 vols. London: Longmans, Green, Reader, and Dyer, 1867. 4 vols. London: Longmans, Green, Reader, and Dyer, 1875.

Essays on Some Unsettled Questions of Political Economy. London: J. W. Parker, 1844.

An Examination of Sir William Hamilton's Philosophy. London: Longman, Green, Longman, Roberts & Green, 1865.

On Liberty. London: J. W. Parker and Son, 1859.

Principles of Political Economy. London: J. W. Parker and Son, 1848. The definitive edition is that edited by John M. Robson, with an Introduction by V. W. Bladen. 2 vols. Toronto: University of Toronto Press, 1965.

The Spirit of the Age. A series of articles from *The Examiner* (January–May 1831). Reprinted, with an Introduction by F. A. Hayek. Chicago: University of Chicago Press, 1942.

The Subjection of Women. London: Longmans, Green, Reader, and Dyer, 1869.

A System of Logic. 2 vols. London: J. W. Parker, 1843. The definitive edition is the eighth, published in 1872, reissued by Longmans, Green in 1959.

Thoughts on Parliamentary Reform. London: J. W. Parker and *Son*, 1859.

Three Essays on Religion. London: Longmans, Green, Reader, and Dyer, 1874.

Utilitarianism. London: Parker, Son, and Bourn, 1863. Reprinted from *Fraser's Magazine* (October–December 1861).

III. *Correspondence, Journals, Early Drafts*

The Earlier Letters of John Stuart Mill: 1812–1848. Edited by Francis E. Mineka. 2 vols. Toronto: University of Toronto Press, 1963.

The Early Draft of John Stuart Mill's "Autobiography." Edited by Jack Stillinger. Urbana: University of Illinois Press, 1961.

John Mill's Boyhood Visit to France: Being a Journal and Notebook Written by John Stuart Mill in France, 1820–21. Edited by Anna Jean Mill. Toronto: University of Toronto Press, 1960.

John Stuart Mill and Harriet Taylor: Their Friendship and Subsequent Marriage. Edited by F. A. Hayek. Chicago: University of Chicago Press, 1951.

The Letters of John Stuart Mill. Edited by Hugh S. R. Elliot. 2 vols. London: Longmans, Green and Co., 1910.

WORKS ABOUT MILL

The following list includes only critical writings that deal with Mill's literary criticism.

Abrams, M. H. *The Mirror and the Lamp: Romantic Theory and the Critical Tradition.* New York: Oxford University Press, 1953. Deals with Mill's contribution to the development of the expressive theory of poetry.

Alexander, Edward. *Matthew Arnold and John Stuart Mill.* New York: Columbia University Press, 1965. Shows similarity between the views of Arnold and Mill on the importance of literature in modern culture and sees Mill as a blend of humanism and liberalism.

———. "Mill's Theory of Culture: The Wedding of Literature and Democracy," *University of Toronto Quarterly*, XXXV (October 1965), 75–88. Discusses the role of literature in Mill's social and political theory.

Cooney, Seamus. " 'The Heart of That Mystery': A Note on John Stuart Mill's Theory of Poetry," *Victorian News Letter*, No. 21 (Spring 1962), pp. 20–23. The article takes as its point of departure Mill's letter to Caryle of April 11–12, 1833 (see below, p. 300).

Hainds, J. R. "J. S. Mill's *Examiner* Articles on Art," *Journal of the History of Ideas*, XI (1950), 215–234. Reprints, with some comment, several of Mill's reviews of theatrical performances and songbooks; a useful complement to the literary essays.

———. "J. S. Mill's Views on Art." Unpublished doctoral dissertation, Northwestern University, 1939.

Haines, L. F. "Mill and 'Pauline': The 'Review' that 'Retarded' Browning's Fame," *Modern Language Notes*, LIX (June 1944), 410–412.

Houghton, Walter E. *The Victorian Frame of Mind: 1830–1870.* New Haven: Yale University Press, 1957. Stresses the essentially Romantic ideal of human nature in Mill's writings.

Kitchel, Anna T. *George Lewes and George Eliot: A Review of Records.* New York: The John Day Company, 1933. Presents

Mill's letters to Lewes and uses them to illustrate the intimacy of their relationship and the nature of Mill's influence over the younger man.

Mill, Anna Jean. "John Stuart Mill's Visit to Wordsworth," *Modern Language Review*, XLIV (July 1949), 341–350.

Mineka, Francis E. *The Dissidence of Dissent: The Monthly Repository, 1806–1838.* Chapel Hill: University of North Carolina Press, 1944. Discusses Mill's *Repository* essays on literature.

McMahon, A. B. "Annotated Copy of Browning's Pauline," *Dial*, XXXI (1901), 229–230.

Ong, Walter J. "Mill's Pariah Poet," *Philological Quarterly*, XXIX (July 1950), 333–344. Criticizes Mill for not completely disavowing his Utilitarian background in his reaction against Benthamism.

Packe, Michael St. John. *The Life of John Stuart Mill.* New York: The Macmillan Company, 1954. The standard life of Mill; sets the reviews of Browning and Tennyson against the background of Mill's varied youthful activities.

Pater, Walter Horatio. *Appreciations: With an Essay on Style.* London: Macmillan and Company, 1889. The "Wordsworth" essay concludes with some interesting comment on Mill's appreciation of Wordsworth.

Robson, John M. "J. S. Mill's Theory of Poetry," *University of Toronto Quarterly*, XXIX (July 1960), 420–438. Shows the place of Mill's theory of poetry in his ethical philosophy and demonstrates his lifelong concern with the importance of literature.

Shannon, Edgar F. *Tennyson and the Reviewers: A Study of His Literary Reputation and of the Influence of the Critics upon His Poetry 1827–1851.* Cambridge: Harvard University Press, 1952. Mill is one of the critics whose influence upon Tennyson is studied.

Sharpless, Francis P. "The Literary Criticism of John Stuart Mill." Unpublished doctoral dissertation, Princeton University, 1963. Traces the process by which Mill tried to reconcile his poetic and imaginative interests with his inherited Utilitarian philosophy, and discusses at length Mill's conception of the philosopher-poet.

———. "William Johnson Fox and Mill's Essays on Poetry," *Victorian News Letter*, No. 27 (Spring 1965), pp. 18–21. Shows the relationship between the critical writings of Mill and the clergyman.

Warren, Alba H., Jr. *English Poetic Theory: 1825–1865*. Princeton: Princeton University Press, 1950. Analyzes "Thoughts on Poetry and Its Varieties," the revised version of Mill's 1833 essays on poetry; concludes they are "full of half-truths" which are nevertheless valuable for the study of Victorian poetry.

Woods, Thomas. *Poetry and Philosophy: A Study of the Thought of John Stuart Mill*. London: Hutchinson, 1961. Assesses the influence of poetry, especially Wordsworth's, upon Mill's thought.

NOTE ON THE TEXT

In the case of essays which we know Mill to have seen through the press at least twice, once in periodical form and a second time in *Dissertations and Discussions*, I have used the later versions. Actually, they rarely vary substantially from the original, for the reason that Mill states in the Preface to *Dissertations and Discussions* (1859):

> Every one whose mind is progressive, or even whose opinions keep up with the changing facts that surround him, must necessarily, in looking back to his own writings during a series of years, find many things, which, if they were to be written again, he would write differently, and some, even, which he has altogether ceased to think true. From these last I have endeavoured to clear the present pages. Beyond this, I have not attempted to render papers written at so many different, and some of them at such distant, times, a faithful representation of my present state of opinion and feeling. I leave them in all their imperfection, as memorials of the states of mind in which they were written, in the hope that they may possibly be useful to such readers as are in a corresponding stage of their own mental progress.

I have adhered to the original titles of these essays because they are always more accurate and informative than those Mill gave to the reprinted versions in *Dissertations and Discussions.*

The text of the *Autobiography* presents a special problem. In 1924 Columbia University Press published what purported to be the "definitive" edition of the *Autobiography*, inasmuch as it was based on the Columbia University Library manuscript, the final holograph version of the *Autobiography*. Unfortunately, as Professor Jack Stillinger has pointed out, the published edition departs from the manuscript in some nine hundred particulars, including at least fifty-four substantive variants.[1] I have therefore resorted to the Columbia manuscript in order to establish an authentic text for those parts of the *Autobiography* that appear in this volume. I should like to acknowledge the kindness of the Columbia University Library in making the manuscript available for my use.

1 "The Text of John Stuart Mill's *Autobiography*," *Bulletin of the John Rylands Library*, XLIII (1960), 220–242.

Mill's letters from the years 1812–1848 have been selected from the excellent scholarly edition of Professor Francis E. Mineka and may be fully relied on for authenticity. Professor F. A. Hayek's edition of the correspondence between Mill and Harriet Taylor, from which I have taken five letters, provides a reliable, scholarly text, but it should be noted that the informal nature of these often hastily scribbled letters made necessary, as Professor Hayek explains in his Introduction, "a reasonable compromise between faithfully reproducing the general character of the manuscripts and achieving easy readability." Letters written during the last twenty-five years of Mill's life come from the collected edition of Mill's correspondence edited by Hugh S. R. Elliot and published in 1910. This collection is not edited according to the strict canons of "modern" (i.e., post–1920) literary scholarship, but it will have to serve until the edition of Mill's later (1849–1873) letters, now being prepared by Professor Mineka and Professor Dwight N. Lindley, is published. Bracketed words or phrases or dates in the letters printed in this volume are editorial insertions.

Throughout this volume, Mill's notes are indicated by asterisks and daggers, and the present editor's notes by numerical superscripts.

JOHN STUART MILL

Literary Essays

On the Present State of Literature

1827 or *1828*

If this lecture was indeed delivered in 1827 or 1828, it is of interest, apart from its intrinsic value, as Mill's earliest public statement about literature and also as being roughly contemporaneous with his mental crisis. Certainly the remark about Wordsworth being the only living poet of the first rank might be expected from someone who had just recovered his mental health through the reading of Wordsworth's poetry.

Although Mill's abrupt dismissal of the subject of poetry here may seem odd, considering that almost all his literary essays of a few years later were to deal with poetry, it is both understandable because of its date and consistent with his lifelong view that prose was a more usable medium than poetry for expressing the conflicts of the nineteenth century. We must remember that in 1827 Wordsworth and Coleridge were many years past their prime, Keats, Byron, and Shelley were dead, and Tennyson had not yet appeared on the scene.

The lecture's main argument is that a decline in the spirit and quality of literature has resulted from the peculiar characteristics of modern civilization. In advancing this view, "On the Present State of Literature" is a forerunner of such fuller and more serious attempts to measure the effects of modern society upon the cultural life as *The Spirit of the Age* (1831) and "Civilization" (1836). As he often did in the years immediately following his mental crisis, Mill here dwells upon the evil effects of the movement toward social democracy. Modern writers debase both subject matter and style, he charges, by their attempts to appeal to that vast audience which reads but does not think.

WHEN I PROPOSED this question, I wondered rather what subject it might be useful to the society [1] to discuss, than what I

First published in *The Adelphi*, I (January 1924).

[1] London Debating Society, organized in 1825 by Mill and some of his friends.

myself was equal to, not to mention other deficiencies (for the extent of my reading was never adequate to so vast a question), and now after a lapse of six months I have entirely lost the train of thought which suggested it. Fortunately the duty of an opener is rather to indicate the topics than to discuss them. I leave it to others to institute an elaborate comparison between our old and new writers and between our own and those of any other country. I myself would rather hint at the principal vices which appear to me to distinguish the literature of the day and the circumstances peculiar to our own times by which those vices seem to me to have been generated.

The word literature has several acceptations: in its most confined sense it means poetry and novels, in its widest every written or spoken composition. Conformably to what I think the established usage, I shall use it in a sense intermediate beween these two extremes, not confining it to works of imagination only nor yet extending it to comprehend works of pure science and philosophy, in which I confess we rank higher than at any former period. I include in literature all which can be denominated popular publications, all which address themselves to the general reader, whether they are intended for amusement only or profess to contain discussions on political, moral, or, in the narrow sense of the word, literary subjects. In these compositions, we are to distinguish two things, the matter and the manner. The literature of any country may be properly said to have deteriorated, if its tendency in regard to the opinions and sentiments which it inculcates has grown worse, and if it is less distinguished than formerly by the beauties of composition and style. In both these respects I am inclined to think that our literature has declined and is declining. In order to establish this, it is not necessary that I should deny that we possess at present writers of merit, perhaps equal in their respective lines to any who have preceded them. When we speak of the character of our literature, we do not mean that of particular writers but the general spirit and quality of the mass: if this has degenerated, our literature has degenerated and my case is made out.

I say little about poetry because nobody will contest that we have no one poet of the first rank, unless it be Wordsworth, and he will probably never write any more. No new poets have arisen or seem likely to arise to succeed those who have gone off the stage or speedily will. I am not sure that I am able to assign any cause of our being thus left without poets, as it seems probable that we soon shall be, and if I were to attempt it it would lead me into a longer discussion than the society would be disposed to listen to. I therefore leave the fact to speak for itself and shall confine myself to our prose writers of whose degeneracy I feel myself more capable of divining the cause.

The influence of literature upon civilization is a topic which has frequently been insisted upon, and certainly not oftener than its importance deserves. The influence of civilization upon literature, though not less remarkable, has not perhaps received from philosophers all the attention which is its due. We all see how individuals (the writer) act upon masses (the readers), but it is not so obvious at first sight to what a prodigious extent masses react upon individuals, and we are perhaps too ready to ascribe the peculiar modes of thinking which are prevalent in every age to its literary men, without considering that the majority of literary men take their colour from the age in which they live.

Every man is a man long before he is a poet or a philosopher. Thousands of impressions are made upon the mind from without before it acquires the power of originating a single one from within. Every man, long before he begins to think or to write, has imbibed more or less of the opinions, the sentiments, the modes of thinking and acting, the habits and associations of that portion of mankind among whom his lot is cast. We all know the power of early impressions over the human mind and how often the direction which they give decides the whole character, the whole life of the man. The greatest men of every age, generally bear a family likeness to their contemporaries: the most splendid monuments of genius which literature can boast of bear almost universally in a greater or less degree the stamp of their age. But over the vast majority of literary men the spirit of their age rules absolutely supreme, because they studiously endeavour to resemble it, and not only imitate but are apt to caricature its leading peculiarities.

It is the demand in literature, as in most other things, which calls forth the supply. Among mental as well as among physical endowments, that is most cultivated which is most admired. When the public bestowed so much of its admiration upon skill in cutting throats that it had very little to spare for anything else, all the ardent characters betook themselves to the trade of blood, and made it their pride to be distinguished chiefly by the warlike virtues. At other times, when the chief source of reputation was oratorical or poetical merit everybody who possessed or thought he possessed genius was an orator or a poet. There have always been men, who, without much aiming at reputation, wrote chiefly to please themselves or to improve their readers. But the grand object of writers in general is success. The qualities most calculated to ensure success constitute the sole idea they have of merit: they cultivate in their own minds a habit of being pleased with that which they find pleasing those to whom they address themselves: their aim is to be read and admired, and the degree in which that aim is successful, is the test by which they try their own merits and those of others. The weaker minds cannot resist the contagion of the common opinion or the common taste: and such of the stronger as prefer the honour and profit of pleasing others to the satisfaction of pleasing themselves, set the example to their numerous imitators of sailing with the stream.

Assuming therefore as an indisputable truth, that the writers of every age are for the most part what the readers make them, it becomes important to the present question to consider who formed the reading public formerly, and who compose it now.

The present age is very remarkably distinguished from all other ages by the number of persons who can read, and, what is of more consequence, by the number who do. Our working classes have learned to read, and our idle classes have learned to find pleasure in reading, and to devote a part of that time to it which they formerly spent in amusements of a grosser kind. That human nature will be a gainer, and that in a high degree, by this change, no one can be more firmly convinced than I am: but it will perhaps be found that the benefit lies rather in the ultimate than in the immediate effects. Reading is necessary; but no wise or even sensible man was ever made by reading alone. The proper use of reading is to be subservient to thinking. It is by those who read to think, that knowledge is advanced, prejudices dispelled and the physical and moral condition of mankind is improved. I cannot however perceive that the general diffusion (so remarkable in our own day) of the taste for reading, has yet been accompanied by any marked increase in taste for the severer exercises of the intellect; that such will one day be its effect may fairly be presumed; but it has not yet declared itself: and it is to the immense multiplication in the present day of those who read but do not think that I should be disposed to ascribe what I view as the degeneracy of our literature.

In former days the literate and the learned formed a class apart: and few concerned themselves with literature and philosophy except those who had leisure and inclination to form their philosophical opinions by study and meditation and to cultivate their literary taste by the assiduous perusal of the most approved models. Those whose sole occupation was pleasure, did not seek it in books, but in the gaieties of a court, or in field sports and debauchery. The public for which authors wrote was a small but, to a very considerable degree, an instructed public; and their suffrages were only to be gained by thinking to a certain extent profoundly and by writing well. The authors who were then in highest reputation are chiefly those to whom we now look back as the ablest thinkers and best writers of their time. No doubt there were many blockheads among the reading public in those days, as well as in our own, and the blockheads often egregiously misplaced their admiration, as blockheads are wont: but the applause of the blockhead was not then the object aimed at even by those who obtained it, and they did not constitute so large and influential a clan of readers, as to tempt any writer of talent to lay himself out for their admiration. If an author failed in obtaining the suffrages of men of knowledge and taste it was for want of powers not from the misapplication of them. The case is now altered. We live in a refined age, and there is a corresponding refinement in our amusements. It is now the height of *mauvais ton* [2] to be drunk, neither is it any longer considered decorous among gentlemen that the staple of their conversation should consist of bawdy. Reading has become one of the most approved and fashionable methods of killing time, and the number of persons who have skimmed the surface of literature is far greater than at any previous period of our history. Our writers, therefore, find that the greatest success is now to be obtained by writing for the many; and endeavouring all they can to bring themselves down to the level of the many, both in their matter and in the manner of expressing it.

It is notorious that half-instructed persons can never appreciate the highest order of excellence either in thought or in composition. Of deep thought, no one can properly judge but those who think: profound and original ideas can only be properly understood by him who will take the trouble to go through in his own mind the process of thought by which they were arrived at: and a book which gives the trouble of thought, is by those unused to think speedily laid aside as incomprehensible and dull. In like manner the beauties of the highest order in a literary composition are such as cannot be apprehended and felt without the exercise of the thinking faculty. I may instance the works of two of the most highly gifted minds which their respective nations have produced, Demosthenes and Milton. Of these may indeed be affirmed what Quintilian has said with somewhat less justice of Cicero [3]: *sciat etc.* . . .[4] In neither of them is there anything to captivate

---

[2] Vulgarity.

[3] Demosthenes (384–322 B.C.), Greek orator, passionately admired by Mill.—Quintilian (A.D. *ca.* 35–*ca.* 95), great Latin rhetorician.—Marcus Tullius Cicero (106–43 B.C.), Roman orator, politician, and philosopher.

[4] This allusion has not been identified.

a vulgar mind: and if not overawed by their reputation, the dunces and coxcombs would unanimously agree in voting Demosthenes commonplace and Milton a bore.

A literature, therefore, of which the chief aim is to be read and applauded by the half-instructed many, is altogether precluded from the higher excellences both of thought and of composition. To obtain the character of a sound or brilliant thinker and a fine writer among superficial people it is a very different set of qualities which must be cultivated.

People are in general much better pleased with the man who persuades them that they have always been right, than with the man who tells them that they are wrong. No one, except the very few, with whom truth is a consideration paramount to all others, is pleased with any person for convincing him that he has been in error: and if to think is always, to most people, a labour too irksome to be borne, more especially will they turn a deaf ear to the man who bids them think when the consequence intended is their being disabused of their favourite opinions, opinions, too, which they perhaps have an interest in sticking to. There remain two paths to reputation and success. One is, to advocate strenuously and if possible enthusiastically the reigning opinions, all, but especially those in which any influential part of the community has an interest: to heap insult and opprobrium on all who dissent from those opinions and to keep those who profess them well supplied with reasons to make themselves and others better satisfied with those opinions than before. Of the class of writers who pursue this plan —a class comprising the great bulk of our moral and political writers—the greatest living example is Dr. Southey.[5] The other, for there is another mode of obtaining among half-instructed persons a reputation for talent, is by dealing in paradoxes. There are two ways of being a paradox-monger. One is by professing opinions which were not likely to occur to anybody. But a still better way, is by maintaining opinions so perfectly silly, that they are at once rejected by everybody. The source of reputation in this case, besides the strangeness of

[5] Robert Southey (1774–1843), Romantic poet who rejected his youthful radicalism in favor of a conservative social philosophy.

the opinion, is the surprise which everyone feels on finding that there is anything plausible to be said in behalf of so very gross and palpable an absurdity. If a man shows any talent in the defence of it he is accordingly set down as at least a very clever and ingenious person; and if he has managed well and made choice of a paradox which flatters any of the passions or inclinations common to mankind or to any influential class or party among mankind he makes a crowd of proselytes and at once establishes his reputation as a profound and original thinker. Among those who in our own day have most distinguished themselves in this field it would be unjust to refuse the first place to the celebrated Mr. Jeffrey,[6] who has shown by his celebrated argument against the progressiveness of human nature and by many other paradoxes besides, that he stands foremost among mankind in the art of saying something very plausible in a case so bad that hardly anybody besides himself would have fancied that anything could be said for it at all.

So much for the matter of our modern writers: now as to their style. It is sufficiently notorious that the kind of writing which is preferred by instructed and cultivated minds, is not that which pleases the half-instructed and pseudo-refined; and although whatever gives pleasure to anybody is so far good, our standard of taste, if we have one, must be founded on what it is incident to minds of the highest degree of cultivation to approve and admire. Now it has always been laid down by them as a rule that the chief excellence of style is to express the meaning exactly and without any appearance of effort, to express it in short as a man of sense and education, filled with his subject and quite indifferent to display, might be supposed to express it spontaneously. Everyone who has been accustomed in writing to make this unaffected simplicity his model, knows how prodigiously it transcends every other style in difficulty: he knows that really to write without effort, is by no means the way to appear without effort, and that when

[6] Francis Jeffrey (1773–1850), chief reviewer and, after May 1803, sole editor of the *Edinburgh Review*. He treated literature from the Whig point of view and was a harsh critic of the Lake poets.

even a man of talent gives the reins to his imagination, and uses the first expressions which occur to him, what he writes will either be feeble and vapid in general with a brilliant passage now and then, or else such stuff as is in *Blackwood's Magazine*.[7] A practised writer knows the immense labour of the *ars celandi artem*[8]: how much more art it requires to speak naturally than to speak affectedly: in what rude and inappropriate language a thought first suggests itself to the mind, and what pains are necessary to make the word suit the idea so exactly that the one shall appear to have been immediately suggested by the other. It is when this attempt is most completely successful that common readers are least capable of appreciating it. It is when a thought is very felicitously expressed that every dunce who reads it thinks he could have expressed it as well. The vulgar taste in style is like the vulgar taste in most other things: everything is admired, in proportion as it deviates from Nature; and, therefore, from what the dunce who pretends to judge of it thinks would have occurred to himself. A ranting player who tears a passion to rags is generally more admired by persons unacquainted with the external indications of real passion than a chaste and natural actor, because in him the art is not perceived, his imitation of Nature appears Nature itself, and where they can perceive no difficulty they ascribe no merit. So in style, a half-cultivated taste is always caught by gaudy, affected, and meretricious ornament, contributing nothing either to the clearness of the idea or the vividness of the leading image; the effusion of a mind not in earnest; the play of an imagination occupied with everything in the world except the subject. The writers whom the vulgar admire are those who deal in conceits with Mr. Moore, or commonplace metaphor with Mr. Jeffrey, or extravagant and far-fetched metaphors with Mr. Hazlitt or the Rev. Mr. Irving. And those

[7] *Blackwood's Edinburgh Magazine* was founded in 1817 to express Tory views on literature and to promote the fortunes of William Blackwood's publishing house; it was long known for its flippant and cruel satire.

[8] "Art concealing art."

who do not aim at this kind of style become careless and aim at no style at all. We have at this time many tolerable writers, but scarcely one who has attained distinguished excellence in style. I must except Sir W. Scott, who, in his peculiar department, description of external Nature, is without a rival, though in descriptions of human emotions and passions Richardson far excels him. But whom have we to compare in wit and idiomatic English with Dr. South, in easy, quiet, unaffected humour with Addison and Goldsmith, in grave Cervantes-like irony with Fielding, in nervous simplicity and poignant satire with Swift, in pathos, though stained by much affectation, with Sterne? Whom have we who can equal Hume in graceful narrative, Bolingbroke in brilliant and animated declamation, Mandeville in copious and appropriate though homely illustration, and which of our authors can rank with Berkeley [9] for the felicitous expression of abstruse thoughts, or can match in exuberance of fancy corrected by the severest judgment that wonderful master of figurative eloquence, Lord Bacon?

I say nothing of what are commonly called our old writers, because my knowledge of them is not extensive, but the writers I have named are sufficient to exemplify the superiority in point of mere writing of other ages to our own.

It remains to mention one feature which particularly marks the literature of the present day, and which I think has con-

---

[9] Thomas Moore (1779–1852), nationalistic Irish poet.—William Hazlitt (1778–1830), one of the foremost essayists and critics of the Romantic period.—Edward Irving (1792–1834), Scottish preacher who founded a sect called the Catholic Apostolic Church; he was expelled from Church of Scotland in 1833 for his teachings.—Sir Walter Scott (1771–1832), great Scottish novelist and poet.—Samuel Richardson (1689–1761), English novelist.—Robert South (1634–1716), distinguished clergyman and preacher, best known for *Sermons Preached upon Several Occasions* (1679).—Joseph Addison (1672–1719), English essayist.—Oliver Goldsmith (1730?–1774), English poet, dramatist, and novelist.—Laurence Sterne (1713–1768), British novelist, clergyman.—Henry St. John, Viscount Bolingbroke (1678–1751), Tory statesman, talented writer and orator.—Bernard Mandeville (1670–1733), English satirical writer on ethical subjects.—George Berkeley (1685–1753), British philosopher and churchman.

tributed more than any other to its degradation. I mean the prevalence of periodical publications. This has operated unfavourably upon our literature in a variety of ways. In the first place periodical works are written more exclusively than any others for the day. They are, therefore, under still stronger inducements than other works, to chime in with the tastes of the day, and the prejudices of the day. All other writers, though they cannot attain immediate, may hope for ultimate reputation and success by being above their age. Periodical writers must have immediate success or none at all. "I hate journals," says Goethe somewhere, "because they are the slaves of the day"; and ample experience confirms the truth of the observation.

It has been said in favour of periodical publications, that they promote a taste for reading, and this praise they undoubtedly deserve: but it may be doubted whether they occasion the reading of much besides themselves. If they cause many to go on to books who begin with newspapers and reviews, they also induce many to satisfy themselves with reviews who would otherwise have read books. And they contribute much to diminish the number of good books. Formerly a young writer appeared before the public under his own colours: if he made his way it was by having sufficient merit to gain a reputation of his own, and he was, therefore, anxious to make his productions as perfect as he was able before he suffered them to see the light. In this manner the taste for literary distinction, not being early or easily gratified, grew into a passion, became deeply rooted in his mind, and if he really possessed talent, rendered him probably for the whole of his life a distinguished literary character. But now every young writer who possesses the moderate degree of cleverness necessary to enable him to compose a readable article for a review, finds he can turn his small capital of intellect to so good an account by writing for periodicals that it would be labour lost to wait till he had made that capital larger: especially as that accuracy of research, that depth of thought, and that highly finished style, which are so essential to a work destined for posterity would not only not contribute to his success, but would obstruct it by taking up his time, and preventing him from composing rapidly. Writing anonymously, he is not afraid of compromising his reputation, and the first crude offspring of his brain, poured forth in a style which will always be good enough if it is grammatical and runs pretty smoothly, passes from hand to hand by virtue of the reputation of the review, and if it have any merit at all gains for the writer such a moderate portion of celebrity as generally appeases the first cravings of his appetite and leaves him lukewarm about the attainment of a higher degree of distinction and averse to the severe application which it would require. I cannot help ascribing partly to this cause the very small number of good prose works which have been published for many years past, except indeed novels, a branch of literature which pays so well that there is always a sufficient motive for producing it.

I have a still heavier charge against periodical literature: it is this which has made literature a trade. Nothing else would have rendered the literary profession sufficiently lucrative to tempt men into it for the mere sake of pecuniary profit. We read in Pope and our other satirists of many dunces whose evil genius persuaded them to write, to the great grief of their relations and injury of their worldly concerns; and who, from a real fondness for the occupation, preferred starving upon the scanty produce of their pen to earning a comfortable livelihood in any honest trade. But we do not find mention made by these authors of any who chose authorship as an advantageous investment of their labour and capital in a commercial point of view; contracted for a stipulated quantity of eloquence and wit, to be delivered on a certain day; were inspired punctually by 12 o'clock in order to be in time for the printer's boy at one; sold a burst of passion at so much per line and gave way to a movement of virtuous indignation as per order received. That a literary man should receive a remuneration for his labour is no more than just, provided he writes in every respect as he would have done, if he had no remuneration to expect. But whatever is a gainful occupation becomes the occupation of many who have nothing beyond the pecuniary gain in view. What is carried on as a trade, soon comes to be carried on upon mere trading principles of profit and loss. When literature is upon this footing it is of all trades almost without exception the most degraded and vile, on account of the insincerity and hypocrisy with which it is necessarily connected. Written composition, like any other form of human discourse, is only endurable so far as the opinions and sentiments which it promulgates are supposed to be the real opinions and genuine sentiments of the writer. The hack author who considers not what sentiments the subject ought to inspire, but only what are the sentiments which are expected of him, and who, after having on due inquiry and examination settled to the satisfaction of his own mind, which side of the question will be the marketable side, proceeds thereupon to brandish his mercenary thunders, and burst forth with the artificial transports of a bought enthusiasm; the occupation of a street-walking prostitute is surely far more respectable. The present times have brought forth a plentiful harvest of this kind of handicrafts. It is fortunate indeed if scribes of this sort do nothing worse than this, in the way of their profession. There are literary. . . .

Attack on Literature

1831

The ambiguously titled article is here published for the first time since it appeared anonymously in 1831. The "Attack on Literature" which provoked Mill to this spirited defense of the value of literature was occasioned by an offer from Lord Grey, the Prime Minister, of a grant of two hundred pounds from treasury funds to Samuel Taylor Coleridge (who refused). The writer, whose attack appeared in the *Brighton Guardian*, could not see why men of letters are more deserving of support than any other class of entertainers, or of men in general. Do not all things receive their due reward in the free competition of the market place? What source of value is there but that which is determined by supply and demand?

Mill was peculiarly sensitive to such crude misapplications of his own *laissez-faire* philosophy. His father had instructed him in the *laissez-faire* economics of Adam Smith and the Scottish economist David Ricardo (who was perhaps James Mill's most intimate friend); he himself was to write one of the classic expositions of the system; and, despite much speculation about his growing sympathy for socialism in later years, he was to the end of his life firmly convinced of the necessity of competition. Yet early in his career he came to see the danger of the mentality which is incapable of conceiving any values other than those determined by the market. In the *Autobiography* he reminds his readers that as early as 1832 he had written an article (published in *The Jurist* in 1833 and reprinted in *Dissertations and Discussions* as "The Right and Wrong of State Interference with Corporation and Church Property") in which he "urged strenuously the importance of having a provision for education, not dependent on the mere demand of the market, that is, on the knowledge and discernment of average parents, but calculated to establish and keep up a higher standard of instruction than is likely to be spontaneously demanded by the buyers of the article" (*Autobiography*, p. 128). In other words, there is such a thing as intrinsic value, which is quite independent of the workings of supply and demand. And as with literature, so with education: just those writers who try to improve rather than to flatter mankind are the least likely to be rewarded for their labors with either money or gratitude.

In the year 1824, a Society was instituted, under the name of the Royal Society of Literature. With what definite views it was established, or what purposes of utility the association, as such, has ever promoted, we know not; and the members themselves, possibly, know as little. There were annexed, however, to the Institution, ten pensions, of a hundred guineas each, from the Privy Purse; to be held by as many persons, distinguished in the world of letters. And the individuals who were first selected to hold these moderate stipends were the following (we quote from the *Englishman's Magazine*):*—"Samuel Taylor Coleridge; the Rev. Edward Davies; Dr. Jamieson, the indefatigable compiler of the Scottish Dictionary; the Rev. T. R. Malthus; Matthias, the author of the *Pursuits of Literature;* James Millingen, Esq.; Sir William Ouseley; William Roscoe; the Rev. Henry J. Todd; and Sharon Turner." [1]

Perhaps no act of the late king,[2] which is known to the public, was altogether so creditable to him as the grant of these

First published in *The Examiner*, No. 1219 (Sunday, June 12, 1831), pp. 369–371.

* The *first* account of the affair appeared in *The Law Magazine.* (Mill's note.)

[1] Rev. Edward Davies (1756–1831), Welsh antiquary.—Dr. John Jamieson (1759–1838), antiquary and philologist; published *Etymological Dictionary of the Scottish Language* in 1808.—Thomas Robert Malthus (1766–1834), English economist, author of *An Essay on the Principle of Population* (1798).—Thomas James Mathias (1754?–1835), satirist and Italian scholar. His *Pursuits of Literature* (1794–1797) was a long poetic satire of those who go in for literature as a trade.—James Millingen (1774–1845), archaeologist.—Sir William Ouseley (1767–1842), orientalist. —William Roscoe (1753–1831), historian.—Rev. Henry J. Todd (1763–1845), editor of Milton.—Sharon Turner (1768–1847), historian.

[2] George IV.

pensions. While the debates on the Civil List are fresh in the recollection of our readers, we need scarcely remind them, that, of what is called the Privy Purse, a large part is granted by Parliament avowedly for purposes of liberality and munificence. These pensions were among the best examples which England had long seen, of well-directed munificence. They were too inconsiderable to excite the cupidity of tax-eating idlers. Several of the persons on whom they were bestowed, were in circumstances which rendered the accession to their incomes of real importance. The individuals were not selected on any narrow or exclusive principle; but had distinguished themselves in different modes, and in different walks of literature and philosophy. All, however, were men of reputation in their several departments; all, as writers, had proposed to themselves higher objects than merely to amuse; and none of them could possibly have acquired affluence, or even respectable subsistence, by such works as those to which they had dedicated themselves. A. or B. may think some of the number undeserving of what was bestowed upon them, and may imagine that he himself could have pointed out individuals better entitled to be so provided for. This was inevitable. We ourselves, as well as other people, could have suggested emendations in the list; but the giver was not bound to please us, or to please A. or B., but to satisfy the body of educated and cultivated Englishmen: and taking, as is proper, for the standard, the prevalent opinions and feelings, at the time when the grant was made, of the bulk of those whose approbation had the best title to be considered, it would be difficult to point out ten persons, the selection of whom, as the objects of the Royal liberality, would have been in every respect so unobjectionable.

These pensions, however, his present MAJESTY[3] has, it appears, seen fit to discontinue. It, undoubtedly, rests with the KING himself to decide in what manner that portion of his revenues which is set apart for acts of generosity, can be most worthily employed; and it is proper that, in the choice of objects, he should follow his own opinion, and not ours. On

[3] William IV.

this subject it would be disrespectful to express more than regret, and our firm conviction that the one thousand guineas per annum which the Privy Purse will save by the stoppage of this annual bounty, will be expended, we know not how indeed, but most assuredly in a less useful manner, and for the benefit of less meritorious persons. We might be permitted to add, (what has been insisted upon with great force by some of our contemporaries) that when the odious Pension List, the wages of political, if not even of personal prostitution–the purchase-money of despotic power–the fragments of a nation's spoil which the feasters have flung from their richly-furnished table to allay the hunger of some of the baser and more subordinate of their tools;–when this monument of iniquity has just been screened from revision, on the ground that, although there had been no promise, persons naturally expect to keep what they have once got;–the moment is ill chosen for resuming the scanty pittance which men, whose lives had been devoted to usefulness, had every rational ground to calculate upon retaining for their few remaining years. But it is in this spirit that an English government usually economizes. Whatever is enormous and unearned, it leaves undisturbed to the possessors. Its retrenchments bear uniformly and exclusively upon the ill-paid and the deserving.

But, as ROUSSEAU well observes, one bad maxim is worse than a thousand bad actions,–because it leads to ten thousand. A report that Lord GREY, at the instigation of Lord BROUGHAM,[4] had tendered to Mr. COLERIDGE a grant of two hundred pounds from the Treasury (which, however, Mr. COLERIDGE declined), has furnished the *Brighton Guardian* with the occasion of an article, equal in length to half a page of *The Times;* the Vandalism of which, inconceivable, if *any* Vandalism could be inconceivable, provokes us to take up the pen. The matter with which the article is filled, is indeed, or should be, very little formidable, did the writer merely state the opinion of one rather perverse individual. But, unfortunately, this per-

[4] Charles Grey, second Earl Grey (1764–1845), Prime Minister 1830–1834.–Henry Brougham (1778–1868), Lord Chancellor in 1831.

verse person is but one man who is bold enough to utter what the whole tribe of the dunces are intimately persuaded of in their hearts, but do not dare to avow. They will soon, however, pluck up courage to proclaim and act upon it, if they find themselves countenanced by one or two persons (as this writer has proved himself to be) not untinctured with letters. It is, therefore, of some importance to analyse a performance, more abounding in the ideas and feelings characteristic of uncultivated minds, than is often the case with the productions of an understanding even superficially cultivated.

The object of the writer is to establish, that men of letters ought, in no case, to be provided for at the national expense. And though this is, in our opinion, a mischievous error, it is shared by too many superior men in the present day, to be matter of serious reproach to any one. It is a maxim in perfect harmony with the *laissez faire* spirit of the prevailing philosophy—with the idea by which, either consciously or unconsciously, nine-tenths of the men who can read and write, are at present possessed—viz. that every person, however uneducated or ill-educated, is the best judge of what is most for his own advantage, better even than the man whom he would delegate to make laws for him. The scope of the received doctrines is, to make mankind retrograde, for a certain space, towards the state of nature; by limiting the ends and functions of the social union, as strictly as possible, to those of a mere police. The idea that political society is a combination among mankind for the purpose of helping one another in every way in which help can be advantageous, is yet a stranger to the immense majority of understandings.

But if the conclusion at which this writer arrives, is common to him with many wiser men than himself, this is not precisely the case with the premises by which he supports it; for he goes the full length of averring that literary men are of no use; that the improvement of mankind is not, in the slightest degree, owing to them or their writings; and that we should be as far, or farther, advanced in wisdom and virtue than we now are, if the whole tribe had long since become extinct.

He begins by accounting for the high estimation in which literary men are held. It arises, he says, from the fact, that "literary men are the penholders of society, and they praise themselves and praise their pursuits." In part also it is "a sort of traditionary sentiment." After the breaking up of the Roman empire, all the knowledge of past times existed in a dead language; and was accessible only to literary men, who, consequently, met with "respect, and even veneration." "There was, at the period of what is called the revival of learning in Europe, a considerable mine of valuable knowledge opened by literary men." This, however, is no longer the case; because, peradventure, we now know everything; or, at least, one of us knows no more than another. Literature "is praised and honoured for what it once did,—not for what it now does." He then holds forth as follows:—

Do literary men, or does literature now improve and instruct mankind? To a certain extent, we admit that it does both. But amusement is afforded to thousands of people by *Punch*[5] in the street, by a clown at the theatre, and by the shows at Vauxhall;[6] and we have never heard any person venture to assert, that a fellow playing on Pan-pipes, making faces, performing extraordinary leaps, or rattling his chin till it sounded like a pair of symbols [cymbals], was a proper object for the national bounty, and ought to be pensioned in his old age, if he dissipated the halfpence or shillings he collected from the crowds. A man who writes a novel, or a play, or a poem, in respect of amusement, and in respect of being entitled to public rewards, is on the same footing as a mountebank or a puppet-showman. It is very possible that this amusement may be combined with some sentiments that may make the heart better; and it is equally possible, which we believe is in fact more generally the case, that the amusement is only made the vehicle of perverted sentiments, of conveying impurity into the mind, and of promoting the cause of vice, rather than of virtue. The use of literature, then, comes to consist in the truth

[5] The clown, not the humor magazine, which was not founded until 1841.

[6] Vauxhall Gardens was a pleasure resort and center for popular entertainments.

and accurate knowledge which it contains. Unfortunately, however, those who have taught mankind truth have been prosecuted, not pensioned. De Foe, Horne Tooke, Thomas Paine,[7] and a number of other writers, who have been the means of making useful, moral, and scientific truths known to the world, have been punished by the government, not rewarded. Governments always have been, and ever will be,—precisely because they are the offspring of conquest or of fraud, not of reason,—ready to prohibit literary men from searching after truth; so that if we should admit that literature, in the abstract, might be harmless, existing literature must have been mischievous. That system of corruption, which we are all now eager to pull down, has in fact long been supported by the majority of literary men. By all who have been pensioned,—by all who have sought any other patronage than that of the public, this miserable system has been favourably regarded, and they have endeavoured, and do endeavour, to uphold it.

Now, if this man's insight into human nature, and into the future destination of mankind, does not enable him to form the conception of any other government than one which is "the offspring of conquest or of fraud, not of reason"–if his mind is fully made up that the human race shall for ever, in spite of themselves, have their necks under the feet of men disposed to restrain and persecute those who search after truth–it is natural that he should look with small favour on any literary labours which such governments are likely to esteem deserving of reward. For our part, we do not hold it to be a law of nature that governments shall endeavour to stop the progress of the human mind. We do not believe that, even in the present vicious constitution of political society, the majority of civilized governments have any such purpose, or are actuated by any such spirit. And we look forward to a time,

---

[7] Daniel De Foe (1660–1731), a pamphleteer and journalist as well as a novelist, was imprisoned under Queen Anne for expression of anti-Tory sentiment in *The Shortest Way with Dissenters* (1702).–Horne Tooke (1736–1812), political associate of Paine, author or several works of political theory; in 1792 he organized the London Corresponding Society, considered revolutionary by the king.–Thomas Paine (1737–1809), political theorist of the American Revolution; he was prosecuted for attacks on English institutions in 1792.

and no very distant one, in which all the more vulgar and subordinate purposes of government will merge in one grand purpose of advancing the progress of civilization. Proceeding upon premises so different from those of our contemporary, no wonder that we should quarrel with his conclusion.

> We must, however, [says he] go a step further in speaking of literature, and say that it has little or no influence over the progress of society. It is the consequence, not the cause, of civilization. Literary men and philosophers may flatter themselves that they possess a great power over the hearts and minds of their fellow-men, and over the progress of society; but experience teaches a different lesson. Man is taught by events, not by books, which too often obscure the most plain facts.

For "it is now upwards of three hundred years since Sir Thomas More[8] made those beautiful observations on punishing theft by death:" and theft still continues to be thus punished. "It is now also a hundred and thirty-nine years since Sir Dudley North[9] published in his Discourses on Trade;" and he wrote in vain, till there arose "a want of markets for our produce:" and "it is upwards of two hundred years since Lord Bacon taught that man was but the minister and interpreter of nature;" notwithstanding which, literary men are constantly recommending alterations in the structure of society; which, according to this writer, is a gross absurdity, since "human society, in its complicated relations, is as much a part of creation as minerals or flowers;" a proposition which is about as good an argument against improvements in the social science, as it would be against improvements in mining or horticulture.

So, because a man of genius may have an idea too far in advance of his age to gain many converts in it, men of genius have no more influence upon the destinies of society than dunces have. Because Sir Thomas More did not convince mankind of the barbarism of capital punishment, the labours of

---

[8] Thomas More (1478–1535), author of *Utopia* (1516), statesman and humanist.

[9] Dudley North (1641–1691), financier and economist, one of the earliest advocates of free trade.

Beccaria, of Voltaire, of Bentham, of Romilly,[10] in the same cause, have been useless and of none effect. Because Sir Dudley North perceived the advantages of free trade, while the politicians of the world, both practical and theoretical, did not read him, or were too stupid, or too much engrossed by other subjects, to understand him, *therefore* the truth which he detected would by this time have been incorporated in our laws, if Adam Smith, and Say, and Ricardo,[11] and all men resembling them, had never existed. And this, because "man is taught by events, not books;" and events, it seems, never have any need of an interpreter; their language is as intelligible to any blockhead, who is not deaf, as to the greatest genius. If Newton had never lived, his next-door neighbour, no doubt, might have seen an apple fall, and in due time would have evolved the Principia, for man is taught by events.

This "ignorance of what mankind owe to books" (if we may borrow an expression from Mr. Coleridge) is most pitiable. We contend, in opposition to our contemporary, that mankind, instead of not being indebted to men of highly-cultivated intellects for any of the steps of their progress, are indebted to them for every step. Events might have spoken, or even cried aloud, but they would have spoken a foreign language: mankind could not have profited, and do not profit, even by the lessons of their personal experience, until a man of genius arises to construe those lessons for them. Before the press existed, the leading minds of a nation could bring them-

[10] Cesare Bonesana, Marchese di Beccaria (1738–1794), Italian criminologist and jurist.—Jeremy Bentham (1748–1832), philosopher and political reformer, urged that effectiveness as a preventive measure, rather than vengeance, be the end of criminal punishments and so helped greatly to reduce the number of crimes punishable by death.—Sir Samuel Romilly (1757–1818), celebrated barrister, friend of Bentham and advocate of penal law reform.

[11] Adam Smith (1723–1790), Scottish economist, author of *An Inquiry into the Nature and Causes of the Wealth of Nations* (1776); he advocated free trade, as did his followers Say and Ricardo.—Jean Baptiste Say (1767–1832), French economist, popularizer of Smith's theories.—David Ricardo (1772–1823), British economist, close friend of James Mill.

selves into contact with the national mind only by means of speech. The forum, the theatre, the pulpit, the school, were then the sources of illumination and mental culture. Since the discovery of printing, books are the medium by which the ideas, the mental habits, and the feelings, of the most exalted and enlarged minds are propagated among the inert, unobserving, unmeditative mass. And we challenge our adversary to a historical trial of the fact. From the Reformation to the present Parliamentary Reform Bill, he will not find one great moral or social improvement, the origin of which cannot be distinctly traced to the labours of men of letters. No one man of genius, it is probable, was ever indispensable; because, what he did, it is likely might have been done by some other: but by another man of genius. Had it not been for a few great minds, mankind would never have emerged from the savage state. Let the series of great minds be once broken off, and it is not clear that we shall not relapse into barbarism.

But mark the pseudo-metaphysical theory, which serves as a pedestal to this fine philosophical system. "Instead of society being modelled on, or formed by, the opinions of literary men or philosophers, all their opinions, as far as they are correct, are modelled on what they behold in the world. Every thought they possess, if correct, is a mere copy of external nature; and yet it is assumed, that by some little legerdemain arrangement of their reflections, they influence the course of the intellectual world:" and, we presume, whatever is "in the world," and in "external nature," is as visible to one man's optics as to another's. This style of philosophizing will carry us far. Every picture which Raphael ever painted, "if correct, is a mere copy of external nature;" of that nature, too, which we can see with our bodily eyes, not solely with those of our minds: *argal*,[12] every man who has eyes, could have painted the Transfiguration.[13] Lavoisier's[14] discovery of the composition of

[12] Perversion of Latin *ergo* (therefore); hence, a clumsy piece of reasoning.

[13] By Raphael (Vatican, Rome).

[14] Antoine Laurent Lavoisier (1743–1794), French chemist and physicist.

water, was "modelled on what he beheld in the world;" the hydrogen and the oxygen were always before us, in every rivulet, and in every cistern, "and yet it is assumed, that by some little arrangement" of retorts and gas apparatus, he "influenced the course" of the science of chemistry, and of the arts to which it is applied.

Finally, our contemporary adds:

> It is clear, we think, whether looked at theoretically or as a matter of fact, that literature and literary men are of no more use to society, no more instrumental in promoting its improvement, than is any other class or any other art; and therefore, we conclude, no more to be pensioned and provided for out of the people's purse than is the weaver, for his skill in cloth-making. The best reward for both is the common market of the world; and what will not sell there that is worth no man's labour.

From this we may learn, that the sale of a book is always in exact proportion to its utility; and mankind are as well able to discern, and as eager to seek, that which will enlarge and elevate their minds, as that which will please and beautify their bodies. The person whose mind is capable of conceiving an opinion of this sort, must be a precious observer of his age and of human nature.

If we were now to state our own opinion with respect to a public provision for literary men, we should suggest to this writer a distinction which, it would seem, is not "heard of in his philosophy." [15] We should remind him, that there are literary men, and literary works, whose object is solely to give immediate pleasure, and other literary men and literary works that aim at producing a permanent impression upon the mind. The first we should, with him, regard as being on the same footing in respect to public rewards, with "a mountebank or a puppet-show man:" not because amusement in itself is not a worthy object of pursuit, but because it is one for which mankind are always willing to pay the full value. Accordingly, the amusement of the poor, who cannot afford to pay for it, *is* a fit object of public provision; and doubtless, as civilization advances, will be so considered.

[15] *Hamlet*, I. v. 167.

In addition, however, to these writers, whose aim is only to please mankind, there is another sort, who endeavour to educate them: to batter down obstinate prejudices; to throw light on the dark places; to discover and promulgate ideas, which must be meditated for years before they will be appreciated; to form mankind to closer habits of thought; to shame them out of whatever is mean and selfish in their behaviour; to elevate their tastes; to inspire them with nobler and more beneficent desires; to teach them that there are virtues which they have never conceived, and pleasures beyond what they have ever enjoyed. These, by the leave of our contemporary, are the labours, for which "the best reward" is not always "the common market of the world." This is a literature which deserves a public provision, and which, unfortunately, is too apt to require one; because such are not the services which mankind are apt at first to requite with either their money or their thanks.

But no enemy to a cause ever did more for its injury, than is done to this cause by its friends, when they talk of giving "encouragement to literature." The phrase grates upon our ears. Literature needs no encouragement. The man who engages in literature from the motive of money, is false to his mission. It is the curse of literature, that it is a trade. He who would inspire others with high desires, must himself be inspired with them. He would teach mankind to love truth and virtue for themselves, and shall *he* need any other stimulus than the love of truth and virtue, in order to inculcate them? What is due to literary men is not encouragement, but subsistence. They ask not to be rewarded,—they ask to be kept alive, while they continue to enlighten and civilize the world. They ask this, in order that they may not, like so many of the first men of our own country, be compelled to renounce or suspend the labours for which none others are fit, and devote their lives to some merely gainful occupation, in order that they may have bread to eat: or still worse, that they may not be compelled by penury and dire dependance, which eat up so many minds fit for better things, to prostitute their noble calling by base compliances—to pander to selfishness and malignity, instead of wrestling with them; to give utterance to the opinion which they hold not, to counterfeit the emotion which they feel not, to find justification for the evil-doer, instead of bringing him to shame—to become confounded with the meanest of mankind, by sycophancy and base hypocrisy—or if they sink not to this depth of infamy, at least to waste their highest powers, by mixing among the herd of those who write merely to amuse.

It is most true, as our contemporary affirms, that the majority of our literary men have long been of the low description, which we have just attempted to characterize. But why is this? For several reasons, one of the chief of which is, that such men, in this country, have *not* any public provision. In Germany and France, where, through the universities and various other institutions, a man of letters or science easily obtains, by the sacrifice, of a small part of his time, a respectable subsistence—there, even under arbitrary governments, the lettered class are really the highest and most cultivated minds of their several nations. With us, they are dependent, for subsistence, upon the sale of their works, and must consequently adapt themselves to the taste of those who will buy. The buying class, until lately, have been the aristocracy: which explains why, as our adversary says, our corrupt institutions have "long been supported by the majority of literary men." When, subsequently to this, the mass of the people became buyers, books were written which were addressed chiefly to them. As the people had not the sinister interests of the aristocracy, the writings which were addressed to them did not assume the same particular form of noxiousness and wickedness, as those which were written for the ruling classes: but they assumed other forms. And so it will be, if, by the Reform Bill and its consequences, all the corruptions of our government are done away. The people, as well as the aristocracy, like better to have their opinions confirmed, than corrected. The people as well as the aristocracy prefer those who chime in with their feelings, to those who endeavour to improve them. After the Reform Bill as before, it will be easier and more gainful to take men as they now are, with their vices and weaknesses, and to give them the food which pleases their vitiated palates, than to form their tastes and their constitutions to healthier nourishment. And such will be the character of all literature, which is got up for "the common market of the world;" until mankind shall have attained a degree of civilization, to which Parliamentary Reform may remove some of the obstacles, but which of itself it gives not, nor ever can give.

But to prevent these evils, it is not necessary that any thing should be added to the fiscal burdens by which we are already weighed down. It is not requisite that the people should be taxed to give pensions to men of literature and science. The endowments of our universities, now squandered upon idle monks, are an ample fund already existing; a large portion of which (the Fellowships) already is expended under that pretext, and is of right appropriate to that purpose and to no other. And a time, we trust, is coming, when to that, and no other purpose, it will be applied.

On Genius

1832

"On Genius" is the earliest statement of Mill's humanism. Cast in the form of a letter, it is outwardly a mild refutation of the "modernist" position taken by an anonymous contributor to the *Monthly Repository* who had maintained that modern civilization, far from frustrating genius, provided it with more material and knowledge with which to work. Mill, or "Antiquus," as he signs himself, is a partisan, though hardly a zealous one, of the ancients in their quarrel with the moderns. The real question, he argues, is not whether ancients or moderns have a more comprehensive or accurate or up-to-date knowledge of the universe; it is whether the moderns or the ancients have succeeded better in the cultivation of the intellect.

The idea of such cultivation is a key to the humanistic bias of the essay. Men, argues Mill, are to be judged not by what they produce but by what they are. Cultivation of the intellect is more important than advancement of knowledge, and genius should not be equated with the acquisition of new knowledge. Contrary to a facile theory of progressivism, genius is not cumulative, and a modern man does not have more of it than an ancient simply by virtue of coming later into the world; it will be as difficult of attainment—and as easy—in the future as it is now.

For those acquainted with Mill's better-known works, perhaps the most striking characteristic of this essay of 1832 is the consistency of its humanistic utterances with those of *On Liberty* (1859) and the Inaugural Address of 1867. However his other opinions may have altered in the course of his career—and Mill has often been berated for his doctrinal inconsistencies—he remained firmly convinced of the primacy of being over doing and of cultivation over production. The present essay's injunction to judge man by what he is, not by what he does, is repeated in *On Liberty's* eloquent attack upon "machinery"; its strictures upon modern education are echoed, and complemented, by the reaffirmation in the Inaugural Address of the virtues of a liberal education founded upon the classics.

Addressed to the Author of an Article, entitled "Some Considerations respecting the Comparative Influence of Ancient and Modern Times on the Development of Genius;" and of its continuation, headed, "On the Intellectual Influences of Christianity." [1]

SIR,—You have turned your attention, and that of the readers of the *Monthly Repository*, to a question, with which, if we well consider its significance, none of the controversies which fill the present age with flame and fury is comparable in interest. You have shown that, without being indifferent to politics, you can see a deeper problem in the existing aspect of human affairs, than the adjustment of a ten-pound franchise; and that with no inclination to undervalue the intellect of these "latter days," you do not write it down transcendant because steam-carriages can run twenty-five miles an hour on an iron railway; because little children are taught to march round a room and sing psalms, or because mechanics can read the *Penny Magazine*.[2] You do not look upon man as having attained the perfection of his nature, when he attains the perfection of a wheel's or a pulley's nature, to go well as a part of some vast machine, being in himself nothing. You do not esteem the higher endowments of the intellect and heart to be given by God, or valuable to man, chiefly as means to his obtaining, first, bread; next, beef to his bread; and, as the last felicitous consummation, wine and fine linen. Rather, you seem to consider the wants which point to these bodily necessaries or indulgences, as having for their chief use that they call into existence and into exercise those loftier qualities. You

First published in the *Monthly Repository*, VI (October 1832).

[1] The articles to which Mill is responding appeared in the *Monthly Repository* in the two previous months (VI, 556–564, 627–634).

[2] A publication sponsored by the Society for the Diffusion of Useful Knowledge, the *Penny Magazine* first appeared in March 1832 and by the year's end had a sale of 200,000 copies. Its purpose was to offer practical instruction and useful information; it published no stories.

judge of man, not by what he does, but by what he is. For, though man is formed for action, and is of no worth further than by virtue of the work which he does; yet (as has been often said, by one of the noblest spirits of our time) [3] the works which most of us are appointed to do on this earth are in themselves little better than trivial and contemptible: the sole thing which is indeed valuable in them, is the *spirit* in which they are done. Nor is this mere mysticism; the most absolute utilitarianism must come to the same conclusion. If life were aught but a struggle to overcome difficulties; if the multifarious labours of the *durum genus hominum* [4] were performed for us by supernatural agency, and there were no demand for either wisdom or virtue, but barely for stretching out our hands and enjoying, small would be our enjoyment, for there would be nothing which man could any longer prize in man. Even men of pleasure know that the means are often more than the end: the delight of fox-hunting does not consist in catching a fox. Whether, according to the ethical theory we adopt, wisdom and virtue be precious in themselves, or there be nothing precious save happiness, it matters little; while we know that where these higher endowments are not, happiness can never be, even although the purposes for which they might seem to have been given, could, through any mechanical contrivance, be accomplished without them.

To one who believes these truths, and has obtained thus much of insight into what the writer to whom I have already alluded would call "the significance of man's life," it was a fitting inquiry what are really the intellectual characteristics of this age; whether our mental light—let us account for the fact as we may—has not lost in intensity, at least a part of what it has gained in diffusion; whether our "march of intellect" be not rather a march towards doing without intellect, and supplying our deficiency of giants by the united efforts of a constantly increasing multitude of dwarfs. Such, too, is actually

---

[3] Professor Mineka suggests that Mill has Goethe in mind here.
[4] "Sturdy human race."

the problem which you have proposed. Suffer, then, one who has also much meditated thereon, to represent to you in what points he considers you to have failed in completely solving, and even in adequately conceiving the question.

Have you not misplaced the gist of the inquiry, and confined the discussion within too narrow bounds, by countenancing the opinion which limits the province of genius to the discovery of truths never before known, or the formation of combinations never before imagined? Is not this confounding the mere *accidents* of Genius with its essentials, and determining the order of precedence among minds, not by their powers, but by their opportunities and chances? Is genius any distinct faculty? Is it not rather the very faculty of thought itself? And is not the act of *knowing* anything not directly within the cognizance of our senses (provided we really *know* it, and do not take it upon trust), as truly an exertion of genius, though of a less *degree* of genius, as if the thing had never been known by any one else?

Philosophic genius is said to be the discovery of new truth. But what is new truth? That which has been known a thousand years may be new truth to you or me. There are born into the world every day several hundred thousand human beings, to whom all truth whatever is new truth. What is it to him who was born yesterday, that somebody who was born fifty years ago knew something? The question is, how *he* is to know it. There is one way; and nobody has ever hit upon more than one—by *discovery*.

There is a language very generally current in the world, which implies that knowledge can be *vicarious;* that when a truth has become known to *any one*, all who follow have nothing to do but passively to receive it; as if one man, by reading or listening, could transport another man's knowledge ready manufactured into his own skull. As well might he try the experiment upon another man's eyesight. Those who have no eyesight of their own, or who are so placed that they cannot conveniently use it, must believe upon trust; they cannot *know*. A man who knows may tell me what he knows, as far as words go, and I may learn to parrot it after him; but if I would *know* it, I must place my mind in the same state in which he has placed his; I must make the thought my own thought; I must verify the fact by my own observation, or by interrogating my own consciousness.

The exceptions and qualifications with which this doctrine must be taken, and which are more apparent than real, will readily present themselves. For example, it will suggest itself at once that the truth of which I am now speaking is *general* truth. To know an *individual* fact may be no exercise of mind at all; merely an exercise of the senses. The sole exercise of mind may have been in bringing the fact sufficiently close for the senses to judge of it; and *that* merit may be peculiar to the first discoverer: there may be talent in finding where the thief is hid, but none at all in being able to see him when found. The same observation applies in a less degree to some *general* truths. To know a general truth is, indeed, always an operation of the *mind:* but some physical truths may be brought to the test of sensation by an experiment so simple, and the conclusiveness of which is so immediately apparent, that the trifling degree of mental power implied in drawing the proper inference from it, is altogether eclipsed by the ingenuity which contrived the experiment, and the sagacious forecast of an undiscovered truth which set that ingenuity to work: qualities, the place of which may now be supplied by mere imitation.

So, again, in a case of mere *reasoning* from assumed premises, as, for instance, in mathematics, the process bears so strong an analogy to a merely mechanical operation, that the first discoverer alone has any real difficulty to contend against; the second may follow the first with very little besides patience and continued attention. But these seeming exceptions do not trench in the least upon the principle which I have ventured to lay down. If the first discovery alone requires genius, it is because the first discovery alone requires any but the simplest and most commonplace exercise of thought. Though genius be no peculiar mental power, but only mental power possessed in a peculiar degree, what implies no mental power at all, requires to be sure no genius.

But can this be said of the conviction which comes by the comparison and appreciation of numerous and scattered proofs? Can it, above all, be said of the knowledge of supersensual things, of man's mental and moral nature, where the appeal is to internal consciousness and self-observation, or to the experience of our common life interpreted by means of the key which self-knowledge alone can supply? The most important phenomena of human nature cannot even be conceived, except by a mind which has actively studied itself. Believed they may be, but as a blind man believes the existence and properties of colour. To *know* these truths is always to *discover* them. Every one, I suppose, of adult years, who has any capacity of knowledge, can remember the impression which he experienced when he *discovered* some truths which he thought he had known for years before. He had only believed them; they were not the fruits of his own consciousness, or of his own observation; he had taken them upon trust, or he had taken upon trust the premises from which they were inferred. If he had happened to forget them, they had been lost altogether; whereas the truths which we *know* we can discover again and again *ad libitum.*[5]

It is with truths of this order as with the ascent of a mountain. Every person who climbs Mont Blanc exerts the same identical muscles as the first man who reached the summit; all that the first climber can do is to encourage the others and lend them a helping hand. What he has partly saved them the necessity of, is *courage:* it requires less hardihood to attempt to do what somebody has done before. It is an advantage also to have some one to point out the way and stop us when we are going wrong. Though one man cannot *teach* another, one man may *suggest* to another. I may be indebted to my predecessor for setting my own faculties to work; for hinting to me what questions to ask myself, and in what order; but it is not given to one man to *answer* those questions for another. Each

[5] "At pleasure"; "as one wishes."

person's own reason must work upon the materials afforded by that same person's own experience. Knowledge comes only from within; all that comes from without is but *questioning*, or else it is mere *authority*.

Now, the capacity of extracting the knowledge of general truth from our own consciousness, whether it be by simple *observation*, by that kind of self-observation which is called *imagination*, or by a more complicated process of analysis and induction, is *originality;* and where truth is the result, whoever says Originality says Genius. The man of the greatest philosophic genius does no more than this, evinces no higher faculty; whoever thinks at all, thinks to that extent, originally. Whoever knows anything of his own knowledge, not immediately obvious to the senses, manifests more or less of the same faculty which made a Newton or a Locke.[6] Whosoever does this same thing systematically—whosoever, to the extent of his opportunity, gets at his convictions by his own faculties, and not by reliance on any other person whatever—that man, in proportion as his conclusions have truth in them, is an *original thinker*, and is, as much as anybody ever was, a *man* of *genius;* nor matters it though he should never chance to find out anything which somebody had not found out before him. There may be no hidden truths left for him to find, or he may accidentally miss them; but if he have courage and opportunity he *can* find hidden truths; for he has found all those which he knows, many of which were as hidden to *him* as those which are still unknown.

If the genius which *discovers* is no peculiar faculty, neither is the genius which *creates*. It was genius which produced the Prometheus Vinctus,[7] the Oration on the Crown,[8] the Minerva,[9] or the Transfiguration; [10] and is it not genius which

[6] Sir Isaac Newton (1642–1727), English physicist, mathematician, and philosopher.—John Locke (1632–1704), philosopher, founder of English empiricism.

[7] *Prometheus Bound*, play by Aeschylus (525–456 B.C.).

[8] By the Greek orator Demosthenes (384–322 B.C.).

[9] The statue of Athene, identified with the Roman Minerva, by Phidias (500–*ca.* 432 B.C.), Greek sculptor.

[10] By Raphael (Vatican, Rome).

comprehends them? Without genius, a work of genius may be *felt*, but it cannot possibly be understood.

The property which distinguishes every work of genius in poetry and art from incoherency and vain caprice is, that it is *one*, *harmonious*, and a *whole:* that its parts are connected together as standing in a common relation to some leading and central idea or purpose. This idea or purpose it is not possible to extract from the work by any mechanical rules. To transport ourselves from the point of view of a spectator or reader, to that of the poet or artist himself, and from that central point to look round and see how the details of the work all conspire to the same end, all contribute to body forth the same general conception, is an exercise of the same powers of imagination, abstraction, and discrimination (though in an inferior degree) which would have enabled ourselves to produce the selfsame work. Do we not accordingly see that as much genius is often displayed in explaining the design and bringing out the hidden significance of a work of art, as in creating it? I have sometimes thought that *conceptive* genius is, in certain cases, even a higher faculty than *creative*. From the data afforded by a person's conversation and life, to frame a connected outline of the inward structure of that person's mind, so as to know and feel what the man is, and how life and the world paint themselves to his conceptions; still more to decipher in that same manner the mind of an age or a nation, and gain from history or travelling a vivid conception of the mind of a Greek or Roman, a Spanish peasant, an American, or a Hindu, is an effort of genius, superior, I must needs believe, to any which was ever shown in the creation of a fictitious character, inasmuch as the imagination is limited by a particular set of conditions, instead of ranging at pleasure within the bounds of human nature.

If there be truth in the principle which the foregoing remarks are intended to illustrate, there is ground for considerable objection to the course of argument which you have adopted in the article which gave occasion to the present letter. You argue, throughout, on the obstacles which oppose the growth and manifestation of genius, as if the future discoverer had to travel to the extreme verge of the ground already rescued from the dominion of doubt and mystery, before he can find any scope for the faculty thereafter to be developed in him,—as if he had first to learn all that has already been known, and then to commence an entirely new series of intellectual operations in order to enlarge the field of human knowledge. Now I conceive, on the contrary, that the career of the discoverer is only the career of the learner, carried on into untrodden ground; and that he has only to continue to do exactly what he ought to have been doing from the first, what he *has* been doing if he be really qualified to be a discoverer. You might, therefore, have spared yourself the inquiry, whether new truths, in as great abundance as ever, are within reach, and whether the approach to them is longer and more difficult than heretofore. According to my view, genius stands not in need of access to new truths, but is always where knowledge is, being itself nothing but a mind with capacity to know. There will be as much room and as much necessity for genius when mankind shall have found out everything attainable by their faculties, as there is now; it will still remain to distinguish the man who knows from the man who takes upon trust—the man who can feel and understand truth, from the man who merely assents to it, the active from the merely passive mind. Nor needs genius be a rare gift bestowed on few. By the aid of suitable culture all might possess it, although in unequal degrees.

The question, then, of 'the comparative influence of ancient and modern times on the development of genius,' is a simpler, yet a larger and more commanding question, than you seem to have supposed. It is no other than this: have the moderns, or the ancients, made most use of the faculty of thought, and which of the two have cultivated it the most highly? Did the ancients *think* and find out for themselves what they ought to believe and to do, taking nothing for granted?—and do the moderns, in comparison, merely *remember* and *imitate*, believing either nothing, or what is told them, and doing either nothing, or what is set down for them?

To this great question I am hardly able to determine

whether you have said aye or no. You are pleading for the moderns against those who place the ancients above them, for civilization and refinement against the charge of being impediments to genius; yet you seem incidentally to admit that inferiority in the higher endowments, which it appeared to be your object to disprove. Your only salvo [11] for the admission is, that, if the fact be so, it must be our own fault. Assuredly it is always our own fault. It is just as possible to be a great man now as it ever was, would but any one try. But that does not explain why we do not try, and why others, mere men like ourselves, *did;* any more than we can explain why the Turks are not as good sailors as the English, by saying that it is all their own fault.

I cannot say that I think you have much advanced the question by terminating where you do. If you were writing to Pagans, it might have been to the purpose to tell them that they would find in Christianity a corrective to their faults and ills; or if we had been superior to the ancients instead of inferior, as in numerous other respects we really are, Christianity might have been assigned as the cause. But to refer us to Christianity as the fountain of intellectual vigour, in explanation of our having fallen off in intellectual vigour since we embraced Christianity, will scarcely be satisfactory. In proportion as our religion gives us an advantage over our predecessors, must an inferiority to them be the more manifest if we have fallen below them after all. If genius, as well as other blessings, be among the natural fruits of Christianity, there must be some reason why Christianity has been our faith for 1500 years, without our having yet begun to reap this benefit. The important question to have resolved would have been, what is the obstacle? The solution of this difficulty I have sought in vain from your two articles—permit me now to seek it from yourself.

I complain of what you have omitted, rather than of what you have said. I have found in your general observations much that is *true*, much that is wise, and eternally profitable to my-

11 "Excuse"; "justification."

self and to all men. The fact which you announce, of the intimate connexion of intellectual with moral greatness, of all soundness and comprehensiveness of intellect with the sublime impartiality resulting from an ever-present and overruling attachment to duty and to truth, is deeply momentous; and, though many have known it heretofore, you also speak as one who knows it,—who therefore has discovered it in himself. It is as true now as it was of yore, that 'the righteousness of the righteous man guideth his steps.'[12] But Christianity, since it first visited the earth, has made many righteous men according to their lights, many in whom the spiritual part prevailed as far as is given to man over the animal and worldly, yet we have not proportionally abounded in men of genius.

There must, then, be some defect in our mental training, which has prevented us from turning either Christianity or our other opportunities to the account we might. Christianity, and much else, cannot have been so taught or so learnt as to make us thinking beings. Is it not that these things have *only* been taught and learnt, but have *not* been *known?*—that the truths which we have inherited still remain traditional, and no one among us, except here and there a man of genius, has made them truly his own?

The ancients, in this particular, were very differently circumstanced. When the range of human experience was still narrow—when, as yet, few facts had been observed and recorded, and there was nothing or but little to learn by rote, those who had curiosity to gratify, or who desired to acquaint themselves with nature and life, were fain to look into things, and not pay themselves with opinions; to see the objects themselves, and not their mere images reflected from the minds of those who had formerly seen them. Education *then* consisted not in giving what is called knowledge, that is, grinding down other men's ideas to a convenient size, and administering them in the form of *cram*—it was a series of exercises to form the thinking faculty itself, that the mind, being active and vigorous, might go forth and know.

[12] Proverbs 11:5.

Such was the education of Greece and Rome, especially Greece. Her philosophers were not formed, nor did they form their scholars, by placing a suit of ready-made truths before them, and helping them to put it on. They helped the disciple to form to himself an intellect fitted to seek truth for itself and to find it. No Greek or Roman schoolboy learnt anything by rote, unless it were verses of Homer or songs in honour of the gods. Modern superciliousness and superficiality have treated the disputations of the sophists as they have those of the schoolmen, with unbounded contempt: the contempt would be better bestowed on the tuition of Eton or Westminster.[13] Those disputations were a kind of mental gymnastics, eminently conducive to acuteness in detecting fallacies; consistency and circumspection in tracing a principle to its consequences; and a faculty of penetrating and searching analysis. They became ridiculous only when, like all other successful systems, they were imitated by persons incapable of entering into their spirit, and degenerated into foppery and *charlatanerie*. With powers thus formed, and no possibility of parroting where there was scarcely anything to parrot, what a man knew was his own, got at by using his own senses or his own reason; and every new acquisition strengthened the powers, by the exercise of which it had been gained.

Nor must we forget to notice the fact to which you have yourself alluded, that the life of a Greek was a perpetual conflict of adverse intellects, struggling with each other, or struggling with difficulty and necessity. Every man had to play his part upon a stage where *cram* was of no use—nothing but genuine *power* would serve his turn. The studies of the closet were combined with, and were intended as, a preparation for the pursuits of active life. There was no *littérature des salons*,[14] no dilettantism in ancient Greece: wisdom was not something to be prattled about, but something to be done. It was this which, during the bright days of Greece, prevented

[13] Famous English public schools.

[14] Literature of the drawing rooms; fashionable, polite literature.

theory from degenerating into vain and idle refinements, and produced that rare combination which distinguishes the great minds of that glorious people,—of profound speculation, and business-like matter-of-fact common sense. It was not the least of the effects of this union of theory and practice, that in the good times of Greece there is no vestige of anything like sentimentality. Bred to action, and passing their lives in the midst of it, all the speculations of the Greeks were for the sake of action, all their conceptions of excellence had a direct reference to it.

This was the education to form great statesmen, great orators, great warriors, great poets, great architects, great sculptors, great philosophers; because, once for all, it formed *men* and not mere knowledge-boxes; and the men, being men, had minds, and could apply them to the work, whatever it might be, which circumstances had given them to perform. But this lasted not long: demolishing the comparatively weak attempts of their predecessors, two vast intellects arose, the one the greatest observer of his own or any age, the other the greatest dialectician, and both almost unrivalled in their powers of metaphysical analysis,—Aristotle and Plato. No sooner, by the exertions of these gigantic minds, and of others their disciples or rivals, was a considerable body of truth, or at least of opinion, got together—no sooner did it become *possible* by mere memory to seem to know something, and to be able for some purposes even to use that knowledge, as men use the rules of arithmetic who have not the slightest notion of the grounds of them, than men found out how much easier it is to remember than to think, and abandoned the pursuit of intellectual power itself for the attempt, without possessing it, to appropriate its results. Even the reverence which mankind had for these great men became a hinderance to following their example. Nature was studied not in nature, but in Plato or Aristotle, in Zeno or Epicurus.[15] Discussion became the mere rehearsal of a lesson got by rote. The attempt to think for oneself fell into

[15] Zeno of Citium (*ca.* 336–*ca.* 264 B.C.), Greek philosopher, founder of Stoicism.—Epicurus (*ca.* 342–*ca.* 270 B.C.), Greek philosopher.

disuse; and, by ceasing to exercise the power, mankind ceased to possess it.

It was in this spirit that, on the rise of Christianity, the doctrines and precepts of Scripture began to be studied. For this there was somewhat greater excuse, as, where the authority was that of the Omniscient, the confirmation of fallible reason might appear less necessary. Yet the effect was fatal. The interpretation of the Gospel was handed over to grammarians and language-grinders. The words of him whose speech was in figures and parables were iron-bound and petrified into inanimate and inflexible *formulae*. Jesus was likened to a logician, framing a rule to meet all cases, and provide against all possible evasions, instead of a poet, orator, and *vates*,[16] whose object was to purify and spiritualize the mind, so that, under the guidance of its purity, its own lights might suffice to find the law of which he only supplied the spirit, and suggested the general scope. Hence, out of the least dogmatical of books, have been generated so many dogmatical religions—each claiming to be found in the book, and none in the mind of man; they are above thought, and thought is to have nothing to do with them; until religion, instead of a spirit pervading the mind, becomes a crust encircling it, nowise penetrating the obdurate mass within, but only keeping out such rays of precious light or genial heat as might haply have come from elsewhere.

And after all which has been done to break down these vitiating, soul-debasing prejudices, against which every great mind of the last two centuries has protested, where are we now? Are not the very first general propositions that are presented for a child's acceptance, theological dogmas, presented not as truths believed by others, and which the child will hereafter be encouraged to know for itself, but as doctrines which it is to believe before it can attach any meaning to them, or be chargeable with the greatest guilt? At school, what is the child taught, except to repeat by rote, or at most to apply technical rules, which are lodged, not in his reason, but in his

16 A seer.

memory? When he leaves school, does not everything which a young person sees and hears conspire to tell him, that it is not expected he shall think, but only that he shall profess no opinion on any subject different from that professed by other people? Is there anything a man can do, short of swindling or forgery, (*à fortiori*[17] a woman,) which will so surely gain him the reputation of a dangerous, or, at least, an unaccountable person, as daring, without either rank or reputation as a warrant for the eccentricity, to make a practice of forming his opinions for himself?

Modern education is all *cram*—Latin cram, mathematical cram, literary cram, political cram, theological cram, moral cram. The world already knows everything, and has only to tell it to its children, who, on their part, have only to hear, and lay it to rote (not to *heart*). Any purpose, any idea of training the mind itself, has gone out of the world. Nor can I yet perceive many symptoms of amendment. Those who dislike what is taught, mostly—if I may trust my own experience—dislike it not for being *cram*, but for being other people's cram, and not theirs. Were they the teachers, they would teach different doctrines, but they would teach them *as* doctrines, not as subjects for impartial inquiry. Those studies which only train the faculties, and produce no fruits obvious to the sense, are fallen into neglect. The most valuable kind of mental gymnastics, logic and metaphysics, have been more neglected and undervalued for the last thirty years, than at any time since the revival of letters. Even the ancient languages, which, when rationally taught, are, from their regular and complicated structure, to a certain extent a lesson of logical classification and analysis, and which give access to a literature more rich than any other, in all that forms a vigorous intellect and a manly character, are insensibly falling into disrepute as a branch of liberal education. Instead of them, we are getting the ready current coin of modern languages, and physical science taught empirically, by committing to memory its results.

17 "With stronger reason," "more conclusively."

Whatever assists in feeding the body, we can see the use of; not so if it serves the body only by forming the mind.

Is it any wonder that, thus educated, we should decline in genius? That the ten centuries of England or France cannot produce as many illustrious names as the hundred and fifty years of little Greece? The wonder is, that we should have produced so many as we have, amidst such adverse circumstances. We have had some true philosophers, and a few genuine poets; two or three great intellects have revolutionized physical science; but in almost every branch of literature and art we are deplorably behind the earlier ages of the world. In art, we hardly attempt anything except spoiled copies of antiquity and the middle ages. We are content to copy them, because that requires less trouble and less cultivated faculties than to comprehend them. If we had genius to enter into the *spirit* of ancient art, the same genius would enable us to clothe that spirit in ever-new forms.

Where, then, is the remedy? It is in the knowledge and clear comprehension of the evil. It is in the distinct recognition, that the end of education is not to *teach*, but to fit the mind for learning from its own consciousness and observation; that we have occasion for this power under ever-varying circumstances, for which no routine or rule of thumb can possibly make provision. As the memory is trained by remembering, so is the reasoning power by reasoning; the imaginative by imagining; the analytic by analysing; the inventive by finding out. Let the education of the mind consist in calling out and exercising these faculties: never trouble yourself about giving knowledge—train the *mind*—keep it supplied with materials, and knowledge will come of itself. Let all *cram* be ruthlessly discarded. Let each person be made to feel that in other things he may believe upon trust—if he find a trustworthy authority—but that in the line of his peculiar duty, and in the line of the duties common to all men, it is his business to *know*. Let the feelings of society cease to stigmatize independent thinking, and divide its censure between a lazy dereliction of the duty and privilege of thought, and the overweening self-conceit of a half-thinker, who rushes to his conclusions without taking the trouble to understand the thoughts of other men. Were all this done, there would be no complaint of any want of genius in modern times. But when will that hour come? Though it come not at all, yet is it not less your duty and mine to strive for it,—and first to do what is certainly and absolutely in our power, to realize it in our own persons.

I am, Sir, yours respectfully,

ANTIQUUS.[18]

---

18 "The ancient."

Browning's *Pauline*

1833

Pauline (1833) was Robert Browning's first published poem. He asked his friend W. J. Fox, editor of the *Monthly Repository*, to help him publicize it, and Fox did so by writing a favorable review himself and by giving *his* friend Mill a copy of the poem to review. Although Mill wrote reviews of it for both the *Examiner* and Tait's *Edinburgh Magazine*, neither was published. We do not have the reviews themselves but we do have Mill's marginal annotations in his copy of the poem and his general estimate of it written on the flyleaf. When Mill returned the annotated copy to Fox, he warned his friend that "on the whole the observations are not flattering to the author—perhaps too strong in the *expression* to be shown to him."

But Browning did see the copy and was affected by the criticism. W. C. De Vane goes so far as to say that "this critique changed the course of Browning's poetical career" (*A Browning Handbook*, p. 47). That Browning took Mill's strictures seriously is evident in the elaborate answers he wrote beneath Mill's marginal criticisms. In his introductory note to *Pauline* in the 1868 edition of his poems, Browning acknowledged that Mill's criticism had taught him the folly of baring his soul in the public-confessional mode of Shelley and had led him to start writing a kind of poetry "dramatic in principle, and so many utterances of so many imaginary persons, not mine."

With considerable poetic powers, the writer seems to me possessed with a more intense and morbid self-consciousness than I ever knew in any sane human being. I should think it a sincere confession, though of a most unlovable state, if the "Pauline" were not evidently a mere phantom. All about her is full of inconsistency—he neither loves her nor fancies he loves her, yet insists upon *talking* love to her. If she *existed* and loved him, he treats her most ungenerously and unfeelingly. All his aspirings and yearnings and regrets point to other things, never to her; then he *pays her off* toward the end by a piece of flummery, amounting to the modest request that she will love him and live with him and give herself up to him *without* his *loving her—moyennant quoi*[1] he will think her and call her everything that is handsome, and he promises her that she shall find it mighty pleasant. Then he leaves off by saying he knows he shall have changed his mind by to-morrow, and despite "these intents which seem so fair," but that having been thus visited once no doubt he will be again—and is therefore "in perfect joy," bad luck to him! as the Irish say. A cento[2] of most beautiful passages might be made from this poem, and the psychological history of himself is powerful and truthful—*truth-like* certainly, all but the last stage. *That*, he evidently has not yet got into. The self-seeking and self-worshipping state is well described—beyond that, I should think the writer had made, as yet, only the next step, viz. into despising his own state. I even question whether part even of that self-disdain is not *assumed*. He is evidently *dissatisfied*, and feels part of the badness of his state; he does not write as if it were purged out of him. If he once could muster a hearty hatred of his selfishness it would *go;* as it is, he feels only the *lack* of *good*, not the positive evil. He feels not remorse, but only disappointment; a mind in that state can only be regenerated by some new passion, and I know not what to wish for him but that he may meet with a *real* Pauline.

Meanwhile he should not attempt to show how a person may be *recovered* from this morbid state,—for *he* is hardly convalescent, and "what should we speak of but that which we know?"

---

[1] "In return for which."

[2] Literary composition formed of selections.

What is Poetry?

1833

Although Mill told Carlyle in a letter that "What is Poetry?" simply embodied some loose thoughts which he had long had in mind about poetry and art, the article can usefully be viewed as a conscious attempt to refute the charges made against poetry by Jeremy Bentham, Mill's own teacher. Bentham had argued that the poet's business "consists in stimulating our passions and exciting our prejudices. . . . The poet must see everything through colored media, and strive to make everyone else do the same." [1]

Mill sought to exonerate poetry by offering a new definition of it. He had to show, first, that genuine poetry does not have designs upon its audience, that it is distinct from both eloquence and rhetoric because it does not try to instill convictions in the reader or rouse him to action. Therefore Mill defines poetry as soliloquy, speech that is uttered without awareness of (though it may be overheard by) an audience. In order to lay to rest the Benthamite suspicion of poetry as being merely a branch of rhetoric, he removes the poet from his audience into solitude.

Bentham had also criticized poetry for its untruthfulness; and to satisfy Bentham on this point Mill had, secondly, to make the poet independent of the external world. He admits that poetry must indeed stand the test of truth, but of truth to the inner and not the outer world. The poet must truthfully depict the state of his own mind, not the face of visible nature. In order to allay the objections of the positivists, for the traditional aesthetic theory of imitation Mill substitutes an aesthetics of expression.

But despite his rejection of rhetoric and didacticism as poetically impure, Mill still thinks of poetry as serving a moral function. Although the true poet must remain unconscious of an audience while he is writing, he may show the finished product to others. Then true poetry will produce its moral effect, not by arguing for certain doctrines but by working, albeit unintentionally, upon the emotions of readers. The poet having rendered his emotion with perfect integrity, the reader will benefit from sharing

[1] *The Works of Jeremy Bentham* (Edinburgh, 1838–1843), II, 254.

it as he never could benefit from sharing an emotion artificially manufactured for his consumption.

It has often been asked, What is Poetry? And many and various are the answers which have been returned. The vulgarest of all—one with which no person possessed of the faculties to which Poetry addresses itself can ever have been satisfied—is that which confounds poetry with metrical composition: yet to this wretched mockery of a definition, many have been led back, by the failure of all their attempts to find any other that would distinguish what they have been accustomed to call poetry, from much which they have known only under other names.

That, however, the word 'poetry' imports something quite peculiar in its nature, something which may exist in what is called prose as well as in verse, something which does not even require the instrument of words, but can speak through the other audible symbols called musical sounds, and even through the visible ones which are the language of sculpture, painting, and architecture; all this, we believe, is and must be felt, though perhaps indistinctly, by all upon whom poetry in any of its shapes produces any impression beyond that of tickling the ear. The distinction between poetry and what is not poetry, whether explained or not, is felt to be fundamental: and where every one feels a difference, a difference there must be. All other appearances may be fallacious, but the appearance of a difference is a real difference. Appearances too, like other things, must have a cause, and that which can cause anything, even an illusion, must be a reality. And hence, while a half-philosophy disdains the classifications and distinctions indicated by popular language, philosophy carried to its highest point frames new ones, but rarely sets aside the old, content with correcting and regularizing them. It cuts fresh channels for thought, but does not fill up such as it finds ready-made; it

First published in the *Monthly Repository*, VII (January 1833).

traces, on the contrary, more deeply, broadly, and distinctly, those into which the current has spontaneously flowed.

Let us then attempt, in the way of modest inquiry, not to coerce and confine nature within the bounds of an arbitrary definition, but rather to find the boundaries which she herself has set, and erect a barrier round them; not calling mankind to account for having misapplied the word 'poetry,' but attempting to clear up the conception which they already attach to it, and to bring forward as a distinct principle that which, as a vague feeling, has really guided them in their employment of the term.

The object of poetry is confessedly to act upon the emotions; and therein is poetry sufficiently distinguished from what Wordsworth affirms to be its logical opposite, namely, not prose, but matter of fact or science.[1] The one addresses itself to the belief, the other to the feelings. The one does its work by convincing or persuading, the other by moving. The one acts by presenting a proposition to the understanding, the other by offering interesting objects of contemplation to the sensibilities.

This, however, leaves us very far from a definition of poetry. This distinguishes it from one thing, but we are bound to distinguish it from everything. To bring thoughts or images before the mind for the purpose of acting upon the emotions, does not belong to poetry alone. It is equally the province (for example) of the novelist: and yet the faculty of the poet and that of the novelist are as distinct as any other two faculties; as the faculties of the novelist and of the orator, or of the poet and the metaphysician. The two characters may be united, as characters the most disparate may; but they have no natural connexion.

Many of the greatest poems are in the form of fictitious narratives, and in almost all good serious fictions there is true poetry. But there is a radical distinction between the interest felt in a story as such, and the interest excited by poetry; for the one is derived from incident, the other from the represen-

[1] Preface to *Lyrical Ballads*, 1800.

tation of feeling. In one, the source of the emotion excited is the exhibition of a state or states of human sensibility; in the other, of a series of states of mere outward circumstances. Now, all minds are capable of being affected more or less by representations of the latter kind, and all, or almost all, by those of the former; yet the two sources of interest correspond to two distinct, and (as respects their greatest development) mutually exclusive, characters of mind.

At what age is the passion for a story, for almost any kind of story, merely as a story, the most intense? In childhood. But that also is the age at which poetry, even of the simplest description, is least relished and least understood; because the feelings with which it is especially conversant are yet undeveloped, and not having been even in the slightest degree experienced, cannot be sympathized with. In what stage of the progress of society, again, is storytelling most valued, and the story-teller in greatest request and honour?—In a rude state like that of the Tartars and Arabs at this day, and of almost all nations in the earliest ages. But in this state of society there is little poetry except ballads, which are mostly narrative, that is, essentially stories, and derive their principal interest from the incidents. Considered as poetry, they are of the lowest and most elementary kind: the feelings depicted, or rather indicated, are the simplest our nature has; such joys and griefs as the immediate pressure of some outward event excites in rude minds, which live wholly immersed in outward things, and have never, either from choice or a force they could not resist, turned themselves to the contemplation of the world within. Passing now from childhood, and from the childhood of society, to the grown-up men and women of this most grown-up and unchildlike age—the minds and hearts of greatest depth and elevation are commonly those which take greatest delight in poetry; the shallowest and emptiest, on the contrary, are, at all events, not those least addicted to novel-reading. This accords, too, with all analogous experience of human nature. The sort of persons whom not merely in books, but in their lives, we find perpetually engaged in hunting for excitement from without, are invariably those who do not possess, either in the vigour of their intellectual powers or in the depth of their sensibilities, that which would enable them to find ample excitement nearer home. The most idle and frivolous persons take a natural delight in fictitious narrative; the excitement it affords is of the kind which comes from without. Such persons are rarely lovers of poetry, though they may fancy themselves so, because they relish novels in verse. But poetry, which is the delineation of the deeper and more secret workings of human emotion, is interesting only to those to whom it recals what they have felt, or whose imagination it stirs up to conceive what they could feel, or what they might have been able to feel, had their outward circumstances been different.

Poetry, when it is really such, is truth; and fiction also, if it is good for anything, is truth: but they are different truths. The truth of poetry is to paint the human soul truly: the truth of fiction is to give a true picture of life. The two kinds of knowledge are different, and come by different ways, come mostly to different persons. Great poets are often proverbially ignorant of life. What they know has come by observation of themselves; they have found within them one highly delicate and sensitive specimen of human nature, on which the laws of emotion are written in large characters, such as can be read off without much study. Other knowledge of mankind, such as comes to men of the world by outward experience, is not indispensable to them as poets: but to the novelist such knowledge is all in all; he has to describe outward things, not the inward man; actions and events, not feelings; and it will not do for him to be numbered among those who, as Madame Roland said of Brissot,[2] know man but not *men*.

All this is no bar to the possibility of combining both elements, poetry and narrative or incident, in the same work, and calling it either a novel or a poem; but so may red and white

---

[2] Manon Phlipon Roland de la Platière (1754–1793), a French revolutionist, said this of Jacques Pierre Brissot de Warville (1754–1793), her fellow revolutionist and victim of the guillotine.

combine on the same human features, or on the same canvas. There is one order of composition which requires the union of poetry and incident, each in its highest kind—the dramatic. Even there the two elements are perfectly distinguishable, and may exist of unequal quality, and in the most various proportion. The incidents of a dramatic poem may be scanty and ineffective, though the delineation of passion and character may be of the highest order; as in Goethe's admirable Torquato Tasso; [3] or again, the story as a mere story may be well got up for effect, as is the case with some of the most trashy productions of the Minerva press: [4] it may even be, what those are not, a coherent and probable series of events, though there be scarcely a feeling exhibited which is not represented falsely, or in a manner absolutely commonplace. The combination of the two excellencies is what renders Shakespeare so generally acceptable, each sort of readers finding in him what is suitable to their faculties. To the many he is great as a story-teller, to the few as a poet.

In limiting poetry to the delineaton of states of feeling, and denying the name where nothing is delineated but outward objects, we may be thought to have done what we promised to avoid—to have not found, but made a definition, in opposition to the usage of language, since it is established by common consent that there is a poetry called descriptive. We deny the charge. Description is not poetry because there is descriptive poetry, no more than science is poetry because there is such a thing as a didactic poem. But an object which admits of being described, or a truth which may fill a place in a scientific treatise, may also furnish an occasion for the generation of poetry, which we thereupon choose to call descriptive or didactic. The poetry is not in the object itself, nor in the scientific truth itself, but in the state of mind in which the one and the other may be contemplated. The mere delineation of the dimensions and colours of external objects is not poetry, no more than a geometrical ground-plan of St. Peter's or

[3] Verse play of 1790.

[4] Publishers of sentimental novels.

Westminster Abbey is painting. Descriptive poetry consists, no doubt, in description, but in description of things as they appear, not as they are; and it paints them not in their bare and natural lineaments, but seen through the medium and arrayed in the colours of the imagination set in action by the feelings. If a poet describes a lion, he does not describe him as a naturalist would, nor even as a traveller would, who was intent upon stating the truth, the whole truth, and nothing but the truth. He describes him by imagery, that is, by suggesting the most striking likenesses and contrasts which might occur to a mind contemplating the lion, in the state of awe, wonder, or terror, which the spectacle naturally excites, or is, on the occasion, supposed to excite. Now this is describing the lion professedly, but the state of excitement of the spectator really. The lion may be described falsely or with exaggeration, and the poetry be all the better; but if the human emotion be not painted with scrupulous truth, the poetry is bad poetry, *i.e.* is not poetry at all, but a failure.

Thus far our progress towards a clear view of the essentials of poetry has brought us very close to the last two attempts at a definition of poetry which we happen to have seen in print, both of them by poets and men of genius. The one is by Ebenezer Elliott,[5] the author of Corn-Law Rhymes, and other poems of still greater merit. 'Poetry,' says he, 'is impassioned truth.' The other is by a writer in Blackwood's Magazine, and comes, we think, still nearer the mark. He defines poetry, 'man's thoughts tinged by his feelings.' There is in either definition a near approximation to what we are in search of. Every truth which a human being can enunciate, every thought, even every outward impression, which can enter into his consciousness, may become poetry when shown through any impassioned medium, when invested with the colouring of joy, or grief, or pity, or affection, or admiration, or reverence, or awe, or even hatred or terror: and, unless so coloured, nothing,

[5] Ebenezer Elliott (1781–1849), author of the "Corn-Law Rhymes" (1831), was a political poet whom Mill wrongly supposed to be a member of the working class.

be it as interesting as it may, is poetry. But both these definitions fail to discriminate between poetry and eloquence. Eloquence, as well as poetry, is impassioned truth; eloquence, as well as poetry, is thoughts coloured by the feelings. Yet common apprehension and philosophic criticism alike recognise a distinction between the two: there is much that every one would call eloquence, which no one would think of classing as poetry. A question will sometimes arise, whether some particular author is a poet; and those who maintain the negative commonly allow, that though not a poet, he is a highly eloquent writer. The distinction between poetry and eloquence appears to us to be equally fundamental with the distinction between poetry and narrative, or between poetry and description, while it is still farther from having been satisfactorily cleared up than either of the others.

Poetry and eloquence are both alike the expression or utterance of feeling. But if we may be excused the antithesis, we should say that eloquence is *heard*, poetry is *over*heard. Eloquence supposes an audience; the peculiarity of poetry appears to us to lie in the poet's utter unconsciousness of a listener. Poetry is feeling confessing itself to itself, in moments of solitude, and embodying itself in symbols which are the nearest possible representations of the feeling in the exact shape in which it exists in the poet's mind. Eloquence is feeling pouring itself out to other minds, courting their sympathy, or endeavouring to influence their belief or move them to passion or to action.

All poetry is of the nature of soliloquy. It may be said that poetry which is printed on hot-pressed paper and sold at a bookseller's shop, is a soliloquy in full dress, and on the stage. It is so; but there is nothing absurd in the idea of such a mode of soliloquizing. What we have said to ourselves, we may tell to others afterwards; what we have said or done in solitude, we may voluntarily reproduce when we know that other eyes are upon us. But no trace of consciousness that any eyes are upon us must be visible in the work itself. The actor knows that there is an audience present; but if he act as though he knew it, he acts ill. A poet may write poetry not only with the intention of printing it, but for the express purpose of being paid for it; that it should *be* poetry, being written under such influences, is less probable; not, however, impossible; but no otherwise possible than if he can succeed in excluding from his work every vestige of such lookings-forth into the outward and every-day world, and can express his emotions exactly as he has felt them in solitude, or as he is conscious that he should feel them though they were to remain for ever unuttered, or (at the lowest) as he knows that others feel them in similar circumstances of solitude. But when he turns round and addresses himself to another person; when the act of utterance is not itself the end, but a means to an end,—viz. by the feelings he himself expresses, to work upon the feelings, or upon the belief, or the will, of another,—when the expression of his emotions, or of his thoughts tinged by his emotions, is tinged also by that purpose, by that desire of making an impression upon another mind, then it ceases to be poetry, and becomes eloquence.

Poetry, accordingly, is the natural fruit of solitude and meditation; eloquence, of intercourse with the world. The persons who have most feeling of their own, if intellectual culture has given them a language in which to express it, have the highest faculty of poetry; those who best understand the feelings of others, are the most eloquent. The persons, and the nations, who commonly excel in poetry, are those whose character and tastes render them least dependent upon the applause, or sympathy, or concurrence of the world in general. Those to whom that applause, that sympathy, that concurrence are most necessary, generally excel most in eloquence. And hence, perhaps, the French, who are the least poetical of all great and intellectual nations, are among the most eloquent: the French, also, being the most sociable, the vainest, and the least self-dependent.

If the above be, as we believe, the true theory of the distinction commonly admitted between eloquence and poetry; or even though it be not so, yet if, as we cannot doubt, the distinction above stated be a real *bonâ fide* distinction, it will be found to hold, not merely in the language of words, but in all other language, and to intersect the whole domain of art.

Take, for example, music: we shall find in that art, so peculiarly the expression of passion, two perfectly distinct styles; one of which may be called the poetry, the other the oratory of music. This difference, being seized, would put an end to much musical sectarianism. There has been much contention whether the music of the modern Italian school, that of Rossini [6] and his successors, be impassioned or not. Without doubt, the passion it expresses is not the musing, meditative tenderness, or pathos, or grief of Mozart or Beethoven. Yet it is passion, but garrulous passion—the passion which pours itself into other ears; and therein the better calculated for dramatic effect, having a natural adaptation for dialogue. Mozart also is great in musical oratory; but his most touching compositions are in the opposite style—that of soliloquy. Who can imagine 'Dove sono' [7] *heard?* We imagine it *over*heard.

Purely pathetic music commonly partakes of soliloquy. The soul is absorbed in its distress, and though there may be bystanders, it is not thinking of them. When the mind is looking within, and not without, its state does not often or rapidly vary; and hence the even, uninterrupted flow, approaching almost to monotony, which a good reader, or a good singer, will give to words or music of a pensive or melancholy cast. But grief taking the form of a prayer, or of a complaint, becomes oratorical; no longer low, and even, and subdued, it assumes a more emphatic rhythm, a more rapidly returning accent; instead of a few slow equal notes, following one after another at regular intervals, it crowds note upon note, and often assumes a hurry and bustle like joy. Those who are familiar with some of the best of Rossini's [8] serious compositions, such as the air 'Tu che i miseri conforti,' in the opera of

[6] Gioacchino Antonio Rossini (1792–1868), Italian operatic composer.

[7] "Dove sono i bei momenti" ("Where are those wondrous moments?"), an aria from Mozart's *Marriage of Figaro.*

[8] Gioacchino Antonio Rossini (1792–1868), Italian composer whose operas include *Tancredi* (1813) and *La Gazza Ladra* (*The Thieving Magpie,* 1817).

'Tancredi,' or the duet 'Ebben per mia memoria,' in 'La Gazza Ladra,' will at once understand and feel our meaning. Both are highly tragic and passionate; the passion of both is that of oratory, not poetry. The like may be said of that most moving invocation in Beethoven's 'Fidelio'—

> 'Komm, Hoffnung, lass das letzte Stern
> Der Müde nicht erbleichen;' [9]

in which Madame Schröder Devrient [10] exhibited such consummate powers of pathetic expression. How different from Winter's [11] beautiful 'Paga fui,' the very soul of melancholy exhaling itself in solitude; fuller of meaning, and, therefore, more profoundly poetical than the words for which it was composed—for it seems to express not simple melancholy, but the melancholy of remorse.

If, from vocal music, we now pass to instrumental, we may have a specimen of musical oratory in any fine military symphony or march: while the poetry of music seems to have attained its consummation in Beethoven's Overture to Egmont, so wonderful in its mixed expression of grandeur and melancholy.

In the arts which speak to the eye, the same distinctions will be found to hold, not only between poetry and oratory, but between poetry, oratory, narrative, and simple imitation or description.

Pure description is exemplified in a mere portrait or a mere landscape—productions of art, it is true, but of the mechanical rather than of the fine arts, being works of simple imitation, not creation. We say, a mere portrait, or a mere landscape, because it is possible for a portrait or a landscape, without ceasing to be such, to be also a picture; like Turner's landscapes, and the great portraits by Titian or Vandyke.[12]

---

9 "Come, hope, do not let weariness pale the last star."

10 Wilhelmine Schröder-Devrient (1804–1860), German operatic singer.

11 Peter von Winter (1754–1825), German composer.

12 Joseph Mallord William Turner (1775–1851), English landscape painter, championed by Ruskin in *Modern Painters*.—Titian (Tiziano Vecellio, 1477–1576), celebrated Venetian painter.—Sir Anthony Vandyke (1599–1641), Flemish painter of portraits and religious subjects.

Whatever in painting or sculpture expresses human feeling —or character, which is only a certain state of feeling grown habitual—may be called, according to circumstances, the poetry, or the eloquence, of the painter's or the sculptor's art: the poetry, if the feeling declares itself by such signs as escape from us when we are unconscious of being seen; the oratory, if the signs are those we use for the purpose of voluntary communication.

The narrative style answers to what is called historical painting, which it is the fashion among connoisseurs to treat as the climax of the pictorial art. That it is the most difficult branch of the art we do not doubt, because, in its perfection, it includes the perfection of all the other branches: as in like manner an epic poem, though in so far as it is epic (*i.e.* narrative) it is not poetry at all, is yet esteemed the greatest effort of poetic genius, because there is no kind whatever of poetry which may not appropriately find a place in it. But an historical picture as such, that is, as the representation of an incident, must necessarily, as it seems to us, be poor and ineffective. The narrative powers of painting are extremely limited. Scarcely any picture, scarcely even any series of pictures, tells its own story without the aid of an interpreter. But it is the single figures which, to us, are the great charm even of an historical picture. It is in these that the power of the art is really seen. In the attempt to narrate, visible and permanent signs are too far behind the fugitive audible ones, which follow so fast one after another, while the faces and figures in a narrative picture, even though they be Titian's, stand still. Who would not prefer one Virgin and Child of Raphael, to all the pictures which Rubens,[13] with his fat, frouzy Dutch Venuses, ever painted? Though Rubens, besides excelling almost every one in his mastery over the mechanical parts of his art, often shows real genius in *grouping* his figures, the peculiar problem of historical painting. But then, who, except a mere student of drawing

[13] Raphael (Rafaello Sanzio, 1483–1520), one of the greatest Italian artists of the Renaissance.—Peter Paul Rubens (1577–1640), one of the foremost painters of the Flemish school.

and colouring, ever cared to look twice at any of the figures themselves? The power of painting lies in poetry, of which Rubens had not the slightest tincture—not in narrative, wherein he might have excelled.

The single figures, however, in an historical picture, are rather the eloquence of painting than the poetry: they mostly (unless they are quite out of place in the picture) express the feelings of one person as modified by the presence of others. Accordingly the minds whose bent leads them rather to eloquence than to poetry, rush to historical painting. The French painters, for instance, seldom attempt, because they could make nothing of, single heads, like those glorious ones of the Italian masters, with which they might feed themselves day after day in their own Louvre. They must all be historical; and they are, almost to a man, attitudinizers. If we wished to give any young artist the most impressive warning our imagination could devise against that kind of vice in the pictorial, which corresponds to rant in the histrionic art, we would advise him to walk once up and once down the gallery of the Luxembourg.[14] Every figure in French painting or statuary seems to be showing itself off before spectators: they are not poetical, but in the worst style of corrupted eloquence.

[From the original (1833) version of "What is Poetry?" Mill cut the following concluding passage:]

The best are stiff and unnatural; the worst resemble figures of cataleptic patients. The French artists fancy themselves imitators of the classics, yet they seem to have no understanding and no feeling of that *repose*, which was the peculiar and pervading character of Grecian art, until it began to decline: a repose tenfold more indicative of strength than all their stretching and straining; for strength, as Thomas Carlyle says, does not manifest itself in spasms.

There are some productions of art which it seems at first difficult to arrange in any of the classes above illustrated. The

[14] Mill expresses his disdain for the galleries of the Luxembourg Palace.

direct aim of art as such, is the production of the *beautiful;* and as there are other things beautiful besides states of mind, there is much of art which may seem to have nothing to do with either poetry or eloquence as we have defined them. Take for instance a composition of Claude, or Salvator Rosa. There is here *creation* of new beauty: by the grouping of natural scenery, conformably indeed to the laws of outward nature, but not after any actual model; the result being a beauty more perfect and faultless than is perhaps to be found in any actual landscape. Yet there is a character of poetry even in these, without which they could not be so beautiful. The unity, and wholeness, and æsthetic congruity of the picture still lies in singleness of expression; but it is expression in a different sense from that in which we have hitherto employed the term. The objects in an imaginary landscape cannot be said, like the words of a poem or the notes of a melody, to be the actual utterance of a feeling; but there must be some feeling with which they harmonize, and which they have a tendency to raise up in the spectator's mind. They must inspire a feeling of grandeur, a loveliness, a cheerfulness, a wildness, a melancholy, a terror. The painter must surround his principal objects with such imagery as would spontaneously arise in a highly imaginative mind, when contemplating those objects under the impression of the feelings which they are intended to inspire. This, if it be not poetry, is so nearly allied to it, as scarcely to require being distinguished.

In this sense we may speak of the poetry of architecture. All architecture, to be impressive, must be the expression or symbol of some interesting idea, some thought, which has power over the emotions. The reason why modern architecture is so paltry, is simply that it is not the expression of any idea; it is a mere parroting of the architectural tongue of the Greeks, or of our Teutonic ancestors, without any conception of a meaning.

To confine ourselves, for the present, to religious edifices: these partake of poetry, in proportion as they express, or harmonize with, the feelings of devotion. But those feelings are different according to the conception entertained of the beings, by whose supposed nature they are called forth. To the Greek, these beings were incarnations of the greatest conceivable physical beauty, combined with supernatural power: and the Greek temples express this, their predominant character being graceful strength; in other words, solidity, which is power, and lightness which is also power, accomplishing with small means what seemed to require great; to combine all in one word, *majesty*. To the Catholic, again, the Deity was something far less clear and definite; a being of still more resistless power than the heathen divinities; greatly to be loved; still more greatly to be feared; and wrapped up in vagueness, mystery, and incomprehensibility. A certain solemnity, a feeling of doubting and trembling hope, like that of one lost in a boundless forest who thinks he knows his way but is not sure, mixes itself in all the genuine expressions of Catholic devotion. This is eminently the expression of the pure Gothic cathedral; conspicuous equally in the mingled majesty and gloom of its vaulted roofs and stately aisles, and in the 'dim religious light' which steals through its painted windows.

There is no generic distinction between the imagery which is the *expression* of feeling and the imagery which is felt to *harmonize* with feeling. They are identical. The imagery in which feeling utters itself forth from within, is also that in which it delights when presented to it from without. All art, therefore, in proportion as it produces its effects by an appeal to the emotions partakes of poetry, unless it partakes of oratory, or of narrative. And the distinction which these three words indicate, runs through the whole field of the fine arts.

The above hints have no pretension to the character of a theory. They are merely thrown out for the consideration of thinkers, in the hope that if they do not contain the truth, they may do somewhat to suggest it. Nor would they, crude as they are, have been deemed worthy of publication, in any country but one in which the philosophy of art is so completely neglected, that whatever may serve to put any inquiring mind upon this kind of investigation, cannot well, however imperfect in itself, fail altogether to be of use.

The Two Kinds of Poetry

1833

In "The Two Kinds of Poetry" Mill continues the general discussion of poetry begun in "What is Poetry?" (In 1859 he reprinted both essays under the single title, "Thoughts of Poetry and Its Varieties.") In trying to answer the question whether there are poetic natures, Mill recognizes a certain kind of temperament which is peculiarly suited for the production of poetry but does not necessarily produce it. At first he seems to subscribe to the conventional English distinction between the poetry of nature and the poetry of culture, but then he argues that only those persons may be called poets whose ideas are linked by emotions. In everyone else poetry, instead of being habitual and characteristic, must be artificially induced.

Once he has agreed to speak of two kinds of poet, Mill proposes Wordsworth and Shelley as representatives of each. In comparing these poets, Mill must have been disturbed by conflicting loyalties. He owed his mental health to Wordsworth, but he respected Shelley as the favorite poet of Harriet Taylor. In Wordsworth, he argues, the thought rather than the emotion is of first importance; the emotion serves only as a means for coloring and conveying the thought. Shelley is the chief representative of the natural poets because, lacking the consecutiveness of thought needed for a long poem, he succeeds best in the short lyric. His poetry, says Mill, is both inspired and nourished by emotions. The main prerequisite for such poetry is simply an unusually high degree of susceptibility to pleasure and pain; its production depends not upon the acquisition of knowledge and technical skill but upon the poet's ability to keep intact his peculiar sensibility.

But Mill takes note of the dangers as well as the blessings of uneducated sensibility. He points out that the powerful emotions which often disturb the poet's equilibrium of judgment and undermine his respect for truth also supply the stuff from which all motives, including the desire for truth, spring. He maintains that the poetic sensibility is a great amoral force which must be educated, not simply thwarted. The most impassioned natures have the greatest desire for truth. If their emotions are fortified by an adequate intellectual culture, they usually become the most powerful intellects; but if their natural endowments are corrupted, they become dangerous. The essay thus combines a celebration of emotion with a warning against undisciplined emotion in a way that is characteristic of Mill's attempt to harmonize his newly discovered respect for the feelings with his older commitment to the life of the mind.

NASCITUR POËTA [1] is a maxim of classical antiquity, which has passed to these latter days with less questioning than most of the doctrines of that early age. When it originated, the human faculties were occupied, fortunately for posterity, less in examining how the works of genius are created, than in creating them: and the adage, probably, had no higher source than the tendency common among mankind to consider all power which is not visibly the effect of practice, all skill which is not capable of being reduced to mechanical rules, as the result of a peculiar gift. Yet this aphorism, born in the infancy of psychology, will perhaps be found, now when that science is in its adolescence, to be as true as an epigram ever is, that is, to contain some truth: truth, however, which has been so compressed and bent out of shape, in order to tie it up into so small a knot of only two words that it requires an almost infinite amount of unrolling and laying straight, before it will resume its just proportions.

We are not now intending to remark upon the grosser misapplications of this ancient maxim, which have engendered so many races of poetasters. The days are gone by, when every raw youth whose borrowed phantasies have set themselves to a borrowed tune, mistaking, as Coleridge says, an ardent desire of poetic reputation for poetic genius, while unable to disguise from himself that he had taken no means whereby he might

First published in the *Monthly Repository*, VII (October 1833).

[1] *Poeta nascitur, non fit* ("A poet is born, not made").

become a poet, could fancy himself a born one. Those who would reap without sowing, and gain the victory without fighting the battle, are ambitious now of another sort of distinction, and are born novelists, or public speakers, not poets. And the wiser thinkers understand and acknowledge that poetic excellence is subject to the same necessary conditions with any other mental endowment; and that to no one of the spiritual benefactors of mankind is a higher or a more assiduous intellectual culture needful than to the poet. It is true, he possesses this advantage over others who use the 'instrument of words,' [2] that, of the truths which he utters, a larger proportion are derived from personal consciousness, and a smaller from philosophic investigation. But the power itself of discriminating between what really is consciousness, and what is only a process of inference completed in a single instant–and the capacity of distinguishing whether that of which the mind is conscious be an eternal truth, or but a dream–are among the last results of the most matured and perfect intellect. Not to mention that the poet, no more than any other person who writes, confines himself altogether to intuitive truths, nor has any means of communicating even these but by words, every one of which derives all its power of conveying a meaning, from a whole host of acquired notions, and facts learnt by study and experience.

Nevertheless, it seems undeniable in point of fact, and consistent with the principles of a sound metaphysics, that there are poetic *natures*. There is a mental and physical constitution or temperament, peculiarly fitted for poetry. This temperament will not of itself make a poet, no more than the soil will the fruit; and as good fruit may be raised by culture from indifferent soils, so may good poetry from naturally unpoetical minds. But the poetry of one who is a poet by nature, will be clearly and broadly distinguishable from the poetry of mere culture. It may not be truer; it may not be more useful; but it will be different: fewer will appreciate it, even though many

[2] Wordsworth, "To B. R. Haydon: High is our Calling, Friend!" (line 2).

should affect to do so; but in those few it will find a keener sympathy, and will yield them a deeper enjoyment.

One may write genuine poetry, and not be a poet; for whosoever writes out truly any human feeling, writes poetry. All persons, even the most unimaginative, in moments of strong emotion, speak poetry; and hence the drama is poetry, which else were always prose, except when a poet is one of the characters. What *is* poetry, but the thoughts and words in which emotion spontaneously embodies itself? As there are few who are not, at least for some moments and in some situations, capable of some strong feeling, poetry is natural to most persons at some period of their lives. And any one whose feelings are genuine, though but of the average strength,—if he be not diverted by uncongenial thoughts or occupations from the indulgence of them, and if he acquire by culture, as all persons may, the faculty of delineating them correctly,— has it in his power to be a poet, so far as a life passed in writing unquestionable poetry may be considered to confer that title. But *ought* it to do so? Yes, perhaps, in a collection of 'British Poets.' But 'poet' is the name also of a variety of man, not solely of the author of a particular variety of book: now, to have written whole volumes of real poetry is possible to almost all kinds of characters, and implies no greater peculiarity of mental construction, than to be the author of a history, or a novel.

Whom, then, shall we call poets? Those who are so constituted, that emotions are the links of association by which their ideas, both sensuous and spiritual, are connected together. This constitution belongs (within certain limits) to all in whom poetry is a pervading principle. In all others, poetry is something extraneous and superinduced: something out of themselves, foreign to the habitual course of their everyday lives and characters; a world to which they may make occasional visits, but where they are sojourners, not dwellers, and which, when out of it, or even when in it, they think of, peradventure, but as a phantom-world, a place of *ignes fatui*[3] and spec-

[3] "Delusive hopes," will o' the wisps.

tral illusions. Those only who have the peculiarity of association which we have mentioned, and which is a natural though not an universal consequence of intense sensibility, instead of seeming not themselves when they are uttering poetry, scarcely seem themselves when uttering anything to which poetry is foreign. Whatever be the thing which they are contemplating, if it be capable of connecting itself with their emotions, the aspect under which it first and most naturally paints itself to them, is its poetic aspect. The poet of culture sees his object in prose, and describes it in poetry; the poet of nature actually sees it in poetry.

This point is perhaps worth some little illustration; the rather, as metaphysicians (the ultimate arbiters of all philosophical criticism), while they have busied themselves for two thousand years, more or less, about the few *universal* laws of human nature, have strangely neglected the analysis of its *diversities*. Of these, none lie deeper or reach further than the varieties which difference of nature and of education makes in what may be termed the habitual bond of association. In a mind entirely uncultivated, which is also without any strong feelings, objects whether of sense or of intellect arrange themselves in the mere casual order in which they have been seen, heard, or otherwise perceived. Persons of this sort may be said to think chronologically. If they remember a fact, it is by reason of a fortuitous coincidence with some trifling incident or circumstance which took place at the very time. If they have a story to tell, or testimony to deliver in a witness-box, their narrative must follow the exact order in which the events took place: *dodge* them, and the thread of association is broken; they cannot go on. Their associations, to use the language of philosophers, are chiefly of the successive, not the synchronous kind, and whether successive or synchronous, are mostly casual.

To the man of science, again, or of business, objects group themselves according to the artificial classifications which the understanding has voluntarily made for the convenience of thought or of practice. But where any of the impressions are vivid and intense, the associations into which these enter are the ruling ones: it being a well-known law of association, that the stronger a feeling is, the more quickly and strongly it associates itself with any other object or feeling. Where, therefore, nature has given strong feelings, and education has not created factitious tendencies stronger than the natural ones, the prevailing associations will be those which connect objects and ideas with emotions, and with each other through the intervention of emotions. Thoughts and images will be linked together, according to the similarity of the feelings which cling to them. A thought will introduce a thought by first introducing a feeling which is allied with it. At the centre of each group of thoughts or images will be found a feeling; and the thoughts or images will be there only because the feeling was there. The combinations which the mind puts together, the pictures which it paints, the wholes which Imagination constructs out of the materials supplied by Fancy, will be indebted to some dominant *feeling*, not as in other natures to a dominant *thought*, for their unity and consistency of character, for what distinguishes them from incoherencies.

The difference, then, between the poetry of a poet, and the poetry of a cultivated but not naturally poetic mind, is, that in the latter, with however bright a halo of feeling the thought may be surrounded and glorified, the thought itself is always the conspicuous object; while the poetry of a poet is Feeling itself, employing Thought only as the medium of its expression. In the one, feeling waits upon thought; in the other, thought upon feeling. The one writer has a distinct aim, common to him with any other didactic author; he desires to convey the thought, and he conveys it clothed in the feelings which it excites in himself, or which he deems most appropriate to it. The other merely pours forth the overflowing of his feelings; and all the thoughts which those feelings suggest are floated promiscuously along the stream.

It may assist in rendering our meaning intelligible, if we illustrate it by a parallel between the two English authors of our own day, who have produced the greatest quantity of true and enduring poetry, Wordsworth and Shelley. Apter instances could not be wished for; the one might be cited as the type, the *exemplar*, of what the poetry of culture may accomplish: the other as perhaps the most striking example ever known of the poetic temperament. How different, accordingly, is the poetry of these two great writers! In Wordsworth, the poetry is almost always the mere setting of a thought. The thought may be more valuable than the setting, or it may be less valuable, but there can be no question as to which was first in his mind: what he is impressed with, and what he is anxious to impress, is some proposition, more or less distinctly conceived; some truth, or something which he deems such. He lets the thought dwell in his mind, till it excites, as is the nature of thought, other thoughts, and also such feelings as the measure of his sensibility is adequate to supply. Among these thoughts and feelings, had he chosen a different walk of authorship (and there are many in which he might equally have excelled), he would probably have made a different selection of media for enforcing the parent thought: his habits, however, being those of poetic composition, he selects in preference the strongest feelings, and the thoughts with which most of feeling is naturally or habitually connected. His poetry, therefore, may be defined to be, his thoughts, coloured by, and impressing themselves by means of, emotions. Such poetry, Wordsworth has occupied a long life in producing. And well and wisely has he so done. Criticisms, no doubt, may be made occasionally both upon the thoughts themselves, and upon the skill he has demonstrated in the choice of his media: for, an affair of skill and study, in the most rigorous sense, it evidently was. But he has not laboured in vain: he has exercised, and continues to exercise, a powerful, and mostly a highly beneficial influence over the formation and growth of not a few of the most cultivated and vigorous of the youthful minds of our time, over whose heads poetry of the opposite description would have flown, for want of an original organization, physical or mental, in sympathy with it.

On the other hand, Wordsworth's poetry is never bounding,

never ebullient; has little even of the appearance of spontaneousness: the well is never so full that it overflows. There is an air of calm deliberateness about all he writes, which is not characteristic of the poetic temperament: his poetry seems one thing, himself another; he seems to be poetical because he wills to be so, not because he cannot help it: did he will to dismiss poetry, he need never again, it might almost seem, have a poetical thought. He never seems *possessed* by any feeling; no emotion seems ever so strong as to have entire sway, for the time being, over the current of his thoughts. He never, even for the space of a few stanzas, appears entirely given up to exultation, or grief, or pity, or love, or admiration, or devotion, or even animal spirits. He now and then, though seldom, attempts to write as if he were; and never, we think, without leaving an impression of poverty: as the brook which on nearly level ground quite fills its banks, appears but a thread when running rapidly down a precipitous declivity. He has feeling enough to form a decent, graceful, even beautiful decoration to a thought which is in itself interesting and moving; but not so much as suffices to stir up the soul by mere sympathy with itself in its simplest manifestation, nor enough to summon up that array of 'thoughts of power' which in a richly stored mind always attends the call of really intense feeling. It is for this reason, doubtless, that the genius of Wordsworth is essentially unlyrical. Lyric poetry, as it was the earliest kind, is also, if the view we are now taking of poetry be correct, more eminently and peculiarly poetry than any other: it is the poetry most natural to a really poetic temperament, and least capable of being successfully imitated by one not so endowed by nature.

Shelley is the very reverse of all this. Where Wordsworth is strong, he is weak; where Wordsworth is weak, he is strong. Culture, that culture by which Wordsworth has reared from his own inward nature the richest harvest ever brought forth by a soil of so little depth, is precisely what was wanting to Shelley: or let us rather say, he had not, at the period of his deplorably early death, reached sufficiently far in that intellectual progression of which he was capable, and which, if it has done so much for greatly inferior natures, might have made of him the most perfect, as he was already the most gifted of our poets. For him, voluntary mental discipline had done little: the vividness of his emotions and of his sensations had done all. He seldom follows up an idea; it starts into life, summons from the fairy-land of his inexhaustible fancy some three or four bold images, then vanishes, and straight he is off on the wings of some casual association into quite another sphere. He had scarcely yet acquired the consecutiveness of thought necessary for a long poem; his more ambitious compositions too often resemble the scattered fragments of a mirror; colours brilliant as life, single images without end, but no picture. It is only when under the overruling influence of some one state of feeling, either actually experienced, or summoned up in the vividness of reality by a fervid imagination, that he writes as a great poet; unity of feeling being to him the harmonizing principle which a central idea is to minds of another class, and supplying the coherency and consistency which would else have been wanting. Thus it is in many of his smaller, and especially his lyrical poems. They are obviously written to exhale, perhaps to relieve, a state of feeling, or of conception of feeling, almost oppressive from its vividness. The thoughts and imagery are suggested by the feeling, and are such as it finds unsought. The state of feeling may be either of soul or of sense, or oftener (might we not say invariably?) of both: for the poetic temperament is usually, perhaps always, accompanied by exquisite senses. The exciting cause may be either an object or an idea. But whatever of sensation enters into the feeling, must not be local, or consciously organic; it is a condition of the whole frame, not of a part only. Like the state of sensation produced by a fine climate, or indeed like all strongly pleasurable or painful sensations in an impassioned nature, it pervades the entire nervous system. States of feeling, whether sensuous or spiritual, which thus possess the whole being, are the fountains of that which we have called the poetry of poets; and which is little else than a pouring forth of the thoughts and images that pass across the mind while some permanent state of feeling is occupying it.

To the same original fineness of organization, Shelley was doubtless indebted for another of his rarest gifts, that exuberance of imagery, which when unrepressed, as in many of his poems it is, amounts to a fault. The susceptibility of his nervous system, which made his emotions intense, made also the impressions of his external senses deep and clear: and agreeably to the law of association by which, as already remarked, the strongest impressions are those which associate themselves the most easily and strongly, these vivid sensations were readily recalled to mind by all objects or thoughts which had co-existed with them, and by all feelings which in any degree resembled them. Never did a fancy so teem with sensuous imagery as Shelley's. Wordsworth economizes an image, and detains it until he has distilled all the poetry out of it, and it will not yield a drop more: Shelley lavishes his with a profusion which is unconscious because it is inexhaustible.

If, then, the maxim *Nascitur poëta,* mean, either that the power of producing poetical compositions is a peculiar faculty which the poet brings into the world with him, which grows with his growth like any of his bodily powers, and is as independent of culture as his height, and his complexion; or that any natural peculiarity whatever is implied in producing poetry, real poetry, and in any quantity—such poetry too, as, to the majority of educated and intelligent readers, shall appear quite as good as, or even better than, any other; in either sense the doctrine is false. And nevertheless, there *is* poetry which could not emanate but from a mental and physical constitution peculiar, not in the kind, but in the degree of its susceptibility: a constitution which makes its possessor capable of greater happiness than mankind in general, and also of greater unhappiness; and because greater, so also more various. And such poetry, to all who know enough of nature to own it as being in nature, is much more poetry, is poetry in a far higher sense, than any other; since the common element of all poetry, that which constitutes poetry, human feeling, enters far more largely into this than into the poetry of culture. Not only because the natures which we have called poetical, really feel more, and consequently have more feeling to express; but because, the capacity of feeling being so great, feeling, when excited and not voluntarily resisted, seizes the helm of their thoughts, and the succession of ideas and images becomes the mere utterance of an emotion; not, as in other natures, the emotion a mere ornamental colouring of the thought.

Ordinary education and the ordinary course of life are constantly at work counteracting this quality of mind, and substituting habits more suitable to their own ends: if instead of substituting they were content to superadd, there would be nothing to complain of. But when will education consist, not in repressing any mental faculty or power, from the uncontrolled action of which danger is apprehended, but in training up to its proper strength the corrective and antagonist power?

In whomsoever the quality which we have described exists, and is not stifled, that person is a poet. Doubtless he is a greater poet in proportion as the fineness of his perceptions, whether of sense or of internal consciousness, furnished him with an ampler supply of lovely images—the vigour and richness of his intellect, with a greater abundance of moving thoughts. For it is through these thoughts and images that the feeling speaks, and through their impressiveness that it impresses itself, and finds response in other hearts; and from these media of transmitting it (contrary to the laws of physical nature) increase of intensity is reflected back upon the feeling itself. But all these it is possible to have, and not be a poet; they are mere materials, which the poet shares in common with other people. What constitutes the poet is not the imagery nor the thoughts, nor even the feelings, but the law according to which they are called up. He is a poet, not because he has ideas of any particular kind, but because the succession of his ideas is subordinate to the course of his emotions.

Many who have never acknowledged this in theory, bear testimony to it in their particular judgments. In listening to an oration, or reading a written discourse not professedly poetical, when do we begin to feel that the speaker or author is putting off the character of the orator or the prose writer, and is passing into the poet? Not when he begins to show strong feeling; *then* we merely say, he is in earnest, he feels what he says; still less when he expresses himself in imagery; then, unless illustration be manifestly his sole object, we are apt to say, this is affectation. It is when the feeling (instead of passing away, or, if it continue, letting the train of thoughts run on exactly as they would have done if there were no influence at work but the mere intellect) becomes itself the originator of another train of association, which expels or blends with the former; when (for example) either his words, or the mode of their arrangement, are such as we spontaneously use only when in a state of excitement, proving that the mind is at least as much occupied by a passive state of its own feelings, as by the desire of attaining the premeditated end which the discourse has in view.*

Our judgments of authors who lay actual claim to the title of poets, follow the same principle. Whenever, after a writer's meaning is fully understood, it is still matter of reasoning and discussion whether he is a poet or not, he will be found to be wanting in the characteristic peculiarity of association so often adverted to. When, on the contrary, after reading or hearing one or two passages, we instinctively and without hesitation cry out, This is a poet, the probability is, that the passages are strongly marked with this peculiar quality. And we may add that in such case, a critic who, not having sufficient feeling to respond to the poetry, is also without sufficient philosophy to understand it though he feel it not, will be apt to pronounce,

* And this, we may remark by the way, seems to point to the true theory of poetic diction; and to suggest the true answer to as much as is erroneous of Wordsworth's celebrated doctrine on that subject. For on the one hand, *all* language which is the natural expression of feeling, is really poetical, and will be felt as such, apart from conventional associations; but on the other, whenever intellectual culture has afforded a choice between several modes of expressing the same emotion, the stronger the feeling is, the more naturally and certainly will it prefer the language which is most peculiarly appropriated to itself, and kept sacred from the contact of more vulgar objects of contemplation. (Mill's note.)

not 'this is prose,' but 'this is exaggeration,' 'this is mysticism,' or, 'this is nonsense.'

Although a philosopher cannot, by culture, make himself, in the peculiar sense in which we now use the term, a poet, unless at least he have that peculiarity of nature which would probably have made poetry his earliest pursuit; a poet may always, by culture, make himself a philosopher. The poetic laws of association are by no means incompatible with the more ordinary laws; are by no means such as *must* have their course, even though a deliberate purpose require their suspension. If the peculiarities of the poetic temperament were uncontrollable in any poet, they might be supposed so in Shelley; yet how powerfully, in the Cenci, does he coerce and restrain all the characteristic qualities of his genius; what severe simplicity, in place of his usual barbaric splendour; how rigidly does he keep the feelings and the imagery in subordination to the thought.

The investigation of nature requires no habits or qualities of mind, but such as may always be acquired by industry and mental activity. Because at one time the mind may be so given up to a state of feeling, that the succession of its ideas is determined by the present enjoyment or suffering which pervades it, this is no reason but that in the calm retirement of study, when under no peculiar excitement either of the outward or of the inward sense, it may form any combinations, or pursue any trains of ideas, which are most conducive to the purposes of philosophic inquiry; and may, while in that state, form deliberate convictions, from which no excitement will afterwards make it swerve. Might we not go even further than this? We shall not pause to ask whether it be not a misunderstanding of the nature of passionate feeling to imagine that it is inconsistent with calmness; whether they who so deem of it, do not mistake passion in the militant or antagonistic state, for the type of passion universally; do not confound passion struggling towards an outward object, with passion brooding over itself. But without entering into this deeper investigation; that capacity of strong feeling, which is supposed necessarily to disturb the judgment, is also the material out of which all *motives* are made; the motives, consequently, which lead human beings to the pursuit of truth. The greater the individual's capability of happiness and of misery, the stronger interest has that individual in arriving at truth; and when once that interest is felt, an impassioned nature is sure to pursue this, as to pursue any other object, with greater ardour; for energy of character is commonly the offspring of strong feeling. If, therefore, the most impassioned natures do not ripen into the most powerful intellects, it is always from defect of culture, or something wrong in the circumstances by which the being has originally or successively been surrounded. Undoubtedly strong feelings require a strong intellect to carry them, as more sail requires more ballast: and when, from neglect, or bad education, that strength is wanting, no wonder if the grandest and swiftest vessels make the most utter wreck.

Where, as in some of our older poets, a poetic nature has been united with logical and scientific culture, the peculiarity of association arising from the finer nature so perpetually alternates with the associations attainable by commoner natures trained to high prefection, that its own particular law is not so conspicuously characteristic of the result produced, as in a poet like Shelley, to whom systematic intellectual culture, in a measure proportioned to the intensity of his own nature, has been wanting. Whether the superiority will naturally be on the side of the philosopher-poet or of the mere poet—whether the writings of the one ought, as a whole, to be truer, and their influence more beneficent, than those of the other—is too obvious in principle to need statement: it would be absurd to doubt whether two endowments are better than one; whether truth is more certainly arrived at by two processes, verifying and correcting each other, than by one alone. Unfortunately, in practice the matter is not quite so simple; there the question often is, which is least prejudicial to the intellect, uncultivation or malcultivation. For, as long as education consists chiefly of the mere inculcation of traditional opinions, many of which, from the mere fact that the human intellect has not yet reached perfection, must necessarily be false; so long as even those who are best taught, are rather taught to know the thoughts of others than to think, it is not always clear that the poet of acquired ideas has the advantage over him whose feeling has been his sole teacher. For, the depth and durability of wrong as well as of right impressions, is proportional to the fineness of the material; and they who have the greatest capacity of natural feeling are generally those whose artificial feelings are the strongest. Hence, doubtless, among other reasons, it is, that in an age of revolutions in opinion, the cotemporary poets, those at least who deserve the name, those who have any individuality of character, if they are not before their age, are almost sure to be behind it. An observation curiously verified all over Europe in the present century. Nor let it be thought disparaging. However urgent may be the necessity for a breaking up of old modes of belief, the most strong-minded and discerning, next to those who head the movement, are generally those who bring up the rear of it.[4]

[4] The original version of the present essay concluded with the signature "Antiquus" and the following note:

"This signature is only used to identify the authorship of the present article with that of a paper headed "What is Poetry?" in a former number of the "Repository." The writer had a reason for the title when he first adopted it; but he has discarded it in his later articles, as giving a partial, and so far a false, notion of the spirit by which he would wish his thoughts and writings to be characterized. As Wordsworth says,

'*Past* and *future* are the wings
On whose support, harmoniously conjoined,
Moves the great spirit of human knowledge;'

and though the present as often goes amiss for lack of what time and change have deprived us of, as of what they have yet to bring, a title which points only one way is unsuitable to a writer who attempts to look both ways. In future, when a signature is employed, it will be the single letter A."

Tennyson's Poems

1835

As soon as he read them, Mill proclaimed Tennyson's poems "the best . . . which have appeared since the best days of Coleridge." At a time when Tennyson had received acclaim as a poet from his friends alone, Mill predicted a high place for him among English poets.

But Tennyson, Mill warned, would achieve this place only if he developed his powers of thought to equal his great natural powers of execution. Mill thus develops a theme of the two earlier essays on poetry, the second of which he once thought of putting at the head of the review of Tennyson's poems. But there are definite differences of emphasis. Now, instead of positing two kinds of poet, Mill sees in every poet both the element of nature and that of culture; the ideal poet is a harmonious blending of the two. Moreover, he is now ready to deal more harshly with undisciplined poetic emotion than he had in the earlier essay.

His remarks on Tennyson show that he is losing sympathy for the type of poet exemplified by Shelley, for this essay, unlike previous ones, makes emotion subservient to thought. Poetry, Mill argues, seeks to transmute thoughts into equivalent poetic feelings in order to communicate them, for feelings are all that poetry can deal with and communicate directly. But the task of perfecting men by purifying their emotions is "the work of cultivated reason," and the poet's success in this task will depend upon the value of his thoughts as well as on his ability to impress them on the feelings of mankind. The mastery of that part of poetry which is not simply the result of poetic temperament, asserts Mill, depends upon the cultivation of the intellect. Nor is it enough for the poet to refrain from the facile anti-intellectualism of the pretenders to poetry; he must consciously involve himself in philosophic studies.

What praise Mill now has for Shelley is faint; at best it is the kind he accorded to "half-thinkers" in philosophy. As a poet without intellectual powers who remained content merely to exercise his natural gift, Shelley was an incomplete and unsatisfactory poet. Mill criticizes him (as, three years later, he was to criticize Bentham) for relying wholly upon the stuff of his own mind and temper, upon subjective, private, perhaps eccentric material. Discerning a causal relation between intellectual failure and the inability to deal with a tangible and generally available subject, Mill has come to see that the spontaneous overflow of powerful feeling cannot by itself suffice to produce great poetry.

1. *Poems, chiefly Lyrical, by Alfred Tennyson. Effingham Wilson. 1830.*
2. *Poems. By Alfred Tennyson. Moxon. 1833.*

TOWARDS the close of the year 1830 appeared a small volume of poems, the work of a young and unknown author, and which, with considerable faults (some of them of a bad kind), gave evidence of powers such as had not for many years been displayed by any new aspirant to the character of a poet. This first publication was followed in due time by a second, in which the faults of its predecessor were still visible, but were evidently on the point of disappearing; while the positive excellence was not only greater and more uniformly sustained, but of a higher order. The imagination of the poet, and his reason, had alike advanced: the one had become more teeming and vigorous, while its resources had been brought more habitually and completely under the command of the other.

The notice which these poems have hitherto received from the more widely-circulated and influential organs of criticism consists, so far as we are aware, of two articles—a review of the first publication, in Blackwood's Magazine,[1] and of the second, in the Quarterly Review.[2] The article in Blackwood, along with the usual flippancy and levity of that journal, evinced one of its better characteristics—a genuine appreciation and willing recognition of genius. It was not to be expected that a writer in 'Blackwood' could accomplish a criticism

First published in *London and Westminster Review*, XXX (July 1835).

[1] By "Christopher North" (Professor John Wilson), XXXI (May 1832), 721–741.

[2] By John Wilson Croker, XLIX (April 1833), 81–96.

on a volume of poetry, without cutting capers and exhibiting himself in postures, as Drawcansir[3] says, 'because he dare.' The article on Mr. Tennyson is throughout in a strain of mocking exaggeration. Some reviewers write to extol their author, others to laugh at him; this writer was desirous to do both—first to make the book appear beyond all measure contemptible, next in the highest degree admirable—putting the whole force of his mind alternately into these two purposes. If we can forgive this audacious sporting with his reader and his subjects, the critique is otherwise not without merit. The praise and blame, though shovelled out rather than measured, are thrown into the right places; the real merits and defects of the poems are pointed out with discrimination, and a fair enough impression left of the proportion between the two; and it is evident that if the same writer were to review Mr. Tennyson's second publication, his praise, instead of being about equally balanced by his censure, would be but slightly qualified by it.

Of Mr. Tennyson's two volumes, the second was the only one which fell into the hands of the Quarterly Reviewer; and his treatment of it, compared with the notice taken by Blackwood of its more juvenile predecessor, forms a contrast, characteristic of the two journals. Whatever may be in other respects our opinion of Blackwood's Magazine, it is impossible to deny to its principal writers (or writer) a certain susceptibility of sense, a geniality of temperament. Their mode of writing about works of genius is that of a person who derives much enjoyment from them, and is grateful for it. Genuine powers of mind, with whatever opinions connected, seldom fail to meet with response and recognition from these writers. The Quarterly Review, on the other hand, both under its original and under its present management,[4] has been no less

[3] In *The Rehearsal* (1672) by George Villiers (1628–1687), Drawcansir is a boasting and vainglorious bully. The name became a synonym for a braggart.

[4] Mill probably refers to William Gifford and John Gibson Lockhart, the first and third editors of the review. J. T. Coleridge was for a time the second editor.

characterised by qualities directly the reverse of these. Every new claim upon its admiration, unless forced upon it by the public voice, or recommended by some party interest, it welcomes, not with a friendly extension of the hand, but with a curl of the lip: the critic (as we figure him to ourselves) taking up the book, in trusting anticipation of pleasure, not from the book, but from the contemplation of his own cleverness in making it contemptible. He has not missed the opportunity of admiring himself at the expense of Mr. Tennyson: although, as we have not heard that these poems have yet, like those of Mr. Robert Montgomery,[5] reached the eleventh edition, nor that any apprehension is entertained of danger to the public taste from their extravagant popularity, we may well be astonished that performances so utterly worthless as this critic considers them, should have appeared to him deserving of so much attention from so superior a mind. The plan he adopts is no new one, but abundantly hacknied: he selects the few bad passages (not amounting to three pages in the whole), and such others as, by being separated from the context, may be made to look ridiculous; and, in a strain of dull irony, of which all the point consists in the ill-nature, he holds forth these as a specimen of the work. A piece of criticism, resembling, in all but their wit, the disgraceful articles in the early Numbers of the Edinburgh Review, on Wordsworth and Coleridge.[6]

Meanwhile, these poems have been winning their way, by slow approaches, to a reputation, the exact limits and measure of which it would be hazardous at present to predict, but which, we believe, will not ultimately be inconsiderable. Desiring, so far as may depend upon us, to accelerate this progress, and also not without a desire to exhibit, to any who still have

---

[5] Robert Montgomery (1807–1855), a poet whose book *The Omnipresence of Deity* (1828) went through twelve editions in a year. In his review of Tennyson's poems in *The Englishman's Magazine* for August 1831, Arthur Henry Hallam, Tennyson's closest friend, began with an attack on Montgomery.

[6] Mill refers to Francis Jeffrey's persistent attacks on the Lake poets.

faith in the Quarterly Review, the value of its critical judgments, we propose to lay before those of our readers who are still unacquainted with the poems, such specimens as may justify the terms in which we have spoken of them—interspersing or subjoining a few remarks on the character and the present state of developement of Mr. Tennyson's poetic endowment.

Of all the capacities of a poet, that which seems to have arisen earliest in Mr. Tennyson, and in which he most excels, is that of scene-painting, in the higher sense of the term: not the mere power of producing that rather vapid species of composition usually termed descriptive poetry—for there is not in these volumes one passage of pure description: but the power of *creating* scenery, in keeping with some state of human feeling; so fitted to it as to be the embodied symbol of it, and to summon up the state of feeling itself, with a force not to be surpassed by anything but reality. Our first specimen, selected from the earlier of the two volumes, will illustrate chiefly this quality of Mr. Tennyson's productions. We do not anticipate that this little poem will be equally relished at first by all lovers of poetry: and indeed if it were, its merit could be but of the humblest kind; for sentiments and imagery which can be received at once, and with equal ease, into every mind, must necessarily be trite. Nevertheless, we do not hesitate to quote it at full length. The subject is Mariana, the Mariana of 'Measure for Measure,' living deserted and in solitude in the 'moated grange.' The ideas which these two words suggest, impregnated with the feelings of the supposed inhabitant, have given rise to the following picture:—

'With blackest moss the flower-pots
   Were thickly crusted, one and all,
The rusted nails fell from the knots
   That held the peach to the garden-wall.
The broken sheds looked sad and strange,
   Unlifted was the clinking latch,
   Weeded and worn the ancient thatch
Upon the lonely moated grange.
      She only said, "My life is dreary,

He cometh not," she said;
She said, "I am aweary, aweary;
I would that I were dead!"

'Her tears fell with the dews at even,
Her tears fell ere the dews were dried,
She could not look on the sweet heaven,
Either at morn or eventide.
After the flitting of the bats,
When thickest dark did trance the sky,
She drew her casement-curtain by,
And glanced athwart the glooming flats.
She only said, "The night is dreary,
He cometh not," she said:
She said, "I am aweary, aweary,
I would that I were dead!"

'Upon the middle of the night,
Waking she heard the night-fowl crow:
The cock sung out an hour ere light:
From the dark fen the oxen's low
Came to her: without hope of change,
In sleep she seemed to walk forlorn,
Till cold winds woke the grey-eyed morn
About the lonely moated grange.
She only said, "The day is dreary,
He cometh not," she said;
She said, "I am aweary, aweary,
I would that I were dead!"

'About a stone-cast from the wall,
A sluice with blackened waters slept,
And o'er it many, round and small,
The clustered marishmosses crept.
Hard by a poplar shook alway,
All silver-green with gnarled bark,
For leagues no other tree did dark
The level waste, the rounding grey.
She only said, "My life is dreary,
He cometh not," she said;
She said, "I am aweary, aweary,
I would that I were dead!"

'And ever when the moon was low,
  And the shrill winds were up an' away,
In the white curtain, to and fro,
  She saw the gusty shadow sway.
But when the moon was very low,
  And wild winds bound within their cell,
  The shadow of the poplar fell
Upon her bed, across her brow.
    She only said, "The night is dreary,
      He cometh not," she said;
    She said, "I am aweary, aweary,
      I would that I were dead!"

'All day within the dreamy house,
  The doors upon their hinges creaked,
The blue-fly sung i' the pane; the mouse
  Behind the mouldering wainscot shrieked,
Or from the crevice peered about.
  Old faces glimmered through the doors,
  Old footsteps trod the upper floors,
Old voices called her from without.
    She only said, "My life is dreary,
      He cometh not," she said;
    She said, "I am aweary, aweary,
      I would that I were dead!"

'The sparrow's chirrup on the roof,
  The slow clock ticking, and the sound
Which to the wooing wind aloof
  The poplar made, did all confound
Her sense; but most she loathed the hour
    When the thickmoted sunbeam lay
    Athwart the chambers, and the day
Downsloped was westering in his bower.
    Then, said she, "I am very dreary,
      He will not come," she said;
    She wept, "I am aweary, aweary,
      Oh God, that I were dead!"'

In the one peculiar and rare quality which we intended to illustrate by it, this poem appears to us to be pre-eminent. We do not, indeed, defend all the expressions in it, some of which seem to have been extorted from the author by the tyranny of rhyme; and we might find much more to say against the poem, if we insisted upon judging of it by a wrong standard. The nominal subject excites anticipations which the poem does not even attempt to fulfil. The humblest poet, who is a poet at all, could make more than is here made of the situation of a maiden abandoned by her lover. But that was not Mr. Tennyson's idea. The love-story is secondary in his mind. The words 'he cometh not' are almost the only words which allude to it at all. To place ourselves at the right point of view, we must drop the conception of Shakespeare's Mariana, and retain only that of a 'moated grange,' and a solitary dweller within it, forgotten by mankind. And now see whether poetic imagery ever conveyed a more intense conception of such a place, or of the feelings of such an inmate. From the very first line, the rust of age and the solitude of desertion are, on the whole, picture. Words surely never excited a more vivid feeling of physical and spiritual dreariness: and not dreariness alone–for that might be felt under many other circumstances of solitude–but the dreariness which speaks not merely of being far from human converse and sympathy, but of being *deserted* by it.

Our next specimen shall be of a character remote from this. It is the second of two poems, 'The May Queen' and 'New Year's Eve'–the one expressing the wild, overflowing spirits of a light-hearted girl, just chosen Queen of the May; the latter, the feelings of the same girl some months afterwards, when dying by a gradual decay. We regret that the opening of the latter poem must lose in our pages the effect of contrast produced by its immediately succeeding the former:—

'If you're waking, call me early, call me early, mother dear,
For I would see the sun rise upon the glad Newyear.
It is the last Newyear that I shall ever see,
Then ye may lay me low i' the mould, and think no more o' me.

'To-night I saw the sun set: he set and left behind
The good old year, the dear old time, and all my peace of mind;
And the Newyear's coming up, mother, but I shall never see
The may upon the blackthorn, the leaf upon the tree.

'Last May we made a crown of flowers: we had a merry day;
Beneath the hawthorn on the green they made me Queen of May;
And we danced about the maypole and in the hazel-copse,
Till Charles's wain came out above the tall white chimney-tops.

'There's not a flower on all the hills: the frost is on the pane:
I only wish to live till the snow-drops come again:
I wish the snow would melt and the sun come out on high—
I long to see a flower so before the day I die.

'The building rook will caw from the windy tall elmtree
And the tufted plover pipe along the fallow lea,
And the swallow will come back again with summer o'er the wave,
But I shall lie alone, mother, within the mouldering grave.

'Upon the chancel-casement, and upon that grave o' mine,
In the early early morning the summer sun will shine,
Before the red cock crows from the farm upon the hill,
When you are warm-asleep, mother, and all the world is still.

'When the flowers come again, mother, beneath the waning light,
Ye'll never see me more in the long gray fields at night;
When from the dry dark wold the summer airs blow cool,
On the oat-grass and the sword-grass, and the bulrush in the pool.

'Ye'll bury me, my mother, just beneath the hawthorn shade,
And ye'll come sometimes and see me where I am lowly laid.
I shall not forget ye, mother, I shall hear ye when ye pass,
With your feet above my head in the long and pleasant grass.

'I have been wild and wayward, but ye'll forgive me now;
Ye'll kiss me, my own mother, upon my cheek and brow;
Nay—nay, ye must not weep, nor let your grief be wild,
Ye should not fret for me, mother, ye have another child.

'If I can I'll come again, mother, from out my resting place;
Though ye'll not see me, mother, I shall look upon your face;
Though I cannot speak a word, I shall hearken what ye say,
And be often—often with ye when ye think I'm far away.

'Goodnight, goodnight, when I have said goodnight for evermore,
And ye see me carried out from the threshold of the door;
Don't let Effie come to see me till my grave be growing green:
She'll be a better child to you than ever I have been.

'She'll find my garden tools upon the granary floor:
Let her take 'em: they are hers: I shall never garden more:
But tell her, when I'm gone, to train the rosebush that I set,
About the parlour-window and the box of mignonette.

'Good-night, sweet mother: call me when it begins to dawn.
All night I lie awake, but I fall asleep at morn;
But I would see the sun rise upon the glad Newyear,
So, if you're waking, call me, call me early, mother dear.'

This poem is fitted for a more extensive popularity than any other in the two volumes. Simple, genuine pathos, arising out of the situations and feelings common to mankind generally, is of all kinds of poetic beauty that which can be most universally appreciated; and the genius implied in it is, in consequence, apt to be overrated, for it is also of all kinds that which can be most easily produced. In this poem there is not only the truest pathos, but (except in one passage*) perfect harmony and keeping.

The next poem which we shall quote is one of higher pretensions. Its length exceeds the usual dimensions of an extract. But the idea which would be given of the more perfect of Mr. Tennyson's poems, by detached passages, would be not merely an incomplete but a false idea. There is not a stanza in the following poem which can be felt or even understood as the poet intended, unless the reader's imagination and feelings are already in the state which results from the passage next preceding, or rather from all which precedes. The very breaks, which divide the story into parts, all tell.

If every one approached poetry in the spirit in which it ought to be approached, willing to feel it first and examine it afterwards, we should not premise another word. But there is a class of readers, (a class, too, on whose verdict the early success of a young poet mainly depends,) who dare not enjoy until they have first satisfied themselves that they have a warrant for enjoying; who read a poem with the critical under-

* We allude to the second line of the second stanza. The concluding words of the line appear to us altogether out of keeping with the rest of the poem. (Mill's note.)

standing first, and only when they are convinced that it is right to be delighted, are willing to give their spontaneous feelings fair play. The consequence is, that they lose the general effect, while they higgle about the details, and never place themselves in the position in which, even with their mere understandings, they can estimate the poem as a whole. For the benefit of such readers, we tell them beforehand, that this is a tale of enchantment; and that they will never enter into the spirit of it unless they surrender their imagination to the guidance of the poet, with the same easy credulity with which they would read the 'Arabian Nights,' or, what this story more resembles, the tales of magic of the middle ages.

Though the agency is supernatural, the scenery, as will be perceived, belongs to the actual world. No reader of any imagination will complain, that the precise nature of the enchantment is left in mystery.

THE LEGEND OF THE LADY OF SHALOTT.
'Part the First.

'On either side the river lie
Long fields of barley and of rye,
That clothe the wold, and meet the sky;
And thro' the field the road runs by
        To manytower'd Camelot.
The yellowleavèd waterlily,
The green-sheathèd daffodilly,
Tremble in the water chilly,
        Round about Shalott.

'Willows whiten, aspens shiver,
The sunbeam-showers break and quiver
In the stream that runneth ever
By the island in the river,
        Flowing down to Camelot.
Four grey walls and four grey towers
Overlook a space of flowers,
And the silent isle imbowers
        The Lady of Shalott.

'Underneath the bearded barley,
The reaper, reaping late and early,
Hears her ever chanting cheerly,
Like an angel, singing clearly,
O'er the stream of Camelot.
Piling the sheaves in furrows airy,
Beneath the moon, the reaper weary
Listening whispers, " 'Tis the fairy
Lady of Shalott."

'The little isle is all inrailed
With a rose-fence, and overtrailed
With roses: by the marge unhailed
The shallop flitteth silken-sailed,
Skimming down to Camelot.
A pearl garland winds her head:
She leaneth on a velvet bed,
Full royally apparallèd,
The Lady of Shalott.

'Part the Second.

'No time has she to sport and play:
A charmed web she weaves alway,
A curse is on her, if she stay
Her weaving, either night or day,
To look down to Camelot.
She knows not what the curse may be;
Therefore she weaveth steadily,
Therefore no other care hath she,
The Lady of Shalott.

'She lives with little joy or fear.
Over the water, running near,
The sheepbell tinkles in her ear.
Before her hangs a mirror clear,
Reflecting towered Camelot.
And, as the mazy web she whirls,
She sees the surly village-churls,
And the red-cloaks of market-girls,
Pass onward from Shalott.

'Sometimes a troop of damsels glad,
An abbot or an ambling pad,
Sometimes a curly shepherd lad,
Or longhaired page, in crimson clad,
Goes by to towered Camelot.
And sometimes thro' the mirror blue,
The knights come riding, two and two.
She hath no loyal knight and true,
The Lady of Shalott.

'But in her web she still delights
To weave the mirror's magic sights:
For often thro' the silent nights,
A funeral, with plumes and lights
And music, came from Camelot.
Or, when the moon was overhead,
Came two young lovers, lately wed:
"I am half-sick of shadows," said
The Lady of Shalott.

'Part the Third.

'A bow-shot from her bower-eaves
He rode between the barley-sheaves:
The sun came dazzling thro' the leaves,
And flamed upon the brazen greaves
Of bold Sir Launcelot.
A redcross knight for ever kneeled
To a lady in his shield,
That sparkled on the yellow field,
Beside remote Shalott.

'The gemmy bridle glittered free,
Like to some branch of stars we see
Hung in the golden galaxy.
The bridle-bells rang merrily
As he rode down from Camelot.
And, from his blazoned baldric slung,
A mighty silver bugle hung,
And, as he rode, his armour rung,
Beside remote Shalott.

'All in the blue unclouded weather,
Thickjewelled shone the saddle-leather.
The helmet, and the helmet-feather,
Burned like one burning flame together,
        As he rode down from Camelot.
As often thro' the purple night,
Below the starry clusters bright,
Some bearded meteor, trailing light,
        Moves over green Shalott.

'His broad clear brow in sunlight glowed.
On burnished hooves his war-horse trode.
From underneath his helmet flowed
His coalblack curls, as on he rode,
        As he rode down from Camelot.
From the bank, and from the river,
He flashed into the crystal mirror,
"Tirra lirra, tirra lirra,"
        Sang Sir Launcelot.*

'She left the web: she left the loom:
She made three paces thro' the room:
She saw the waterflower bloom:
She saw the helmet and the plume:
        She looked down to Camelot.
Out flew the web, and floated wide,
The mirror cracked from side to side,
"The curse is come upon me," cried
        The Lady of Shalott.

'Part the Fourth.

'In the stormy eastwind straining,
The pale-yellow woods were waning,
The broad stream in his banks complaining,
Heavily the low sky raining
        Over towered Camelot:
Outside the isle a shallow boat

* In this most striking passage, which we should have thought would have commanded admiration from every one who can read, all that the Quarterly Reviewer could see is, that the rhymes are incorrect! (Mill's note.)

Beneath a willow lay afloat,
Below the carven stern she wrote,
The Lady of Shalott.

'A cloudwhite crown of pearl she dight.
All raimented in snowy white
That loosely flew, (her zone in sight,
Clasped with one blinding diamond bright,)
Her wide eyes fixed on Camelot,
Though the squally eastwind keenly
Blew, with folded arms serenely
By the water stood the queenly
Lady of Shalott.

'With a steady, stony glance—
Like some bold seer in a trance,
Beholding all his own mischance,
Mute, with a glassy countenance—
She looked down to Camelot.
It was the closing of the day,
She loosed the chain, and down she lay,
The broad stream bore her far away,
The Lady of Shalott.

'As when to sailors while they roam,
By creeks and outfalls far from home,
Rising and dropping with the foam,
From dying swans wild warblings come,
Blown shoreward; so to Camelot
Still as the boathead wound along,
The willowy hills and fields among,
They heard her chanting her deathsong,
The Lady of Shalott.

A longdrawn carol, mournful, holy,
She chanted loudly, chanted lowly,
Till her eyes were darkened wholly,
And her smooth face sharpened slowly*

* This exquisite line, the egregious critic of the Quarterly distinguishes by italics as specially absurd! proving thereby what is his test of the truth of a description, even of a physical fact. He does not ask himself, Is the fact so? but, Have I ever seen the expression in the verses of any former poet of celebrity? (Mill's note.)

> Turned to towered Camelot:
> For ere she reached upon the tide
> The first house by the waterside,
> Singing in her song she died,
> The Lady of Shalott.
>
> 'Under tower and balcony,
> By gardenwall and gallery,
> A pale, pale corpse she floated by,
> Deadcold, between the houses high,
> Dead into towered Camelot.
> Knight and burgher, lord and dame,
> To the plankèd wharfage came,
> Below the stern they read her name,
> "The Lady of Shalott"' †

In powers of narrative and scene-painting combined, this poem must be ranked among the very first of its class. The delineation of outward objects, as in the greater number of Mr. Tennyson's poems, is, not picturesque, but (if we may use the term) statuesque; with brilliancy of colour superadded. The forms are not, as in painting, of unequal degrees of definiteness; the tints do not melt gradually into each other, but each individual object stands out in bold relief, with a clear decided outline. This statue-like precision and distinctness, few artists have been able to give to so essentially vague a language as that of words: but if once this difficulty be got over, scene-painting by words has a wider range than either painting or sculpture; for it can represent (as the reader must have seen in the foregoing poem), not only with the vividness and strength of the one, but with the clearness and definiteness of the other, objects in motion. Along with all this, there is in the poem all that power of making a few touches do the whole work, which excites our admiration in Coleridge. Every line suggests so much more than it says, that much may be left unsaid: the concentration, which is the soul of narrative, is obtained, with-

† We omit the remaining stanza, which seems to us a 'lame and impotent conclusion,' where no conclusion was required. (Mill's note.)

out the sacrifice of reality and life. Where the march of the story requires that the mind should pause, details are specified; where rapidity is necessary, they are all brought before us at a flash. Except that the versification is less exquisite, the 'Lady of Shalott' is entitled to a place by the side of the 'Ancient Mariner,' and 'Christabel.'

Mr. Tennyson's two volumes contain a whole picture-gallery of lovely women: but we are drawing near to the limits of allowable quotation. The imagery of the following passage from the poem of 'Isabel,' in the first volume, is beautifully typical of the nobler and gentler of two beings, upholding, purifying, and, as far as possible, assimilating to itself the grosser and ruder:—

'A clear stream flowing with a muddy one,
Till in its onward current it absorbs
With swifter movement and in purer light
The vexed eddies of its wayward brother—
A leaning and upbearing parasite,
Clothing the stem, which else had fallen quite,
With clustered flowerbells and ambrosial orbs
Of rich fruitbunches leaning on each other.'

We venture upon a long extract from what we consider the finest of these ideal portraits, the 'Eleänore.' The reader must not, in this case, look for the definiteness of the 'Lady of Shalott;' there is nothing statuesque here. The object to be represented being more vague, there is greater vagueness and dimness in the expression. The loveliness of a graceful woman, words cannot make us see, but only feel. The individual expressions in the poem, from which the following is an extract, may not always bear a minute analysis; but ought they to be subjected to it? They are mere colours in a picture; nothing in themselves, but everything as they conduce to the general result.

'How may fullsailed verse express,
How may measured words adore
The fullflowing harmony

Of thy swanlike stateliness,
                Eleänore?
      The luxuriant symmetry
Of thy floating gracefulness,
                Eleänore?
    Every turn and glance of thine,
    Every lineament divine,
                Eleänore,
And the steady sunset glow
  That stays upon thee? For in thee
      Is nothing sudden, nothing single;
  Like two streams of incense free
    From one censer, in one shrine,
      Thought and motion mingle,
Mingle ever. Motions flow
To one another, even as tho'
They were modulated so
  To an unheard melody,
Which lives about thee, and a sweep
  Of richest pauses, evermore
Drawn from each other mellowdeep—
  Who may express thee, Eleänore?

'I stand before thee, Eleänore;
  I see thy beauty gradually unfold,
Daily and hourly, more and more.
I muse, as in a trance, the while
  Slowly, as from a cloud of gold,
Comes out thy deep ambrosial smile.
I muse, as in a trance, whene'er
  The languors of thy lovedeep eyes
Float on to me. I would I were
  So tranced, so rapt in ecstacies,
To stand apart, and to adore,
Gazing on thee for evermore,
Serene, imperial Eleänore!

'Sometimes, with most intensity
Gazing, I seem to see
Thought folded over thought, smiling asleep,
Slowly awakened, grow so full and deep

In thy large eyes, that, overpowered quite,
I cannot veil, or droop my sight,
But am as nothing in its light.
As though a star, in inmost heaven set,
Ev'n while we gaze on it,
Should slowly round its orb, and slowly grow
To a full face, there like a sun remain
Fixed—then as slowly fade again,
And draw itself to what it was before,
So full, so deep, so slow
Thought seems to come and go
In thy large eyes, imperial Eleänore.

'As thunderclouds that, hung on high
Did roof noonday with doubt and fear,
Floating through an evening atmosphere
Grow golden all about the sky;
In thee all passion becomes passionless,
Touched by thy spirit's mellowness,
Losing his fire and active might
In a silent meditation,
Falling into a still delight
And luxury of contemplation:
As waves that from the outer deep
Roll into a quiet cove,
There fall away, and lying still,
Having glorious dreams in sleep,
Shadow forth the banks at will;
Or sometimes they swell and move,
Pressing up against the land,
With motions of the outer sea:
And the selfsame influence
Controlleth all the soul and sense
Of Passion gazing upon thee.
His bowstring slackened, languid Love,
Leaning his cheek upon his hand,
Droops both his wings, regarding thee,
And so would languish evermore,
Serene, imperial Eleänore.'

It has for some time been the fashion, though a fashion now happily on the decline, to consider a poet as a poet, only so far as he is supposed capable of delineating the more violent passions; meaning by violent passions, states of excitement approaching to monomania, and characters predisposed to such states. The poem which follows will show how powerfully, without the slightest straining, by a few touches which do not seem to cost him an effort, Mr. Tennyson can depict such a state and such a character.

THE SISTERS.

'We were two daughters of one race:
She was the fairest in the face:
    The wind is blowing in turret an' tree.
They were together, and she fell;
Therefore revenge became me well.
    O the Earl was fair to see!

'She died: she went to burning flame:
She mixed her ancient blood with shame.
    The wind is howling in turret an' tree.
Whole weeks and months, and early and late,
To win his love I lay in wait:
    O the Earl was fair to see!

'I made a feast; I bad him come:
I won his love, I brought him home.
    The wind is roaring in turret an' tree.
And after supper, on a bed,
Upon my lap he laid his head:
    O the Earl was fair to see!

'I kissed his eyelids into rest;
His ruddy cheek upon my breast.
    The wind is raging in turret an' tree.
I hated him with the hate of hell,
But I loved his beauty passing well.
    O the Earl was fair to see!

'I rose up in the silent night:
I made my dagger sharp and bright.

The wind is raving in turret an' tree.
As half-asleep his breath he drew,
Three times I stabbed him through and through.
O the Earl was fair to see!

'I curled and combed his comely head,
He looked so grand when he was dead.
The wind is blowing in turret an' tree.
I wrapped his body in the sheet
And laid him at his mother's feet.
O the Earl was fair to see!'

The second publication contains several classical subjects treated with more or less felicity. The story of the Judgment of Paris,[7] recited by Oenone, his deserted love, is introduced in the following stately manner:—

'There is a dale in Ida, lovelier
Than any in old Ionia, beautiful
With emerald slopes of sunny sward, that lean
Above the loud glenriver, which hath worn
A path through steepdown granite walls below,
Mantled with flowering tendriltwine. In front
The cedarshadowy valleys open wide.
Far-seen, high over all the Godbuilt wall
And many a snowycolumned range divine,
Mounted with awful sculptures—men and Gods,
The work of Gods—bright on the dark blue sky
The windy citadel of Ilion
Shone, like the crown of Troas. Hither came
Mournful Oenone, wandering forlorn
Of Paris, once her playmate. Round her neck,
Her neck all marblewhite and marblecold,
Floated her hair or seemed to float in rest;

[7] Oenone, a nymph, was the daughter of Mt. Ida and the river Simois. Paris was devoted to her until he was asked to decide the contest of Hera, Aphrodite, and Athena for the golden apple marked "For the fairest." He preferred the possession of the fairest woman, promised him by Aphrodite, to power and riches, or wisdom and fame, promised by Hera and Athena, respectively. Aphrodite rewarded him with Helen of Troy, and Oenone was deserted.

She, leaning on a vine-entwinèd stone,
Sang to the stillness, till the mountain-shadow
Sloped downward to her seat from the upper cliff.'*

The length to which our quotations have extended, and the unsatisfactoriness of short extracts, prevent us from giving any specimen of one of the finest of Mr. Tennyson's poems, the 'Lotos-eaters.' The subject is familiar to every reader of the Odyssey.[8] The poem is not of such sustained merit in the execution as some of the others; but the general impression resembles an effect of climate in a landscape: we see the objects through a drowsy, relaxing, but dreamy atmosphere, and the inhabitants seem to have inhaled the like. Two lines near the commencement touch the key-note of the poem:—

'In the afternoon they came unto a land
Wherein it seemèd always afternoon.'

The above extracts by no means afford an idea of all the variety of beauty to be found in these volumes. But the specimens we have given may, we hope, satisfy the reader, that if he explore further for himself, his search will be rewarded. We shall only subjoin a few remarks, tending to an estimation of Mr. Tennyson's general character as a writer and as a poet.

---

* The small critic of the Quarterly finds fault with the frequent repetition, in Oenone's recital, of the following two verses:—

'O mother Ida, many-fountained Ida,
Dear mother Ida, hearken ere I die.'

To return continually to the same *refrain* is, as the reader must have observed even in our extracts, a frequent practice of Mr. Tennyson, and one which, though occasionally productive of great beauty, he carries to a faulty excess. But on this occasion, if ever, it was allowable. A subject from Greek poetry surely justifies imitation of the Greek poets. Repetitions similar to this are, as everybody knows, universal among the pastoral and elegiac poets of Greece, and their Roman imitators: and this poem is both pastoral and elegiac. (Mill's note.)

[8] In the *Odyssey*, Odysseus and his men are carried by a storm to the coast of North Africa, onto the land of the Lotos-eaters. He must then use force to drag his companions away and prevent them from forgetting their homes for love of the sweet lotos food.

There are in the character of every true poet, two elements, for one of which he is indebted to nature, for the other to cultivation. What he derives from nature, is fine senses: a nervous organization, not only adapted to make his outward impressions vivid and distinct (in which, however, practice does even more than nature), but so constituted, as to be, more easily than common organizations, thrown, either by physical or moral causes, into *states* of enjoyment or suffering, especially of enjoyment: states of a certain duration; often lasting long after the removal of the cause which produced them; and not local, nor consciously physical, but, in so far as organic, pervading the entire nervous system. This peculiar kind of nervous susceptibility seems to be the distinctive character of the poetic temperament. It constitutes the capacity for poetry; and not only produces, as has been shown from the known laws of the human mind, a predisposition to the poetic associations, but supplies the very materials out of which many of them are formed.* What the poet will afterwards construct out of these materials, or whether he will construct anything of value to any one but himself, depends upon the direction given, either by accident or design, to his habitual associations. Here, therefore, begins the province of culture; and, from this point upwards, we may lay it down as a principle, that the achievements of any poet in his art will be in proportion to the growth and perfection of his thinking faculty.

Every great poet, every poet who has extensively or permanently influenced mankind, has been a great thinker;—has had a philosophy, though perhaps he did not call it by that name;—has had his mind full of thoughts, derived not merely from passive sensibility, but from trains of reflection, from observation, analysis, and generalization; however remote the sphere

---

* It may be thought, perhaps, that among the gifts of nature to a poet, ought also to be included a vivid and exuberant imagination. We believe, however, that vividness of imagination is no further a gift of nature, than in so far as it is a natural consequence of vivid sensations. All besides this, we incline to think, depends on habit and cultivation. (Mill's note.)

of his observation and meditation may have lain from the studies of the schools. Where the poetic temperament exists in its greatest degree, while the systematic culture of the intellect has been neglected, we may expect to find, what we do find in the best poems of Shelley—vivid representations of states of passive and dreamy emotion, fitted to give extreme pleasure to persons of similar organization to the poet, but not likely to be sympathized in, because not understood, by any other persons; and scarcely conducing at all to the noblest end of poetry as an intellectual pursuit, that of acting upon the desires and characters of mankind through their emotions, to raise them towards the perfection of their nature. This, like every other adaptation of means to ends, is the work of cultivated reason; and the poet's success in it will be in proportion to the intrinsic value of his thoughts, and to the command which he has acquired over the materials of his imagination, for placing those thoughts in a strong light before the intellect, and impressing them on the feelings.

The poems which we have quoted from Mr. Tennyson prove incontestably that he possesses, in an eminent degree, the natural endowment of a poet—the poetic temperament. And it appears clearly, not only from a comparison of the two volumes, but of different poems in the same volume, that, with him, the other element of poetic excellence—intellectual culture—is advancing both steadily and rapidly; that he is not destined, like so many others, to be remembered for what he might have done, rather than for what he did; that he will not remain a poet of mere temperament, but is ripening into a true artist. Mr. Tennyson may not be conscious of the wide difference in maturity of intellect, which is apparent in his various poems. Though he now writes from greater fulness and clearness of thought, it by no means follows that he has learnt to detect the absence of those qualities in some of his earlier effusions. Indeed, he himself, in one of the most beautiful poems of his first volume (though, as a work of art, very imperfect), the 'Ode to Memory,' confesses a parental predilection for the 'first-born' of his genius. But to us it is evident, not only that his second volume differs from his first as early manhood from youth, but that the various poems in the first volume belong to different, and even distant stages of intellectual development;—distant, not perhaps in years—for a mind like Mr. Tennyson's advances rapidly—but corresponding to very different states of the intellectual powers, both in respect of their strength and of their proportions.

From the very first, like all writers of his natural gifts, he luxuriates in sensuous* imagery; his nominal subject sometimes lies buried in a heap of it. From the first, too, we see his intellect, with every successive degree of strength, struggling upwards to shape this sensuous imagery to a spiritual meaning †; to bring the materials which sense supplies, and fancy summons up, under the command of a central and controlling thought or feeling. We have seen, by the poem of 'Mariana,' with what success he could occasionally do this, even in the period which answers to his first volume; but that volume contains various instances in which he has attempted the same thing, and failed. Such, for example, are, in our opinion, the opening poem, 'Claribel,' and the verses headed 'Elegiacs.' In both, there is what is commonly called imagination—namely, fancy: the imagery and the melody actually haunt us; but there is no harmonizing principle in either;—no appropriateness to the spiritual elements of the scene. If the one poem had been called 'A solitary Place in a Wood,' and the other, 'An

* *Sensuous*, a word revived by Coleridge, as he himself states, 'from our elder classics.' It is used by Milton, who, in his little tract on Education, says of poetry, as compared with rhetoric, that it is 'less subtile and fine, but more simple, *sensuous*, and passionate.' The word *sensual* is irretrievably diverted to another meaning; and a term seems to be required, which (without exciting any ethical associations) shall denote all things pertaining to the bodily senses, in contradistinction to things pertaining to the intellect and the mental feelings. To this use, the word *sensuous* seems as well adapted as any other which could be chosen. (Mill's note.)

† We conceive ourselves warranted, both by usage and the necessity of the case, in using the word *spiritual* as the converse of *sensuous*. It is scarcely necessary to say that we do not mean *religious*. (Mill's note.)

Evening Landscape,' they would not have lost, but gained. In another poem, in the same volume, called 'A Dirge,' and intended for a person who, when alive, had suffered from calumny—a subject which a poet of maturer powers would have made so much of, Mr. Tennyson merely glances at the topics of thought and emotion which his subject suggested, and expatiates in the mere scenery about the grave.*

Some of the smaller poems have a fault which in any but a very juvenile production would be the worst fault of all: they are altogether without meaning: none at least can be discerned in them by persons otherwise competent judges of poetry; if the author had any meaning, he has not been able to express it. Such, for instance, are the two songs on the Owl; such, also, are the verses headed 'The How and the Why,' in the first volume, and the lines on To-day and Yesterday, in the second. If in the former of these productions Mr. Tennyson aimed at

* There are instances in the volume, of far worse failures than these. Such are the two poems 'The Merman' and 'The Mermaid.' When a poet attempts to represent to us any of the beings either of religious or of popular mythology, we expect from him, that, under the conditions prescribed by the received notion of those beings, some mode of spiritual existence will be figured, which we shall recognise as in harmony with the general laws of spirit, but exhibiting those laws in action among a new set of elements. The faculty of thus bringing home to us a coherent conception of beings unknown to our experience, not by logically *characterizing* them, but by a living *representation* of them, such as they would, in fact, *be*, if the hypothesis of their possibility could be realized—is what is meant, when anything is meant, by the words creative imagination. Mr. Tennyson not only fails in this, but makes nothing even of the sensuous elements of the scene: he does not even produce, what he in no other instance misses—a suitable representation of outward scenery. He is actually puerile.

Of the two productions (the most juvenile, we should think, of the set)—'An English War Song,' and 'National Song,' we can only say, that unless they are meant for bitter ridicule of vulgar nationality, and of the poverty of intellect which usually accompanies it, their appearance here is unaccountable. The sonnet, 'Buonaparte,' in the second volume, though not so childish in manner, has still something of the same spirit which was manifested in the two just cited (if they are to be taken as serious.) (Mill's note.)

shadowing forth the vague aspirations to a knowledge beyond the reach of man—the yearnings for a solution of all questions, soluble or insoluble, which concern our nature and destiny—the impatience under the insufficiency of the human faculties to penetrate the secret of our being here, and being what we are—which are natural in a certain state of the human mind; if this was what he sought to typify, he has only proved that he knows not the feeling—that he has neither experienced it, nor realized it in imagination. The questions which a Faust calls upon earth and heaven, and all powers supernal and infernal, to resolve for him, are not the ridiculous ones which Mr. Tennyson asks himself in these verses.

But enough of faults which the poet has almost entirely thrown off merely by the natural expansion of his intellect. We have alluded to them chiefly to show how rapidly progressive that intellect has been.* There are traces, we think, of a continuance of the same progression, throughout the second as well as the first volume.

In the art of painting a picture to the inward eye, the improvement is not so conspicuous as in other qualities; so high a degree of excellence having been already attained in the first volume. Besides the poems which we have quoted, we may refer, in that volume, to those entitled, 'Recollections of the Arabian Nights,' 'The Dying Swan,' 'The Kraken,' and 'The Sleeping Beauty.' The beautiful poems (songs they are called, but are not) 'In the glooming light,' and 'A spirit haunts the

* With the trifling exceptions already mentioned, the only pieces in the second volume which we could have wished omitted are, the little piece of childishness beginning 'O darling room,' and the verses to Christopher North, which express, in rather a common-place way, the author's resentment against a critique, which merited no resentment from him, but rather (all things considered) a directly contrary feeling.

One or two poems, of greater pretension than the above, may be considered not indeed as absolute, but as comparative failures. Among these we must place the second poem in the volume (which affords to the Quarterly critic the opportunities for almost his only just criticisms); and even, notwithstanding its fine sonorous opening, the 'Hesperides.' (Mill's note.)

year's last hours,' are (like the 'Mariana') not mere pictures, but states of emotion, embodied in sensuous imagery. From these, however, to the command over the materials of outward sense for the purpose of bodying forth states of feeling, evinced by some of the poems in the second volume, especially 'The Lady of Shalott' and 'The Lotos-eaters,' there is a considerable distance; and Mr. Tennyson seems, as he proceeded, to have raised his aims still higher—to have aspired to render his poems not only vivid representations of spiritual states, but symbolical of spiritual truths. His longest poem, 'The Palace of Art,' is an attempt of this sort. As such, we do not think it wholly successful, though rich in beauties of detail; but we deem it of the most favourable augury for Mr. Tennyson's future achievements, since it proves a continually increasing endeavour towards the highest excellence, and a constantly rising standard of it.

We predict, that, as Mr. Tennyson advances in general spiritual culture, these higher aims will become more and more predominant in his writings; that he will strive more and more diligently, and, even without striving, will be more and more impelled by the natural tendencies of an expanding character, towards what has been described as the highest object of poetry, 'to incorporate the everlasting reason of man in forms visible to his sense, and suitable to it.' For the fulfilment of this exalted purpose, what we have already seen of him authorizes us to foretell with confidence, that powers of execution will not fail him; it rests with himself to see that his powers of thought may keep pace with them. To render his poetic endowment the means of giving impressiveness to important truths, he must, by continual study and meditation, strengthen his intellect for the discrimination of such truths; he must see that his theory of life and the world be no chimera of the brain, but the well-grounded result of solid and mature thinking;—he must cultivate, and with no half devotion, philosophy as well as poetry.

It may not be superfluous to add, that he should guard himself against an error, to which the philosophical speculations of poets are peculiarly liable—that of embracing as truth, not the conclusions which are recommended by the strongest evidence, but those which have the most poetical appearance;—not those which arise from the deductions of impartial reason, but those which are most captivating to an imagination, biassed perhaps by education and conventional associations. That whatever philosophy he adopts will leave ample materials for poetry, he may be well assured. Whatever is comprehensive, whatever is commanding, whatever is on a great scale, is poetical. Let our philosophical system be what it may, human feelings exist: human nature, with all its enjoyments and sufferings, its strugglings, its victories and defeats, still remain to us; and these are the materials of all poetry. Whoever, in the greatest concerns of human life, pursues truth with unbiassed feelings, and an intellect adequate to discern it, will not find that the resources of poetry are lost to him because he has learnt to use, and not abuse them. They are as open to him as they are to the sentimental weakling, who has no test of the true but the ornamental. And when he once has them under his command, he can wield them for purposes, and with a power, of which neither the dilettante nor the visionary have the slightest conception.

We will not conclude without reminding Mr. Tennyson, that if he wishes his poems to live, he has still much to do in order to perfect himself in the merely mechanical parts of his craft. In a prose-writer, great beauties bespeak forgiveness for innumerable negligences; but poems, especially short poems, attain permanent fame only by the most finished perfection in the details. In some of the most beautiful of Mr. Tennyson's productions there are awkwardnesses and feeblenesses of expression, occasionally even absurdities, to be corrected; and which generally might be corrected without impairing a single beauty. His powers of versification are not yet of the highest order. In one great secret of his art, the adaptation of the music of his verse to the character of his subject, he is far from being a master: he often seems to take his metres almost at random. But this is little to set in the balance against so much excellence; and needed not have been mentioned, except to indicate to Mr. Tennyson the points on which some of his warmest admirers see most room and most necessity for further effort on his part, if he would secure to himself the high place in our poetic literature for which so many of the qualifications are already his own.

A.

From Civilization—Signs of the Times

1836

In "Civilization" Mill deals with a question that had beset the minds of sensitive progressives at least since the philosopher Jean Jacques Rousseau confronted it in the form of a question proposed in 1749, by the academy of Dijon, as the theme for an essay competition: "Has the restoration of the sciences contributed to purifying or to corrupting manners?" In his prize-winning response, *Discourse on the Moral Effects of the Arts and Sciences,* Rousseau came out vehemently on the side of nature as against civilization; and three years later he developed the doctrines of primitivism in a book on the social origin of inequality in which, as his philosophical antagonist Voltaire uncharitably put it, he used unexampled cleverness "in the design of making us all stupid."

Mill, like Voltaire, was on the side of civilization. In the *Autobiography* (page 76) he calls the Utilitarians a nineteenth-century version of the eighteenth-century French *philosophes.* And in the present essay he states clearly his opinion "that civilization is a good; that it is the cause of much good, and not incompatible with any." But he had also participated in that Romantic reaction against the Enlightenment which had its fountainhead in Rousseau; and "Civilization" may be viewed as an attempt to reconcile the antithetical views of these two philosophies on the question of progress. Mill believes that "civilization" is a good, but not the sole good, and that progress is possible, but not inevitable.

The essay suggests two kinds of solution to the special problems of modern civilization: larger and more effective co-operative ventures among individuals, and such reforms of educational and political institutions as will reinvigorate individual character. Among Mill's specific proposals are several to which he would often return, and some, such as the idea of a literary academy, which he would later reject. The ideas put forth on education were to become matters of principle with him, and they were substantially repeated forty years later in the Inaugural Address at St. Andrews.

THE WORD Civilization, like many other terms of the philosophy of human nature, is a word of double meaning. It sometimes stands for *human improvement* in general, and sometimes for *certain kinds* of improvement in particular.

We are accustomed to call a country more civilized if we think it more improved; more eminent in the best characteristics of Man and Society; farther advanced in the road to perfection; happier, nobler, wiser. This is one sense of the word civilization. But in another sense it stands for that kind of improvement only, which distinguishes a wealthy and powerful nation from savages or barbarians. It is in this sense that we may speak of the vices or the miseries of civilization; and that the question has been seriously propounded, whether civilization is on the whole a good or an evil? Assuredly, we entertain no doubt on this point; we hold that civilization is a good, that it is the cause of much good, and not incompatible with any; but we think there is other good, much even of the highest good, which civilization in this sense does not provide for, and some which it has a tendency (though that tendency may be counteracted) to impede.

The inquiry into which these considerations would lead, is calculated to throw light upon many of the characteristic features of our time. The present era is pre-eminently the era of civilization in the narrow sense; whether we consider what has already been achieved, or the rapid advances making towards still greater achievements. We do not regard the age as either equally advanced or equally progressive in many of the other kinds of improvement. In some it appears to us stationary, in some even retrograde. Moreover, the irresistible consequences of a state of advancing civilization; the new position in which that advance has placed, and is every day more and more placing, mankind; the entire inapplicability of old rules to this new position, and the necessity, if we would either realize the benefits of the new state or preserve those of the old, that we should adopt many new rules, and new courses of action; are

First published in the *London and Westminster Review*, XXV (April 1836).

topics which seem to require a more comprehensive examination than they have usually received.

We shall on the present occasion use the word civilization only in the restricted sense: not that in which it is synonymous with improvement, but that in which it is the direct converse or contrary of rudeness or barbarism. Whatever be the characteristics of what we call savage life, the contrary of these, or the qualities which society puts on as it throws off these, constitute civilization. Thus, a savage tribe consists of a handful of individuals, wandering or thinly scattered over a vast tract of country: a dense population, therefore, dwelling in fixed habitations, and largely collected together in towns and villages, we term civilized. In savage life there is no commerce, no manufactures, no agriculture, or next to none: a country rich in the fruits of agriculture: commerce, and manufactures, we call civilized. In savage communities each person shifts for himself; except in war (and even then very imperfectly), we seldom see any joint operations carried on by the union of many; nor do savages, in general, find much pleasure in each other's society. Wherever, therefore, we find human beings acting together for common purposes in large bodies, and enjoying the pleasures of social intercourse, we term them civilized. In savage life there is little or no law, or administration of justice; no systematic employment of the collective strength of society, to protect individuals against injury from one another; every one trusts to his own strength or cunning, and where that fails, he is generally without resource. We accordingly call a people civilized, where the arrangements of society, for protecting the persons and property of its members, are sufficiently perfect to maintain peace among them; *i.e.* to induce the bulk of the community to rely for their security mainly upon social arrangements, and renounce for the most part, and in ordinary circumstances, the vindication of their interests (whether in the way of aggression or of defence) by their individual strength or courage.

These ingredients of civilization are various, but consideration will satisfy us that they are not improperly classed together. History, and their own nature, alike show that they begin together, always co-exist, and accompany each other in their growth. Wherever there has arisen sufficient knowledge of the arts of life, and sufficient security of property and person, to render the progressive increase of wealth and population possible, the community becomes and continues progressive in all the elements which we have just enumerated. These elements exist in modern Europe, and especially in Great Britain, in a more eminent degree, and in a state of more rapid progression, than at any other place or time. We propose to consider some of the consequences which that high and progressive state of civilization has already produced, and of the further ones which it is hastening to produce.

The most remarkable of those consequences of advancing civilization, which the state of the world is now forcing upon the attention of thinking minds, is this: that power passes more and more from individuals, and small knots of individuals, to masses: that the importance of the masses becomes constantly greater, that of individuals less.

. . . .

It is not solely on the private virtues, that this growing insignificance of the individual in the mass, is productive of mischief. It corrupts the very fountain of the improvement of public opinion itself; it corrupts public teaching; it weakens the influence of the more cultivated few over the many. Literature has suffered more than any other human production by the common disease. When there were few books, and when few read at all save those who had been accustomed to read the best authors, books were written with the well-grounded expectation that they would be read carefully, and if they deserved it, would be read often. A book of sterling merit, when it came out, was sure to be heard of, and might hope to be read, by the whole reading class; it might succeed by its real excellencies, though not got up to strike at once; and even if so got up, unless it had the support of genuine merit, it fell into oblivion. The rewards were then for him who wrote *well,* not *much;* for the laborious and learned, not the crude and ill-informed writer. But now the case is reversed. 'This is a reading age; and precisely because it is so reading an age, any book which is the result of profound meditation is, perhaps, less likely to be duly and profitably read than at a former period. The world reads too much and too quickly to read well. When books were few, to get through one was a work of time and labour: what was written with thought was read with thought, and with a desire to extract from it as much of the materials of knowledge as possible. But when almost every person who can spell, can and will write, what is to be done? It is difficult to know what to read, except by reading everything; and so much of the world's business is now transacted through the press, that it is necessary to know what is printed, if we desire to know what is going on. Opinion weighs with so vast a weight in the balance of events, that ideas of no value in themselves are of importance from the mere circumstance that they *are* ideas, and have a *bonâ fide* existence as such anywhere out of Bedlam. The world, in consequence, gorges itself with intellectual food, and in order to swallow the more, *bolts* it. Nothing is now read slowly, or twice over. Books are run through with no less rapidity, and scarcely leave a more durable impression, than a newspaper article. It is for this, among other causes, that so few books are produced of any value. The lioness in the fable boasted that though she produced only one at a birth, that one was a lion. But if each lion only counted for one, and each leveret for one, the advantage would all be on the side of the hare. When every unit is individually weak, it is only multitude that tells. What wonder that the newspapers should carry all before them? A book produces hardly a greater effect than an article, and there can be 365 of these in one year. He, therefore, who should and would write a book, and write it in the proper manner of writing a book, now dashes down his first hasty thoughts, or what he mistakes for thoughts, in a periodical. And the public is in the predicament of an indolent man, who cannot bring himself to apply his mind vigorously to his own affairs, and over whom, therefore, not he who speaks most wisely, but he who speaks most frequently, obtains the influence.'*

Hence we see that literature is becoming more and more ephemeral: books, of any solidity, are almost gone by; even reviews are not now considered sufficiently light; the attention cannot sustain itself on any serious subject, even for the space of a review-article. In the more attractive kinds of literature, novels and magazines, though the demand has so greatly increased, the supply has so outstripped it, that even a novel is seldom a lucrative speculation. It is only under circumstances of rare attraction that a bookseller will now give anything to an author for copyright. As the difficulties of success thus progressively increase, all other ends are more and more sacrificed for the attainment of it; literature becomes more and more a mere reflection of the current sentiments, and has almost entirely abandoned its mission as an enlightener and improver of them.[1]

There are now in this country, we may say, but two modes left in which an individual mind can hope to produce much direct effect upon the minds and destinies of his countrymen generally; as a member of parliament, or an editor of a London newspaper. In both these capacities much may still be done by an individual, because, while the power of the collective body is very great, the number of participants in it does not admit of much increase. One of these monopolies will be opened to competition when the newspaper stamp is taken off; whereby the importance of the newspaper press in the aggregate, considered as the voice of public opinion, will be increased, and the influence of any one writer in helping to form that opinion necessarily diminished. This we might regret, did we not remember to what ends that influence is now used, and is sure to

---

* From a paper by the author, not included in the present collection. (Mill's note. The paper referred to is a review of "Austin's Lectures on Jurisprudence," *Tait's Magazine* [December 1832].)

[1] This passage is markedly similar in message and tone to "Attack on Literature."

be so while newspapers are a mere investment of capital for the sake of mercantile profit.

Is there, then, no remedy? Are the decay of individual energy, the weakening of the influence of superior minds over the multitude, the growth of charlatanerie, and the diminished efficacy of public opinion as a restraining power,–are these the price we necessarily pay for the benefits of civilization; and can they only be avoided by checking the diffusion of knowledge, discouraging the spirit of combination, prohibiting improvements in the arts of life, and repressing the further increase of wealth and of production? Assuredly not. Those advantages which civilization cannot give–which in its uncorrected influence it has even a tendency to destroy–may yet coexist with civilization; and it is only when joined to civilization that they can produce their fairest fruits. All that we are in danger of losing we may preserve, all that we have lost we may regain, and bring to a perfection hitherto unknown; but not by slumbering, and leaving things to themselves, no more than by ridiculously trying our strength against their irresistible tendencies: only by establishing counter-tendencies, which may combine with those tendencies, and modify them.

The evils are, that the individual is lost and becomes impotent in the crowd, and that individual character itself becomes relaxed and enervated. For the first evil, the remedy is, greater and more perfect combination among individuals; for the second, national institutions of education, and forms of polity calculated to invigorate the individual character.

The former of these desiderata, as its attainment depends upon a change in the habits of society itself, can only be realized by degrees, as the necessity becomes felt; but circumstances are even now to a certain extent forcing it on. In Great Britain especially (which so far surpasses the rest of the old world in the extent and rapidity of the accumulation of wealth) the fall of profits, consequent upon the vast increase of population and capital, is rapidly extinguishing the class of small dealers and small producers, from the impossibility of living on their diminished profits, and is throwing business of all kinds more and more into the hands of large capitalists—whether these be rich individuals, or joint-stock companies formed by the aggregation of many small capitals. We are not among those who believe that this progress is tending to the complete extinction of competition, or that the entire productive resources of the country will within any assignable number of ages, if ever, be administered by, and for the benefit of, a general association of the whole community. But we believe that the multiplication of competitors in all branches of business and in all professions—which renders it more and more difficult to obtain success by merit alone, more and more easy to obtain it by plausible pretence—will find a limiting principle in the progress of the spirit of co-operation; that in every over-crowded department there will arise a tendency among individuals so to unite their labour or their capital, that the purchaser or employer will have to choose, not among innumerable individuals, but among a few groups. Competition will be as active as ever, but the number of competitors will be brought within manageable bounds.

Such a spirit of co-operation is most of all wanted among the intellectual classes and professions. The amount of human labour, and labour of the most precious kind, now wasted, and wasted too in the cruelest manner, for want of combination, is incalculable. What a spectacle, for instance, does the medical profession present! One successful practitioner burthened with more work than mortal man can perform, and which he performs so summarily that it were often better let alone;—in the surrounding streets twenty unhappy men, each of whom has been as laboriously and expensively trained as he has to do the very same thing, and is possibly as well qualified, wasting their capabilities and starving for want of work. Under better arrangements these twenty would form a corps of subalterns marshalled under their more successful leader; who (granting him to be really the ablest physician of the set, and not merely the most successful impostor) is wasting time in physicking people for headaches and heartburns, which he might with better economy of mankind's resources turn over to his subordinates, while he employed his maturer powers and greater experience in studying and treating those more obscure and difficult cases upon which science has not yet thrown sufficient light, and to which ordinary knowledge and abilities would not be adequate. By such means every person's capacities would be turned to account, and the highest minds being kept for the highest things, these would make progress, while ordinary occasions would be no losers.

But it is in literature, above all, that a change of this sort is of most pressing urgency. There the system of individual competition has fairly worked itself out, and things can hardly continue much longer as they are. Literature is a province of exertion upon which more, of the first value to human nature, depends, than upon any other; a province in which the highest and most valuable order of works, those which most contribute to form the opinions and shape the characters of subsequent ages, are, more than in any other class of productions, placed beyond the possibility of appreciation by those who form the bulk of the purchasers in the book-market; insomuch that, even in ages when these were a far less numerous and more select class than now, it was an admitted point that the only success which writers of the first order could look to was the verdict of posterity. That verdict could, in those times, be confidently expected by whoever was worthy of it; for the good judges, though few in number, were sure to read every work of merit which appeared; and as the recollection of one book was not in those days immediately obliterated by a hundred others, they remembered it, and kept alive the knowledge of it to subsequent ages. But in our day, from the immense multitude of writers (which is now not less remarkable than the multitude of readers), and from the manner in which the people of this age are obliged to read, it is difficult for what does not strike during its novelty, to strike at all: a book either misses fire altogether, or is so read as to make no permanent impression; and the good equally with the worthless are forgotten by the next day.

For this there is no remedy, while the public have no guidance beyond booksellers' advertisements, and the ill-considered and hasty criticisms of newspapers and small periodicals, to direct them in distinguishing what is not worth reading from what is. The resource must in time be, some organized co-operation among the leading intellects of the age, whereby works of first-rate merit, of whatever class, and of whatever tendency in point of opinion, might come forth with the stamp on them, from the first, of the approval of those whose names would carry authority. There are many causes why we must wait long for such a combination; but (with enormous defects, both in plan and in execution) the Society for the Diffusion of Useful Knowledge [2] was as considerable a step towards it, as could be expected in the present state of men's minds, and in a first attempt. Literature has had in this country two ages; it must now have a third. The age of patronage, as Johnson a century ago proclaimed, is gone. The age of booksellers, it has been proclaimed by Mr. Carlyle, has well nigh died out.[3] In the first there was nothing intrinsically base, nor in the second anything inherently independent and liberal. Each has done great things; both have had their day. The time is perhaps coming when authors, as a collective guild, will be their own patrons and their own booksellers.

These things must bide their time. But the other of the two great desiderata, the regeneration of individual character among our lettered and opulent classes, by the adaptation to that purpose of our institutions, and, above all, of our educational institutions, is an object of more urgency, and for which more might be immediately accomplished, if the will and the understanding were not alike wanting.

This, unfortunately, is a subject on which, for the inculcation of rational views, everything is yet to be done; for, all that we

---

[2] Founded by Lord Brougham, prominent Whig statesman, in 1827 for the purpose of educating the lower classes.

[3] See Carlyle's review of J. W. Croker's 1831 edition of *Boswell's Life of Johnson,* published in *Fraser's Magazine* in May 1832.

would inculcate, all that we deem of vital importance, all upon which we conceive the salvation of the next and all future ages to rest, has the misfortune to be almost equally opposed to the most popular doctrines of our own time, and to the prejudices of those who cherish the empty husk of what has descended from ancient times. We are at issue equally with the admirers of Oxford and Cambridge, Eton and Westminster, and with the generality of their professed reformers. We regard the system of those institutions, as administered for two centuries past, with sentiments little short of utter abhorrence. But we do not conceive that their vices would be cured by bringing their studies into a closer connexion with what it is the fashion to term 'the business of the world;' by dismissing the logic and classics which are still professedly taught, to substitute modern languages and experimental physics. We would have classics and logic taught far more really and deeply than at present, and we would add to them other studies more alien than any which yet exist to the 'business of the world,' but more germane to the great business of every rational being–the strengthening and enlarging of his own intellect and character. The empirical knowledge which the world demands, which is the stock in trade of money-getting life, we would leave the world to provide for itself; content with infusing into the youth of our country a spirit, and training them to habits, which would ensure their acquiring such knowledge easily, and using it well. These, we know, are not the sentiments of the vulgar; but we believe them to be those of the best and wisest of all parties: and we are glad to corroborate our opinion by a quotation from a work written by a friend to the Universities, and by one whose tendencies are rather Conservative than Liberal; a book which, though really, and not in form merely, one of fiction, contains much subtle and ingenious thought, and the results of much psychological experience, combined, we are compelled to say, with much caricature, and very provoking (though we are convinced unintentional) distortion and misinterpretation of the opinions of some of those with whose philosophy that of the author does not agree.

'You believe' (a clergyman *loquitur*[4]) 'that the University is to prepare youths for a successful career in society: I believe the sole object is to give them that manly character which will enable them to resist the influences of society. I do not care to prove that I am right, and that any university which does not stand upon this basis will be rickety in its childhood, and useless or mischievous in its manhood; I care only to assert that this was the notion of those who founded Oxford and Cambridge. I fear that their successors are gradually losing sight of this principle—are gradually beginning to think that it is their business to turn out clever lawyers and serviceable Treasury clerks—are pleased when the world compliments them upon the goodness of the article with which they have furnished it—and that this low vanity is absorbing all their will and their power to create great men, whom the age will scorn, and who will save it from the scorn of the times to come.'

'One or two such men,' said the Liberal, 'in a generation, may be very useful; but the University gives us two or three thousand youths every year. I suppose you are content that a portion shall do week-day services.'

'I wish to have a far more hard-working and active race than we have at present,' said the clergyman; 'men more persevering in toil, and less impatient of reward; but all experience, a thing which the schools are not privileged to despise, though the world is—all experience is against the notion, that the means to procure a supply of good ordinary men is to attempt nothing higher. I know that nine-tenths of those whom the University sends out must be hewers of wood and drawers of water; but, if I train the ten-tenths to be so, depend upon it the wood will be badly cut, the water will be spilt. Aim at something noble; make your system such that a great man may be formed by it, and there will be a manhood in your little men of which you do not dream. But when some skilful rhetorician, or lucky rat, stands at the top of the ladder—when the University, instead of disclaiming the creature, instead of pleading, as an excuse for themselves, that the healthiest mother may, by accident, produce a shapeless abortion, stands shouting, that the world may know what great things they can do, "we taught the boy!"—when the hatred which worldly men will bear to religion always, and to learning whenever it teaches us to soar and not to grovel, is met, not with a frank defiance, but rather with a deceit-

[4] "Speaks."

ful argument to show that trade is the better for them; is it wonderful that a puny beggarly feeling should pervade the mass of our young men? that they should scorn all noble achievements, should have no higher standard of action than the world's opinion, and should conceive of no higher reward than to sit down amidst loud cheering, which continues for several moments?'*

Nothing can be more just or more forcible than the description here given of the objects which University education should aim at: we are at issue with the writer, only on the proposition that these objects ever were attained, or ever could be so, consistently with the principle which has always been the foundation of the English Universities; a principle, unfortunately, by no means confined to them. The difficulty which continues to oppose either such reform of our old academical institutions, or the establishment of such new ones, as shall give us an education capable of forming great minds, is, that in order to do so it is necessary to begin by eradicating the idea which nearly all the upholders and nearly all the impugners of the Universities rootedly entertain, as to the objects not merely of academical education, but of education itself. What is this idea? That the object of education is, not to qualify the pupil for judging what is true or what is right, but to provide that he shall think true what we think true, and right what we think right—that to teach, means to inculcate our own opinions, and that our business is not to make thinkers or inquirers, but disciples. This is the deep-seated error, the inveterate prejudice, which the real reformer of English education has to struggle against. Is it astonishing that great minds are not produced, in a country where the test of a great mind is, agreeing in the opinions of the small minds? where every institution for spiritual culture which the country has—the Church, the Universities, and almost every dissenting community—are consti-

* From the novel of 'Eustace Conway,' attributed to Mr. Maurice. (Mill's note. Frederick Denison Maurice [1805–1872], follower of Coleridge, friend of Mill, originator of the Christian Socialist movement. The excerpt is from chapter six of the second volume of his novel, *Eustace Conway, or The Brother and Sister* [1834]. See *Autobiography*, pp. 107–110, for Mill's estimate of Maurice.)

tuted on the following as their avowed principle: that the object is, *not* that the individual should go forth determined and qualified to seek truth ardently, vigorously, and disinterestedly; *not* that he be furnished at setting out with the needful aids and facilities, the needful materials and instruments for that search, and then left to the unshackled use of them; *not* that, by a free communion with the thoughts and deeds of the great minds which preceded him, he be inspired at once with the courage to dare all which truth and conscience require, and the modesty to weigh well the grounds of what others think, before adopting contrary opinions of his own: *not* this–no; but that the triumph of the system, the merit, the excellence in the sight of God which it possesses, or which it can impart to its pupil, is, that his speculations shall terminate in the adoption, in words, of a particular set of opinions. That provided he adhere to these opinions, it matters little whether he receive them from authority or from examination; and worse, that it matters little by what temptations of interest or vanity, by what voluntary or involuntary sophistication with his intellect, and deadening of his noblest feelings, that result is arrived at; that it even matters comparatively little whether to his mind the words are mere words, or the representatives of realities–in what sense he receives the favoured set of propositions, or whether he attaches to them any sense at all. Were ever great minds thus formed? Never. The few great minds which this country has produced have been formed in spite of nearly everything which could be done to stifle their growth. And all thinkers, much above the common order, who have grown up in the Church of England, or in any other Church, have been produced in latitudinarian epochs, or while the impulse of intellectual emancipation which gave existence to the Church had not quite spent itself. The flood of burning metal which issued from the furnace, flowed on a few paces before it congealed.

That the English Universities have, throughout, proceeded on the principle, that the intellectual association of mankind must be founded upon articles, *i.e.* upon a promise of belief in certain opinions; that the scope of all they do is to prevail upon their pupils, by fair means or foul, to acquiesce in the opinions which are set down for them; that the abuse of the human faculties so forcibly denounced by Locke [5] under the name of 'principling' their pupils, is their sole method in religion, politics, morality, or philosophy–is vicious indeed, but the vice is equally prevalent without and within their pale, and is no farther disgraceful to them than inasmuch as a better doctrine has been taught for a century past by the superior spirits, with whom in point of intelligence it was their duty to maintain themselves on a level. But, that when this object was attained they cared for no other; that if they could make churchmen, they cared not to make religious men; that if they could make Tories, whether they made patriots was indifferent to them; that if they could prevent heresy, they cared not if the price paid were stupidity–this constitutes the peculiar baseness of those bodies. Look at them. While their sectarian character, while the exclusion of all who will not sign away their freedom of thought, is contended for as if life depended upon it, there is hardly a trace in the system of the Universities that any other object whatever is seriously cared for. Nearly all the professorships have degenerated into sinecures. Few of the professors ever deliver a lecture. One of the few great scholars who have issued from either University for a century (and he was such before he went thither), the Rev. Connop Thirlwall,[6] has published to the world that in his University at least,

---

[5] See "On Genius," note 7. In 1684 Locke was "sent down" from Christ Church, Oxford, for sedition.

[6] Connop Thirlwall (1797–1875) was a churchman (he was to become Bishop of St. David's) and a leader of the historical revival in England, his major contribution being the eight-volume *History of Greece* (1835–1844). In 1834 Thirlwall's connection with Trinity College, Cambridge, was broken after a dispute over a parliamentary bill to admit Dissenters to the university. In answering the argument that evils would arise from mixing students of varied religious opinions, Thirlwall wrote that at Cambridge "our colleges are not theological seminaries. We have no theological colleges, no theological tutors, no theological students. . . ." He added that the colleges were not even "schools of

even theology—even Church of England theology—is not taught; and his dismissal, for this piece of honesty, from the tutorship of his college, is one among the daily proofs how much safer it is for twenty men to neglect their duty, than for one man to impeach them of the neglect. The only studies really encouraged are classics and mathematics; neither of them a useless study, though the last, as an exclusive instrument for fashioning the mental powers, greatly overrated; but Mr. Whewell,[7] a high authority against his own University, has published a pamphlet, chiefly to prove that the kind of mathematical attainment by which Cambridge honours are gained, expertness in the use of the calculus, is not that kind which has any tendency to produce superiority of intellect.* The mere shell and husk of the syllogistic logic at the one University, the wretchedest smattering of Locke and Paley at the other, are all of moral or psychological science that is

---

religious instruction" and attacked college lectures in divinity and compulsory chapel attendance. On May 21, 1834, Dr. Christopher Wordsworth, Master of Trinity, asked Thirlwall to resign from his position as assistant-tutor. Many years later, ironically, he concurred in the prosecution for heresy of the contributors to *Essays and Reviews* (1860).

[7] William Whewell, D.D. (1794–1866), Professor of Moral Philosophy at Cambridge in 1837, later became Master of Trinity. Mill considered him a formidable representative of the deductive mode of philosophizing, and the two men engaged in a philosophic quarrel of fifteen years' duration.

* The erudite and able writer in the 'Edinburgh Review' [Sir William Hamilton], who has expended an almost superfluous weight of argument and authority in combating the position incidentally maintained in Mr. Whewell's pamphlet, of the great value of mathematics as an exercise of the mind, was, we think, bound to have noticed the fact that the far more direct object of the pamphlet was one which partially coincided with that of its reviewer. We do not think that Mr. Whewell has done well what he undertook: he is vague, and is always attempting to be a profounder metaphysician than he can be; but the main proposition of his pamphlet is true and important, and he is entitled to no little credit for having discerned that important truth, and expressed it so strongly. (Mill's note.)

taught at either.† As a means of educating the many, the Universities are absolutely null. The youth of England are not educated. The attainments of any kind required for taking all the degrees conferred by these bodies are, at Cambridge, utterly contemptible; at Oxford, we believe, of late years, somewhat higher, but still very low. Honours, indeed, are not gained but by a severe struggle; and if even the candidates for honours were mentally benefited, the system would not be worthless. But what have the senior wranglers done, even in mathematics? Has Cambridge produced, since Newton, one great mathematical genius? We do not say an Euler, a Laplace, or a Lagrange,[8] but such as France has produced a score of during the same period. How many books which have thrown light upon the history, antiquities, philosophy, art, or literature of the ancients, have the two Universities sent forth since the Reformation? Compare them, not merely with Germany, but even with Italy or France. When a man is pronounced by them to have excelled in their studies, what do the Universities do? They give him an income, not for continuing to learn, but for having learnt; not for doing anything, but for what he has already done: on condition solely of living like a monk, and putting on the livery of the Church at the end of seven years. They bribe men by high rewards to get their arms ready, but do not require them to fight.*

† We should except, at Oxford, the Ethics, Politics, and Rhetoric of Aristotle. These are part of the course of classical instruction, and are so far an exception to the rule, otherwise pretty faithfully observed at both Universities, of cultivating only the least useful parts of ancient literature. (Mill's note.)

[8] Leonhard Euler (1707–1783), Swiss mathematician.—Pierre Simon, Marquis de Laplace (1749–1827), French astronomer and mathematician, evolved the scientific form of the nebular hypothesis—Joseph Louis, Comte Lagrange (1736–1813), French mathematician and astronomer.

* Much of what is here said of the Universities, has, in a great measure, ceased to be true. The Legislature has at last asserted its right of interference; and even before it did so, the bodies had already entered into a course of as decided improvement as any other English institu-

Are these the places of education which are to send forth minds capable of maintaining a victorious struggle with the debilitating influences of the age, and strengthening the weak side of Civilization by the support of a higher Cultivation? This, however, is what we require from these institutions; or, in their default, from others which should take their place. And the very first step towards their reform should be to unsectarianize them wholly—not by the paltry measure of allowing Dissenters to come and be taught orthodox sectarianism, but by putting an end to sectarian teaching altogether. The principle itself of dogmatic religion, dogmatic morality, dogmatic philosophy, is what requires to be rooted out; not any particular manifestation of that principle.

The very corner-stone of an education intended to form great minds, must be the recognition of the principle, that the object is to call forth the greatest possible quantity of intellectual *power*, and to inspire the intensest *love of truth;* and this without a particle of regard to the results to which the exercise of that power may lead, even though it should conduct the pupil to opinions diametrically opposite to those of his teachers. We say this, not because we think opinions unimportant, but because of the immense importance which we attach to them; for in proportion to the degree of intellectual power and love of truth which we succeed in creating, is the certainty that (whatever may happen in any one particular instance) in the aggregate of instances true opinions will be the result; and intellectual power and practical love of truth are alike impossible where the reasoner is shown his conclusions, and informed beforehand that he is expected to arrive at them.

We are not so absurd as to propose that the teacher should not set forth his own opinions as the true ones, and exert his utmost powers to exhibit their truth in the strongest light. To abstain from this would be to nourish the worse intellectual habit of all, that of not finding, and not looking for, certainty in anything. But the teacher himself should not be held to any

tions. But I leave these pages unaltered, as matter of historical record, and as an illustration of tendencies. (Mill's note, added in 1859.)

creed; nor should the question be whether his own opinions are the true ones, but whether he is well instructed in those of other people, and, in enforcing his own, states the arguments for all conflicting opinions fairly. In this spirit it is that all the great subjects are taught from the chairs of the German and French Universities. As a general rule, the most distinguished teacher is selected, whatever be his particular views, and he consequently teaches in the spirit of free inquiry, not of dogmatic imposition.

Such is the principle of all academical instruction which aims at forming great minds. The details cannot be too various and comprehensive. Ancient literature would fill a large place in such a course of instruction; because it brings before us the thoughts and actions of many great minds, minds of many various orders of greatness, and these related and exhibited in a manner tenfold more impressive, tenfold more calculated to call forth high aspirations, than in any modern literature. Imperfectly as these impressions are made by the current modes of classical teaching, it is incalculable what we owe to this, the sole ennobling feature in the slavish, mechanical thing which the moderns call education. Nor is it to be forgotten among the benefits of familiarity with the monuments of antiquity, and especially those of Greece, that we are taught by it to appreciate and to admire intrinsic greatness, amidst opinions, habits, and institutions most remote from ours; and are thus trained to that large and catholic toleration, which is founded on understanding, not on indifference—and to a habit of free, open sympathy with powers of mind and nobleness of character, howsoever exemplified. Were but the languages and literature of antiquity so taught that the glorious images they present might stand before the student's eyes as living and glowing realities—that, instead of lying a *caput mortuum* [9] at the bottom of his mind, like some foreign substance in no way influencing the current of his thoughts or the tone of his feelings, they might circulate through it, and become assimilated, and be part and parcel of himself!—then should we see how

[9] "Dead head," i.e., worthless residue.

little these studies have yet done for us, compared with what they have yet to do.

An important place in the system of education which we contemplate would be occupied by history: because it is the record of all great things which have been achieved by mankind, and because when philosophically studied it gives a certain largeness of conception to the student, and familiarizes him with the action of great causes. In no other way can he so completely realize in his own mind (howsoever he may be satisfied with the proof of them as abstract propositions) the great principles by which the progress of man and the condition of society are governed. Nowhere else will the infinite varieties of human nature be so vividly brought home to him, and anything cramped or one-sided in his own standard of it so effectually corrected; and nowhere else will he behold so strongly exemplified the astonishing pliability of our nature, and the vast effects which may under good guidance be produced upon it by honest endeavour. The literature of our own and other modern nations should be studied along with the history, or rather as part of the history.

In the department of pure intellect, the highest place will belong to logic and the philosophy of mind: the one, the instrument for the cultivation of all sciences; the other, the root from which they all grow. It scarcely needs be said that the former ought not to be taught as a mere system of technical rules, nor the latter as a set of concatenated abstract propositions. The tendency, so strong everywhere, is strongest of all here, to receive opinions into the mind without any real understanding of them, merely because they seem to follow from certain admitted premises, and to let them lie there as forms of words, lifeless and void of meaning. The pupil must be led to interrogate his own consciousness, to observe and experiment upon himself: of the mind, by any other process, little will he ever know.

With these should be joined all those sciences, in which great and certain results are arrived at by mental processes of some length or nicety: not that all persons should study all these sciences, but that some should study all, and all some. These may be divided into sciences of mere ratiocination, as mathematics; and sciences partly of ratiocination, and partly of what is far more difficult, comprehensive observation and analysis. Such are, in their *rationale*, even the sciences to which mathematical processes are applicable: and such are all those which relate to human nature.The philosophy of morals, of government, of law, of political economy, of poetry and art, should form subjects of systematic instruction, under the most eminent professors who could be found; these being chosen, not for the particular doctrines they might happen to profess, but as being those who were most likely to send forth pupils qualified in point of disposition and attainments to choose doctrines for themselves. And why should not religion be taught in the same manner? Not until then will one step be made towards the healing of religious differences: not until then will the spirit of English religion become catholic instead of sectarian, favourable instead of hostile to freedom of thought and the progress of the human mind.

With regard to the changes, in forms of polity and social arrangements, which, in addition to reforms in education, we conceive to be required for regenerating the character of the higher classes; to express them even summarily would require a long discourse. But the general idea from which they all emanate, may be stated briefly. Civilization has brought about a degree of security and fixity in the possession of all advantages once acquired, which has rendered it possible for a rich man to lead the life of a Sybarite,[10] and nevertheless enjoy throughout life a degree of power and consideration which could formerly be earned or retained only by personal activity. We cannot undo what civilization has done, and again stimulate the energy of the higher classes by insecurity of property, or danger of life or limb. The only adventitious motive it is in the

10 A lover of luxury, a voluptuary; literally, an inhabitant of ancient Sybaris, a Greek city whose people were known for their voluptuousness.

power of society to hold out, is reputation and consequence; and of this as much use as possible should be made for the encouragement of desert. The main thing which social changes can do for the improvement of the higher classes—and it is what the progress of democracy is insensibly but certainly accomplishing—is gradually to put an end to every kind of unearned distinction, and let the only road open to honour and ascendancy be that of personal qualities.

From The French Revolution

1837

Mill had both helped and hindered Thomas Carlyle's progress in writing *The French Revolution.* It is well known that after reading the manuscript of Carlyle's first volume Mill carelessly allowed his maid to burn it as waste paper, thus putting Carlyle to the trouble of rewriting it. To what extent Mill helped Carlyle in his research is not so well known. Mill had long been a close student of French affairs and of the French Revolution in particular. He abandoned the idea of writing his own history of the revolution only when he became convinced of the impossibility of speaking frankly to the English public on the subject of Christianity. Subsequently, he turned over all of his materials and imparted much of his knowledge to Carlyle.

As he usually did when he wanted to promote the success of a book he liked, Mill included in his review long quotations (many of which are omitted here) from Carlyle's work. Indeed, after he had written it, he told a friend that the article "reads damned bad—not so the extracts, which are splendid."

But the modern reader is not likely to share Mill's opinion. For him the article's main interest lies in Mill's development of the argument, first stated in "What is Poetry?," that poetry can be purified of rhetoric and still act as a moral force. Mill's distinction, in this review, between the author who keeps his opinions distinct from his presentation and the author who intentionally confuses them is analogous to the distinction in "What Is Poetry?" between the poet and the rhetorician. The integrity of Carlyle's "evidence" is preserved because it is not tainted by rhetorical intentions. According to Mill, Carlyle acquaints his reader with men and events before he expresses any opinion of them, whereas other historians allow their prejudices and opinions to determine the character of their descriptions and presentations.

The French Revolution: A History. In three volumes. By Thomas Carlyle. Small 8vo., Fraser, 1837.

This is not so much a history, as an epic poem; and notwithstanding, or even in consequence of this, the truest of histories. It is the history of the French Revolution, and the poetry of it, both in one; and on the whole no work of greater genius, either historical or poetical, has been produced in this country for many years.

It is a book on which opinion will be for some time divided; nay, what talk there is about it, while it is still fresh, will probably be oftenest of a disparaging sort; as indeed is usually the case, both with men's works and with men themselves, of distinguished originality. For a thing which is unaccustomed, must be a very small thing indeed, if mankind can at once see into it and be sure that it is good: when, therefore, a considerable thing, which is also an unaccustomed one, appears, those who will hereafter approve, sit silent for a time, making up their minds; and those only to whom the mere novelty is a sufficient reason for disapproval, speak out. We need not fear to prophesy that the suffrages of a large class of the very best qualified judges will be given, even enthusiastically, in favour of the volumes before us; but we will not affect to deny that the sentiment of another large class of readers (among whom are many entitled to the most respectful attention on other subjects) will be far different; a class comprehending all who are repelled by quaintness of manner. For a style more peculiar than that of Mr Carlyle, more unlike the jog-trot characterless uniformity which distinguishes the English style of this age of Periodicals, does not exist. Nor indeed can this style be wholly defended even by its admirers. Some of its peculiarities are mere mannerisms, arising from some casual association of ideas, or some habit accidentally picked up; and what is worse, many sterling thoughts are so disguised in phraseology borrowed from the spiritualist school of German poets and meta-

---

First published in *London and Westminster Review*, XXVII (July 1837).

physicians, as not only to obscure the meaning, but to raise, in the minds of most English readers, a not unnatural nor inexcusable presumption of there being no meaning at all. Nevertheless, the presumption fails in this instance (as in many other instances); there is not only a meaning, but generally a true, and even a profound meaning; and, although a few dicta about the "mystery" and the "infinitude" which are in the universe and in man, and such like topics, are repeated in varied phrases greatly too often for our taste, this must be borne with, proceeding, as one cannot but see, from feelings the most solemn, and the most deeply rooted which can lie in the heart of a human being. These transcendentalisms, and the accidental mannerisms excepted, we pronounce the style of this book to be not only good, but of surpassing excellence; excelled, in its kind, only by the great masters of epic poetry; and a most suitable and glorious vesture for a work which is itself, as we have said, an epic poem.

To any one who is perfectly satisfied with the best of the existing histories, it will be difficult to explain wherein the merit of Mr Carlyle's book consists. If there be a person who, in reading the histories of Hume, Robertson, and Gibbon[1] (works of extraordinary talent, and the works of great writers) has never felt that this, after all, is not history—and that the lives and deeds of his fellow-creatures must be placed before him in quite another manner, if he is to know them, or feel them to be real beings, who once were alive, beings of his own flesh and blood, not mere shadows and dim abstractions; such a person, for whom plausible talk *about* a thing does as well as an image of the thing itself, feels no need of a book like Mr Carlyle's; the want, which it is peculiarly fitted to supply, does not yet consciously exist in his mind. That such a want,

[1] David Hume (1711–1776), best known as a philosopher, published his *History of England* during the years 1754–1762.—William Robertson (1721–1793) published *History of Scotland* in 1759, *History of Charles V* in 1769, and *History of America* in 1777.—Edward Gibbon (1737–1794) published his *Decline and Fall of the Roman Empire* between 1776 and 1788.

however, is generally felt, may be inferred from the vast number of historical plays and historical romances, which have been written for no other purpose than to satisfy it. Mr Carlyle has been the first to shew that all which is done for history by the best historical play, by Schiller's Wallenstein,[2] for example, or Vitet's admirable trilogy,* may be done in a strictly true narrative, in which every incident rests on irrefragable authority; may be done, by means merely of an apt selection and a judicious grouping of authentic facts.

It has been noted as a point which distinguishes Shakespeare from ordinary dramatists, that *their* characters are logical abstractions, his are human beings: that their kings are nothing but kings, their lovers nothing but lovers, their patriots, courtiers, villains, cowards, bullies, are each of them that, and that alone; while his are real men and women, who have these qualities, but have them in addition to their full share of all other qualities (not incompatible), which are incident to human nature. In Shakespeare, consequently, we feel we are in a world of realities; we are among such beings as really could exist, as do exist, or have existed, and as we can sympathise with; the faces we see around us are human faces, and not mere rudiments of such, or exaggerations of single features. This quality, so often pointed out as distinctive of Shakespeare's plays, distinguishes Mr Carlyle's history. Never before did we take up a book calling itself by that name, a book

[2] Friedrich von Schiller (1759–1805) was a German poet, dramatist, historian, and philosopher. *Wallenstein*, a dramatic trilogy of 1798–1799, dealt with the Thirty Years' War.

* *Les Barricades; Les Etats de Blois;* and *La Mort de Henri III*, three prose plays or rather series of dramatic scenes, illustrative of the League and the period of the religious wars in France. A work scarcely heard of in this country, but which well deserves to be so. The author, like so many of the rising literary notabilities of France (from M. Guizot downwards), is now unhappily withdrawn from literature, by place-hunting, and *doctrinaire* politics. (Mill's note. Ludovic Vitet [1802–1873], French dramatist and politician, published a series of dramatic sketches in 1844 under the title of *La Ligue*. They dealt with the League, an organization of French Catholics for the suppression of Protestantism which existed from 1576–1598.)

treating of past times, and professing to be true, and find ourselves actually among human beings. We at once felt, that what had hitherto been to us mere abstractions, had become realities; the "forms of things unknown," which we fancied we knew, but knew their names merely, were, for the first time, with most startling effect, "bodied forth" and "turned into shape." Other historians talk to us indeed of human beings; but what do they place before us? Not even stuffed figures of such, but rather their algebraical symbols; a few phrases, which present no image to the fancy, but by adding up the dictionary meanings of which, we may hunt out a few qualities, not enough to form even the merest outline of what the men *were*, or possibly *could* have been; furnishing little but a canvas, which, if we ourselves can paint, we may fill with almost any picture, and if we cannot, it will remain for ever blank.

Take, for example, Hume's history; certainly, in its own way, one of the most skilful specimens of narrative in modern literature, and with some pretensions also to philosophy. Does Hume throw his own mind into the mind of an Anglo-Saxon, or an Anglo-Norman? Does any reader feel, after having read Hume's history, that he can now picture to himself what human life was, among the Anglo-Saxons? how an Anglo-Saxon would have acted in any supposable case? what were his joys, his sorrows, his hopes and fears, his ideas and opinions on any of the great and small matters of human interest? Would not the sight, if it could be had, of a single table or pair of shoes made by an Anglo-Saxon, tell us, directly and by inference, more of his whole way of life, more of how men thought and acted among the Anglo-Saxons, than Hume, with all his narrative skill, has contrived to tell us from all his materials?

Or descending from the history of civilization, which in Hume's case may have been a subordinate object, to the history of political events: did any one ever gain from Hume's history anything like a picture of what may actually have been passing, in the minds, say, of Cavaliers or of Roundheads during the civil wars? Does any one feel that Hume has made him figure to himself with any precision what manner of men these were; how far they were like ourselves, how far different; what things they loved and hated, and what sort of conception they had formed of the things they loved and hated? And what kind of a notion can be framed of a period of history, unless we begin with that as a preliminary? Hampden, and Strafford, and Vane, and Cromwell,[3] do these, in Hume's pages, appear to us like beings who actually trod this earth, and spoke with a human voice, and stretched out human hands in fellowship with other human beings; or like the figures in a phantasmagoria, colourless, impalpable, gigantic, and in all varieties of attitude, but all resembling one another in being shadows? And suppose he had done his best to assist us in forming a conception of these leading characters: what would it have availed, unless he had placed us also in the atmosphere which they breathed? What wiser are we for looking out upon the world through Hampden's eyes, unless it be the same world which Hampden looked upon? and what help has Hume afforded us for this? Has he depicted to us, or to himself, what all the multitude of people were about, who surrounded Hampden; what the whole English nation were feeling, thinking, or doing? Does he shew us what impressions from without were coming to Hampden—what materials and what instruments were given him to work with? If not, we are well qualified, truly, from Hume's information, to erect ourselves into judges of any part of Hampden's conduct!

Another very celebrated historian, we mean Gibbon—not a

---

[3] John Hampden (1594–1643), English statesman and cousin of Cromwell; Charles I's attempt to arrest this hero of the parliamentary cause helped precipitate the Civil War.—Thomas Wentworth, first Earl of Strafford (1593–1641), leading adviser to Charles I, whose rule he enforced as Lord Deputy of Ireland (1632–1639).—Sir Henry Vane (1613–1662), Puritan administrator, sat in Short and Long Parliaments, negotiated the Solemn League and Covenant with Scotland, served under Cromwell; he was executed for treason by the Restoration government.—Oliver Cromwell (1599–1658), leader of the Puritan cause, defeated Charles I at Naseby in 1645, invaded Scotland in 1650, defeating Charles II and Royalist Scots, and became Lord Protector in 1653.

man of mere science and analysis, like Hume, but with some (though not the truest or profoundest) artistic feeling of the picturesque, and from whom, therefore, rather more might have been expected—has with much pains succeeded in producing a tolerably graphic picture of here and there a battle, a tumult, or an insurrection; his book is full of movement and costume, and would make a series of very pretty ballets at the Opera-house, and the ballets would give us fully as distinct an idea of the Roman empire, and how it declined and fell, as the book does. If we want that, we must look for it anywhere but in Gibbon. One touch of M. Guizot [4] removes a portion of the veil which hid from us the recesses of private life under the Roman empire, lets in a ray of light which penetrates as far even as the domestic hearth of a subject of Rome, and shews us the government at work making that desolate; but no similar gleam of light from Gibbon's mind ever reaches the subject; *human life*, in the times he wrote about, is not what he concerned himself with.

On the other hand, there are probably many among our readers who are acquainted (though it is not included in Coleridge's admirable translation) with that extraordinary piece of dramatic writing, termed 'Wallenstein's Camp.' One of the greatest of dramatists, the historian of the Thirty Years' War, aspired to do, in a dramatic fiction, what even *his* genius had not enabled him to do in his history—to delineate the great characters, and, above all, to embody the general spirit of that period. This is done with such life and reality through ten acts, that the reader feels when it is over as if all the prominent personages in the play were people whom he had known from his childhood; but the author did not trust to this alone: he prefixed to the ten acts, one introductory act, intended to

[4] François Guizot (1787–1874), French statesman and historian, the leading intellectual exponent of the bourgeois monarchy of Louis Philippe. Mill alludes to a lecture on the fall of the Roman Empire which Guizot reprinted as the first piece in *Essays on the History of France*. The contrast between Guizot and Gibbon is articulated by Mill in "Guizot's Essays and Lectures on History," *Dissertations and Discussions*, II, 224–227.

exhibit, not the characters, but the element they moved in. It is there, in this preliminary piece, that Schiller really depicts the Thirty Years' War; without that, even the other ten acts, splendid as they are, would not have sufficiently realized it to our conception, nor would the Wallensteins and Piccolominis and Terzskys [5] of that glorious tragedy have been themselves, comparatively speaking, intelligible.

What Schiller must have done, in his own mind, with respect to the age of Wallenstein, to enable him to frame that fictitious delineation of it, Mr Carlyle, with a mind which looks still more penetratingly into the deeper meanings of things than Schiller's, has done with respect to the French Revolution. And he has communicated his picture of it with equal vividness; but he has done it by means of real, not fictitious incidents. And therefore is his book, as we said, at once the authentic History and the Poetry of the French Revolution.

It is indeed a favourite doctrine of Mr Carlyle, and one which he has enforced with great strength of reason and eloquence in other places,[6] that all poetry suitable to the present age must be of this kind: that poetry has not naturally any thing to do with fiction, nor is fiction in these days even the most appropriate vehicle and vesture of it; that it should, and will, employ itself more and more, not in inventing unrealities, but in bringing out into ever greater distinctness and impressiveness the poetic aspect of realities. For what is it, in the fictitious subjects which poets usually treat, that makes those subjects poetical? Surely not the dry, mechanical *facts* which

---

[5] Albrecht von Wallenstein (1583–1634), imperialist generalissimo in the Thirty Years' War. Emperor Ferdinand II rewarded him for his victories by making him a duke in 1625 and later instigated his murder in order to punish him for his defeats and his involvement in secret peace negotiations.—Octavio Piccolomini (1599–1656), Italian general, one of the conspirators who murdered Wallenstein. Max Piccolomini, another character in the play, was invented by Schiller.—Count Adam Erdmann Trčzka (*ca.* 1600–*ca.* 1650), one of Wallenstein's principal officers.

[6] For example, in the essay "Biography," published in *Fraser's Magazine* in April 1832.

compose the story; but the *feelings*—the high and solemn, the tender or mournful, even the gay and mirthful contemplations, which the story, or the manner of relating it, awaken in our minds. But would not all these thoughts and feelings be far more vividly aroused if the facts were *believed;* if the men, and all that is ascribed to them, had actually *been;* if the whole were no play of imagination, but a truth? In every real fact, in which any of the great interests of human beings are implicated, there lie the materials of all poetry; there is, as Mr Carlyle has said, the fifth act of a tragedy in every peasant's deathbed; the life of every heroic character is a heroic poem, were but the man of genius found, who could *so* write it! Not falsification of the reality is wanted, not the representation of it as being any thing which it is not; only a deeper understanding of what it is; the power to conceive, and to represent, not the mere outside surface and costume of the thing, nor yet the mere logical definition, and *caput mortuum*[7] of it—but an image of the thing itself in the concrete, with all that is loveable or hateable or admirable or pitiable or sad or solemn or pathetic, in it, and in the things which are implied in it. That is, the thing must be presented as it can exist only in the mind of a great poet: of one gifted with the two essential elements of the poetic character—creative imagination, which, from a chaos of scattered hints and confused testimonies, can summon up the Thing to appear before it as a completed whole: and that depth and breadth of feeling which makes all the images that are called up appear arrayed in whatever, of all that belongs to them, is naturally most affecting and impressive to the human soul.

We do not envy the person who can read Mr Carlyle's three volumes, and not recognize in him both these endowments in a most rare and remarkable degree. What is equally important to be said—he possesses in no less perfection that among the qualities necessary for his task, seemingly the most opposite to these, and in which the man of poetic imagination might be thought likeliest to be deficient; the quality of the historical

---

[7] "Dead head," i.e., worthless residue.

day-drudge. A more pains-taking or accurate investigator of facts, and sifter of testimonies, never wielded the historical pen. We do not say this at random, but from a most extensive acquaintance with his materials, with his subject, and with the mode in which it has been treated by others.

Thus endowed, and having a theme the most replete with every kind of human interest, epic, tragic, elegiac, even comic and farcical, which history affords, and so near to us withal, that the authentic details of it are still attainable; need it be said, that he has produced a work which deserves to be memorable? a work which, whatever may be its immediate reception, "will not willingly be let die;" whose reputation will be a growing reputation, its influence rapidly felt, for it will be read by the writers; and perhaps every historical work of any note, which shall hereafter be written in this country, will be different from what it would have been if this book were not.

. . . .

And what (it may be asked) are Mr Carlyle's *opinions?*

If this means, whether is he Tory, Whig, or Democrat; is he for things as they are, or for things *nearly* as they are; or is he one who thinks that subverting things as they are, and setting up Democracy is the main thing needful? we answer, he is none of all these. We should say that he has appropriated and made part of his own frame of thought, nearly all that is good in all these several modes of thinking. But it may be asked, what opinion has Mr Carlyle formed of the French Revolution, as an event in universal history; and this question is entitled to an answer. It should be, however, premised, that in a history upon the plan of Mr Carlyle's, the opinions of the writer are a matter of secondary importance. In reading an ordinary historian, we want to know his opinions, because it is mainly his *opinions* of things, and not the things themselves, that he sets before us; or if any features of the things themselves, those chiefly, which his *opinions* lead him to consider as of importance. Our readers have seen sufficient in the extracts we have made for them, to be satisfied that this is not Mr

Carlyle's method. Mr Carlyle brings the thing before us in the *concrete*—clothed, not indeed in *all* its properties and circumstances, since these are infinite, but in as many of them as can be authentically ascertained and imaginatively realized: not prejudging that some of those properties and circumstances will prove instructive and others not, a prejudgment which is the fertile source of misrepresentation and one-sided historical delineation without end. Every one knows, who has attended (for instance) to the sifting of a complicated case by a court of justice, that as long as our image of the fact remains in the slightest degree vague and hazy and undefined, we cannot tell but that what we do *not* yet distinctly see may be precisely that on which all turns. Mr Carlyle, therefore, brings us *acquainted* with persons, things, and events, before he suggests to us what to think of them: nay, we see that this is the very process by which he arrives at his own thoughts; he paints the thing to himself—he constructs a picture of it in his own mind, and does not, till afterwards, make any logical propositions about it at all. This done, his logical propositions concerning the thing may be true, or may be false; the thing is there, and any reader may find a totally different set of propositions in it if he can; as he might in the reality, if *that* had been before him.

We, for our part, do not always agree in Mr Carlyle's opinions either on things or on men. But we hold it to be impossible that any person should set before himself a perfectly true picture of a great historical event, as it actually happened, and yet that his judgment of it should be radically wrong. Differing partially from some of Mr Carlyle's detached views, we hold his theory, or theorem, of the Revolution, to be the true theory; true as far as it goes, and wanting little of being as complete as any theory of so vast and complicated a phenomenon can be. Nay, we do not think that any rational creature, now that the thing can be looked at calmly, now that we have nothing to hope or to fear from it, can form any second theory on the matter.

Mr Carlyle's view of the Revolution is briefly this: That it was the breaking down of a great Imposture: which had not always been an Imposture, but had been becoming such for several centuries.

Two bodies—the King and Feudal Nobility, and the Clergy—held their exalted stations, and received the obedience and allegiance which were paid to them, by virtue solely of their affording *guidance* to the people: the one, directing and keeping order among them in their conjunct operations towards the pursuit of their most important temporal interests; the other, ministering to their spiritual teaching and culture. These are the grounds on which alone any government either claims obedience or finds it: for the obedience of twenty-five millions to a few hundred thousand never yet was yielded to avowed tyranny.

Now, this guidance, the original ground of all obedience, the privileged classes *did* for centuries give. The King and the Nobles led the people in war, and protected and judged them in peace, being the fittest persons to do so who then existed; and the Clergy did teach the best doctrine, did inculcate and impress upon the people the best rule of life then known, and did believe in the doctrine and in the rule of life which they taught, and manifested their belief by their actions, and believed that, in teaching it, they were doing the highest thing appointed to mortals. So far as they did this, both spiritual and temporal rulers deserved and obtained reverence, and willing loyal obedience. But for centuries before the French Revolution, the sincerity which once was in this scheme of society was gradually dying out. The King and the Nobles afforded less and less of any real guidance, of any real protection to the people; and even ceased more and more to fancy that they afforded any. All the important business of society went on without them, nay, mostly in spite of their hindrance. The appointed spiritual teachers ceased to do their duty as teachers, ceased to practise what they taught, ceased to believe it, but alas, not to cant about it, or to receive wages as teachers of it. Thus the whole scheme of society and government in France became one great Lie: the places of honour and power being all occupied by persons whose sole claim to occupy them was the pretence of being what they were not, of doing what they did not, nor even for a single moment attempted to do. All other vileness and profligacy in the rulers of a country were but the inevitable consequences of this inherent vice in the condition of their existence. And, this continuing for centuries, the government growing ever more and more consciously a Lie, the people ever more and more perceiving it to be such, the day of reckoning, which comes for all impostures, came for this: the Good would no longer obey such rulers, the Bad ceased to be in awe of them, and both together rose up and hurled them into chaos.

Such is Mr Carlyle's idea of what the Revolution was. And now, as to the melancholy turn it took, the horrors which accompanied it, the iron despotism by which it was forced to wind itself up, and the smallness of its positive results, compared with those which were hoped for by the sanguine in its commencement.

Mr Carlyle's theory of these things is also a simple one: That the men, most of them good, and many of them among the most instructed of their generation, who attempted at that period to regenerate France, failed in what it was impossible that any one should succeed in: namely, in attempting to found a government, to create a new order of society, a new set of institutions and habits, among a people having no convictions to base such order of things upon. That the existing government, habits, state of society, were bad, this the people were thoroughly convinced of, and rose up as one man, to declare, in every language of deed and word, that they would no more endure it. What was, was bad; but what was good, nobody had determined; no *opinion* on that subject had rooted itself in the people's minds; nor was there even any person, or any body of persons, deference for whom was rooted in their minds and whose word they were willing to take for all the rest. Suppose, then, that the twelve hundred members of the Constituent Assembly[8] had even been gifted with perfect

[8] A body, at first called the National Assembly, composed mainly of deputies of the third estate, which pressed for sweeping political and social reforms. In 1791 it drafted a constitution with the famous Declaration of the Rights of Man as preamble.

knowledge what arrangement of society was best:—how were they to get time to establish it? Or how were they to hold the people in obedience to it when established? A people with no pre-conceived reverence, either for it or for them; a people like slaves broke from their fetters—with all man's boundless desires let loose in indefinite expectation, and all the influences of habit and imagination which keep mankind patient under the denial of what they crave for, annihilated for the time, never to be restored but in some quite different shape?

Faith, doubtless, in representative institutions, there was, and of the firmest kind; but unhappily this was not enough: for all that representative institutions themselves can do, is to give practical effect to the faith of the people in something else. What is a representative constitution? Simply a set of contrivances for ascertaining the convictions of the people; for enabling them to declare what men they have faith in; or, failing such, what things the majority of them will insist upon having done to them—by what *rule* they are willing to be governed. But what if the majority have not faith in any men, nor know even in the smallest degree what things they wish to have done, in what manner they would be governed? This was the condition of the French people. To have made it otherwise was possible, but required time; and time, unhappily, in a Revolution, is not given. A great man, indeed, may do it, by inspiring at least faith in himself, which may last till the tree he has planted has taken root, and can stand alone; such apparently was Solon,* and such perhaps, had he lived, might have been Mirabeau: [9] nay, in the absence of other greatness, even a great quack may temporarily do it; as Napoleon, himself a

* A more definite, as well as, we think, a juster idea of this great man, than we have met with elsewhere, may be found in Mr Bulwer's "Athens;" a book which, if it be completed as it has been begun, will, by its effect in correcting prejudices which have been most sedulously fostered, and diffusing true notions on one of the most interesting of all parts of the world's history, entitle its author to no humble meed of praise. (Mill's note.)

[9] Honoré Gabriel Riquetti, Comte de Mirabeau (1749–1791), statesman and revolutionist who wanted to create a constitutional monarchy.

mixture of great man and great quack, did in some measure exemplify. Revolutions sweep much away, but if any Revolution since the beginning of the world ever founded anything, towards which the minds of the people had not been growing for generations previous, it has been founded by some individual man.

Much more must be added to what has now been said, to make the statement of Mr Carlyle's opinions on the French Revolution anything like complete; nor shall we any further set forth, either such of those opinions as we agree in, or those, far less numerous, from which we disagree. Nevertheless, we will not leave the subject without pointing out what appears to us to be the most prominent defect in our author's general mode of thinking. His own method being that of the artist, not of the man of science–working as he does by figuring things to himself as wholes, not dissecting them into their parts–he appears, though perhaps it is but appearance, to entertain something like a contempt for the opposite method; and to go as much too far in his distrust of analysis and generalization, as others (the Constitutional party, for instance, in the French Revolution) went too far in their reliance upon it.

Doubtless, in the infinite complexities of human affairs, any general theorem which a wise man will form concerning them, must be regarded as a mere approximation to truth; an approximation obtained by striking an average of many cases, and consequently not exactly fitting any one case. No wise man, therefore, will stand upon his theorem only–neglecting to look into the specialties of the case in hand, and see what features *that* may present which may take it out of any theorem, or bring it within the compass of more theorems than one. But the far greater number of people–when they have got a formula by rote, when they can bring the matter in hand within some maxim "in that case made and provided" by the traditions of the vulgar, by the doctrines of their sect or school, or by some generalization of their own–do not think it necessary to let their mind's eye rest upon the thing itself at all; but deliberate and act, not upon knowledge of the thing, but upon a hearsay of it; being (to use a frequent illustration of our author) provided with spectacles, they fancy it not needful to use their eyes. It should be understood that general principles are not intended to dispense with thinking and examining, but to help us to think and examine. When the object itself is out of our reach, and we cannot examine into it, we must follow general principles, because, by doing so, we are not so likely to go wrong, and almost certain not to go so far wrong, as if we floated on the boundless ocean of mere conjecture; but when we are not driven to guess, when we have means and appliances for observing, general principles are nothing more or other than helps towards a better use of those means and appliances.

Thus far we and Mr Carlyle travel harmoniously together; but here we apparently diverge. For, having admitted that general principles (or *formulae*, as our author calls them, after old Mirabeau,[10] the crabbed *ami des hommes*[11]) are helps to observation, not substitutes for it, we must add, that they are *necessary* helps, and that without general principles no one ever observed a particular case to any purpose. For, except by general principles, how do we bring the light of past experience to bear upon the new case? The essence of past experience lies embodied in those logical, abstract propositions, which our author makes so light of:—there, and no where else. From them we learn what has ordinarily been found true, or even recal what we ourselves have found true, in innumerable unnamed and unremembered cases, more or less resembling the present. We are hence taught, at the least, what we shall *probably* find true in the present case; and although this, which is only a probability, may be lazily acquiesced in and acted upon without further inquiry as a certainty, the risk even so is infinitely less than if we began without a theory, or even a probable hypothesis. Granting that all the facts of the particular instance are within the reach of observation, how difficult is

10 Victor Riquetti, Marquis de Mirabeau (1715–1789), leader of the Physiocrats, father of the revolutionist, friend of Rousseau.

11 "Friend of men."

the work of observing, how almost impossible that of disentangling a complicated case, if, when we begin, no one view of it appears to us more probable than another. Without a hypothesis to commence with, we do not even know what end to begin at, what points to enquire into. Nearly every thing that has ever been ascertained by scientific observers, was brought to light in the attempt to test and verify some theory. To start from a theory, but not to see the object through the theory; to bring light with us, but also to receive other light from whencesoever it comes; such is the part of the philosopher, of the true practical *seer* or person of insight.

Connected with the tendency which we fancy we perceive in our author, to undervalue general principles, is another tendency which we think is perceptible in him, to set too low a value on what constitutions and forms of government can do. Be it admitted once for all, that no form of government will enable you, as our author has elsewhere said, "given a world of rogues, to produce an honesty by their united action;" nor when a people are wholly without faith either in man or creed, has any representative constitution a charm to render them governable well, or even governable at all. On the other hand, Mr Carlyle must no less admit, that when a nation *has* faith in any men, or any set of principles, representative institutions furnish the only regular and peaceable mode in which that faith can quietly declare itself, and those men, or those principles, obtain the predominance. It is surely no trifling matter to have a legalized means whereby the guidance will always be in the hands of the Acknowledged Wisest, who, if not always the really wisest, are at least those whose wisdom, such as it may be, is the most available for the purpose. Doubtless it is the natural law of representative governments that the power is shared, in varying proportions, between the really skilfullest and the skilfullest quacks; with a tendency, in easy times, towards the preponderance of the quacks, in the "times which try men's souls," towards that of the true men. Improvements enough may be expected as mankind improve, but that the best and wisest shall always be accounted such, *that* we need not expect; because the quack can always steal, and vend for his own profit, as much of the good ware as is marketable. But is not all this to the full as likely to happen in every other kind of government as in a representative one? with these differences in favour of representative government, which will be found perhaps to be its only real and universal pre-eminence: That it alone is government by consent—government by mutual compromise and compact; while all others are, in one form or another, governments by constraint: That it alone proceeds by quiet muster of opposing strengths, when that which is really weakest sees itself to be such, and peaceably gives way; a benefit never yet realized but in countries inured to a representative government; elsewhere nothing but actual blows can show who is strongest, and every great dissension of opinion must break out into a civil war.

We have thus briefly touched upon the two principal points on which we take exception, not so much to any opinion of the author, as to the tone of sentiment which runs through the book; a tone of sentiment which otherwise, for justness and nobleness, stands almost unrivalled in the writings of our time. A deep catholic sympathy with human nature, with all natural human feelings, looks out from every page of these volumes; justice administered in love, to all kind of human beings, bad and good; the most earnest exalted feeling of moral distinctions, with the most generous allowances for whatever partial confounding of these distinctions, either natural weakness or perverse circumstances can excuse. No greatness, no strength, no goodness or lovingness, passes unrecognized or unhonoured by him. All the sublimity of "the simultaneous death-defiance of twenty-five millions" speaks itself forth in his pages—not the less impressively, because the unspeakable folly and incoherency, which always in real life are not one step from, but actually pervade, the sublimities of so large a body (and did so most notably in this instance) are no less perceptible to his keen sense of the ludicrous. We presume it is this which has caused the book to be accused, even in print,[12] of "flippancy,"

[12] In the *Atheneum* for May 20, 1837.

a term which appears to us singularly misapplied. For is not this mixture and confused entanglement of the great and the contemptible, precisely what we meet with in nature? and would not a history, which did not make us not only see this, but feel it, be deceptive; and give an impression which would be the more false, the greater the general vivacity and vigour of the delineation? And indeed the capacity to see and feel what is loveable, admirable, in a thing, and what is laughable in it, at the same time, constitutes humour; the quality to which we owe a Falstaff, a Parson Adams,[13] an Uncle Toby,[14] and Mause Headriggs [15] and Barons of Bradwardine [16] without end. You meet in this book with passages of grave drollery (drollery unsought for, arising from the simple statement of facts, and a true natural feeling of them) not inferior to the best in Mr Peacock's novels [17]; and immediately or soon after comes a soft note as of dirge music, or solemn choral song of old Greek tragedy, which makes the heart too full for endurance, and forces you to close the book and rest for a while.

Again, there are aphorisms which deserve to live for ever; characters drawn with a few touches, and indicating a very remarkable insight into many of the obscurest regions of human nature; much genuine philosophy, disguised though it often be in a poetico-metaphysical vesture of a most questionable kind; and, in short, new and singular but not therefore absurd or unpractical views taken of many important things. A most original book; original not least in its complete sincerity, its disregard of the merely conventional: every idea and sentiment is given out exactly as it is thought and felt, fresh from the soul of the writer, and in such language (conformable to precedent or not) as is most capable of representing it in the form in which it exists there. And hence the critics have begun

13 In Henry Fielding's *Joseph Andrews* (1742).

14 In Laurence Sterne's *Tristram Shandy* (1760–1767).

15 In Walter Scott's *Old Mortality* (1816).

16 In Scott's *Waverley* (1814).

17 Thomas Love Peacock (1785–1866) was best known for the satirical novels *Headlong Hall* (1816), *Nightmare Abbey* (1818), and *Crotchet Castle* (1831).

to call the style "affected;" a term which conventional people, whether in literature or society, invariably bestow upon the unreservedly natural.*

In truth, every book which is eminently original, either in matter or style, has a hard battle to fight before it can obtain even pardon for its originality, much less applause. Well, therefore, may this be the case when a book is original, not in matter only or in style only, but in both; and, moreover, written in prose, with a fervour and exaltation of feeling which is only tolerated in verse, if even there. And when we consider that Wordsworth, Coleridge, and others of their time, whose deviation from the beaten track was but a stone's throw compared with Mr Carlyle, were ignominiously hooted out of court by the wise tribunals which in those days dispensed justice in such matters, and had to wait for a second generation before the sentence could be reversed, and their names placed among the great names of our literature, we might well imagine that the same or a worse fate awaits Mr Carlyle; did we not believe that those very writers, aided by circumstances, have made straight the way for Mr Carlyle and for much else. This very phenomenon, of the different estimation of Wordsworth and Coleridge, now, and thirty years ago, is among the indica-

* A curious instance of this occurred lately. Mr. D'Israeli, a writer of considerable literary daring, tried in his novel, "Henrietta Temple," one of the boldest experiments he had yet ventured upon; that of making his lovers and his other characters speak naturally the language of real talk, not dressed-up talk; such language as all persons talk who are not in the presence of an audience. A questionable experiment—allowable as an experiment, but scarcely otherwise; for the reader does not want pure nature, but nature idealised; nobody wants the verbiage, the repetitions and slovenlinesses, of real conversation, but only the substance of what is interesting in such conversation, divested of these. There was much which might have been said by critics against Mr. D'Israeli's experiment; but what did they say? "Affectation!"—that was their cry. Natural conversation in print looked so unnatural to men of artificiality; it was so unlike all their experience—of books! (Mill's note. Benjamin Disraeli [1804–1881] was first elected to Parliament in 1837, the same year in which he published *Henrietta Temple*. He became Prime Minister in 1867 and managed passage of the Second Reform Bill of that year.)

tions of one of the most conspicuous new elements which have sprung up in the European mind during those years: an insatiable demand for realities, come of conventionalities and formalities what may; of which desire the literary phasis is, a large tolerance for every feeling which is natural and not got-up, for every picture taken from the life and not from other pictures, however it may clash with traditionary notions of elegance or congruity. The book before us needs to be read with this catholic spirit; if we read it captiously, we shall never have done finding fault. But no true poet, writing sincerely and following the promptings of his own genius, can fail to be contemptible to any who desire to find him so; and if even Milton's Areopagitica, of which now, it would seem, no one dares speak with only moderate praise, were now first to issue from the press, it would be turned from with contempt by every one who will think or speak disparagingly of this work of Mr Carlyle. . . .

From A Prophecy

1838

"A Prophecy" was originally part of "Letters from Palmyra," a review of William Ware's historical novel, *Letters of Lucius Manlius Piso, from Palmyra, to His Friend, Marcus Curtius, at Rome* (1837). It stands out as the shortest excerpt among those miscellaneous periodical essays which Mill thought worthy of preserving in volume form; it occupies but three pages (the first two of which are reprinted here) in the first volume of *Dissertations and Discussions.*

Obviously Mill lifted the piece out of the review in order to make a specific point—simply, that the function of literature is not primarily to represent people as they are but to create characters who suggest, through their actions and sentiments, what people may and should become. Mill, the utilitarian and democrat, recommends literature's incarnations of chivalry and heroism as the best remedies for the shortcomings peculiar to a society constructed upon utilitarian and democratic principles.

THE TIME was, when it was thought that the best and most appropriate office of fictitious narrative was to awaken high aspirations, by the representation in interesting circumstances, of characters conformable indeed to human nature, but whose actions and sentiments were of a more generous and loftier cast than are ordinarily to be met with by everybody in everyday life. But nowadays nature and probability are thought to be violated, if there be shown to the reader, in the personages with whom he is called upon to sympathize, characters on a larger scale than himself, or than the persons he is accus-

First published in *London and Westminster Review,* XXVIII (January 1838).

tomed to meet at a dinner or a quadrille party. Yet, from such representations, familiar from early youth, have not only the noblest minds in modern Europe derived much of what made them noble, but even the commoner spirits what made them understand and respond to nobleness. And *this* is education. It would be well if the more narrow-minded portion, both of the religious and of the scientific education-mongers, would consider whether the books which they are banishing from the hands of youth, were not instruments of national education to the full as powerful as the catalogues of physical facts and theological dogmas which they have substituted—as if science and religion were to be taught, not by imbuing the mind with their spirit, but by cramming the memory with summaries of their conclusions. Not what a boy or a girl can repeat by rote, but what they have learnt to love and admire, is what forms their character. The chivalrous spirit has almost disappeared from books of education; the popular novels of the day teach nothing but (what is already too soon learnt from actual life) lessons of worldliness, with at most the huckstering virtues which conduce to getting on in the world; and for the first time perhaps in history, the youth of both sexes of the educated classes are universally growing up unromantic. What will come in mature age from such a youth, the world has not yet had time to see. But the world may rely upon it, that Catechisms, whether Pinnock's [1] or the Church of England's, will be found a poor substitute for those old romances, whether of chivalry or of faëry, which, if they did not give a true picture of actual life, did not give a false one, since they did not profess to give any, but (what was much better) filled the youthful imagination with pictures of heroic men, and of what are at least as much wanted, heroic women. The book before us does this: and greatly is any book to be valued,

[1] Pinnock's *Catechisms* were short popular manuals, arranged in question-and-answer form, of the different departments of knowledge. They took their name from their publisher, William Pinnock (1782–1843).

which in this age, and in a form suited to it, does its part towards keeping alive the chivalrous spirit, which was the best part of the old romances; towards giving to the aspirations of the young and susceptible a noble direction, and keeping present to the mind an exalted standard of worth, by placing before it heroes and heroines worthy of the name. . . .

From Poems and Romances of Alfred de Vigny

1838

Among his various literary articles in the *London and Westminster Review*, Mill said, "the one which contained most thought was on Alfred de Vigny" (*The Early Draft of John Stuart Mill's "Autobiography,"* p. 165). Since a large part of the article is devoted to retelling Vigny's stories of military men and poets, we must suppose that Mill set a very high value upon the article's discussions of the characteristics that distinguish Conservative from Liberal poets, of the fate of poets in society, and of the occasions when, and the reasons why, verse may be preferable to prose.

Mill's point of view in the essay is neither that of the ideologue who sees nothing in poetry *but* politics nor that of the aesthete who refuses to admit even the possibility that a political revolution can give a poet's genius its distinguishing mark. Mill relegates mere political poetry to the inferior status of oratory. He is concerned with the spirit and sympathies with which a poet may be imbued by his allegiance to Liberalism or to Conservatism.

After a long enumeration of the distinguishing features of both kinds of poet, Mill classifies Alfred de Vigny as a poet of Royalist and Conservative sympathies who has fallen on an age of revolution. His portrait of such a poet, torn between a dying world that commanded his allegiance and a flourishing world from which he feels estranged, might well fit Matthew Arnold and other poets not heard of at the time Mill wrote.

In this essay, Mill insists that wherever, as in France, both poetry and politics are taken seriously, they will inevitably be related. He thus speaks with the same voice that was later to be heard from the great Victorian critics, such as Ruskin and Arnold, who often showed a happy inability to discuss poetry or art without at the same time discussing politics. But perhaps Mill goes further than Ruskin or Arnold would have liked when he defends those French artists who are too much in earnest to sacrifice the chance of doing some work in the world through their art to mere considerations of beauty.

WRITINGS OF ALFRED DE VIGNY.*

In the French mind (the most active national mind in Europe at the present moment) one of the most stirring elements, and among the fullest of promise for the futurity of France and of the world, is the Royalist, or Carlist,[1] ingredient. We are not now alluding to the attempts of M. de Genoude,[2] and that portion of the Carlist party of which the 'Gazette de France' [3] is the organ, to effect an alliance between legitimacy and universal suffrage; nor to the eloquent anathemas hurled against the existing institutions of society by a man of a far superior order, the Abbé de la Mennais,[4] whose original fervour of Roman Catholic absolutism has given place to a no less fervour of Roman Catholic ultra-Radicalism. These things too have their importance as symptoms, and even intrinsically are not altogether without their value. But we would speak rather of the somewhat less obvious inward working, which (ever since the Revolution of 1830 annihilated the Carlist party as a power in the State) has been going on in the minds of that accom-

First published in the *London and Westminster Review*, XXIX (April 1838).

* Consisting of—1. Souvenirs de Servitude et de Grandeur Militaire. 2. Cinq-Mars; ou, une Conjuration sous Louis XIII. 3. Stello; ou, les Consultations du Docteur Noir. 4. Poëmes. 5. Le More de Venise, tragédie traduite de Shakespeare en Vers Francais. 6. La Maréchale d'Ancre, drame. 7. Chatterton, drame. (Mill's note.)

[1] Loyal to Charles X, deposed by the Revolution of 1830.

[2] Antoine Eugène Genoud (1792–1849), French journalist, revived *Gazette de France* in 1825.

[3] The oldest French newspaper, founded in 1631 and periodically revived under various names, appeared as the *Gazette de France* between 1797 and 1848. At the Restoration it assumed a militant political role as a royalist journal championing universal suffrage.

[4] Félicité Robert de la Mennais (1782–1854), a Roman Catholic apologist who led a liberal group that opposed royal government and encouraged ultramontanism; he eventually left the Church.

plished and numerous portion of the educated youth of France, whose family connexions or early mental impressions ranked them with the defeated party; who had been brought up, as far as the age permitted, in the old ideas of monarchical and Catholic France; were allied by their feelings or imaginations with whatever of great and heroic those old ideas had produced in the past; had not been sullied by participation in the selfish struggles for Court favour and power, of which the same ideas were the pretext in the present—and to whom the Three Days were really the destruction of something which they had loved and revered, if not for itself, at least for the reminiscences associated with it.

These reflections present themselves naturally when we are about to speak of the writings of Alfred de Vigny, one of the earliest in date, and one of the most genuine, true-hearted, and irreproachable in tendency and spirit, of the new school of French literature, termed the romantic. It would, in fact, be impossible to understand M. de Vigny's writings, especially the later and better portion, or to enter sympathizingly into the peculiar feelings which pervade them, without this clue. M. de Vigny is, in poetry and art, as a still more eminent man, M. de Tocqueville, is in philosophy, a result of the influences of the age upon a mind and character trained up in opinions and feelings opposed to those of the age. Both these writers, educated in one set of views of life and society, found, when they attained manhood, another set predominant in the world they lived in, and, at length, after 1830, enthroned in its high places. The contradictions they had thus to reconcile—the doubts and perplexities and misgivings which they had to find the means of overcoming before they could see clearly between these cross-lights—were to them that, for want of which so many otherwise well-educated and naturally-gifted persons grow up hopelessly commonplace. To go through life with a set of opinions ready-made and provided for saving them the trouble of thought, was a destiny that could not be theirs. Unable to satisfy themselves with either of the conflicting formulas which were given them for the interpretation of what lay in the world before them, they learnt to take formulas for what they were worth, and to look into the world itself for the philosophy of it. They looked with both their eyes, and saw much there, which was neither in the creed they had been taught, nor in that which they found prevailing around them: much that the prejudices, either of Liberalism or of Royalism, amounted to a disqualification for the perception of, and which would have been hid from themselves if the atmosphere of either had surrounded them both in their youth and in their maturer years.

That this conflict between a Royalist education, and the spirit of the modern world, triumphant in July 1830, must have gone for something in giving to the speculations of a philosopher like M. de Tocqueville the catholic spirit and comprehensive range which distinguish them, most people will readily admit. But, that the same causes must have exerted an analogous influence over a poet and artist, such as Alfred de Vigny is in his degree; that a political revolution can have given to the genius of a poet what principally distinguishes it—may not appear so obvious, at least to those who, like most Englishmen, rarely enter into either politics or poetry with their whole soul. Worldly advancement, or religion, are an Englishman's real interests: for Politics, except in connexion with one of those two objects, and for Art, he keeps only bye-corners of his mind, which naturally are far apart from each other: and it is but a small minority among Englishmen who can comprehend, that there are nations among whom Politics, or the pursuit of social well-being, and Poetry, or the love of beauty and of imaginative emotion, are passions as intense, as absorbing—influencing as much the whole tendencies of the character, and constituting as large a part of the objects in life of a considerable portion of the cultivated classes, as either the religious feelings, or those of worldly interest. Where both politics and poetry, instead of being either a trade or a pastime, are taken completely *au sérieux*,[5] each will be more or less coloured by the other; and that close relation between an au-

[5] "In earnest," "seriously."

thor's politics and his poetry, which with us is only seen in the great poetic figures of their age, a Shelley, a Byron, or a Wordsworth, is broadly conspicuous in France (for example), through the whole range of her literature.

It may be worth while to employ a moment in considering what are the general features which, in an age of revolutions, may be expected to distinguish a Royalist or Conservative from a Liberal or Radical poet or imaginative writer. We are not speaking of political poetry, of Tyrtæus or Körner,[6] of Corn-Law Rhymes,[7] or sonnets on the Vaudois [8] or on Zaragoza [9]; these are rather oratory than poetry. We have nothing to do with the Radical poet as the scourge of the oppressor, or with the Tory one as the denouncer of infidelity or jacobinism. They are not poets by virtue of what is negative or combative in their feelings, but by what is positive and sympathizing. The pervading spirit, then, of the one, will be love of the Past; of the other, faith in the Future. The partialities of the one will be towards things established, settled, regulated; of the other, towards human free-will, cramped and fettered in all directions, both for good and ill, by those establishments and regulations. Both, being poets, will have a heroic sympathy with heroism; but the one will respond most readily to the heroism of endurance and self-control, the other to that of action and struggle. Of the virtues and beauties of our common humanity, the one will view with most affection those which have their natural growth under the shelter of fixed habits and firmly settled opinions: local and family attach-

[6] Tyrtaeus was a celebrated Greek elegiac poet of the seventh century B.C. When the Spartans asked the Athenians for a general to help their cause, they were sent the lame Tyrtaeus. By the power of his poetry, he healed the divisions among the Spartans and roused them to victory. —Karl Theodor Körner (1791–1813), German patriotic poet.

[7] By Ebenezer Elliott; see "What Is Poetry?," note 5.

[8] The French name for the Waldensians, often supposed to be the earliest Protestant sect; the Duke of Savoy's brutal attack on them (1655) provoked Milton's famous sonnet.

[9] A city in northeastern Spain. Mill may refer to sonnets commemorating the city's heroic defense against the French siege of 1808 in the Peninsular War.

ments, tranquil tastes and pleasures, those gentle and placid feelings towards man and nature, ever most easy to those upon whom is not imposed the burthen of being their own protectors and their own guides. Greater reverence, deeper humility, the virtues of abnegation and forbearance carried to a higher degree, will distinguish his favourite personages: while, as subjection to a common faith and law brings the most diverse characters to the same standard, and tends more or less to efface their differences, a certain monotony of goodness will be apparent, and a degree of distaste for *prononcé*[10] characters, as being nearly allied to ill-regulated ones. The sympathies of the Radical or Movement poet will take the opposite direction. Active qualities are what he will demand, rather than passive; those which fit persons for making changes in the circumstances which surround them, rather than for accommodating themselves to those circumstances. Sensible he must of course be of the necessity of restraints, but since he is dissatisfied with those which exist, his dislike of established opinions and institutions turns naturally into sympathy with all things, not in themselves bad, which those opinions and institutions restrain, that is, with all natural human feelings. Free and vigorous developments of human nature, even when he cannot refuse them his disapprobation, will command his sympathy: a more marked individuality will usually be conspicuous in his creations; his heroic characters will be all armed for conflict, full of energy and strong self-will, of grand conceptions and brilliant virtues, but, in habits of virtue, often below those of the Conservative school: there will not be so broad and black a line between his good and bad personages; his characters of principle will be more tolerant of his characters of mere passion. Among human affections, the Conservative poet will give the preference to those which can be invested with the character of duties; to those of which the objects are as it were marked out by the arrangements either of nature or of society, we ourselves exercising no choice: as the parental—the filial—the conjugal after the irrevocable

10 "Pronounced."

union, or a solemn betrothment equivalent to it, and with due observance of all decencies, both real and conventional. The other will delight in painting the affections which choose their own objects, especially the most powerful of these, passionate love; and of that, the more vehement oftener than the more graceful aspects; will select by preference its subtlest workings, and its most unusual and unconventional forms; will show it at war with the forms and customs of society, nay even with its laws and its religion, if the laws and tenets which regulate that branch of human relations are among those which have begun to be murmured against. By the Conservative, feelings and states of mind which he disapproves will be indicated rather than painted; to lay open the morbid anatomy of human nature will appear to him contrary to good taste always, and often to morality: and inasmuch as feelings intense enough to threaten established decorums with any danger of violation will most frequently have the character of morbidness in his eyes, the representation of passion in the colours of reality will commonly be left to the Movement poet. To him, whatever exists will appear, from that alone, fit to be represented: to probe the wounds of society and humanity is part of his business, and he will neither shrink from exhibiting what is in nature, because it is morally culpable, nor because it is physically revolting. Even in their representations of inanimate nature there will be a difference. The pictures most grateful and most familiar to the one will be those of a universe at peace within itself—of stability and duration—of irresistible power serenely at rest, or moving in fulfilment of the established arrangements of the universe: whatever suggests unity of design, and the harmonious co-operation of all the forces of nature towards ends intended by a Being in whom there is no variableness nor shadow of change. In the creations of the other, nature will oftener appear in the relations which it bears to the individual, rather than to the scheme of the universe; there will be a larger place assigned to those of its aspects which reflect back the troubles of an unquiet soul, the impulses of a passionate, or the enjoyments of a voluptuous one;

and on the whole, here too the Movement poet will extend so much more widely the bounds of the permitted, that his sources both of effect and of permanent interest will have a far larger range; and he will generally be more admired than the other, by all those by whom he is not actually condemned.

There is room in the world for poets of both these kinds; and the greatest will always partake of the nature of both. A comprehensive and catholic mind and heart will doubtless feel and exhibit all these different sympathies, each in its due proportion and degree; but what that due proportion may happen to be, is part of the larger question which every one has to ask of himself at such periods, viz., whether it were for the good of humanity at the particular era, that Conservative or Radical feeling should most predominate? For there is a perpetual antagonism between these two; and until human affairs are much better ordered than they are likely to be for some time to come, each will require to be, in a greater or less degree, tempered by the other: nor until the ordinances of law and of opinion are so framed as to give full scope to all individuality not positively noxious, and to restrain all that is noxious, will the two classes of sympathies ever be entirely reconciled.

Suppose, now, a poet of conservative sympathies, surprised by the shock of a revolution, which sweeps away the surviving symbols of what was great in the Past, and decides irrevocably the triumph of new things over the old: what will be the influence of this event on his imagination and feelings? To us it seems that they will become both sadder and wiser. He will lose that blind faith in the Past, which previously might have tempted him to fight for it with a mistaken ardour, against what is generous and worthy in the new doctrines. The fall of the objects of his reverence, will naturally, if he has any discernment, open his mind to the perception of that in them whereby they deserved to fall. But while he is thus disenchanted of the old things, he will not have acquired that faith in the new, which animated the Radical poet. Having it not before, there is nothing in the triumph of those new things which can inspire him with it: institutions and creeds fall by their own badness, not by the goodness of that which strikes the actual blow. The destiny of mankind, therefore, will naturally appear to him in rather sombre colours; gloomy he may not be, but he will everywhere tend to the elegiac, to the contemplative and melancholy rather than to the epic and active; his song will be a subdued and plaintive symphony, more or less melodious according to the measure of his genius, on the old theme of blasted hopes and defeated aspirations. Yet there will now be nothing partial or one-sided in his sympathies: no sense of a conflict to be maintained, of a position to be defended against assailants, will warp the impartiality of his pity—will make him feel that there are wrongs and sufferings which must be dissembled, inconsistencies which must be patched up, vanities which he must attempt to consider serious, false pretences which he must try to mistake for truths, lest he should be too little satisfied with his own cause to do his duty as a combatant for it: he will no longer feel obliged to treat all that part of human nature which rebelled against the old ideas, as if it were accursed—all those human joys and sufferings, hopes and fears, which were the strength of the new doctrines, and which the old ones did not take sufficient account of, as if they were unworthy of his sympathy. His heart will open itself freely and largely to the love of all that is loveable, to pity of all that is pitiable: every cry of suffering humanity will strike a responsive chord in his breast; whoever carries nobly his own share of the general burthen of human life, or generously helps to lighten that of others, is sure of his homage; while he has a deep fraternal charity for the erring and disappointed—for those who have aspired and fallen—who have fallen because they have aspired, because they too have felt those infinite longings for something greater than merely to live and die, which he as a poet has felt—which, as a poet, he cannot but have been conscious that he would have purchased the realization of by an even greater measure of error and suffering—and which, as a poet disenchanted, he knows too well the pain of renouncing, not to feel a deep indulgence for those who are victims of their inability to make the sacrifice.

In this ideal portraiture may be seen the genuine lineaments of Alfred de Vigny. The same features may, indeed, be traced more or less, in the greater part of the Royalist literature of young France; even in Balzac all these characteristics are distinctly visible, blended of course with his individual peculiarities, and modified by them. But M. de Vigny is a more perfect type, because he, more entirely than most others, writes from his real feelings, and not from mere play of fancy. Many a writer in France, of no creed at all, and who therefore gives himself all the latitude of a Movement poet, is a Royalist with his imagination merely, for the sake of the picturesque effect of donjons and cloisters, crusaders and troubadours. And in retaliation many a Liberal or Republican critic will stand up stiffly for the old school in literature, for the *grand siècle*,[11] because, like him, it takes its models from Greece or Rome; and will keep no terms with the innovators who find anything grand and poetical in the middle ages, or who fancy that barons or priests may look well in rhyme. But this is accident; an exception to the ordinary relation between political opinions and poetic tendencies. A Radical who finds his political *beau ideal*[12] still farther back in the Past than the Royalist finds his, is not the type of a Radical poet; he will more resemble the Conservative poet of ages back: less of the Movement spirit may be found in him, than in many a nominal Royalist whose Royalist convictions have no very deep root. But when we would see the true character of a Royalist poet, we must seek for it in one like M. de Vigny, a conservative in feeling, and not in mere fancy, and a man (if we may judge from his writings) of rare simplicity of heart, and freedom from egotism and self-display. The most complete exemplification of the feelings and views of things which we have described as naturally belonging to the Royalist poet of young France, will

11 "Great century," the age of Louis XIV.

12 Ideal of consummate beauty or of perfection.

be found in his productions, subsequent to the Revolution of 1830. But we must first see him as he was before 1830, and in writings in which the qualities we have enumerated had as yet manifested themselves only in a small degree.

Count Alfred de Vigny was born on the 27th of March 1799, at Loches in Touraine, that province which has given birth to so many of the literary celebrities of France. His father was an old cavalry officer of ancient lineage, who had served in the Seven Years War,[13] and whose stories of his illustrious friends Chevert and d'Assas, and of the great Frederic [14] (who was not a little indebted even for his victories, to the *prestige* he exercised over the enthusiastic imaginations of the French officers who fought against him), were the earliest nourishment of the son's childish aspirations. In the latter years of Napoleon our author was a youth at college; and he has described, in the first chapter of his 'Souvenirs de Servitude Militaire,' [15] the restless and roving spirit, the ardour for military glory and military adventure, the contempt of all pursuits and wishes not terminating in a Marshal's bâton, which were the epidemic diseases of every French schoolboy during those years when 'the beat of drum,' to use his own expression, 'drowned the voice of the teacher,' and of which M. de Vigny confesses, in all humility, that the traces in himself are not entirely effaced. On the fall of Napoleon, he entered, at six-

---

[13] A world-wide conflict fought from 1756 to 1763 in Europe, North America, and India between, on the one side, France, Austria, Russia, Saxony, Sweden, and (after 1762) Spain and, on the other, Prussia, England, and Hanover. The two main issues were colonial rivalry in America and India, and the struggle between Austria and Prussia for supremacy in Germany.

[14] François de Chevert (1695–1769), lieutenant-general of the armies of the French king.—Louis, Chevalier d'Assas (1733–1760), captain in the French army.—Frederick II (Frederick the Great, 1712–1786), king of Prussia. His successes in the wars of the Austrian Succession and the Seven Years' War made Prussia the first military power of Europe and gave him a reputation as a military genius.

[15] "Memories of Military Servitude."

teen, into the royal guard; accompanied the Bourbons to Ghent during the Hundred Days,[16] and remained in the army up to 1828. Fourteen years a soldier without seeing any service (for he was not even in the brief Spanish campaign)—the alternation of routine duties and enforced idleness, the *ennui* of an active profession without one opportunity for action except in obscure and painful civil broils, would have driven many to find relief in dissipation; M. de Vigny found it in contemplation and solitary thought. 'Those years of my life,' he says, 'would have been wasted, if I had not employed them in attentive and persevering observation, storing up the results for future years. I owe to my military life views of human nature which could never have reached me but under a soldier's uniform. There are scenes which one can only arrive at through disgusts, which, to one not forced to endure them, would be unendurable. . . . Overcome by an *ennui* which I had little expected in that life so ardently desired, it became a necessity for me to rescue at least my nights from the empty and tiresome bustle of a soldier's days. In those nights I enlarged in silence what knowledge I had received from our tumultuous public studies; and thence the origin of my writings.'

M. de Vigny's first publications were poems, of which we shall say a few words presently, and which, whatever be the opinion formed of their absolute merit, are considered by a sober and impartial critic, M. Sainte-Beuve, as of a more completely original character than those of either Lamartine or Victor Hugo.[17] It is, therefore, only in the common course of things, that they were at the time but moderately successful.

---

[16] The period from March 20 to June 28, 1815, when Napoleon attempted to rebuild his empire after returning from Elba. The Waterloo campaign, last action of the Napoleonic Wars, was fought in southern Belgium.

[17] Charles Augustin Sainte-Beuve (1804–1869), French literary historian and highly influential critic.—Alphonse de Lamartine (1790–1869), French poet, novelist, and statesman.—Victor Hugo (1802–1885), one of the foremost French poets of his age; he was also a novelist and dramatist.

The first of his works which attained popularity was 'Cinq-Mars, or a Conspiracy under Louis XIII.,' an historical romance of the school of Sir Walter Scott, then at the height of his popularity in France, and who was breathing the breath of life into the historical literature of France, and, through France, of all Europe.

M. de Vigny has chosen his scene at that passage of French history, which completed the transformation of the feudal monarchy of the middle ages into the despotic and courtly monarchy of Louis XIV.[18] The iron hand of Richelieu, reigning in the name of a master who both feared and hated him, but whom habit and conscious incapacity rendered his slave, had broken the remaining strength of those great lords, once powerful enough to cope single-handed with their sovereign, and several of whom, by confederating, could, to a very late period, dictate for themselves terms of capitulation. The crafty and cruel policy of the minister had mowed down all of those who, by position and personal qualities, stood pre-eminent above the rest. As for those whom, because they could not be dangerous to him, he spared, their restlessness and turbulence, surviving their power, might, during a royal minority, break out once more into impotent and passing tumults, but the next generation of them were and could be nothing but courtiers; an aristocracy still for purposes of rapine and oppression, for resistance to the despotism of the monarch they were as the feeblest of the multitude. A most necessary and salutary transformation in European society, and which, whether completed by the hands of a Richelieu or a Henry the Seventh, was, as M. de Vigny clearly sees (and perhaps no longer laments), the destined and inevitable preparation for the era of modern liberty and democracy.[19] But the

[18] Louis XIV (1638–1715), called *Roi Soleil* (Sun King), occupied the throne of France from 1643–1715, during which time he brought the monarchy to its highest point.

[19] Armand Jean du Plessis, Duc de Richelieu (1585–1642), French prelate and statesman who was virtually dictator of France as the chief adviser of Louis XIII.

Mill suggests a parallel between Richelieu and Henry VII (1457–

age was one of those (there are several of them in history) in which the greatest and most beneficial ends were accomplished by the basest means. It was the age of struggle between unscrupulous intellect and brute force; intellect not yet in a condition to assert its inherent right of supremacy by pure means, and no longer wielding, as in the great era of the Reformation, the noble weapon of an honest popular enthusiasm. Iago prime minister, is the type of the men who crumbled into dust the feudal aristocracies of Europe. In no period were the unseen springs both of the good and the evil that was done, so exclusively the viler passions of humanity: what little of honourable or virtuous feeling might exist in high places during that era, was probably oftenest found in the aristocratic faction so justly and beneficially extirpated; for in the rule of lawless force, some noble impulses are possible in the rulers at least—in that of cunning and fraud, none.

Towards the close of Richelieu's career, when the most difficult part of his task was done, but his sinking health, and the growing jealousy and fear of that master, one word of whom would even then have dismissed him into private life, made the cares of his station press heavier on him, and required a more constant and anxious watchfulness then ever; it was his practice to amuse the frivolous monarch with a perpetual succession of new favourites, who served his purpose till Louis was tired of them, or whom, if any of them proved capable of acquiring a permanent tenure of the royal favour, and of promoting other designs than his own, he well knew how to remove. The last, the most accomplished, and the most unfortunate of these was Henri d'Effiat, Marquis de Cinq-Mars,[20] and of him our author has made the hero of his tale.*

1509), king of England from 1485–1509. Henry's reign is often thought to mark the beginning of modern English history because it marked the end of the Wars of the Roses and the founding of the Tudor dynasty.

20 Henri Coeffier de Ruzé, Marquis de Cinq-Mars (1620–1642) was executed for plotting with Spain against Richelieu.

* [Here followed originally a sketch of the plot of the romance, now omitted as unnecessary.] (Mill's note.)

Such is 'Cinq-Mars, or a Conspiracy under Louis XIII.'—a work not free from the fault, so far as it is a fault, most common in the romantic literature of young France; it partakes somewhat of the 'Literature of Despair;' it too much resembles M. Eugene Sue's[21] early novels, in which every villain dies honoured and prosperous at a good old age, after every innocent person in the tale has been crushed and exterminated by him without pity or remorse—through which the mocking laugh of a chorus of demons seems to ring in our ears that the world is delivered over to an evil spirit, and that man is his creature and his prey. But such is not the character of M. de Vigny's writings, and the resemblance in this single instance is only casual. Still, as a mere work of art, if the end of art be, as conceived by the ancients and by the great German writers, the production of the intrinsically beautiful, Cinq-Mars cannot be commended. A story in which the odious and the contemptible in man and life act so predominant a part, which excites our scorn or our hatred so much more than our pity—comes within a far other category than that of the Beautiful, and can be justified on no canons of taste of which that is the end. But it is not possible for the present generation of France to restrict the purposes of art within this limit. They are too much in earnest. They take life too much *au sérieux*. It may be possible (what some of his more enthusiastic admirers say of Goethe) that a thoroughly earnest mind may struggle upwards through the region of clouds and storms to an untroubled summit, where all other good sympathies and aspirations confound themselves in a serene love and culture of the calmly beautiful—looking down upon the woes and struggles of perplexed humanity with as calm a gaze (though with a more helping arm) as that of him who is most placidly indifferent to human weal. But however this may be, the great majority of persons in earnest will remain always in the intermediate region; will feel themselves more or less militant in this world—having something to pursue in it, different from the Beautiful,

[21] Eugène Sue (1804–1857), novelist best known for *The Mysteries of Paris* (1842–1843) and *The Wandering Jew* (1844–1845).

different from their own mental tranquillity and health, and which they will pursue, if they have the gifts of an artist, by all the resources of art, whatever becomes of canons of criticism, and beauty in the abstract. The writers and readers of works of imagination in France have the desire of amusement as much as English readers, the sense of beauty generally much more; but they have also, very generally, a thirst for something which shall address itself to their real-life feelings, and not to those of imagination merely—which shall give them an idea or a sentiment connected with the actual world. And if a story or a poem is possessed by an Idea—if it powerfully exhibits some form of real life, or some conception respecting human nature or society which may tend to consequences, not only is it not necessarily expected to represent abstract beauty, but it is pardoned for exhibiting even hideousness. These considerations should enable us to understand and tolerate such works as *Le Pere Goriot*, of Balzac, or *Leoni*, of George Sand, and to understand, if we do not tolerate, such as the *Antony* or *Richard Darlington*, of Alexandre Dumas.[22]

Now, among the ideas with which French literature has been possessed for the last ten years, is that of realizing, and bringing home to the imagination, the history and spirit of past ages. Sir Walter Scott, having no object but to please, and having readers who only sought to be pleased, would not have told the story of Richelieu and Cinq-Mars without greatly softening the colouring; and the picture would have been more agreeable than M. de Vigny's, but it would not have been so true to the age. M. de Vigny preferred the truer to the more pleasing, and *his* readers have sanctioned the preference.

Even according to this view of its object, the work has obvious defects. The characters of some of the subordinate personages, Friar Joseph[23] for instance, are even more revolt-

[22] Honoré de Balzac (1799–1850) published *Le Père Goriot* in 1835.—George Sand (1804–1876) published *Leone Leoni* in 1833.—Alexandre Dumas (1803–1871), novelist and playwright. The plays *Antony* and *Richard Darlington* were first produced in 1831.

[23] Friar Joseph (François Le Clerc du Tremblay, 1577–1638), French Capuchin monk, confidant and agent of Richelieu.

ing than the truth of history requires. De Thou,[24] the pious and studious man of retirement, cast out into storms for which he was never meant—the only character of principle in the tale, yet who sacrifices principle as well as life to romantic friendship—is but coldly represented; his goodness is too simple, his attachment too instinctive, too dog-like, and so much intensity of friendship is not sufficiently accounted for; Balzac would have managed these things better. The author also crowds his story too much with characters; he cannot bear that any celebrated personage whom the age affords should be passed over, and consequently introduces many who ought not to have been drawn at all unless they could be drawn truly, and on whom he has not been able to employ the same accurate study as he has on his principal characters. Richelieu and Louis XIII. are historical figures of which he has taken the trouble to form a well-digested conception; but he can know nothing of Milton, whom he introduces, on his way from Italy, reading his 'Paradise Lost,' not written till twenty years after, to Corneille, Descartes, and a crowd of other poets, wits, and philosophers, in the *salon* of the celebrated courtezan, Marion Delorme.[25] But these are minor blemishes. As a specimen of art employed in embodying the character of an age, the merit of 'Cinq-Mars' is very great. The spirit of the age penetrates every nook and corner of it; the same atmosphere which hangs over the personages of the story hangs over us; we feel the eye of the omnipresent Richelieu upon us, and the influences of France in its Catholic and aristocratic days, of ardent, pleasure-loving, laughter-loving, and danger-loving France, all round us. To this merit is to be added, that the representations of feeling are always simple and graceful; the author has not, like so many inferior writers, supplied by the easy resource of mere exaggeration of colouring, the inca-

---

[24] Jacques Auguste de Thou (1553–1617), historian and statesman; drafted Edict of Nantes.

[25] Pierre Corneille (1606–1684), great French classical dramatist.—René Descartes (1596–1650), French philosopher, mathematician, and scientist.—Marion Delorme (1613?–1650), mistress of Cinq-Mars.

pacity to show us anything subtle or profound, any trait we knew not before, in the workings of passion in the human heart. On the whole, 'Cinq-Mars' is admirable as a first production of its kind, but altogether of an inferior order to its successors, the *Grandeur et Servitude Militaire*, and *Stello;* to which we proceed.

Of M. de Vigny's prose works, 'Cinq-Mars' alone was written previous to the Revolution of 1830; and though the royalist tendency of the author's political opinions is manifest throughout—indeed the book is one long protest against the levelling of the feudal aristocracy—it does not, nor does any part of the royalist literature of the last twenty years, entirely answer to our description of the Conservative school of poetry and romance. To find a real Conservative literature in France one must look earlier than the first Revolution, as to study the final transformation of that literature, one must descend below the last. One must distinguish three periods; Conservatism triumphant, Conservatism militant, Conservatism vanquished. The first is represented by Racine, Fénélon,[26] and Voltaire in his tragedies,[27] before he quitted the paths of his predecessors. Jean Jacques Rousseau is the father and founder of the Movement literature of France, and Madame de Stael its second great apostle[28]: in them first the revolt of the modern mind against the social arrangements and doctrines which had descended from of old, spoke with the inspired voice of genius. At the head of the literature of Conservatism in its second or

[26] Jean Racine (1639–1699), great French classical dramatist.—François de Salignac de la Mothe Fénelon (1651–1715), theologian and author; best known for *Télémaque* (1699).

[27] Principally *Zaïre* (1732), *Mahomet* (1742), *Mérope* (1743).

[28] Jean Jacques Rousseau (1712–1778), the Geneva-born philosopher who exerted great influence in France with *La Nouvelle Héloïse* (1761) and *The Social Contract* (1762).—Germaine de Staël (1766–1817), woman of letters, wrote two successful novels—*Delphine* (1802) and *Corinne* (1807)—and a very influential celebration of German romanticism called *De l'Allemagne* (1811).

militant period, stands Chateaubriand[29]: a man whose name marks one of the turning points in the literary history of his country: poetically a Conservative to the inmost core—rootedly feudal and Catholic—whose genius burst into life during the tempest of a revolution which hurled down from their pedestals all his objects of reverence; which saddened his imagination, modified (without impairing) his Conservatism by the addition of its multiform experiences, and made the world to him too full of disorder and gloom, too much a world without harmony, and ill at ease, to allow of his exhibiting the pure untroubled spirit of Conservative poetry as exemplified in Southey,[30] or still more in Wordsworth. To this literature, of Conservatism discouraged but not yet disenchanted, still hopeful and striving to set up again its old idols, 'Cinq-Mars' belongs. From the final and hopeless overthrow of the old order of society in July 1830, begins the era of Conservatism disenchanted—Conservatism which is already in the past tense—which for practical purposes is abandoned, and only contributes its share, as all past associations and experiences do, towards shaping and colouring the individual's impressions of the present.

This is the character which pervades the two principal of M. de Vigny's more recent works, the 'Servitude et Grandeur Militaire,' and 'Stello.' He has lost his faith in Royalism, and in the system of opinions connected with it. His eyes are opened to all the iniquities and hypocrisies of the state of society which is passing away. But he cannot take up with any of the systems of politics, and of either irreligious or religious philosophy, which profess to lay open the mystery of what is to follow, and to guarantee that the new order of society will not have its own iniquities and hypocrisies of as dark a kind. He has no faith in any systems, or in man's power of prophecy;

29 François René, Vicomte de Chateaubriand (1768–1848), founder of French romanticism; published *The Genius of Christianity*, which included *Atala* and *René,* in 1802.

30 See "On the Present State of Literature," note 5.

nor is he sure that the new tendencies of society, take them for all in all, have more to satisfy the wants of a thoughtful and loving spirit, than the old had; at all events not so much more, as to make the condition of human nature a cheerful subject to him. He looks upon life, and sees most things crooked, and (saving whatever assurance his religious impressions may afford to him that in some unknown way all things must be working for good) sees not how they shall be made straight. This is not a happy state of mind, but it is not an unfavourable one to poetry. If the worse forms of it produce a 'Literature of Despair,' the better are seen in a writer like M. de Vigny—who having now no theories of his own or of his teachers to save the credit of, looks life steadily in the face—applies himself to understanding whatever of evil, and of heroic struggle with evil, it presents to his individual experience—and gives forth his pictures of both, with deep feeling, but with the calmness of one who has no point to carry, no quarrel to maintain, over and above the 'general one of every son of Adam with his lot here below.'

M. de Vigny has been a soldier, and he has been, and is, a poet: the situation and feelings of a soldier (especially a soldier not in active service), and, so far as the measure of his genius admits, those of a poet, are what he is best acquainted with, and what, therefore, as a man of earnest mind, not now taking anything on trust, it was most natural he should attempt to delineate. The 'Souvenirs Militaires' are the embodiment of the author's experiences in the one capacity, 'Stello,' in the other. Each consists of three touching and beautifully told stories, founded on fact, in which the life and position of a soldier in modern times, and of a poet at all times, in their relation to society, are shadowed out. In relation to society chiefly; for that is the prominent feature in all the speculations of the French mind; and thence it is that their poetry is so much shallower than ours, and their works of fiction so much deeper; that, of the metaphysics of every mode of feeling and thinking, so little is to be learnt from them, and of its social influences so much.

The soldier, and the poet, appear to M. de Vigny alike misplaced, alike ill at ease, in the present condition of human life. In the soldier he sees a human being set apart for a profession doomed to extinction, and doomed consequently, in the interval, to a continual decrease of dignity and of the sympathies of mankind. War he sees drawing to a close; compromises and diplomatic arrangements now terminate the differences among civilized nations; the army is reduced more and more to mere parade, or the functions of a police; called out from time to time, to shed its own blood and that of malcontent fellow-citizens in tumults where much popular hatred is to be earned, but no glory; disliked by taxpayers for its burthensomeness; looked down upon by the industrious for its enforced idleness: its employers themselves always in dread of its numbers, and jealous of its restlessness, which, in a soldier, is but the impatience of a man who is useless and nobody, for a chance of being useful and of being something. The soldier thus remains with all the burthens, all the irksome restraints of his condition, aggravated, but without the hopes which lighted it up, the excitements which gave it zest. Those alone, says M. de Vigny, who have been soldiers, know what servitude is. To the soldier alone is obedience, passive and active, the law of his life, the law of every day and of every moment; obedience, not stopping at sacrifice, nor even at crime. In him alone is the abnegation of his self-will, of his liberty of independent action, absolute and unreserved; the grand distinction of humanity, the responsibility of the individual as a moral agent, being made over, once for all, to superior authority. The type of human nature which these circumstances create, well deserves the study of the artist and the philosopher. M. de Vigny has deeply meditated on it. He has drawn with delicacy and profundity that mixture of Spartan and stoical impassibility with child-like *insouciance* and *bonhomie*,[31] which is the result, on the one hand, of a life of painful and difficult obedience to discipline—on the other, of a conscience freed from concern or accountability for the quality of the actions of which that

[31] "Indifference," "apathy," and "good nature," "geniality."

life is made up. On the means by which the moral position of the soldier might be raised, and his hardships alleviated, M. de Vigny has ideas worthy of the consideration of him who is yet to come—the statesman who has care and leisure for plans of social amelioration unconnected with party contests and the cry of the hour. His stories, full of melancholy beauty, will carry into thousands of minds and hearts which would otherwise have been unvisited by it, a conception of a soldier's trials and a soldier's virtues in times which, like ours, are not those of martial glory.

The first of these tales at least, if not all the three, if the author's words are to be taken literally, is unvarnished fact. But familiar as the modern French romance-writers have made us with the artifice of assimilating their fictions, for the sake of artistic reality, to actual recollections, we dare not trust these appearances; and we must needs suppose that, though suggested by facts, the stories are indebted to M. de Vigny's invention not only for their details, but for some of their main circumstances. If he had been so fortunate as to meet with facts which, related as they actually occurred, served so perfectly as these do his purposes of illustration, he would hardly have left any possibility of doubt as to their authenticity. He must know the infinite distance, as to power of influencing the mind, between the best contrived and most probable fiction, and the smallest fact.

. . . .

Such is a brief outline of this remarkable book [32]: to which we have felt throughout, and feel still more on looking back, what scanty justice we have done. Among the writings of our day we know not one which breathes a nobler spirit, or in which every detail is conceived and wrought out in a manner more worthy of that spirit. But whoever would know what it is, must read the book itself. No *résumé* can convey any idea of it; the impression it makes is not the sum of the impressions of particular incidents or particular sayings, it is the effect of

[32] *Souvenirs de Servitude et de Grandeur Militaire.*

the tone and colouring of the whole. We do not seem to be listening to the author, to be receiving a 'moral' from any of his stories, or from his characters an 'example' prepense; the poem of human life is opened before us, and M. de Vigny does but chaunt from it, in a voice of subdued sadness, a few strains telling of obscure wisdom and unrewarded virtue; of those antique characters which, without self-glorification or hope of being appreciated, 'carry out,' as he expresses it, 'the sentiment of duty to its extremest consequences,' and whom he avers, as a matter of personal experience, that he has never met with in any walk of life but the profession of arms.

'Stello' [33] is a work of similar merit to the 'Military Recollections,' though, we think, somewhat inferior. The poet, and his condition—the function he has to perform in the world, and its treatment of him—are the subject of the book. Stello, a young poet, having, it would appear, no personal cause of complaint against the world, but subject to fits of nervous despondency, seeks relief under one of these attacks from a mysterious personage, the *docteur noir* [34]; and discloses to him that in his *ennui* and his thirst for activity and excitement, he has almost determined to fling himself into politics, and sacrifice himself for some one of the parties or forms of government which are struggling with one another in the world. The doctor prescribes to him three stories, exhibiting the fate of the poet under every form of government, and the fruitlessness of his expecting from the world, or from men of the world, aught but negligence or contempt. The stories are of

[33] Published in 1832, *Stello* contains three different stories. The first, "Historie d'une puce enragée" ("Tale of the Mad Flea"), is devoted to the tragedy of the poet Nicolas Joseph Gilbert (1751–1780); the second, "Histoire de Kitty Bell," to the fate of the English poet Thomas Chatterton (1752–1770); the third, "Une histoire de la Terreur" ("A Tale of the Terror"), to the death of André Chénier (1762–1794), the French poet executed for his attack on the excesses of the Revolution. In 1835 Vigny returned to the subject of the second of these stories in the play *Chatterton.*

[34] "Black doctor," but usually translated "Doctor Noir."

three poets, all of whom the *docteur noir* has seen die, as, in fact, the same person might have been present at all their deaths: under three different governments—in an absolute monarchy, a constitutional government, and a democratic revolution. Gilbert, the poet and satirist, called from his poverty Gilbert *sans-culotte*,[35] who died mad in a hospital at Paris, he who wrote in the last days of his life the verses beginning

> 'Au banquet de la vie infortuné convive
> J'apparus un jour, et je meurs'—[36]

Chatterton—

> 'the marvellous boy,
> The sleepless soul, who perished in his pride'—[37]

driven to suicide at eighteen by the anguish of disappointment and neglect; and André Chénier, the elder brother of Chénier the revolutionary poet—whose own poems, published not till many years after his death, were at once hailed by the new school of poetry in France as having anticipated what they had since done, and given the real commencement to the new era: he perished by the guillotine only two days before the fall of Robespierre[38]; on the scaffold he exclaimed, striking his forehead, *'Il y avait pourtant quelque chose là!'*[39] The stories adhere strictly to the spirit of history, though not to the literal facts, and are, as usual, beautifully told, especially the last and most elaborate of them, 'André Chénier.' In this tale we are shown the prison of Saint-Lazare during the reign of terror,

---

[35] "Without breeches," a term of reproach given by the aristocrats to the extreme republicans, who wore pantaloons instead of knee breeches.

[36] "I appeared one day, an unhappy guest at the banquet of life, and I am dying."

[37] Wordsworth, "Resolution and Independence," lines 43–44. (Wordsworth has "that" rather than "who.")

[38] Maximilien Robespierre (1758–1794), leading figure of the French Revolution and an organizer of the Terror. He himself was finally tried and guillotined by the Convention.

[39] "There was something there nevertheless!"

and the courtesies and gallantries of polished life still blossoming in the foulness of the dungeon and on the brink of the tomb. Madame de St. Aignan,[40] with her reserved and delicate passion for André Chénier, is one of the most graceful of M. de Vigny's creations. We are brought into the presence of Robespierre and Saint-Just [41]—who are drawn, not indeed like Catoes and Brutuses,[42] though there have been found in our time Frenchmen not indisposed to take that view of them. But the hatred of exaggeration which always characterizes M. de Vigny, does not desert him here: the terrorist chiefs do not figure in his pages as monsters thirsting for blood, nor as hypocrites and impostors with merely the low aims of selfish ambition: either of these representations would have been false to history. He shows us these men as they were, as such men could not but have been; men distinguished, morally, chiefly by two qualities, entire hardness of heart, and the most overweening and bloated self-conceit: for nothing less, assuredly, could lead any man to believe that his individual judgment respecting the public good is a warrant to him for exterminating all who are suspected of forming any other judgment, and for setting up a machine to cut off heads, sixty or seventy every day, till some unknown futurity be accomplished, some Utopia realized.

The lesson which the *docteur noir* finds in these tragical

[40] The Duchess of Saint-Aignan is a major character in that part of *Stello* called "A Tale of the Terror."

[41] Louis de Saint-Just (1767–1794) was, like Robespierre, whom he aided in organizing the Reign of Terror, a staunch believer in Spartan virtue and incorruptibility.

[42] Cato the Censor (Marcus Porcius Cato, 234–149 B.C.), a Roman statesman, represented the austere virtues of old Rome and decried luxury and extravagance. Visiting Carthage in his old age, he returned to insist that it be destroyed and thus brought on the Third Punic War. His great-grandson, Cato the Younger (95–45 B.C.), also known as Marcus Porcius Cato, was known for his incorruptible honesty.

Marcus Junius Brutus (85–42 B.C.), the principal assassin of Julius Caesar. The linking of his name with Cato's suggests the type of the incorruptible and virtuous statesman who is driven to enforce virtue by brutal means.

histories, for the edification of poets, is still that of abnegation: to expect nothing for themselves from changes in society or in political institutions; to renounce for ever the idea that the world will, or can be expected, to fall at their feet and worship them; to consider themselves, once for all, as martyrs, if they are so, and instead of complaining, to take up their cross and bear it.

This counsel is so essentially wise, and so much required everywhere, but above all in France—where the idea that intellect ought to rule the world, an idea in itself true and just, has taken such root that every youth who fancies himself a thinker or an artist thinks that he has a right to everything society has to give, and deems himself the victim of ingratitude because he is not loaded with its riches and honours; M. de Vigny has so genuine a feeling of the true greatness of a poet, of the spirit which has dwelt in all poets deserving the name of great—that he may be pardoned for what there is in his picture of a poet's position and destiny in the actual world, somewhat morbid and overcharged, though with a foundation of universal truth. It is most true that, whether in poetry or in philosophy, a person endowed in any eminent degree with genius—originality—the gift of seeing truths at a greater depth than the world can penetrate, or of feeling deeply and justly things which the world has not yet learnt to feel—that such a person needs not hope to be appreciated, to be otherwise than made light of and evil entreated, in virtue of what is greatest in him, his genius. For (except in things which can be reduced to mathematical demonstration, or made obvious to sense) that which all mankind will be prepared to see and understand tomorrow, it cannot require much genius to perceive to-day; and all persons of distinguished originality, whether thinkers or artists, are subject to the eternal law, that they must themselves create the tastes or the habits of thought by means of which they will afterwards be appreciated. No great poet or philosopher since the Christian era (apart from the accident of a rich patron) could have gained either rank or subsistence *as* a poet or a philosopher; but things are not, and have seldom been, so badly ordered in the world, as that he could not get it in any other way. Chatterton, and probably Gilbert, could have earned an honest livelihood, if their inordinate pride would have accepted it in the common paths of obscure industry. And much as it is to be lamented, for the world's sake more than that of the individual, that they who are equal to the noblest things are not reserved for such,—it is nevertheless true that persons of genius, persons whose superiority is that they can do what others cannot do, can generally also, if they choose, do better than others that which others do, and which others are willing to honour and reward. If they cannot, it is usually from something ill regulated in themselves, something to be cured of which would be for the health even of their own minds; perhaps oftenest because they will not take the pains which less gifted persons are willing to take, though less than half as much would suffice; because the habit of doing with ease things on a large scale, makes them impatient of slow and unattractive toil. It is their own choice, then. If they wish for worldly honour and profit, let them seek it in the way others do; the struggle indeed is hard, and the attainment uncertain, but not specially so to them; on the contrary, they have advantages over most of their competitors. If they prefer their nobler vocation, they have no cause of quarrel with the world because they follow that vocation under the conditions necessarily implied in it. If it were possible that they should from the first have the acclamations of the world, they could not be deserving of them; all they could be doing for the world must be comparatively little: they could not be the great men they fancy themselves.

A story, or a poem, might nevertheless be conceived, which would throw tenfold more light upon the poetic character, and upon the condition of a poet in the world, than any instance, either historical or fictitious, of the world's undervaluing of him. It would exhibit the sufferings of a poet, not from mortified vanity, but from the poetic temperament itself—under arrangements of society made by and for harder natures, and in a world which, for any but the unsensitive, is not a place of contentment ever, nor of peace till after many a hard-fought battle. That M. de Vigny could conceive such a subject in the spirit in which it should be conceived, is clear from the signs by which his Stello recognises himself as a poet. 'Because there is in nature no beauty, nor grandeur, nor harmony, which does not cause in me a prophetic thrill—which does not fill me with a deep emotion, and swell my eyelids with tears divine and inexplicable. Because of the infinite pity I feel for mankind, my companions in suffering, and the eager desire I feel to hold out my hand to them, and raise them incessantly by words of commiseration and of love. Because I feel in my inmost being an invisible and undefinable power which resembles a presentiment of the future, and a revelation of the mysterious causes of the present:' a presentiment which is not always imaginary, but often the instinctive insight of a sensitive nature, which from its finer texture vibrates to impressions so evanescent as to be unfelt by others, and, by that faculty as by an additional sense, is apprised, it cannot tell how, of things without, which escape the cognizance of the less delicately organized.

These *are* the tests, or some of the tests, of a poetic nature; and it must be evident that to such, even when supported by a positive religious faith, and that a cheerful one, this life is naturally, or at least may easily be, a vale of tears; a place in which there is no rest. The poet who would speak of such, must do it in the spirit of those beautiful lines of Shelley—himself the most perfect type of that which he described:—

> 'High, spirit-winged heart, who dost for ever
> Beat thine unfeeling bars with vain endeavour,
> Till those bright plumes of thought, in which arrayed
> It over-soared this low and worldly shade,
> Lie shattered, and thy panting wounded breast
> Stains with dear blood its unmaternal nest!
> I weep vain tears: blood would less bitter be,
> Yet poured forth gladlier, could it profit thee.' [43]

The remainder of M. de Vigny's works are plays and poems.

[43] "Epipsychidion," lines 13–20.

The plays are 'Le More de Venise,' a well-executed and very close translation of Othello; 'La Maréchale d'Ancre,' from the same period of history as Cinq-Mars; and 'Chatterton,' the story in Stello, with the characters more developed, the outline more filled up. Without disparagement to these works, we think the narrative style more suitable than the dramatic to the quality of M. de Vigny's genius. It we had not read these plays, we should not have known how much of the impressiveness of his other writings comes from his own presence in them (if the expression may be allowed), animating and harmonizing the picture, by blending with its natural tints the colouring of his own feelings and character.

Of the poems much were to be said, if a foreigner could be considered altogether a competent judge of them. For our own part we confess that, of the admirable poetry to be found in French literature, that part is most poetry to us, which is written in prose. In regard to verse-writing, we would even exceed the severity of Horace's precept against mediocrity[44]; we hold, that nothing should be written in verse which is not exquisite. In prose, anything may be said which is worth saying at all; in verse, only what is worth saying better than prose can say it. The gems alone of thought and fancy, are worth setting with so finished and elaborate a workmanship; and even of them, those only whose effect is heightened by it: which takes place under two conditions; and in one or other of these two, if we are not mistaken, must be found the origin and justification of all composition in verse. A thought or feeling requires verse for its adequate expression, when in order that it may dart into the soul with the speed of a lightning-flash, the ideas or images that are to convey it require to be pressed closer together than is compatible with the rigid grammatical construction of the prose sentence. One recommendation of verse, therefore, is, that it affords a language more *condensed* than prose. The other is derived from one of the natural laws

---

[44] *Mediocribus esse poetis/Non homines, non di, non concessere columnae.* ("To poets, to be second-rate is a privilege which neither men, nor gods, nor bookstalls ever allowed." *Ars Poetica.*)

of the human mind, in the utterance of its thoughts impregnated with its feelings. All emotion which has taken possession of the whole being—which flows unresistedly, and therefore equably—instinctively seeks a language that flows equably like itself; and must either find it, or be conscious of an unsatisfied want, which even impedes and prematurely stops the flow of the feeling. Hence, ever since man has been man, all deep and sustained feeling has tended to express itself in rhythmical language; and the deeper the feeling, the more characteristic and decided the rhythm; provided always the feeling be sustained as well as deep; for, a *fit* of passion has no natural connexion with verse or music, a *mood* of passion has the strongest. No one, who does not hold this distinction in view, will comprehend the importance which the Greek lawgivers and philosophers attached to music, and which appears inexplicable till we understand how perpetual an aim of their polity it was to subdue *fits* of passion, and to sustain and reinforce *moods* of it.* This view of the origin of rhythmic utterance in general, and verse in particular, naturally demands *short* poems, it being impossible that a feeling so intense as to require a more rhythmical cadence than that of eloquent prose, should sustain itself at its highest elevation for long together; and we think (heretical as the opinion may be) that, except in the ages when the absence of written books occasioned all things to be thrown into verse for facility of memory, or in those other ages in which writing in verse may happen to be a fashion, a

* The Dorian mood
Of flutes and soft recorders; such as raised
To height of noblest temper heroes old
Arming to battle; and, *instead of rage,*
Deliberate valour breathed, firm and unmoved
With dread of death, to flight or foul retreat:
Nor wanting power to mitigate and swage,
With solemn touches, troubled thoughts, and chase
Anguish, and doubt, and fear, and sorrow and pain,
From mortal or immortal minds.'

(*Paradise Lost,* I, 550–559.
Mill's note.)

long poem will always be felt (though perhaps unconsciously) to be something unnatural and hollow; something which it requires the genius of a Homer, a Dante, or a Milton, to induce posterity to read, or at least to read through.

Verse, then, being only allowable where prose would be inadequate; and the inadequacy of prose arising either from its not being sufficiently condensed, or from its not having cadence enough to express sustained passion, which is never long-winded–it follows, that if prolix writing is vulgarly called *prosy* writing, a very true feeling of the distinction between verse and prose shows itself in the vulgarism; and that the one unpardonable sin in a versified composition, next to the absence of meaning, and of true meaning, is diffuseness. From this sin it will be impossible to exculpate M. Alfred de Vigny. His poems, graceful and often fanciful though they be, are, to us, marred by their diffuseness.

Of the more considerable among them, that which most resembles what, in our conception, a poem ought to be, is 'Moïse.' The theme is still the sufferings of the man of genius, the inspired man, the intellectual ruler and seer: not however, this time, the great man persecuted by the world, but the great man honoured by it, and in his natural place at the helm of it, he on whom all rely, whom all reverence–Moses on Pisgah, Moses the appointed of God, the judge, captain and hierarch of the chosen race–crying to God in anguish of spirit for deliverance and rest; that the cares and toils, the weariness and solitariness of heart, of him who is lifted altogether above his brethren, be no longer imposed upon him–that the Almighty may withdraw his gifts, and suffer him to sleep the sleep of common humanity. His cry is heard; when the clouds disperse, which veiled the summit of the mountain from the Israelites waiting in prayer and prostration at its foot, Moses is no more seen: and now, 'marching towards the promised land, Joshua advanced, pale and pensive of mien; for he was already the chosen of the Omnipotent.'

The longest of the poems is 'Eloa; or, the Sister of the Angels;' a story of a bright being, created from a tear of the

Redeemer, and who falls, tempted by pity for the Spirit of Darkness. The idea is fine, and the details graceful, a word we have often occasion to use in speaking of M. de Vigny: but this and most of his other poems are written in the heroic verse,[45] that is to say, he has aggravated the imperfections, for his purpose, of the most prosaic language in Europe, by choosing to write in its most prosaic metre. The absence of prosody, of long and short or accented and unaccented syllables, renders the French language essentially unmusical; while—the unbending structure of its sentence, of which there is essentially but one type for verse and prose, almost precluding inversions and elisions—all the screws and pegs of the prose sentence are retained to encumber the verse. If it is to be raised at all above prose, variety of rhythm must be sought in variety of versification; there is no room for it in the monotonous structure of the heroic metre. Where is it that Racine, always an admirable writer, appears to us more than an admirable *prose* writer? In his irregular metres—in the choruses of Esther and of Athalie.[46] It is not wonderful then if the same may be said of M. de Vigny. We shall conclude with the following beautiful little poem, one of the few which he has produced in the style and measure of lyric verse:—

'Viens sur la mer, jeune fille,
  Sois sans effroi;
Viens sans trésor, sans famille,
  Seule avec moi.
Mon bateau sur les eaux brille,
  Voi ses mâts, voi
Ses pavillons et sa quille.
Ce n'est rien qu'une coquille,
  Mais j'y suis roi.

'Pour l'esclave on fit la terre,
  O ma beauté!

---

[45] In French poetry, verse consisting regularly of rhymed Alexandrines.

[46] Racine made significant departures from his earlier classical tragedies in the biblical tragedies *Esther* (1689) and *Athalie* (1691).

Mais pour l'homme libre, austère
  L'immensité.
Les flots savent un mystère
  De volupté;
Leur soupir involontaire
Veut dire: amour solitaire,
  Et liberté.' [47]

---

[47] "Come to the sea, maid; come fearless, treasureless, parentless, alone with me. My boat glistens on the waves. Look at the masts; look: the colors, the keel! Only a shell, yes—but I am its king. The land was made for slaves, my beautiful! but for the austere, free man, the sea's immensity. The water veils a mystery of sensual delight; its unconscious sigh says: Love in solitude, be free!" (Translation by Professor Samuel N. Rosenberg, Indiana University.)

From Bentham

1838

The essay on Bentham was one of those about which Mill had misgivings years after its publication. He did not change his mind about the justness of the opinions expressed in the essay, but he did come to think, as he says in the *Autobiography*, that the essay had been published too soon. It had exposed the weaknesses of Bentham's doctrines before those doctrines, which also contained great strengths, had done their work in the world. Such a misgiving suggests Mill's relativistic view of ideas, his belief that certain ideas are more needed at certain times and places than at others. Naturally, too, Mill had personal qualms about putting his name to an attack upon his and his father's mentor. Some years before he published this study of Bentham, he had refused to be publicly identified as the author of an article entitled "Remarks on Bentham's Philosophy," which he wrote as one of the appendices to the novelist Edward Bulwer's *England and the English* in 1833.

The essay is full of riches and of contradictions. Mill wishes to condemn Bentham for his narrowness and yet to suggest that narrowness may be a philosophical virtue. He wishes to show that Bentham's philosophy is adequate to the management of the material or business part of social arrangements and yet to show that no theory of society can be sound which is not the outgrowth of a sound theory of individual culture. He wishes to praise Bentham for promoting a democratic theory of government and also to blame him for not occupying himself with the dangers of the tyranny of the majority. At each stage of the essay Mill announces that the unpleasant part of his work is done, and that he can now devote himself to the celebration of Bentham's virtues; yet each time he finds a bit more of the unpleasant work to do.

In the early parts of the essay, Mill praises Bentham for introducing the method of scientific investigation into morals and politics. Bentham's method will guarantee clarity and a kind of certainty, but it is no guarantee for completeness. However scientific a thinker may be, he will be a poor empiricist if he is lacking in experience. Such, argues Mill, was the case with Bentham. Although he dealt brilliantly with his materials, they were few in number because he relied solely upon what his own mind and experience could supply. Since his own nature and experience were far from being representative of the human race, and since he refused to learn from other thinkers, the relevance of his conclusions must be limited.

In explaining why Bentham's experience was an inadequate basis for generalization about human nature, Mill actually blames Bentham for his healthy life and his "failure" to experience dejection, ennui, and "self-consciousness, that daemon of the men of genius of our time, from Wordsworth to Byron, from Goethe to Chateaubriand, and to which this age owes so much both of its cheerful and its mournful wisdom." Bentham had been blamed by many people for many things, but only John Stuart Mill blamed him for his failure to have a nervous breakdown. For Mill's use of Bentham as a foil to the other "seminal thinker," Coleridge, was more than the result of a change in his philosophical tastes. When Mill went through the suffering of his mental crisis, he turned to Coleridge for a poetic explanation of his state. Coleridge had suffered, and the stoical Bentham and James Mill had not; Mill was convinced that much of the truth of human life was concealed from those who had never suffered.

Mill's disaffection from Bentham takes a less private form in his criticism of political and social philosophies that are not conceived in awareness of the importance of national character. Bentham had been convinced of the universal applicability of his codes and constitutions. He "dreamed of setting out for Switzerland, for Spain, for Mexico, for Venezuela, and of landing among a people whose traditional and local prejudices he ignored, like Epimenides at Athens or Plato at Syracuse" (Elie Halévy, *The Growth of Philosophic Radicalism*, trans. Mary Morris [Boston, 1955], p. 298). Mill, on the other hand, made his theory of national character the basis of his political relativism. He believed that laws and institutions must be judged not absolutely but in relation to their greater or lesser applicability to particular countries at particular stages in their development. Hence he favored self-government for Europe but not for India.

But Mill's greatest objection to Bentham is that Bentham never recognizes man as a creature capable of pursuing spiritual perfection as an end in itself, and in fact shows himself unable even to conceive of the idea of perfection. Mill dreads the possibility that the spiritual blindness of this great theoretician of democracy will be institutionalized in the civilization he has helped to create.

THERE ARE two men, recently deceased, to whom their country is indebted not only for the greater part of the important ideas which have been thrown into circulation among its thinking men in their time, but for a revolution in its general modes of thought and investigation. These men, dissimilar in almost all else, agreed in being closet-students—secluded in a peculiar degree, by circumstances and character, from the business and intercourse of the world: and both were, through a large portion of their lives, regarded by those who took the lead in opinion (when they happened to hear of them) with feelings akin to contempt. But they were destined to renew a lesson given to mankind by every age, and always disregarded —to show that speculative philosophy, which to the superficial appears a thing so remote from the business of life and the outward interests of men, is in reality the thing on earth which most influences them, and in the long run overbears every other influence save those which it must itself obey. The writers of whom we speak have never been read by the multitude; except for the more slight of their works, their readers have been few: but, they have been the teachers of the teachers; there is hardly to be found in England an individual of any importance in the world of mind, who (whatever opinions he may have afterwards adopted) did not first learn to think from one of these two; and though their influences have but begun to diffuse themselves through these intermediate channels over society at large, there is already scarcely a publication of any consequence addressed to the educated classes, which, if these persons had not existed, would not have been different from what it is. These men are, Jeremy Bentham and Samuel Taylor

First published in the *London and Westminster Review,* XXIX (August 1838).

Coleridge—the two great seminal minds of England in their age.

No comparison is intended here between the minds or influences of these remarkable men: this were impossible unless there were first formed a complete judgment of each, considered apart. It is our intention to attempt, on the present occasion, an estimate of one of them; the only one, a complete edition of whose works is yet in progress, and who, in the classification which may be made of all writers into Progressive and Conservative, belongs to the same division with ourselves.[1] For although they were far too great men to be correctly designated by either appellation exclusively, yet in the main, Bentham was a Progressive philosopher, Coleridge a Conservative one. The influence of the former has made itself felt chiefly on minds of the Progressive class; of the latter, on those of the Conservative: and the two systems of concentric circles which the shock given by them is spreading over the ocean of mind, have only just begun to meet and intersect. The writings of both contain severe lessons to their own side, on many of the errors and faults they are addicted to: but to Bentham it was given to discern more particularly those truths with which existing doctrines and institutions were at variance; to Coleridge, the neglected truths which lay *in* them.

. . . .

Bentham's contempt, then, of all other schools of thinkers; his determination to create a philosophy wholly out of the materials furnished by his own mind, and by minds like his own; was his first disqualification as a philosopher. His second, was the incompleteness of his own mind as a representative of universal human nature. In many of the most natural and strongest feelings of human nature he had no sympathy; from many of its graver experiences he was altogether cut off; and the faculty by which one mind understands a mind different from itself, and throws itself into the feelings of that other mind, was denied him by his deficiency of Imagination.

[1] That is, Progressive.

With Imagination in the popular sense, command of imagery and metaphorical expression, Bentham was, to a certain degree, endowed. For want, indeed, of poetical culture, the images with which his fancy supplied him were seldom beautiful, but they were quaint and humorous, or bold, forcible, and intense: passages might be quoted from him both of playful irony, and of declamatory eloquence, seldom surpassed in the writings of philosophers. The Imagination which he had not, was that to which the name is generally appropriated by the best writers of the present day; that which enables us, by a voluntary effort, to conceive the absent as if it were present, the imaginary as if it were real, and to clothe it in the feelings which, if it were indeed real, it would bring along with it. This is the power by which one human being enters into the mind and circumstances of another. This power constitutes the poet, in so far as he does anything but melodiously utter his own actual feelings. It constitutes the dramatist entirely. It is one of the constituents of the historian; by it we understand other times; by it Guizot[2] interprets to us the middle ages; Nisard,[3] in his beautiful Studies on the later Latin poets, places us in the Rome of the Caesars; Michelet[4] disengages the distinctive characters of the different races and generations of mankind from the facts of their history. Without it nobody knows even his own nature, further than circumstances have actually tried it and called it out; nor the nature of his fellow-creatures, beyond such generalizations as he may have been enabled to make from his observation of their outward conduct.

By these limits, accordingly, Bentham's knowledge of human nature is bounded. It is wholly empirical; and the empiricism of one who has had little experience. He had neither internal experience nor external; the quiet, even tenor of his

---

[2] See "The French Revolution," note 4, and Mill's comments on Guizot in the Carlyle essay and in "Guizot's Essays and Lectures on History," *Dissertations and Discussions*, II, 218–282.

[3] Désiré Nisard (1806–1888), literary historian and critic.

[4] Jules Michelet (1798–1874), French writer, greatest historian of the romantic school.

life, and his healthiness of mind, conspired to exclude him from both. He never knew prosperity and adversity, passion nor satiety: he never had even the experiences which sickness gives; he lived from childhood to the age of eighty-five in boyish health. He knew no dejection, no heaviness of heart. He never felt life a sore and a weary burthen. He was a boy to the last. Self-consciousness, that dæmon of the men of genius of our time, from Wordsworth to Byron, from Goethe to Chateaubriand, and to which this age owes so much both of its cheerful and its mournful wisdom, never was awakened in him. How much of human nature slumbered in him he knew not, neither can we know. He had never been made alive to the unseen influences which were acting on himself, nor consequently on his fellow-creatures. Other ages and other nations were a blank to him for purposes of instruction. He measured them but by one standard; their knowledge of facts, and their capability to take correct views of utility, and merge all other objects in it. His own lot was cast in a generation of the leanest and barrenest men whom England had yet produced, and he was an old man when a better race came in with the present century. He saw accordingly in man little but what the vulgarest eye can see; recognised no diversities of character but such as he who runs may read. Knowing so little of human feelings, he knew still less of the influences by which those feelings are formed: all the more subtle workings both of the mind upon itself, and of external things upon the mind, escaped him; and no one, probably, who, in a highly instructed age, ever attempted to give a rule to all human conduct, set out with a more limited conception either of the agencies by which human conduct *is*, or of those by which it *should* be, influenced.

. . . .

Man is never recognised by him as a being capable of pursuing spiritual perfection as an end; of desiring, for its own sake, the conformity of his own character to his standard of excellence, without hope of good or fear of evil from other source than his own inward consciousness. Even in the more limited form of Conscience, this great fact in human nature escapes him. Nothing is more curious than the absence of recognition in any of his writings of the existence of conscience, as a thing distinct from philanthropy, from affection for God or man, and from self-interest in this world or in the next. There is a studied abstinence from any of the phrases which, in the mouths of others, import the acknowledgement of such a fact.* If we find the words 'Conscience,' 'Principle,' 'Moral Rectitude,' 'Moral Duty,' in his Table of the Springs of Action,[5] it is among the synonymes of the 'love of reputation;' with an intimation as to the two former phrases, that they are also sometimes synonymous with the *religious* motive, or the motive of *sympathy*. The feeling of moral approbation or disapprobation properly so called, either towards ourselves or our fellow-creatures, he seems unaware of the existence of; and neither the word *self-respect*, nor the idea to which that word is appropriated, occurs even once, so far as our recollection serves us, in his whole writings.

Nor is it only the moral part of man's nature, in the strict sense of the term—the desire of perfection, or the feeling of an approving or of an accusing conscience—that he overlooks; he but faintly recognises, as a fact in human nature, the pursuit of any other ideal end for its own sake. The sense of *honour*, and personal dignity—that feeling of personal exaltation and degradation which acts independently of other people's opinion, or even in defiance of it; the love of *beauty*, the passion of the artist; the love of *order*, of congruity, of consistency in all things, and conformity to their end; the love of *power*, not in the limited form of power over other human beings, but abstract power, the power of making our volitions effectual; the love of *action*, the thirst for movement and activity, a principle

* In a passage in the last volume of his book on Evidence, and possibly in one or two other places, the 'love of justice' is spoken of as a feeling inherent in almost all mankind. It is impossible, without explanations now unattainable, to ascertain what sense is to be put upon casual expressions so inconsistent with the general tenor of his philosophy. (Mill's note.)

[5] Bentham's work by this name was published in 1815.

scarcely of less influence in human life than its opposite, the love of ease:—None of these powerful constituents of human nature are thought worthy of a place among the 'Springs of Action;' and though there is possibly no one of them of the existence of which an acknowledgment might not be found in some corner of Bentham's writings, no conclusions are ever founded on the acknowledgment. Man, that most complex being, is a very simple one in his eyes. Even under the head of *sympathy*, his recognition does not extend to the more complex forms of the feeling—the love of *loving*, the need of a sympathising support, or of objects of admiration and reverence. If he thought at all of any of the deeper feelings of human nature, it was but as idiosyncrasies of taste, with which the moralist no more than the legislator had any concern, further than to prohibit such as were mischievous among the actions to which they might chance to lead. To say either that man should, or that he should not, take pleasure in one thing, displeasure in another, appeared to him as much an act of despotism in the moralist as in the political ruler.

It would be most unjust to Bentham to surmise (as narrow-minded and passionate adversaries are apt in such cases to do) that this picture of human nature was copied from himself; that all those constituents of humanity which he rejected from his table of motives, were wanting in his own breast. The unusual strength of his early feelings of virtue, was, as we have seen, the original cause of all his speculations; and a noble sense of morality, and especially of justice, guides and pervades them all. But having been early accustomed to keep before his mind's eye the happiness of mankind (or rather of the whole sentient world), as the only thing desirable in itself, or which rendered anything else desirable, he confounded all disinterested feelings which he found in himself, with the desire of general happiness: just as some religious writers, who loved virtue for its own sake as much perhaps as men could do, habitually confounded their love of virtue with their fear of hell. It would have required greater subtlety than Bentham possessed, to distinguish from each other, feelings which, from long habit, always acted in the same direction; and his want of imagination prevented him from reading the distinction, where it is legible enough, in the hearts of others.

Accordingly, he has not been followed in this grand oversight by any of the able men who, from the extent of their intellectual obligations to him, have been regarded as his disciples. They may have followed him in his doctrine of utility, and in his rejection of a moral sense as the test of right and wrong: but while repudiating it as such, they have, with Hartley,[6] acknowledged it as a fact in human nature; they have endeavoured to account for it, to assign its laws: nor are they justly chargeable either with undervaluing this part of our nature, or with any disposition to throw it into the background of their speculations. If any part of the influence of this cardinal error has extended itself to them, it is circuitously, and through the effect on their minds of other parts of Bentham's doctrines.

Sympathy, the only disinterested motive which Bentham recognised, he felt the inadequacy of, except in certain limited cases, as a security for virtuous action. Personal affection, he well knew, is as liable to operate to the injury of third parties, and requires as much to be kept under government, as any other feeling whatever: and general philanthropy, considered as a motive influencing mankind in general, he estimated at its true value when divorced from the feeling of duty—as the very weakest and most unsteady of all feelings. There remained, as a motive by which mankind are influenced, and by which they may be guided to their good, only personal interest. Accordingly, Bentham's idea of the world is that of a collection of persons pursuing each his separate interest or pleasure, and the prevention of whom from jostling one another more than is unavoidable, may be attempted by hopes and fears derived from three sources—the law, religion, and public opinion. To these three powers, considered as binding human conduct, he gave the name of *sanctions:* the *political*

[6] David Hartley (1705–1757), a medical practitioner, developed a physiological psychology in *Observations on Man* (1749).

sanction, operating by the rewards and penalties of the law; the *religious* sanction, by those expected from the Ruler of the Universe; and the *popular,* which he characteristically calls also the *moral* sanction, operating through the pains and pleasures arising from the favour or disfavour of our fellow-creatures.

Such is Bentham's theory of the world. And now, in a spirit neither of apology nor of censure, but of calm appreciation, we are to inquire how far this view of human nature and life will carry any one:—how much it will accomplish in morals, and how much in political and social philosophy: what it will do for the individual, and what for society.

It will do nothing for the conduct of the individual, beyond prescribing some of the more obvious dictates of worldly prudence, and outward probity and beneficence. There is no need to expatiate on the deficiencies of a system of ethics which does not pretend to aid individuals in the formation of their own character; which recognises no such wish as that of self-culture, we may even say no such power, as existing in human nature; and if it did recognise, could furnish little assistance to that great duty, because it overlooks the existence of about half of the whole number of mental feelings which human beings are capable of, including all those of which the direct objects are states of their own mind.

Morality consists of two parts. One of these is self-education; the training, by the human being himself, of his affections and will. That department is a blank in Bentham's system. The other and co-equal part, the regulation of his outward actions, must be altogether halting and imperfect without the first: for how can we judge in what manner many an action will affect even the worldly interests of ourselves or others, unless we take in, as part of the question, its influence on the regulation of our, or their, affections and desires? A moralist on Bentham's principles may get as far as this, that he ought not to slay, burn, or steal; but what will be his qualifications for regulating the nicer shades of human behaviour, or for laying down even the greater moralities as to those facts in human life which are liable to influence the depths of the character quite independently of any influence on worldly circumstances—such, for instance, as the sexual relations, or those of family in general, or any other social and sympathetic connexions of an intimate kind? The moralities of these questions depend essentially on considerations which Bentham never so much as took into the account; and when he happened to be in the right, it was always, and necessarily, on wrong or insufficient grounds.

It is fortunate for the world that Bentham's taste lay rather in the direction of jurisprudential than of properly ethical inquiry. Nothing expressly of the latter kind has been published under his name, except the 'Deontology'—a book scarcely ever, in our experience, alluded to by any admirer of Bentham without deep regret that it ever saw the light. We did not expect from Bentham correct systematic views of ethics, or a sound treatment of any question the moralities of which require a profound knowledge of the human heart; but we did anticipate that the greater moral questions would have been boldly plunged into, and at least a searching criticism produced of the received opinions; we did not expect that the *petite morale* [7] almost alone would have been treated, and that with the most pedantic minuteness, and on the *quid pro quo* principles which regulate trade. The book has not even the value which would belong to an authentic exhibition of the legitimate consequences of an erroneous line of thought; for the style proves it to have been so entirely rewritten, that it is impossible to tell how much or how little of it is Bentham's. The collected edition, now in progress, will not, it is said, include Bentham's religious writings; these, although we think most of them of exceedingly small value, are at least his, and the world has a right to whatever light they throw upon the constitution of his mind. But the omission of the 'Deontology' would be an act of editorial discretion which we should deem entirely justifiable.

If Bentham's theory of life can do so little for the individual, what can it do for society?

---

[7] Petty, prudential morality of everyday conduct.

It will enable a society which has attained a certain state of spiritual development, and the maintenance of which in that state is otherwise provided for, to prescribe the rules by which it may protect its material interests. It will do nothing (except sometimes as an instrument in the hands of a higher doctrine) for the spiritual interests of society; nor does it suffice of itself even for the material interests. That which alone causes any material interests to exist, which alone enables any body of human beings to exist as a society, is national character: *that* it is, which causes one nation to succeed in what it attempts, another to fail; one nation to understand and aspire to elevated things, another to grovel in mean ones; which makes the greatness of one nation lasting, and dooms another to early and rapid decay. The true teacher of the fitting social arrangements for England, France, or America, is the one who can point out how the English, French, or American character can be improved, and how it has been made what it is. A philosophy of laws and institutions, not founded on a philosophy of national character, is an absurdity. But what could Bentham's opinion be worth on national character? How could he, whose mind contained so few and so poor types of individual character, rise to that higher generalization? All he can do is but to indicate means by which, in any given state of the national mind, the material interests of society can be protected; saving the question, of which others must judge, whether the use of those means would have, on the national character, any injurious influence.

We have arrived, then, at a sort of estimate of what a philosophy like Bentham's can do. It can teach the means of organizing and regulating the merely *business* part of the social arrangements. Whatever can be understood or whatever done without reference to moral influences, his philosophy is equal to; where those influences require to be taken into account, it is at fault. He committed the mistake of supposing that the business part of human affairs was the whole of them; all at least that the legislator and the moralist had to do with. Not that he disregarded moral influences when he perceived them;

but his want of imagination, small experience of human feelings, and ignorance of the filiation and connexion of feelings with one another, made this rarely the case.

The business part is accordingly the only province of human affairs which Bentham has cultivated with any success; into which he has introduced any considerable number of comprehensive and luminous practical principles. That is the field of his greatness; and there he is indeed great. He has swept away the accumulated cobwebs of centuries—he has untied knots which the efforts of the ablest thinkers, age after age, had only drawn tighter; and it is no exaggeration to say of him that over a great part of the field he was the first to shed the light of reason.

We turn with pleasure from what Bentham could not do, to what he did. It is an ungracious task to call a great benefactor of mankind to account for not being a greater—to insist upon the errors of a man who has originated more new truths, has given to the world more sound practical lessons, than it ever received, except in a few glorious instances, from any other individual. The unpleasing part of our work is ended. We are now to show the greatness of the man; the grasp which his intellect took of the subjects with which it was fitted to deal; the giant's task which was before him, and the hero's courage and strength with which he achieved it. Nor let that which he did be deemed of small account because its province was limited: man has but the choice to go a little way in many paths, or a great way in only one. The field of Bentham's labours was like the space between two parallel lines; narrow to excess in one direction, in another it reached to infinity.

. . . .

He is chargeable also with another error, which it would be improper to pass over, because nothing has tended more to place him in opposition to the common feelings of mankind, and to give to his philosophy that cold, mechanical, and ungenial air which characterizes the popular idea of a Benthamite. This error, or rather one-sidedness, belongs to him not as a utilitarian, but as a moralist by profession, and in common with almost all professed moralists, whether religious or philosophical: it is that of treating the *moral* view of actions and characters, which is unquestionably the first and most important mode of looking at them, as if it were the sole one: whereas it is only one of three, by all of which our sentiments towards the human being may be, ought to be, and without entirely crushing our own nature cannot but be, materially influenced. Every human action has three aspects: its *moral* aspect, or that of its *right* and *wrong;* its *æsthetic* aspect, or that of its *beauty;* its *sympathetic* aspect, or that of its *loveableness.* The first addresses itself to our reason and conscience; the second to our imagination; the third to our human fellow-feeling. According to the first, we approve or disapprove; according to the second, we admire or despise; according to the third, we love, pity, or dislike. The morality of an action depends on its foreseeable consequences; its beauty, and its loveableness, or the reverse, depend on the qualities which it is evidence of. Thus, a lie is *wrong,* because its effect is to mislead, and because it tends to destroy the confidence of man in man; it is also *mean,* because it is cowardly—because it proceeds from not daring to face the consequences of telling the truth—or at best is evidence of want of that *power* to compass our ends by straightforward means, which is conceived as properly belonging to every person not deficient in energy or in understanding. The action of Brutus [8] in sentencing his sons was *right,* because it was executing a law essential to the freedom of his country, against persons of whose guilt there was no doubt: it was *admirable,* because it evinced a rare degree of patriotism, courage, and self-control; but there was nothing *loveable* in it; it affords either no presumption in regard to loveable qualities, or a presumption of their deficiency. If one of the sons had engaged in the conspiracy from affection for the other, his action would have been loveable, though neither moral nor admirable. It is not possible for any sophistry to confound these three modes of

---

[8] Lucius Junius Brutus (*fl.* 510 B.C.) helped to end the Tarquin dynasty and is said to have killed his sons for plotting to restore the Tarquins.

viewing an action; but it is very possible to adhere to one of them exclusively, and lose sight of the rest. Sentimentality consists in setting the last two of the three above the first; the error of moralists in general, and of Bentham, is to sink the two latter entirely. This is pre-eminently the case with Bentham: he both wrote and felt as if the moral standard ought not only to be paramount (which it ought), but to be alone; as if it ought to be the sole master of all our actions, and even of all our sentiments; as if either to admire or like, or despise or dislike a person for any action which neither does good nor harm, or which does not do a good or a harm proportioned to the sentiment entertained, were an injustice and a prejudice. He carried this so far, that there were certain phrases which, being expressive of what he considered to be this groundless liking or aversion, he could not bear to hear pronounced in his presence. Among these phrases were those of *good* and *bad taste*. He thought it an insolent piece of dogmatism in one person to praise or condemn another in a matter of taste: as if men's likings and dislikings, on things in themselves indifferent, were not full of the most important inferences as to every point of their character; as if a person's tastes did not show him to be wise or a fool, cultivated or ignorant, gentle or rough, sensitive or callous, generous or sordid, benevolent or selfish, conscientious or depraved.

Connected with the same topic are Bentham's peculiar opinions on poetry. Much more has been said than there is any foundation for, about his contempt for the pleasures of imagination, and for the fine arts. Music was throughout life his favourite amusement; painting, sculpture, and the other arts addressed to the eye, he was so far from holding in any contempt, that he occasionally recognises them as means employable for important social ends; though his ignorance of the deeper springs of human character prevented him (as it prevents most Englishmen) from suspecting how profoundly such things enter into the moral nature of man, and into the education both of the individual and of the race. But towards poetry in the narrower sense, that which employs the language of words, he entertained no favour. Words, he thought, were perverted from their proper office when they were employed in uttering anything but precise logical truth. He says, somewhere in his works,[9] that, 'quantity of pleasure being equal, push-pin is as good as poetry:' but this is only a paradoxical way of stating what he would equally have said of the things which he most valued and admired. Another aphorism is attributed to him, which is much more characteristic of his view of this subject: 'All poetry is misrepresentation.' Poetry, he thought, consisted essentially in exaggeration for effect: in proclaiming some one view of a thing very emphatically, and suppressing all the limitations and qualifications. This trait of character seems to us a curious example of what Mr. Carlyle strikingly calls 'the completeness of limited men.' Here is a philosopher who is happy within his narrow boundary as no man of indefinite range ever was: who flatters himself that he is so completely emancipated from the essential law of poor human intellect, by which it can only see one thing at a time well, that he can even turn round upon the imperfection and lay a solemn interdict upon it. Did Bentham really suppose that it is in poetry only that propositions cannot be exactly true, cannot contain in themselves all the limitations and qualifications with which they require to be taken when applied to practice? We have seen how far his own prose propositions are from realizing this Utopia; and even the attempt to approach it would be incompatible not with poetry merely, but with oratory, and popular writing of every kind. Bentham's charge is true to the fullest extent; all writing which undertakes to make men feel truths as well as see them, does take up one point at a time, does seek to impress that, to drive that home, to make it sink into and colour the whole mind of the reader or hearer. It is justified in doing so, if the portion of truth which it thus enforces be that which is called for by the occasion. All writing addressed to the feelings has a natural tendency to exag-

[9] *The Rationale of Reward* (1825).

geration; but Bentham should have remembered that in this, as in many things, we must aim at too much, to be assured of doing enough.

From the same principle in Bentham came the intricate and involved style, which makes his later writings books for the student only, not the general reader. It was from his perpetually aiming at impracticable precision. Nearly all his earlier, and many parts of his later writings, are models, as we have already observed, of light, playful, and popular style: a Benthamiana might be made of passages worthy of Addison or Goldsmith. But in his later years and more advanced studies, he fell into a Latin or German structure of sentence, foreign to the genius of the English language. He could not bear, for the sake of clearness and the reader's ease, to say, as ordinary men are content to do, a little more than the truth in one sentence, and correct it in the next. The whole of the qualifying remarks which he intended to make, he insisted upon imbedding as parentheses in the very middle of the sentence itself. And thus the sense being so long suspended, and attention being required to the accessory ideas before the principal idea had been properly seized, it became difficult, without some practice, to make out the train of thought. It is fortunate that so many of the most important parts of his writings are free from this defect. We regard it as a *reductio ad absurdum* of his objection to poetry. In trying to write in a manner against which the same objection should not lie, he could stop nowhere short of utter unreadableness, and after all attained no more accuracy than is compatible with opinions as imperfect and one-sided as those of any poet or sentimentalist breathing. Judge then in what state literature and philosophy would be, and what chance they would have of influencing the multitude, if his objection were allowed, and all styles of writing banished which would not stand his test.

We must here close this brief and imperfect view of Bentham and his doctrines; in which many parts of the subject have been entirely untouched, and no part done justice to, but which at least proceeds from an intimate familiarity with his writings, and is nearly the first attempt at an impartial estimate of his character as a philosopher, and of the result of his labours to the world.

After every abatement, and it has been seen whether we have made our abatements sparingly—there remains to Bentham an indisputable place among the great intellectual benefactors of mankind. His writings will long form an indispensable part of the education of the highest order of practical thinkers; and the collected edition of them ought to be in the hands of every one who would either understand his age, or take any beneficial part in the great business of it.*

* Since the first publication of this paper, Lord Brougham's brilliant series of characters has been published, including a sketch of Bentham. Lord Brougham's view of Bentham's characteristics agrees in the main points, so far as it goes, with the result of our more minute examination, but there is an imputation cast upon Bentham, of a jealous and splenetic disposition in private life, of which we feel called upon to give at once a contradiction and an explanation. It is indispensable to a correct estimate of any of Bentham's dealings with the world, to bear in mind that in everything except abstract speculation he was to the last, what we have called him, essentially a boy. He had the freshness, the simplicity, the confidingness, the liveliness and activity, all the delightful qualities of boyhood, and the weaknesses which are the reverse side of those qualities —the undue importance attached to trifles, the habitual mismeasurement of the practical bearing and value of things, the readiness to be either delighted or offended on inadequate cause. These were the real sources of what was unreasonable in some of his attacks on individuals, and in particular on Lord Brougham, on the subject of his Law Reforms; they were no more the effect of envy or malice, or any really unamiable quality, than the freaks of a pettish child, and are scarcely a fitter subject of censure or criticism. (Mill's note.)

From Coleridge

1840

Mill's misgivings about his essay on Coleridge were of a different kind from those about the essay on Bentham. He was aware that, although he had tried to give a semblance of detachment and symmetry to his comparison of Bentham with Coleridge, nothing in the discussion of Coleridge's work was comparable in severity to the strictures upon Bentham in the earlier essay. In fact, beyond a sneer at his contemptible ignorance of political economy, the discussion of Coleridge contains nothing unfavorable to the man at all. Of Coleridge's character, which could hardly survive a fair comparison with Bentham's, Mill says nothing. In the *Autobiography*, he explains this imbalance, saying that he was writing this article for Benthamites, who, if they had heard of Coleridge at all, had heard no good of him; and that he wanted to present the Romantic reaction to the "negative philosophy" of the eighteenth century in the strongest possible light.

In the essay Mill recommends not only a man but also a method —the dialectical and synthetic method of seeking truth. Opposed thinkers like Bentham and Coleridge, he argues, may actually complement each other; each of them is so thoroughly the master of that portion of truth which he does see that he is blind to its incompleteness. It remains for the disinterested bystander to synthesize into the whole truth the partial truths set forth by exponents of antithetical philosophical positions. Bentham is blind to the truth that lies in traditional opinions, and Coleridge is blind to the truth that lies outside them. It seems to be the way of men of genius, Mill says, to be narrow and exclusive, but this should not prevent us from benefiting by their *depth* of vision, for we can supply from other sources what these one-eyed men leave out of view. In all great controversies in social philosophy, Mill maintains, "both sides were in the right in what they affirmed, though wrong in what they denied."

Mill's theory of controversy and of the way in which to extract the whole truth from "the noisy conflict of half-truths" is linked in this essay with a theory of history. Bentham and Coleridge are made the spokesmen of historical epochs as well as of philosophical schools. Coleridge spoke for the nineteenth-century or Romantic reaction to the dominant philosophy of the eighteenth century; like the reaction he represented, he overlooked what was of value in the philosophy he rejected. Mill sees history as a perpetual oscillation between two conflicting modes of thought, a process in which the only progress consists in approaching closer to the center. Mill deplores this alternation between extremes, yet says hopefully that the opposed powers symbolized by Bentham and Coleridge are "opposite poles of one great force of progression."

Mill did not expect, or want, to convert his *Westminster Review* readers into Coleridgian conservatives. But he did want to show them that although they cannot convert conservatives into liberals, they can persuade conservatives that certain liberal goals are not inconsistent with conservative principles. The essay offers several illustrations of the way in which conservative principles may be conducive to the approval of liberal programs. Mill tells us, for example, that one requisite of civil society is the feeling of loyalty to "*something* which is settled, something permanent, and not to be called in question." This sounds ominously conservative until Mill says that in future this loyalty can only take the form of attachment to the principles of individual freedom and social and political equality. Similarly, Coleridge's defense of the Church Establishment was hardly likely to attract liberals until Mill could show, as he does, how the State might, consistently with the principles Coleridge sets forth, remove education from the hands of the clergy and establish a system of secular instruction.

The essay, then, asks liberals to attend to the philosophy of conservatives for the good of both. If they do, they will encourage the development of rationality within conservative ranks, and, more important, they will provide themselves with intelligent critics and worthy opponents.

The name of Coleridge is one of the few English names of our time which are likely to be oftener pronounced, and to become symbolical of more important things, in proportion as

---

First published in the *London and Westminster Review*, XXXIII (March 1840).

the inward workings of the age manifest themselves more and more in outward facts. Bentham excepted, no Englishman of recent date has left his impress so deeply in the opinions and mental tendencies of those among us who attempt to enlighten their practice by philosophical meditation. If it be true, as Lord Bacon affirms, that a knowledge of the speculative opinions of the men between twenty and thirty years of age is the great source of political prophecy, the existence of Coleridge will show itself by no slight or ambiguous traces in the coming history of our country; for no one has contributed more to shape the opinions of those among its younger men, who can be said to have opinions at all.

The influence of Coleridge, like that of Bentham, extends far beyond those who share in the peculiarities of his religious or philosophical creed. He has been the great awakener in this country of the spirit of philosophy, within the bounds of traditional opinions. He has been, almost as truly as Bentham, 'the great questioner of things established [1];' for a questioner needs not necessarily be an enemy. By Bentham, beyond all others, men have been led to ask themselves, in regard to any ancient or received opinion, Is it true? and by Coleridge, What is the meaning of it? The one took his stand *outside* the received opinion, and surveyed it as an entire stranger to it: the other looked at it from within, and endeavoured to see it with the eyes of a believer in it; to discover by what apparent facts it was at first suggested, and by what appearances it has ever since been rendered continually credible—has seemed, to a succession of persons, to be a faithful interpretation of their experience. Bentham judged a proposition true or false as it accorded or not with the result of his own inquiries; and did not search very curiously into what might be meant by the proposition, when it obviously did not mean what he thought true. With Coleridge, on the contrary, the very fact that any doctrine had been believed by thoughtful men, and received by whole nations or generations of mankind, was part of the problem to be solved, was one of the phenomena to be ac-

[1] Mill quotes his own description from the essay on Bentham.

counted for. And as Bentham's short and easy method of referring all to the selfish interests of aristocracies, or priests, or lawyers, or some other species of impostors, could not satisfy a man who saw so much farther into the complexities of the human intellect and feelings—he considered the long or extensive prevalence of any opinion as a presumption that it was not altogether a fallacy; that, to its first authors at least, it was the result of a struggle to express in words something which had a reality to them, though perhaps not to many of those who have since received the doctrine by mere tradition. The long duration of a belief, he thought, is at least proof of an adaptation in it to some portion or other of the human mind; and if, on digging down to the root, we do not find, as is generally the case, some truth, we shall find some natural want or requirement of human nature which the doctrine in question is fitted to satisfy: among which wants the instincts of selfishness and of credulity have a place, but by no means an exclusive one. From this difference in the points of view of the two philosophers, and from the too rigid adherence of each to his own, it was to be expected that Bentham should continually miss the truth which is in the traditional opinions, and Coleridge that which is out of them, and at variance with them. But it was also likely that each would find, or show the way to finding, much of what the other missed.

It is hardly possible to speak of Coleridge, and his position among his cotemporaries, without reverting to Bentham: they are connected by two of the closest bonds of association —resemblance, and contrast. It would be difficult to find two persons of philosophic eminence more exactly the contrary of one another. Compare their modes of treatment of any subject, and you might fancy them inhabitants of different worlds. They seem to have scarcely a principle or a premise in common. Each of them sees scarcely anything but what the other does not see. Bentham would have regarded Coleridge with a peculiar measure of the good-humoured contempt with which he was accustomed to regard all modes of philosophizing different from his own. Coleridge would probably have made

Bentham one of the exceptions to the enlarged and liberal appreciation which (to the credit of *his* mode of philosophizing) he extended to most thinkers of any eminence, from whom he differed. But contraries, as logicians say, are but *quæ in eodem genere maxime distant*, the things which are farthest from one another in the same kind. These two agreed in being the men who, in their age and country, did most to enforce, by precept and example, the necessity of a philosophy. They agreed in making it their occupation to recal opinions to first principles; taking no proposition for granted without examining into the grounds of it, and ascertaining that it possessed the kind and degree of evidence suitable to its nature. They agreed in recognising that sound theory is the only foundation for sound practice, and that whoever despises theory, let him give himself what airs of wisdom he may, is self-convicted of being a quack. If a book were to be compiled containing all the best things ever said on the rule-of-thumb school of political craftsmanship, and on the insufficiency for practical purposes of what the mere practical man calls experience, it is difficult to say whether the collection would be more indebted to the writings of Bentham or of Coleridge. They agreed, too, in perceiving that the groundwork of all other philosophy must be laid in the philosophy of the mind. To lay this foundation deeply and strongly, and to raise a superstructure in accordance with it, were the objects to which their lives were devoted. They employed, indeed, for the most part, different materials; but as the materials of both were real observations, the genuine product of experience—the results will in the end be found not hostile, but supplementary, to one another. Of their methods of philosophizing, the same thing may be said: they were different, yet both were legitimate logical processes. In every respect the two men are each other's 'completing counterpart:' the strong points of each correspond to the weak points of the other. Whoever could master the premises and combine the methods of both, would possess the entire English philosophy of his age. Coleridge used to say that every one is born either a Platonist or an Aristotelian: it may be similarly affirmed, that every Englishman of the present day is by implication either a Benthamite or a Coleridgian; holds views of human affairs which can only be proved true on the principles either of Bentham or of Coleridge. In one respect, indeed, the parallel fails. Bentham so improved and added to the system of philosophy he adopted, that for his successors he may almost be accounted its founder; while Coleridge, though he has left on the system he inclucated, such traces of himself as cannot fail to be left by any mind of original powers, was anticipated in all the essentials of his doctrine by the great Germans[2] of the latter half of the last century, and was accompanied in it by the remarkable series of their French expositors and followers.[3] Hence, although Coleridge is to Englishmen the type and the main source of that doctrine, he is the creator rather of the shape in which it has appeared among us, than of the doctrine itself.

The time is yet far distant when, in the estimation of Coleridge, and of his influence upon the intellect of our time, anything like unanimity can be looked for. As a poet, Coleridge has taken his place. The healthier taste, and more intelligent canons of poetic criticism, which he was himself mainly instrumental in diffusing, have at length assigned to him his proper rank, as one among the great, and (if we look to the powers shown rather than to the amount of actual achievement) among the greatest, names in our literature. But as a philosopher, the class of thinkers has scarcely yet arisen by whom he is to be judged. The limited philosophical public of this country is as yet too exclusively divided between those to whom Coleridge and the views which he promulgated or defended are everything, and those to whom they are nothing. A true thinker can only be justly estimated when his thoughts have worked their way into minds formed in a different school; have been wrought and moulded into consistency with

[2] Principally Friedrich W. J. von Schelling (1775–1854) and August W. von Schlegel (1767–1845).

[3] Principally Chateaubriand and Germaine de Staël (see "Poems and Romances of Alfred de Vigny," notes 28, 29).

all other true and relevant thoughts; when the noisy conflict of half-truths, angrily denying one another, has subsided, and ideas which seemed mutually incompatible, have been found only to require mutual limitations. This time has not yet come for Coleridge. The spirit of philosophy in England, like that of religion, is still rootedly sectarian. Conservative thinkers and Liberals, transcendentalists and admirers of Hobbes and Locke,[4] regard each other as out of the pale of philosophical intercourse; look upon each other's speculations as vitiated by an original taint, which makes all study of them, except for purposes of attack, useless, if not mischievous. An error much the same as if Kepler had refused to profit by Ptolemy's or Tycho's[5] observations, because those astronomers believed that the sun moved round the earth; or as if Priestley and Lavoisier, because they differed on the doctrine of phlogiston,[6] had rejected each other's chemical experiments. It is even a still greater error than either of these. For, among the truths long recognised by Continental philosophers, but which very few Englishmen have yet arrived at, one is, the importance, in the present imperfect state of mental and social science, of antagonist modes of thought: which, it will one day be felt, are as necessary to one another in speculation, as mutually checking powers are in a political constitution. A clear insight, indeed, into this necessity is the only rational or enduring basis of philosophical tolerance; the only condition under which liberality in matters of opinion can be anything better than a polite synonym for indifference between one opinion and another.

---

4 Admirers of Hobbes and Locke would be empiricists.

5 Johannes Kepler (1571–1630), discoverer of laws of planetary motion.—Ptolemy (*fl.* 127–141 or 151), Greco-Egyptian astronomer, mathematician, and geographer.—Tycho Brahe (1546–1601), Danish astronomer.

6 Antoine Laurent Lavoisier (1743–1794), French chemist and physicist, explained combustion as the union of the burning substance with oxygen. Joseph Priestley (1733–1804), English scientist and theologian, said that the flame (phlogiston) was a material part of the substance.

All students of man and society who possess that first requisite for so difficult a study, a due sense of its difficulties, are aware that the besetting danger is not so much of embracing falsehood for truth, as of mistaking part of the truth for the whole. It might be plausibly maintained that in almost every one of the leading controversies, past or present, in social philosophy, both sides were in the right in what they affirmed, though wrong in what they denied; and that if either could have been made to take the other's views in addition to its own, little more would have been needed to make its doctrine correct. Take for instance the question how far mankind have gained by civilization. One observer is forcibly struck by the multiplication of physical comforts; the advancement and diffusion of knowledge; the decay of superstition; the facilities of mutual intercourse; the softening of manners; the decline of war and personal conflict; the progressive limitation of the tyranny of the strong over the weak; the great works accomplished throughout the globe by the cooperation of multitudes: and he becomes that very common character, the worshipper of 'our enlightened age.' Another fixes his attention, not upon the value of these advantages, but upon the high price which is paid for them; the relaxation of individual energy and courage; the loss of proud and self-relying independence; the slavery of so large a portion of mankind to artificial wants; their effeminate shrinking from even the shadow of pain; the dull unexciting monotony of their lives, and the passionless insipidity, and absence of any marked individuality, in their characters; the contrast between the narrow mechanical understanding, produced by a life spent in executing by fixed rules a fixed task, and the varied powers of the man of the woods, whose subsistence and safety depend at each instant upon his capacity of extemporarily adapting means to ends; the demoralizing effect of great inequalities in wealth and social rank; and the sufferings of the great mass of the people of civilized countries, whose wants are scarcely better provided for than those of the savage, while they are bound by a thousand fetters in lieu of the freedom and excitement which are his compensations. One who attends to these things, and to these exclusively, will be apt to infer that savage life is preferable to civilized; that the work of civilization should as far as possible be undone; and from the premises of Rousseau, he will not improbably be led to the practical conclusions of Rousseau's disciple, Robespierre. No two thinkers can be more entirely at variance than the two we have supposed—the worshippers of Civilization and of Independence, of the present and of the remote past. Yet all that is positive in the opinions of either of them is true; and we see how easy it would be to choose one's path, if either half of the truth were the whole of it, and how great may be the difficulty of framing, as it is necessary to do, a set of practical maxims which combine both.

So again, one person sees in a very strong light the need which the great mass of mankind have of being ruled over by a degree of intelligence and virtue superior to their own. He is deeply impressed with the mischief done to the uneducated and uncultivated by weaning them of all habits of reverence, appealing to them as a competent tribunal to decide the most intricate questions, and making them think themselves capable, not only of being a light to themselves, but of giving the law to their superiors in culture. He sees, further, that cultivation, to be carried beyond a certain point, requires leisure; that leisure is the natural attribute of a hereditary aristocracy; that such a body has all the means of acquiring intellectual and moral superiority; and he needs be at no loss to endow them with abundant motives to it. An aristocracy indeed, being human, are, as he cannot but see, not exempt, any more than their inferiors, from the common need of being controlled and enlightened by a still greater wisdom and goodness than their own. For this, however, his reliance is upon reverence for a Higher above them, sedulously inculcated and fostered by the course of their education. We thus see brought together all the elements of a conscientious zealot for an aristocratic government, supporting and supported by an established Christian church. There is truth, and important truth, in this thinker's premises. But there is a thinker of a very different description, in whose premises there is an equal portion of truth. This is he who says, that an average man, even an average member of an aristocracy, if he can postpone the interests of other people to his own calculations or instincts of self-interest, will do so; that all governments in all ages have done so, as far as they were permitted, and generally to a ruinous extent; and that the only possible remedy is a pure democracy, in which the people are their own governors, and can have no selfish interest in oppressing themselves.

Thus it is in regard to every important partial truth; there are always two conflicting modes of thought, one tending to give to that truth too large, the other to give it too small, a place: and the history of opinion is generally an oscillation between these extremes. From the imperfection of the human faculties, it seldom happens that, even in the minds of eminent thinkers, each partial view of their subject passes for its worth, and none for more than its worth. But even if this just balance exist in the mind of the wiser teacher, it will not exist in his disciples, still less in the general mind. He cannot prevent that which is new in his doctrine, and on which, being new, he is forced to insist the most strongly, from making a disproportionate impression. The impetus necessary to overcome the obstacles which resist all novelties of opinion, seldom fails to carry the public mind almost as far on the contrary side of the perpendicular. Thus every excess in either direction determines a corresponding reaction; improvement consisting only in this, that the oscillation, each time, departs rather less widely from the centre, and an ever-increasing tendency is manifested to settle finally in it.

Now the Germano-Coleridgian doctrine is, in our view of the matter, the result of such a reaction. It expresses the revolt of the human mind against the philosophy of the eighteenth century. It is ontological, because that was experimental; conservative, because that was innovative; religious, because so much of that was infidel; concrete and historical, because that was abstract and metaphysical; poetical, because that was matter-of-fact and prosaic. In every respect it flies off in the contrary direction to its predecessor; yet faithful to the general law of improvement last noticed, it is less extreme in its opposition, it denies less of what is true in the doctrine it wars against, than had been the case in any previous philosophic reaction; and in particular, far less than when the philosophy of the eighteenth century triumphed, and so memorably abused its victory, over that which preceded it.

. . . .

No one can calculate what struggles, which the cause of improvement has yet to undergo, might have been spared if the philosophers of the eighteenth century had done anything like justice to the Past. Their mistake was, that they did not acknowledge the historical value of much which had ceased to be useful, nor saw that institutions and creeds, now effete, had rendered essential services to civilization, and still filled a place in the human mind, and in the arrangements of society, which could not without great peril be left vacant. Their mistake was, that they did not recognise in many of the errors which they assailed, corruptions of important truths, and in many of the institutions most cankered with abuse, necessary elements of civilized society, though in a form and vesture no longer suited to the age; and hence they involved, as far as in them lay, many great truths in a common discredit with the errors which had grown up around them. They threw away the shell without preserving the kernel; and attempting to new-model society without the binding forces which hold society together, met with such success as might have been anticipated.

Now we claim, in behalf of the philosophers of the reactionary school—of the school to which Coleridge belongs—that exactly what we blame the philosophers of the eighteenth century for not doing, they have done.

Every reaction in opinion, of course brings into view that portion of the truth which was overlooked before. It was natural that a philosophy which anathematized all that had been going on in Europe from Constantine to Luther, or even to Voltaire, should be succeeded by another, at once a severe critic of the new tendencies of society, and an impassioned vindicator of what was good in the past. This is the easy merit of all Tory and Royalist writers. But the peculiarity of the Germano-Coleridgian school is, that they saw beyond the immediate controversy, to the fundamental principles involved in all such controversies. They were the first (except a solitary thinker here and there) who inquired with any comprehensiveness or depth, into the inductive laws of the existence and growth of human society. They were the first to bring prominently forward the three requisites which we have enumerated, as essential principles of all permanent forms of social existence; as principles, we say, and not as mere accidental advantages inherent in the particular polity or religion which the writer happened to patronize. They were the first who pursued, philosophically and in the spirit of Baconian investigation, not only this inquiry, but others ulterior and collateral to it. They thus produced, not a piece of party advocacy, but a philosophy of society, in the only form in which it is yet possible, that of a philosophy of history; not a defence of particular ethical or religious doctrines, but a contribution, the largest made by any class of thinkers, towards the philosophy of human culture.

The brilliant light which has been thrown upon history during the last half century, has proceeded almost wholly from this school. The disrespect in which history was held by the *philosophes* is notorious; one of the soberest of them, D'Alembert [7] we believe, was the author of the wish that all record whatever of past events could be blotted out. And indeed the ordinary mode of writing history, and the ordinary mode of drawing lessons from it, were almost sufficient to excuse this contempt. But the *philosophes* saw, as usual, what was not true, not what was. It is no wonder that they who looked on the greater part of what had been handed down from the past, as sheer hindrances to man's attaining a well-being which would otherwise be of easy attainment, should content themselves

---

[7] Jean le Rond d'Alembert (1717–1783), French mathematician and philosopher, co-editor of the *Encyclopédie* of 1751.

with a very superificial study of history. But the case was otherwise with those who regarded the maintenance of society at all, and especially its maintenance in a state of progressive advancement, as a very difficult task actually achieved, in however imperfect a manner, for a number of centuries, against the strongest obstacles. It was natural that they should feel a deep interest in ascertaining how this had been effected; and should be led to inquire, both what were the requisites of the permanent existence of the body politic, and what were the conditions which had rendered the preservation of these permanent requisites compatible with perpetual and progressive improvement. And hence that series of great writers and thinkers, from Herder to Michelet,[8] by whom history, which was till then 'a tale told by an idiot, full of sound and fury, signifying nothing,'[9] has been made a science of causes and effects; who, by making the facts and events of the past have a meaning and an intelligible place in the gradual evolution of humanity, have at once given history, even to the imagination, an interest like romance, and afforded the only means of predicting and guiding the future, by unfolding the agencies which have produced and still maintain the Present.*

[8] Johann Gottfried von Herder (1744–1803), German philosopher, poet, historian. His most ambitious work was *Outlines of the Philosophy of Man* (1784–1791).–See also "Bentham," note 4.

[9] *Macbeth,* V. v. 26–28.

* There is something at once ridiculous and discouraging in the signs which daily meet us, of the Cimmerian darkness still prevailing in England (wherever recent foreign literature or the speculations of the Coleridgians have not penetrated) concerning the very existence of the views of general history, which have been received throughout the Continent of Europe for the last twenty or thirty years. A writer in Blackwood's Magazine, certainly not the least able publication of our day, nor this the least able writer in it, lately announced, with all the pomp and heraldry of triumphant genius, a discovery which was to disabuse the world of an universal prejudice, and create 'the philosophy of Roman history.' This is, that the Roman empire perished not from outward violence, but from inward decay; and that the barbarian conquerors were the renovators, not the destroyers of its civilization. Why, there is not a schoolboy in France or Germany who did not

The same causes have naturally led the same class of thinkers to do what their predecessors never could have done, for the philosophy of human culture. For the tendency of their speculations compelled them to see in the character of the national education existing in any political society, at once the principal cause of its permanence as a society, and the chief source of its progressiveness: the former by the extent to which that education operated as a system of restraining discipline; the latter by the degree in which it called forth and invigorated the active faculties. Besides, not to have looked upon the culture of the inward man as the problem of problems, would have been incompatible with the belief which many of these philosophers entertained in Christianity, and the recognition by all of them of its historical value, and the prime part which it has acted in the progress of mankind. But here, too, let us not fail to observe, they rose to principles, and did not stick in the particular case. The culture of the human being had been carried to no ordinary height, and human nature had exhibited many of its noblest manifestations, not in Christian countries only, but in the ancient world, in Athens, Sparta, Rome; nay, even barbarians, as the Germans, or still more unmitigated savages, the wild Indians, and again the Chinese, the Egyptians, the Arabs, all had their own education, their own culture; a culture which, whatever might be its tendency upon the whole, had been successful in some respect or other. Every form of polity, every condition of society, whatever else it had done, had formed its type of national character. What that type was, and how it had been made what it was, were questions which the metaphysician might overlook, the historical philosopher could not. Accordingly, the views respecting the various elements of human culture and the causes influencing the forma-

possess this writer's discovery before him; the contrary opinion has receded so far into the past, that it must be rather a learned Frenchman or German who remembers that it was ever held. If the writer in Blackwood had read a line of Guizot (to go no further than the most obvious sources), he would probably have abstained from making himself very ridiculous, and his country, so far as depends upon him, the laughing-stock of Europe. (Mill's note.)

tion of national character, which pervade the writings of the Germano-Coleridgian school, throw into the shade everything which had been effected before, or which has been attempted simultaneously by any other school. Such views are, more than anything else, the characteristic feature of the Goethian period of German literature; and are richly diffused through the historical and critical writings of the new French school, as well as of Coleridge and his followers.

From Inaugural Address to St. Andrews

1867

Mill was elected to the office of Rector of St. Andrews University in 1865. Not being anxious to perform the attendant duties (which were relatively few), he wished to decline the honor, but he and the university authorities finally agreed to put off the inaugural address until 1867. According to the philosopher Alexander Bain, who did not much care for the lecture, its delivery took almost three hours.

The length of the address is not surprising in view of the variety of subjects Mill tried to cover. He begins by linking education to the hopes that each generation entertains for raising the subsequent generation above its own level. He then makes clear that the proper function of a university is not professional training but the production, by means of a liberal education, of "capable and cultivated human beings." A liberal education, he continues, properly implies training in the method of the sciences, rather than in a particular science, and in the philosophy of knowledge, always assuming that knowledge itself has been gained elsewhere. The end of a liberal education is nothing less than "the strengthening, exalting, purifying, and beautifying of our common nature"; but each department of culture helps to realize this end in its own way, which Mill now proceeds to define.

As might be expected, he says that both literature and science must be studied, and he warns against the dangers of specialization. Perhaps most interesting in the lecture is Mill's justification for the study of ancient literature and language, and his comparison of the merits of ancient and modern literature. Mill argues that the only cure for parochialism is knowledge of the language and literature of another cultivated people, and that the best cure, because it supplies the most of that which is both valuable and wanting to England, is the language and literature of the ancients.

Linked with the defense of the study of ancient literature is the last section of the lecture, which defines the value of aesthetic education. Here Mill asserts that a man who is intellectually astute and morally sound is yet incomplete as a human being if his feelings have not been educated by poetry and art. English contempt for art, he says, is one of the chief reasons for lack of sympathy and comprehension between England and the nations of Europe. He assigns as the causes of this contempt the English business spirit and English Puritanism. Admitting that Puritanism has given the English a kind of moral superiority over their neighbors, he nevertheless charges that Puritan morality is largely of a negative kind, and that the love of good, as distinct from the hatred of evil, cannot be inspired except through that cultivation of feeling and widening of sympathy which is achieved by poetry. The high note of the lecture is struck by Mill's eloquent tribute to poetry's power to inspire moral idealism.

In complying with the custom which prescribes that the person whom you have called by your suffrages to the honorary presidency of your University should embody in an Address a few thoughts on the subjects which most nearly concern a seat of liberal education; let me begin by saying, that this usage appears to me highly commendable. Education, in its larger sense, is one of the most inexhaustible of all topics. Though there is hardly any subject on which so much has been written, by so many of the wisest men, it is as fresh to those who come to it with a fresh mind, a mind not hopelessly filled full with other people's conclusions, as it was to the first explorers of it: and notwithstanding the great mass of excellent things which have been said respecting it, no thoughtful person finds any lack of things both great and small still waiting to be said, or waiting to be developed and followed out to their consequences. Education, moreover, is one of the subjects which most essentially require to be considered by various minds, and from a variety of points of view. For, of all many-sided subjects, it is the one which has the greatest number of sides. Not only does it include whatever we do for ourselves, and whatever is done for us by others, for the express purpose of bring-

---

From *Inaugural Address Delivered to the University of St. Andrews* (London: Longmans, Green, Reader, and Dyer, 1867).

ing us somewhat nearer to the perfection of our nature; it does more: in its largest acceptation, it comprehends even the indirect effects produced on character and on the human faculties, by things of which the direct purposes are quite different; by laws, by forms of government, by the industrial arts, by modes of social life; nay even by physical facts not dependent on human will; by climate, soil, and local position. Whatever helps to shape the human being; to make the individual what he is, or hinder him from being what he is not—is part of his education. And a very bad education it often is; requiring all that can be done by cultivated intelligence and will, to counteract its tendencies. To take an obvious instance; the niggardliness of Nature in some places, by engrossing the whole energies of the human being in the mere preservation of life, and her over-bounty in others, affording a sort of brutish subsistence on too easy terms, with hardly any exertion of the human faculties, are both hostile to the spontaneous growth and development of the mind; and it is at those two extremes of the scale that we find human societies in the state of most unmitigated savagery. I shall confine myself, however, to education in the narrower sense; the culture which each generation purposely gives to those who are to be its successors, in order to qualify them for at least keeping up, and if possible for raising, the level of improvement which has been attained. Nearly all here present are daily occupied either in receiving or in giving this sort of education: and the part of it which most concerns you at present is that in which you are yourselves engaged—the stage of education which is the appointed business of a national University.

The proper function of an University in national education is tolerably well understood. At least there is a tolerably general agreement about what an University is not. It is not a place of professional education. Universities are not intended to teach the knowledge required to fit men for some special mode of gaining their livelihood. Their object is not to make skilful lawyers, or physicians, or engineers, but capable and cultivated human beings. It is very right that there should be public facilities for the study of professions. It is well that there should be Schools of Law, and of Medicine, and it would be well if there were schools of engineering, and the industrial arts. The countries which have such institutions are greatly the better for them; and there is something to be said for having them in the same localities, and under the same general superintendence, as the establishments devoted to education properly so called. But these things are no part of what every generation owes to the next, as that on which its civilization and worth will principally depend. They are needed only by a comparatively few, who are under the strongest private inducements to acquire them by their own efforts; and even those few do not require them until after their education, in the ordinary sense, has been completed. Whether those whose speciality they are, will learn them as a branch of intelligence or as a mere trade, and whether, having learnt them, they will make a wise and conscientious use of them or the reverse, depends less on the manner in which they are taught their profession, than upon what sort of minds they bring to it—what kind of intelligence, and of conscience, the general system of education has developed in them. Men are men before they are lawyers, or physicians, or merchants, or manufacturers; and if you make them capable and sensible men, they will make themselves capable and sensible lawyers or physicians. What professional men should carry away with them from an University, is not professional knowledge, but that which should direct the use of their professional knowledge, and bring the light of general culture to illuminate the technicalities of a special pursuit. Men may be competent lawyers without general education, but it depends on general education to make them philosophic lawyers—who demand, and are capable of apprehending, principles, instead of merely cramming their memory with details. And so of all other useful pursuits, mechanical included. Education makes a man a more intelligent shoemaker, if that be his occupation, but not by teaching him how to make shoes; it does so by the mental exercise it gives, and the habits it impresses.

This, then, is what a mathematician would call the higher limit of University education: its province ends where education, ceasing to be general, branches off into departments adapted to the individual's destination in life. The lower limit is more difficult to define. An University is not concerned with elementary instruction: the pupil is supposed to have acquired that before coming here. But where does elementary instruction end, and the higher studies begin? Some have given a very wide extension to the idea of elementary instruction. According to them, it is not the office of an University to give instruction in single branches of knowledge from the commencement. What the pupil should be taught here (they think), is to methodize his knowledge: to look at every separate part of it in its relation to the other parts, and to the whole; combining the partial glimpses which he has obtained of the field of human knowledge at different points, into a general map, if I may so speak, of the entire region; observing how all knowledge is connected, how we ascend to one branch by means of another, how the higher modifies the lower, and the lower helps us to understand the higher; how every existing reality is a compound of many properties, of which each science or distinct mode of study reveals but a small part, but the whole of which must be included to enable us to know it truly as a fact in Nature, and not as a mere abstraction.

This last stage of general education, destined to give the pupil a comprehensive and connected view of the things which he has already learnt separately, includes a philosophic study of the Methods of the sciences; the modes in which the human intellect proceeds from the known to the unknown. We must be taught to generalize our conception of the resources which the human mind possesses for the exploration of nature; to understand how man discovers the real facts of the world, and by what tests he can judge whether he has really found them. And doubtless this is the crown and consummation of a liberal education: but before we restrict an University to this highest department of instruction–before we confine it to teaching, not knowledge, but the philosophy of knowledge–we must be assured that the knowledge itself has been acquired elsewhere. Those who take this view of the function of an University are not wrong in thinking that the schools, as distinguished from the universities, ought to be adequate to teaching every branch of general instruction required by youth, so far as it can be studied apart from the rest. But where are such schools to be found? Since science assumed its modern character, nowhere: and in these islands even less than elsewhere. This ancient kingdom, thanks to its great religious reformers, had the inestimable advantage, denied to its southern sister, of excellent parish schools, which gave, really and not in pretence, a considerable amount of valuable literary instruction to the bulk of the population, two centuries earlier than in any other country. But schools of a still higher description have been, even in Scotland, so few and inadequate, that the Universities have had to perform largely the functions which ought to be performed by schools; receiving students at an early age, and undertaking not only the work for which the schools should have prepared them, but much of the preparation itself. Every Scottish University is not an University only, but a High School, to supply the deficiency of other schools. And if the English Universities do not do the same, it is not because the same need does not exist, but because it is disregarded. Youths come to the Scottish Universities ignorant, and are there taught. The majority of those who come to the English Universities come still more ignorant, and ignorant they go away.

In point of fact, therefore, the office of a Scottish University comprises the whole of a liberal education, from the foundations upwards. And the scheme of your Universities has, almost from the beginning, really aimed at including the whole, both in depth and in breadth. You have not, as the English Universities so long did, confined all the stress of your teaching, all your real effort to teach, within the limits of two subjects, the classical languages and mathematics. You did not wait till the last few years to establish a Natural Science and a Moral Science Tripos.[1] Instruction in both those departments

[1] Honor examination at Cambridge.

was organized long ago: and your teachers of those subjects have not been nominal professors, who did not lecture: some of the greatest names in physical and in moral science have taught in your Universities, and by their teaching contributed to form some of the most distinguished intellects of the last and present centuries. To comment upon the course of education at the Scottish Universities is to pass in review every essential department of general culture. The best use, then, which I am able to make of the present occasion, is to offer a few remarks on each of those departments, considered in its relation to human cultivation at large: adverting to the nature of the claims which each has to a place in liberal education; in what special manner they each conduce to the improvement of the individual mind and the benefit of the race; and how they all conspire to the common end, the strengthening, exalting, purifying, and beautifying of our common nature, and the fitting out of mankind with the necessary mental implements for the work they have to perform through life.

Let me first say a few words on the great controversy of the present day with regard to the higher education, the difference which most broadly divides educational reformers and conservatives; the vexed question between the ancient languages and the modern sciences and arts; whether general education should be classical—let me use a wider expression, and say literary—or scientific. A dispute as endlessly, and often as fruitlessly agitated as that old controversy which it resembles, made memorable by the names of Swift[2] and Sir William Temple in England and Fontenelle in France[3]—the contest for superiority between the ancients and the moderns. This question, whether we should be taught the classics or the sciences, seems to me, I confess, very like a dispute whether painters should cultivate drawing or colouring, or, to use a more

[2] See *Battle of the Books* (1704).

[3] Sir William Temple (1628–1699), Swift's patron, came out on the side of the ancients in an essay of 1690 on ancient and modern learning. —Bernard le Bovier de Fontenelle (1657–1757), French popularizer of scientific knowledge.

homely illustration, whether a tailor should make coats or trousers. I can only reply by the question, why not both? Can anything deserve the name of a good education which does not include literature and science too? If there were no more to be said than that scientific education teaches us to think, and literary education to express our thoughts, do we not require both? and is not any one a poor, maimed, lopsided fragment of humanity who is deficient in either? We are not obliged to ask ourselves whether it is more important to know the languages or the sciences. Short as life is, and shorter still as we make it by the time we waste on things which are neither business, nor meditation, nor pleasure, we are not so badly off that our scholars need be ignorant of the laws and properties of the world they live in, or our scientific men destitute of poetic feeling and artistic cultivation. I am amazed at the limited conception which many educational reformers have formed to themselves of a human being's power of acquisition. The study of science, they truly say, is indispensable: our present education neglects it: there is truth in this too, though it is not all truth: and they think it impossible to find room for the studies which they desire to encourage, but by turning out, at least from general education, those which are now chiefly cultivated. How absurd, they say, that the whole of boyhood should be taken up in acquiring an imperfect knowledge of two dead languages. Absurd indeed: but is the human mind's capacity to learn, measured by that of Eton and Westminster to teach? I should prefer to see these reformers pointing their attacks against the shameful inefficiency of the schools, public and private, which pretend to teach these two languages and do not. I should like to hear them denounce the wretched methods of teaching, and the criminal idleness and supineness, which waste the entire boyhood of the pupils without really giving to most of them more than a smattering, if even that, of the only kind of knowledge which is even pretended to be cared for. Let us try what conscientious and intelligent teaching can do, before we presume to decide what cannot be done.

Scotland has on the whole, in this respect, been considerably more fortunate than England. Scotch youths have never found it impossible to leave school or the university having learnt somewhat of other things besides Greek and Latin; and why? Because Greek and Latin have been better taught. A beginning of classical instruction has all along been made in the common schools: and the common schools of Scotland, like her Universities, have never been the mere shams that the English Universities were during the last century, and the greater part of the English classical schools still are. The only tolerable Latin grammars for school purposes that I know of, which had been produced in these islands until very lately, were written by Scotchmen. Reason, indeed, is beginning to find its way by gradual infiltration even into English schools, and to maintain a contest, though as yet a very unequal one, against routine. A few practical reformers of school tuition, of whom Arnold [4] was the most eminent, have made a beginning of amendment in many things: but reforms, worthy of the name, are always slow, and reform even of governments and churches is not so slow as that of schools, for there is the great preliminary difficulty of fashioning the instruments: of teaching the teachers. If all the improvements in the mode of teaching languages which are already sanctioned by experience, were adopted into our classical schools, we should soon cease to hear of Latin and Greek as studies which must engross the school years, and render impossible any other acquirements. If a boy learnt Greek and Latin on the same principle on which a mere child learns with such ease and rapidity any modern language, namely, by acquiring some familiarity with the vocabulary by practice and repetition, before being troubled with grammatical rules—those rules being acquired with tenfold greater facility when the cases to which they apply are already familiar to the mind: an average schoolboy, long before the age at which schooling terminates, would be able to read fluently and with intelligent interest any ordinary Latin or Greek author in

[4] Thomas Arnold (1795–1842), headmaster of Rugby, instituted many reforms in public school curriculum and moral tone.

prose or verse, would have a competent knowledge of the grammatical structure of both languages, and have had time besides for an ample amount of scientific instruction. I might go much further; but I am as unwilling to speak out all that I think practicable in this matter, as George Stephenson [5] was about railways, when he calculated the average speed of a train at ten miles an hour, because if he had estimated it higher, the practical men would have turned a deaf ear to him, as that most unsafe character in their estimation, an enthusiast and a visionary. The results have shown, in that case, who was the real practical man. What the results would show in the other case, I will not attempt to anticipate. But I will say confidently, that if the two classical languages were properly taught, there would be no need whatever for ejecting them from the school course, in order to have sufficient time for everything else that need be included therein.

Let me say a few words more on this strangely limited estimate of what it is possible for human beings to learn, resting on a tacit assumption that they are already as efficiently taught as they ever can be. So narrow a conception not only vitiates our idea of education, but actually, if we receive it, darkens our anticipations as to the future progress of mankind. For if the inexorable conditions of human life make it useless for one man to attempt to know more than one thing, what is to become of the human intellect as facts accumulate? In every generation, and now more rapidly than ever, the things which it is necessary that somebody should know are more and more multiplied. Every department of knowledge becomes so loaded with details, that one who endeavours to know it with minute accuracy, must confine himself to a smaller and smaller portion of the whole extent: every science and art must be cut up into subdivisions, until each man's portion, the district which he thoroughly knows, bears about the same ratio to the whole range of useful knowledge that the art of putting on a pin's head does to the field of human industry. Now, if in order to

[5] George Stephenson (1781–1848), English engineer, a noted locomotive builder.

know that little completely, it is necessary to remain wholly ignorant of all the rest, what will soon be the worth of a man, for any human purpose except his own infinitesimal fraction of human wants and requirements? His state will be even worse than that of simple ignorance. Experience proves that there is no one study or pursuit, which, practised to the exclusion of all others, does not narrow and pervert the mind; breeding in it a class of prejudices special to that pursuit, besides a general prejudice, common to all narrow specialities, against large views, from an incapacity to take in and appreciate the grounds of them. We should have to expect that human nature would be more and more dwarfed, and unfitted for great things, by its very proficiency in small ones. But matters are not so bad with us: there is no ground for so dreary an anticipation. It is not the utmost limit of human acquirement to know only one thing, but to combine a minute knowledge of one or a few things with a general knowledge of many things. By a general knowledge I do not mean a few vague impressions. An eminent man, one of whose writings is part of the course of this University, Archbishop Whately,[6] has well discriminated between a general knowledge and a superficial knowledge. To have a general knowledge of a subject is to know only its leading truths, but to know these not superficially but thoroughly, so as to have a true conception of the subject in its great features; leaving the minor details to those who require them for the purposes of their special pursuit. There is no incompatibility between knowing a wide range of subjects up to this point, and some one subject with the completeness required by those who make it their principal occupation. It is this combination which gives an enlightened public: a body of cultivated intellects, each taught by its attainments in its own province what real knowledge is, and knowing enough of other subjects to be able to discern who are those that know them better. The amount of knowledge is not to be lightly estimated, which qualifies us for judging to whom

[6] Richard Whately (1787–1863), a liberal churchman and author of *Logic* (1826) and *Rhetoric* (1828).

we may have recourse for more. The elements of the more important studies being widely diffused, those who have reached the higher summits find a public capable of appreciating their superiority, and prepared to follow their lead. It is thus too that minds are formed capable of guiding and improving public opinion on the greater concerns of practical life. Government and civil society are the most complicated of all subjects accessible to the human mind: and he who would deal competently with them as a thinker, and not as a blind follower of party, requires not only a general knowledge of the leading facts of life, both moral and material, but an understanding exercised and disciplined in the principles and rules of sound thinking, up to a point which neither the experience of life, nor any one science or branch of knowledge, affords. Let us understand, then, that it should be our aim in learning, not merely to know the one thing which is to be our principal occupation, as well as it can be known, but to do this and also to know something of all the great subjects of human interest: taking care to know that something accurately; marking well the dividing line between what we know accurately and what we do not: and remembering that our object should be to obtain a true view of nature and life in their broad outline, and that it is idle to throw away time upon the details of anything which is to form no part of the occupation of our practical energies.

It by no means follows, however, that every useful branch of general, as distinct from professional, knowledge, should be included in the curriculum of school or university studies. There are things which are better learnt out of school, or when the school years, and even those usually passed in a Scottish university, are over. I do not agree with those reformers who would give a regular and prominent place in the school or university course to modern languages. This is not because I attach small importance to the knowledge of them. No one can in our age be esteemed a well-instructed person who is not familiar with at least the French language, so as to read French books with ease; and there is great use in cultivating a familiarity with German. But living languages are so much more easily acquired by intercourse with those who use them in daily life; a few months in the country itself, if properly employed, go so much farther than as many years of school lessons; that it is really waste of time for those to whom that easier mode is attainable, to labour at them with no help but that of books and masters: and it will in time be made attainable, through international schools and colleges, to many more than at present. Universities do enough to facilitate the study of modern languages, if they give a mastery over that ancient language which is the foundation of most of them, and the possession of which makes it easier to learn four or five of the continental languages than it is to learn one of them without it. Again, it has always seemed to me a great absurdity that history and geography should be taught in schools; except in elementary schools for the children of the labouring classes, whose subsequent access to books is limited. Who ever really learnt history and geography except by private reading? and what an utter failure a system of education must be, if it has not given the pupil a sufficient taste for reading to seek for himself those most attractive and easily intelligible of all kinds of knowledge? Besides, such history and geography as can be taught in schools exercise none of the faculties of the intelligence except the memory. An University is indeed the place where the student should be introduced to the Philosophy of History; where Professors who not merely know the facts but have exercised their minds on them, should initiate him into the causes and explanation, so far as within our reach, of the past life of mankind in its principal features. Historical criticism, also—the tests of historical truth—are a subject to which his attention may well be drawn in this stage of his education. But of the mere facts of history, as commonly accepted, what educated youth of any mental activity does not learn as much as is necessary, if he is simply turned loose into an historical library? What he needs on this, and on most other matters of common information, is not that he should be taught it in boyhood, but that abundance of books should be accessible to him.

The only languages, then, and the only literature, to which I would allow a place in the ordinary curriculum, are those of the Greeks and Romans; and to these I would preserve the position in it which they at present occupy. That position is justified, by the great value, in education, of knowing well some other cultivated language and literature than one's own, and by the peculiar value of those particular languages and literatures.

There is one purely intellectual benefit from a knowledge of languages, which I am specially desirous to dwell on. Those who have seriously reflected on the causes of human error, have been deeply impressed with the tendency of mankind to mistake words for things. Without entering into the metaphysics of the subject, we know how common it is to use words glibly and with apparent propriety, and to accept them confidently when used by others, without ever having had any distinct conception of the things denoted by them. To quote again from Archbishop Whately, it is the habit of mankind to mistake familiarity for accurate knowledge. As we seldom think of asking the meaning of what we see every day, so when our ears are used to the sound of a word or a phrase, we do not suspect that it conveys no clear idea to our minds, and that we should have the utmost difficulty in defining it, or expressing, in any other words, what we think we understand by it. Now it is obvious in what manner this bad habit tends to be corrected by the practice of translating with accuracy from one language to another, and hunting out the meanings expressed in a vocabulary with which we have not grown familiar by early and constant use. I hardly know any greater proof of the extraordinary genius of the Greeks, than that they were able to make such brilliant achievements in abstract thought, knowing, as they generally did, no language but their own. But the Greeks did not escape the effects of this deficiency. Their greatest intellects, those who laid the foundation of philosophy and of all our intellectual culture, Plato and Aristotle, are continually led away by words; mistaking the accidents of language for real relations in nature, and supposing that things which have the same name in the Greek tongue must be the same in their own essence. There is a well-known saying of Hobbes, the far-reaching significance of which you will more and more appreciate in proportion to the growth of your own intellect: "Words are the counters of wise men, but the money of fools." [7] With the wise man a word stands for the fact which it represents; to the fool it is itself the fact. To carry on Hobbes' metaphor, the counter is far more likely to be taken for merely what it is, by those who are in the habit of using many different kinds of counters. But besides the advantage of possessing another cultivated language, there is a further consideration equally important. Without knowing the language of a people, we never really know their thoughts, their feelings, and their type of character: and unless we do possess this knowledge, of some other people than ourselves, we remain, to the hour of our death, with our intellects only half expanded. Look at a youth who has never been out of his family circle: he never dreams of any other opinions or ways of thinking than those he has been bred up in; or, if he has heard of any such, attributes them to some moral defect, or inferiority of nature or education. If his family are Tory, he cannot conceive the possibility of being a Liberal; if Liberal, of being a Tory. What the notions and habits of a single family are to a boy who has had no intercourse beyond it, the notions and habits of his own country are to him who is ignorant of every other. Those notions and habits are to him human nature itself; whatever varies from them is an unaccountable aberration which he cannot mentally realize: the idea that any other ways can be right, or as near an approach to right as some of his own, is inconceivable to him. This does not merely close his eyes to the many things which every country still has to learn from others: it hinders every country from reaching the improvement which it could otherwise at-

[7] *Leviathan* (1651), I. iv. 15.

tain by itself. We are not likely to correct any of our opinions or mend any of our ways, unless we begin by conceiving that they are capable of amendment: but merely to know that foreigners think differently from ourselves, without understanding why they do so, or what they really do think, does but confirm us in our self-conceit, and connect our national vanity with the preservation of our own peculiarities. Improvement consists in bringing our opinions into nearer agreement with facts; and we shall not be likely to do this while we look at facts only through glasses coloured by those very opinions. But since we cannot divest ourselves of preconceived notions, there is no known means of eliminating their influence but by frequently using the differently coloured glasses of other people: and those of other nations, as the most different, are the best.

But if it is so useful, on this account, to know the language and literature of any other cultivated and civilized people, the most valuable of all to us in this respect are the languages and literature of the ancients. No nations of modern and civilized Europe are so unlike one another, as the Greeks and Romans are unlike all of us; yet without being, as some remote Orientals are, so totally dissimilar, that the labour of a life is required to enable us to understand them. Were this the only gain to be derived from a knowledge of the ancients, it would already place the study of them in a high rank among enlightening and liberalizing pursuits. It is of no use saying that we may know them through modern writings. We may know something of them in that way; which is much better than knowing nothing. But modern books do not teach us ancient thought; they teach us some modern writer's notion of ancient thought. Modern books do not show us the Greeks and Romans; they tell us some modern writer's opinions about the Greeks and Romans. Translations are scarcely better. When we want really to know what a person thinks or says, we seek it at first hand from himself. We do not trust to another person's impression of his meaning, given in another person's words; we refer to his own. Much more is it necessary to do so when his words are in one language, and those of his reporter in another. Modern phraseology never conveys the exact meaning of a Greek writer; it cannot do so, except by a diffuse explanatory circumlocution which no translator dares use. We must be able, in a certain degree, to think in Greek, if we would represent to ourselves how a Greek thought: and this not only in the abstruse region of metaphysics, but about the political, religious, and even domestic concerns of life. I will mention a further aspect of this question, which, though I have not the merit of originating it, I do not remember to have seen noticed in any book. There is no part of our knowledge which it is more useful to obtain at first hand—to go to the fountain head for—than our knowledge of history. Yet this, in most cases, we hardly ever do. Our conception of the past is not drawn from its own records, but from books written about it, containing not the facts, but a view of the facts which has shaped itself in the mind of somebody of our own or a very recent time. Such books are very instructive and valuable; they help us to understand history, to interpret history, to draw just conclusions from it; at the worst, they set us the example of trying to do all this; but they are not themselves history. The knowledge they give is upon trust, and even when they have done their best, it is not only incomplete but partial, because confined to what a few modern writers have seen in the materials, and have thought worth picking out from among them. How little we learn of our own ancestors from Hume, or Hallam, or Macaulay,[8] compared with what we know if we add to what these tell us, even a little reading of contemporary authors and documents! The most recent historians are so well aware of this, that they fill their pages with extracts from the original materials, feeling that these extracts are the real history, and their comments and thread of narrative are only helps towards understanding it. Now it is part of the great worth to us of our Greek and Latin studies,

[8] Mill refers to David Hume's *History of England* (1754–1762), Henry Hallam's *Constitutional History of England* (1827), and Thomas Babington Macaulay's *History of England* (1848–1861).

that in them we do read history in the original sources. We are in actual contact with cotemporary minds; we are not dependent on hearsay; we have something by which we can test and check the representations and theories of modern historians. It may be asked, why then not study the original materials of modern history? I answer, it is highly desirable to do so; and let me remark by the way, that even this requires a dead language; nearly all the documents prior to the Reformation, and many subsequent to it, being written in Latin. But the exploration of these documents, though a most useful pursuit, cannot be a branch of education. Not to speak of their vast extent, and the fragmentary nature of each, the strongest reason is, that in learning the spirit of our own past ages, until a comparatively recent period, from cotemporary writers, we learn hardly anything else. Those authors, with a few exceptions, are little worth reading on their own account. While, in studying the great writers of antiquity, we are not only learning to understand the ancient mind, but laying in a stock of wise thought and observation, still valuable to ourselves; and at the same time making ourselves familiar with a number of the most perfect and finished literary compositions which the human mind has produced—compositions which, from the altered conditions of human life, are likely to be seldom paralleled, in their sustained excellence, by the times to come.

Even as mere languages, no modern European language is so valuable a discipline to the intellect as those of Greece and Rome, on account of their regular and complicated structure. Consider for a moment what grammar is. It is the most elementary part of logic. It is the beginning of the analysis of the thinking process. The principles and rules of grammar are the means by which the forms of language are made to correspond with the universal forms of thought. The distinctions between the various parts of speech, between the cases of nouns, the moods and tenses of verbs, the functions of particles, are distinctions in thought, not merely in words. Single nouns and verbs express objects and events, many of which can be cognized by the senses: but the modes of putting nouns and verbs together, express the relations of objects and events, which can be cognized only by the intellect; and each different mode corresponds to a different relation. The structure of every sentence is a lesson in logic. The various rules of syntax oblige us to distinguish between the subject and predicate of a proposition, between the agent, the action, and the thing acted upon; to mark when an idea is intended to modify or qualify, or merely to unite with, some other idea; what assertions are categorical, what only conditional; whether the intention is to express similarity or contrast, to make a plurality of assertions conjunctively or disjunctively; what portions of a sentence, though grammatically complete within themselves, are mere members or subordinate parts of the assertion made by the entire sentence. Such things form the subject-matter of universal grammar; and the languages which teach it best are those which have the most definite rules, and which provide distinct forms for the greatest number of distinctions in thought, so that if we fail to attend precisely and accurately to any of these, we cannot avoid committing a solecism in language. In these qualities the classical languages have an incomparable superiority over every modern language, and over all languages, dead or living, which have a literature worth being generally studied.

But the superiority of the literature itself, for purposes of education, is still more marked and decisive. Even in the substantial value of the matter of which it is the vehicle, it is very far from having been superseded. The discoveries of the ancients in science have been greatly surpassed, and as much of them as is still valuable loses nothing by being incorporated in modern treatises: but what does not so well admit of being transferred bodily, and has been very imperfectly carried off even piecemeal, is the treasure which they accumulated of what may be called the wisdom of life: the rich store of experience of human nature and conduct, which the acute and observing minds of those ages, aided in their observations by the greater simplicity of manners and life, consigned to their writings, and most of which retains all its value. The speeches in Thucydides; the Rhetoric, Ethics, and Politics of Aristotle; the Dialogues of Plato; the Orations of Demosthenes; the Satires, and especially the Epistles of Horace; all the writings of Tacitus; the great work of Quintilian,[9] a repertory of the best thoughts of the ancient world on all subjects connected with education; and, in a less formal manner, all that is left to us of the ancient historians, orators, philosophers, and even dramatists, are replete with remarks and maxims of singular good sense and penetration, applicable both to political and to private life: and the actual truths we find in them are even surpassed in value by the encouragement and help they give us in the pursuit of truth. Human invention has never produced anything so valuable in the way both of stimulation and of discipline to the inquiring intellect, as the dialectics of the ancients, of which many of the works of Aristotle illustrate the theory, and those of Plato exhibit the practice. No modern writings come near to these, in teaching, both by precept and example, the way to investigate truth, on those subjects, so vastly important to us, which remain matters of controversy from the difficulty or impossibility of bringing them to a directly experimental test. To question all things; never to turn away from any difficulty; to accept no doctrine either from ourselves or from other people without a rigid scrutiny by negative criticism, letting no fallacy, or incoherence, or confusion of thought, slip by unperceived; above all, to insist upon having the meaning of a word clearly understood before using it, and the meaning of a proposition before assenting to it; these are the lessons we learn from the ancient dialecticians. With all this vigorous management of the negative element, they inspire no scepticism about the reality of truth, or indifference to its pursuit. The noblest enthusiasm, both for the search after truth and for applying it to its highest uses, pervades these writers, Aristotle no less than Plato, though Plato has incomparably the greater power of imparting those feelings to others. In cultivating, therefore, the ancient languages as our best literary education, we are all the while laying an

[9] *Institutio Oratoria.*

admirable foundation for ethical and philosophical culture. In purely literary excellence—in perfection of form—the pre-eminence of the ancients is not disputed. In every department which they attempted, and they attempted almost all, their composition, like their sculpture, has been to the greatest modern artists an example, to be looked up to with hopeless admiration, but of inappreciable value as a light on high, guiding their own endeavours. In prose and in poetry, in epic, lyric, or dramatic, as in historical, philosophical, and oratorical art, the pinnacle on which they stand is equally eminent. I am now speaking of the form, the artistic perfection of treatment: for, as regards substance, I consider modern poetry to be superior to ancient, in the same manner, though in a less degree, as modern science: it enters deeper into nature. The feelings of the modern mind are more various, more complex and manifold, than those of the ancients ever were. The modern mind is, what the ancient mind was not, brooding and self-conscious; and its meditative self-consciousness has discovered depths in the human soul which the Greeks and Romans did not dream of, and would not have understood. But what they had got to express, they expressed in a manner which few even of the greatest moderns have seriously attempted to rival. It must be remembered that they had more time, and that they wrote chiefly for a select class, possessed of leisure. To us who write in a hurry for people who read in a hurry, the attempt to give an equal degree of finish would be loss of time. But to be familiar with perfect models is not the less important to us because the element in which we work precludes even the effort to equal them. They shew us at least what excellence is, and make us desire it, and strive to get as near to it as is within our reach. And this is the value to us of the ancient writers, all the more emphatically, because their excellence does not admit of being copied, or directly imitated. It does not consist in a trick which can be learnt, but in the perfect adaptation of means to ends. The secret of the style of the great Greek and Roman authors, is that it is the perfection of good sense. In the first place, they never use a word without a meaning, or a word which adds nothing to the meaning. They always (to begin with) had a meaning; they knew what they wanted to say; and their whole purpose was to say it with the highest degree of exactness and completeness, and bring it home to the mind with the greatest possible clearness and vividness. It never entered into their thoughts to conceive of a piece of writing as beautiful in itself, abstractedly from what it had to express: its beauty must all be subservient to the most perfect expression of the sense. The *curiosa felicitas* [10] which their critics ascribed in a pre-eminent degree to Horace, expresses the standard at which they all aimed. Their style is exactly described by Swift's definition, "the right words in the right places." [11] Look at an oration of Demosthenes; there is nothing in it which calls attention to itself as style at all: it is only after a close examination we perceive that every word is what it should be, and where it should be, to lead the hearer smoothly and imperceptibly into the state of mind which the orator wishes to produce. The perfection of the workmanship is only visible in the total absence of any blemish or fault, and of anything which checks the flow of thought and feeling, anything which even momentarily distracts the mind from the main purpose. But then (as has been well said) it was not the object of Demosthenes to make the Athenians cry out "What a splendid speaker!" but to make them say "Let us march against Philip!" [12] It was only in the decline of ancient literature that ornament began to be cultivated merely as ornament. In the time of its maturity, not the merest epithet was put in because it was thought beautiful in itself; nor even for a merely descriptive purpose, for epithets purely descriptive were one of the corruptions of style which abound in Lucan,[13] for example: the word had no business there unless it brought out some feature which was wanted, and helped to place the object in the light which the purpose of the composi-

[10] "Nice felicity of expression" (from Petronius, *Satyricon,* 118).
[11] Letter to a young clergyman, January 9, 1720.
[12] Philip II of Macedon (382–336 B.C.).
[13] Marcus Annaeus Lucanus (A.D. 39–65), Latin poet.

tion required. These conditions being complied with, then indeed the intrinsic beauty of the means used was a source of additional effect, of which it behoved them to avail themselves, like rhythm and melody of versification. But these great writers knew that ornament for the sake of ornament, ornament which attracts attention to itself, and shines by its own beauties, only does so by calling off the mind from the main object, and thus not only interferes with the higher purpose of human discourse, which ought, and generally professes, to have some matter to communicate, apart from the mere excitement of the moment, but also spoils the perfection of the composition as a piece of fine art, by destroying the unity of effect. This, then, is the first great lesson in composition to be learnt from the classical authors. The second is, not to be prolix. In a single paragraph, Thucydides can give a clear and vivid representation of a battle, such as a reader who has once taken it into his mind can seldom forget. The most powerful and affecting piece of narrative perhaps in all historical literature, is the account of the Sicilian catastrophe in his seventh book,[14] yet how few pages does it fill! The ancients were concise, because of the extreme pains they took with their compositions; almost all moderns are prolix, because they do not. The great ancients could express a thought so perfectly in a few words or sentences, that they did not need to add any more: the moderns, because they cannot bring it out clearly and completely at once, return again and again, heaping sentence upon sentence, each adding a little more elucidation, in hopes that though no single sentence expresses the full meaning, the whole together may give a sufficient notion of it. In this respect, I am afraid we are growing worse instead of better, for want of time and patience, and from the necessity we are in of addressing almost all writings to a busy and imperfectly prepared public. The demands of modern life are such—the work to be done, the mass to be worked upon, are so vast, that those who have anything particular to say—who have, as the phrase goes, any message to deliver—cannot afford to devote their time to the

[14] Of his history of the Peloponnesian War.

production of masterpieces. But they would do far worse than they do, if there had never been masterpieces, or if they had never known them. Early familiarity with the perfect, makes our most imperfect production far less bad than it otherwise would be. To have a high standard of excellence often makes the whole difference of rendering our work good when it would otherwise be mediocre.

For all these reasons, I think it important to retain these two languages and literatures in the place they occupy, as a part of liberal education, that is, of the education of all who are not obliged by their circumstances to discontinue their scholastic studies at a very early age. But the same reasons which vindicate the place of classical studies in general education, shew also the proper limitation of them. They should be carried as far as is sufficient to enable the pupil, in after life, to read the great works of ancient literature with ease. Those who have leisure and inclination to make scholarship, or ancient history, or general philology, their pursuit, of course require much more; but there is no room for more in general education. The laborious idleness in which the schooltime is wasted away in the English classical schools deserves the severest reprehension. To what purpose should the most precious years of early life be irreparably squandered in learning to write bad Latin and Greek verses? I do not see that we are much the better even for those who end by writing good ones. I am often tempted to ask the favourites of nature and fortune, whether all the serious and important work of the world is done, that their time and energy can be spared for these *nugae difficiles?* [15] I am not blind to the utility of composing in a language, as a means of learning it accurately. I hardly know any other means equally effectual. But why should not prose composition suffice? What need is there of original composition at all? if that can be called original which unfortunate schoolboys, without any thoughts to express, hammer out on compulsion from mere memory, acquiring the pernicious habit which a teacher should consider it one of his first duties to repress, that

[15] "Troublesome trifles."

of merely stringing together borrowed phrases? The exercise in composition, most suitable to the requirements of learners, is that most valuable one, of retranslating from translated passages of a good author: and to this might be added, what still exists in many Continental places of education, occasional practice in talking Latin. There would be something to be said for the time spent in the manufacture of verses, if such practice were necessary for the enjoyment of ancient poetry; though it would be better to lose that enjoyment than to purchase it at so extravagant a price. But the beauties of a great poet would be a far poorer thing than they are, if they only impressed us through a knowledge of the technicalities of his art. The poet needed those technicalities: they are not necessary to us. They are essential for criticizing a poem, but not for enjoying it. All that is wanted is sufficient familiarity with the language, for its meaning to reach us without any sense of effort, and clothed with the associations on which the poet counted for producing his effect. Whoever has this familiarity, and a practised ear, can have as keen a relish of the music of Virgil and Horace, as of Gray, or Burns, or Shelley, though he know not the metrical rules of a common Sapphic or Alcaic.[16] I do not say that these rules ought not to be taught, but I would have a class apart for them, and would make the appropriate exercises an optional, not a compulsory part of the school teaching.

Much more might be said respecting classical instruction, and literary cultivation in general, as a part of liberal education. But it is time to speak of the uses of scientific instruction: or rather its indispensable necessity, for it is recommended by every consideration which pleads for any high order of intellectual education at all.

. . . .

I have now said what I had to say on the two kinds of education which the system of schools and universities is in-

[16] Verse form used by Sappho (*ca.* 600 B.C.), poetess of Lesbos, and a meter invented by Alcaeus (*ca.* 600 B.C.), lyric poet of Mytilene on Lesbos.

tended to promote—intellectual education, and moral education: knowledge and the training of the knowing faculty, conscience and that of the moral faculty. These are the two main ingredients of human culture; but they do not exhaust the whole of it. There is a third division, which, if subordinate, and owing allegiance to the two others, is barely inferior to them, and not less needful to the completeness of the human being; I mean the æsthetic branch; the culture which comes through poetry and art, and may be described as the education of the feelings, and the cultivation of the beautiful. This department of things deserves to be regarded in a far more serious light than is the custom of these countries. It is only of late, and chiefly by a superficial imitation of foreigners, that we have begun to use the word Art by itself, and to speak of Art as we speak of Science, or Government, or Religion: we used to talk of the Arts, and more specifically of the Fine Arts: and even by them were vulgarly meant only two forms of art, Painting and Sculpture, the two which as a people we cared least about—which were regarded even by the more cultivated among us as little more than branches of domestic ornamentation, a kind of elegant upholstery. The very words "Fine Arts" called up a notion of frivolity, of great pains expended on a rather trifling object—on something which differed from the cheaper and commoner arts of producing pretty things, mainly by being more difficult, and by giving fops an opportunity of pluming themselves on caring for it and on being able to talk about it. This estimate extended in no small degree, though not altogether, even to poetry; the queen of arts, but, in Great Britain, hardly included under the name. It cannot exactly be said that poetry was little thought of; we were proud of our Shakespeare and Milton, and in one period at least of our history, that of Queen Anne, it was a high literary distinction to be a poet; but poetry was hardly looked upon in any serious light, or as having much value except as an amusement or excitement, the superiority of which over others principally consisted in being that of a more refined order of minds. Yet the celebrated saying of Fletcher of Saltoun,[17] "Let who will make the laws of a people if I write their songs," might have taught us how great an instrument for acting on the human mind we were undervaluing. It would be difficult for anybody to imagine that "Rule Britannia," [18] for example, or "Scots wha hae," [19] had no permanent influence on the higher region of human character; some of Moore's songs have done more for Ireland than all Grattan's speeches [20]: and songs are far from being the highest or most impressive form of poetry. On these subjects, the mode of thinking and feeling of other countries was not only not intelligible, but not credible, to an average Englishman. To find Art ranking on a complete equality, in theory at least, with Philosophy, Learning, and Science—as holding an equally important place among the agents of civilization and among the elements of the worth of humanity: to find even painting and sculpture treated as great social powers, and the art of a country as a feature in its character and condition, little inferior in importance to either its religion or its government; all this only did not amaze and puzzle Englishmen, because it was too strange for them to be able to realize it, or, in truth, to believe it possible: and the radical difference of feeling on this matter between the British people and those of France, Germany, and the Continent generally, is one among the causes of that extraordinary inability to understand one another, which exists between England and the rest of Europe, while it does not exist to anything like the same degree between one nation of Continental Europe and another. It may be traced to the two influences which have chiefly shaped the British character since the days of the Stuarts: commercial money-getting business, and religious Puritanism. Business, demanding the whole of the faculties,

---

17 Andrew Fletcher (1655–1716), Scottish patriot.

18 By James Thomson (1700–1748), English poet.

19 The opening words of Robert Burns's patriotic song, "Bruce to His Men at Bannockburn."

20 Thomas Moore (1779–1852), nationalistic Irish poet.—Henry Grattan (1746–1820), Irish orator and statesman.

and, whether pursued from duty or the love of gain, regarding as a loss of time whatever does not conduce directly to the end; Puritanism, which looking upon every feeling of human nature, except fear and reverence for God, as a snare, if not as partaking of sin, looked coldly, if not disapprovingly, on the cultivation of the sentiments. Different causes have produced different effects in the Continental nations; among whom it is even now observable that virtue and goodness are generally for the most part an affair of the sentiments, while with us they are almost exclusively an affair of duty. Accordingly, the kind of advantage which we have had over many other countries in point of morals—I am not sure that we are not losing it—has consisted in greater tenderness of conscience. In this we have had on the whole a real superiority, though one principally negative; for conscience is with most men a power chiefly in the way of restraint—a power which acts rather in staying our hands from any great wickedness, than by the direction it gives to the general course of our desires and sentiments. One of the commonest types of character among us is that of a man all whose ambition is self-regarding; who has no higher purpose in life than to enrich or raise in the world himself and his family; who never dreams of making the good of his fellow-creatures or of his country an habitual object, further than giving away, annually or from time to time, certain sums in charity; but who has a conscience sincerely alive to whatever is generally considered wrong, and would scruple to use any very illegitimate means for attaining his self-interested objects. While it will often happen in other countries that men whose feelings and whose active energies point strongly in an unselfish direction, who have the love of their country, of human improvement, of human freedom, even of virtue, in great strength, and of whose thoughts and activity a large share is devoted to disinterested objects, will yet, in the pursuit of these or of any other objects that they strongly desire, permit themselves to do wrong things which the other man, though intrinsically, and taking the whole of his character, farther removed from what a human being ought to be, could not bring himself to commit. It is of no use to debate which of these two states of mind is the best, or rather the least bad. It is quite possible to cultivate the conscience and the sentiments too. Nothing hinders us from so training a man that he will not, even for a disinterested purpose, violate the moral law, and also feeding and encouraging those high feelings, on which we mainly rely for lifting men above low and sordid objects, and giving them a higher conception of what constitutes success in life. If we wish men to practise virtue, it is worth while trying to make them love virtue, and feel it an object in itself, and not a tax paid for leave to pursue other objects. It is worth training them to feel, not only actual wrong or actual meanness, but the absence of noble aims and endeavours, as not merely blamable but also degrading: to have a feeling of the miserable smallness of mere self in the face of this great universe, of the collective mass of our fellow creatures, in the face of past history and of the indefinite future—the poorness and insignificance of human life if it is to be all spent in making things comfortable for ourselves and our kin, and raising ourselves and them a step or two on the social ladder. Thus feeling, we learn to respect ourselves only so far as we feel capable of nobler objects: and if unfortunately those by whom we are surrounded do not share our aspirations, perhaps disapprove the conduct to which we are prompted by them—to sustain ourselves by the ideal sympathy of the great characters in history, or even in fiction, and by the contemplation of an idealized posterity: shall I add, of ideal perfection embodied in a Divine Being? Now, of this elevated tone of mind the great source of inspiration is poetry, and all literature so far as it is poetical and artistic. We may imbibe exalted feelings from Plato, or Demosthenes, or Tacitus, but it is in so far as those great men are not solely philosophers or orators or historians, but poets and artists. Nor is it only loftiness, only the heroic feelings, that are bred by poetic cultivation. Its power is as great in calming the soul as in elevating it—in fostering the milder emotions, as the more exalted. It brings home to us all those aspects of life which take hold of our nature on its unselfish side, and lead us to identify our joy and grief with the good or ill of the system of which we form a part; and all those solemn or pensive feelings, which, without having any direct application to conduct, incline us to take life seriously, and predispose us to the reception of anything which comes before us in the shape of duty. Who does not feel himself a better man after a course of Dante, or of Wordsworth, or, I will add, of Lucretius[21] or the Georgics,[22] or after brooding over Gray's Elegy, or Shelley's Hymn to Intellectual Beauty? I have spoken of poetry, but all the other modes of art produce similar effects in their degree. The races and nations whose senses are naturally finer, and their sensuous perceptions more exercised, than ours, receive the same kind of impressions from painting and sculpture: and many of the more delicately organized among ourselves do the same. All the arts of expression tend to keep alive and in activity the feelings they express. Do you think that the great Italian painters would have filled the place they did in the European mind, would have been universally ranked among the greatest men of their time, if their productions had done nothing for it but to serve as the decoration of a public hall or a private *salon?* Their Nativities and Crucifixions, their glorious Madonnas and Saints, were to their susceptible Southern countrymen the great school not only of devotional, but of all the elevated and all the imaginative feelings. We colder Northerns may approach to a conception of this function of art when we listen to an oratorio of Handel, or give ourselves up to the emotions excited by a Gothic cathedral. Even apart from any specific emotional expression, the mere contemplation of beauty of a high order produces in no small degree this elevating effect on the character. The power of natural scenery addresses itself to the same region of human nature which corresponds to Art. There are few capable of feeling the sublimer order of natural beauty, such as your own Highlands and other mountain regions afford, who are not, at least temporarily, raised by it

[21] Lucretius (*ca.* 99–55 B.C.), Latin philosophical poet.
[22] Virgil's poem about agriculture and farming.

above the littlenesses of humanity, and made to feel the puerility of the petty objects which set men's interests at variance, contrasted with the nobler pleasures which all might share. To whatever avocations we may be called in life, let us never quash these susceptibilities within us, but carefully seek the opportunities of maintaining them in exercise. The more prosaic our ordinary duties, the more necessary it is to keep up the tone of our minds by frequent visits to that higher region of thought and feeling, in which every work seems dignified in proportion to the ends for which, and the spirit in which, it is done; where we learn, while eagerly seizing every opportunity of exercising higher faculties and performing higher duties, to regard all useful and honest work as a public function, which may be ennobled by the mode of performing it—which has not properly any other nobility than what that gives—and which, if ever so humble, is never mean but when it is meanly done, and when the motives from which it is done are mean motives. There is, besides, a natural affinity between goodness and the cultivation of the Beautiful, when it is real cultivation, and not a mere unguided instinct. He who has learnt what beauty is, if he be of a virtuous character, will desire to realize it in his own life—will keep before himself a type of perfect beauty in human character, to light his attempts at self-culture. There is a true meaning in the saying of Goethe, though liable to be misunderstood and perverted, that the Beautiful is greater than the Good; for it includes the Good, and adds something to it: it is the Good made perfect, and fitted with all the collateral perfections which make it a finished and completed thing. Now, this sense of perfection, which would make us demand from every creation of man the very utmost that it ought to give, and render us intolerant of the smallest fault in ourselves or in anything we do, is one of the results of Art cultivation. No other human productions come so near to perfection as works of pure Art. In all other things, we are, and may reasonably be, satisfied if the degree of excellence is as great as the object immediately in view seems to us to be worth: but in Art, the perfection is itself the object. If I were to define Art, I should be inclined to call it the endeavour after perfection in execution. If we meet with even a piece of mechanical work which bears the marks of being done in this spirit—which is done as if the workman loved it, and tried to make it as good as possible, though something less good would have answered the purpose for which it was ostensibly made—we say that he has worked like an artist. Art, when really cultivated, and not merely practised empirically, maintains, what it first gave the conception of, an ideal Beauty, to be eternally aimed at, though surpassing what can be actually attained; and by this idea it trains us never to be completely satisfied with imperfection in what we ourselves do and are: to idealize, as much as possible, every work we do, and most of all, our own characters and lives.

And now, having travelled with you over the whole range of the materials and training which an University supplies as a preparation for the higher uses of life, it is almost needless to add any exhortation to you to profit by the gift. Now is your opportunity for gaining a degree of insight into subjects larger and more ennobling than the minutiæ of a business or a profession, and for acquiring a facility of using your minds on all that concerns the higher interests of man, which you will carry with you into the occupations of active life, and which will prevent even the short intervals of time which that may leave you, from being altogether lost for noble purposes. Having once conquered the first difficulties, the only ones of which the irksomeness surpasses the interest; having turned the point beyond which what was once a task, becomes a pleasure; in even the busiest after-life, the higher powers of your mind will make progress imperceptibly, by the spontaneous exercise of your thoughts, and by the lessons you will know how to learn from daily experience. So, at least, it will be if in your early studies you have fixed your eyes upon the ultimate end from which those studies take their chief value—that of making you more effective combatants in the great fight which never ceases to rage between Good and Evil, and more equal to coping with the ever new problems which the changing course of human nature and human society present to be resolved. Aims like these commonly retain the footing which they have once established in the mind; and their presence in our thoughts keeps our higher faculties in exercise, and makes us consider the acquirements and powers which we store up at any time of our lives, as a mental capital, to be freely expended in helping forward any mode which presents itself of making mankind in any respect wiser or better, or placing any portion of human affairs on a more sensible and rational footing than its existing one. There is not one of us who may not qualify himself so to improve the average amount of opportunities, as to leave his fellow creatures some little the better for the use he has known how to make of his intellect. To make this little greater, let us strive to keep ourselves acquainted with the best thoughts that are brought forth by the original minds of the age; that we may know what movements stand most in need of our aid, and that, as far as depends on us, the good seed may not fall on a rock, and perish without reaching the soil in which it might have germinated and flourished. You are to be a part of the public who are to welcome, encourage, and help forward the future intellectual benefactors of humanity; and you are, if possible, to furnish your contingent to the number of those benefactors. Nor let any one be discouraged by what may seem, in moments of despondency, the lack of time and of opportunity. Those who know how to employ opportunities will often find that they can create them: and what we achieve depends less on the amount of time we possess, than on the use we make of our time. You and your like are the hope and resource of your country in the coming generation. All great things which that generation is destined to do, have to be done by some like you; several will assuredly be done by persons for whom society has done much less, to whom it has given far less preparation, than those whom I am now addressing. I do not attempt to instigate you by the prospect of direct rewards, either earthly or heavenly; the less we think about being rewarded in either way, the better for us. But there is one reward which will not fail you, and which may be called disinterested, because it is not a consequence, but is inherent in the very fact of deserving it; the deeper and more varied interest you will feel in life: which will give it tenfold its value, and a value which will last to the end. All merely personal objects grow less valuable as we advance in life: this not only endures but increases.

From Autobiography

1873

The fame of John Stuart Mill's *Autobiography* has depended largely on the account, given in the fifth chapter, of his mental crisis and his recovery. Men of letters whose knowledge of Benthamism is as superficial as Bentham's knowledge of poetry was have been fond of pointing to Mill's confession as a vindication of the claims of poetry as against those of philosophy. They argue that it re-enforces Dickens' attack upon the Utilitarian system of education in *Hard Times*, a novel published in the same year in which Mill was writing his first draft of the *Autobiography*. Others have found in the account the archetypal Freudian experience, in which the son harbors a death-wish against his father, whom he hopes to supplant in his relations with the mother. Still others are attracted to the chapter because it seems to be an illustration of the validity of the Coleridge-Schelling view of Hamlet as a character whose excessive thought paralyzes him for action. Each of these views, as Mill might have said, contains a partial truth, but the interest of the fifth chapter of the *Autobiography* is greater than that suggested by any single one.

Mill's sudden discovery that his social, political, and philosophical commitments were incapable of giving him happiness is not merely a criticism of a Utilitarian education (and the Utilitarians were not the only Victorians who raised their children to be social reformers) but an attempt to deal with the complex question of the proper relation between thought and action in an age of doubt. Mill's crisis resulted from the overintellectualization of life that was becoming general in the nineteenth century. Such Victorian writers as Carlyle, Arnold, Ruskin, and Newman all discovered that "the habit of analysis has a tendency to wear away the feelings." Mill's condition was therefore unusual only in its intensity, for he had indeed been the victim of an unusual education.

When his crisis came, Mill discovered that a heterodox education like his could only be as strong as those associations which were formed early in life. If analysis had been strong enough to wear down the traditional associations developed through centuries, how much more quickly and destructively could it work upon a set of associations newly formed by innovating social theorists! James Mill's failure as an educator consisted of his inability to secure, in his son's mind, lasting associations between the goals of Benthamite reform and individual happiness.

In Mill's progress toward recovery, two stages may be distinguished. The first is begun by his reading of the section in the eighteenth-century French writer Jean François Marmontel's *Mémoires d'un Père* in which the writer describes his father's death and the way in which, after having taken his father's empty place in his mother's bed, he resolves to assume all the responsibilities of a father to the family. In reading this scene, the Freudian implications of which do not need to be underlined, Mill was moved to tears and thus reassured of his power still to feel. Between the reading of Marmontel and the discovery of Wordsworth, whose poetry completed his recovery, Mill had come to adopt an attitude toward the possibility of happiness which he himself compares to Carlyle's "anti-self-consciousness" theory. It holds that the direct pursuit of happiness is self-defeating because happiness can only come as a by-product of other pursuits. Yet it must be remembered that, unlike Carlyle, Mill still believed in happiness as an end and did not suppose that action, as an escape from thought, was a good in itself. On the contrary, he immediately went on to discuss the experience of Wordsworth's poetry, which taught him the importance of the passive susceptibilities, and the way in which to find happiness in quiet contemplation.

From Chapter IV

YOUTHFUL PROPAGANDISM. THE WESTMINSTER REVIEW.

I conceive that the description so often given of a Benthamite, as a mere reasoning machine, though extremely inapplicable to most of those who have been designated by that title, was during two or three years of my life not altogether untrue of

From *Autobiography of John Stuart Mill* (New York: Columbia University Press, 1924). Reprinted by permission of the publisher.

me. It was perhaps as applicable to me as it can well be to any one just entering into life, to whom the common objects of desire must in general have at least the attraction of novelty. There is nothing very extraordinary in this fact: no youth of the age I then was, can be expected to be more than one thing, and this was the thing I happened to be. Ambition and desire of distinction, I had in abundance; and zeal for what I thought the good of mankind was my strongest sentiment, mixing with and colouring all others. But my zeal was as yet little else, at that period of my life, than zeal for speculative opinions. It had not its root in genuine benevolence, or sympathy with mankind; though these qualities held their due place in my ethical standard. Nor was it connected with any high enthusiasm for ideal nobleness. Yet of this feeling I was imaginatively very susceptible; but there was at that time an intermission of its natural aliment, poetical culture, while there was a superabundance of the discipline antagonistic to it, that of mere logic and analysis. Add to this that, as already mentioned, my father's teachings tended to the undervaluing of feeling. It was not that he was himself cold-hearted or insensible; I believe it was rather from the contrary quality; he thought that feeling could take care of itself; that there was sure to be enough of it if actions were properly cared about. Offended by the frequency with which, in ethical and philosophical controversy, feeling is made the ultimate reason and justification of conduct, instead of being itself called on for a justification, while, in practice, actions, the effect of which on human happiness is mischievous, are defended as being required by feeling, and the character of a person of feeling obtains a credit for desert, which he thought only due to actions, he had a real impatience of attributing praise to feeling or of any but the most sparing reference to it either in the estimation of persons or in the discussion of things. In addition to the influence which this characteristic in him, had on me and others, we found all the opinions to which we attached most importance, constantly attacked on the ground of feeling. Utility was denounced as cold calculation; political economy as hard-hearted; antipopulation doctrines as repulsive to the natural feelings of mankind. We retorted by the word "sentimentality" which, along with "declamation" and "vague generalities," served us as common terms of opprobrium. Although we were generally in the right, as against those who were opposed to us, the effect was that the cultivation of feeling (except the feelings of public and private duty) was not in much esteem among us, and had very little place in the thoughts of most of us, myself in particular. What we principally thought of, was to alter people's opinions; to make them believe according to evidence, and know what was their real interest, which when they once knew, they would, we thought, by the instrument of opinion, enforce a regard to it upon one another. While fully recognizing the superior excellence of unselfish benevolence and love of justice, we did not expect the regeneration of mankind from any direct action on those sentiments, but from the effect of educated intellect, enlightening the selfish feelings. Although this last is prodigiously important as a means of improvement in the hands of those who are themselves impelled by nobler principles of action, I do not believe that any one of the survivors of the Benthamites or Utilitarians of that day, now relies mainly upon it for the general amendment of human conduct.

From this neglect both in theory and in practice of the cultivation of feeling, naturally resulted among other things, an undervaluing of poetry, and of Imagination generally, as an element of human nature. It is, or was, part of the popular notion of Benthamites, that they are enemies of poetry: this was partly true of Bentham himself; he used to say that "all poetry is misrepresentation": but, in the sense in which he said it, the same might have been said of all impressive speech; of all representation or inculcation more oratorical in its character than a sum in arithmetic. An article of Bingham's[1] in the first number of the Westminster Review, in which he offered as an explanation of something which he disliked in Moore,[2]

[1] Peregrine Bingham (1788–1864) often contributed to the *Westminster Review* in its early days.

[2] See "Inaugural Address at St. Andrews," note 20.

that "Mr. Moore *is* a poet, and therefore is *not* a reasoner", did a good deal to attach the notion of hating poetry to the writers in the Review. But the truth was that many of us were great readers of poetry; Bingham himself had been a writer of it, while as regards me (and the same thing might be said of my father) the correct statement would be not that I disliked poetry, but that I was theoretically indifferent to it. I disliked any sentiments in poetry which I should have disliked in prose; and that included a great deal. And I was wholly blind to its place in human culture, as a means of educating the feelings. But I was always personally very susceptible to some kinds of it. In the most sectarian period of my Benthamism I happened to look into Pope's Essay on Man, and though every opinion in it was contrary to mine, I well remember how powerfully it acted on my imagination. Perhaps at that time poetical composition of any higher type than eloquent discussion in verse, might not have produced a similar effect on me: at all events I seldom gave it an opportunity. This, however, was a mere passing state. Long before I had enlarged in any considerable degree, the basis of my intellectual creed, I had obtained in the natural course of my mental progress, poetic culture of the most valuable kind, by means of reverential admiration for the lives and characters of heroic persons; especially the heroes of philosophy. The same inspiring effect which so many of the benefactors of mankind have left on record that they had experienced from Plutarch's Lives,[3] was produced on me by Plato's pictures of Socrates, and by some modern biographies, above all by Condorcet's Life of Turgot;[4] a book well calculated to rouse the best sort of enthusiasm, since it contains one of the wisest and noblest of lives, delineated by one of the wisest and noblest of men. The heroic virtue of these glorious representatives of the opinions with which I sympathized,

---

[3] Plutarch (46–*ca.* 120), Greek biographer and essayist, wrote his *Parallel Lives* to provide examples of wise and noble conduct.

[4] Antoine Nicolas, Marquis de Condorcet (1743–1794), French philosopher and Revolutionist, wrote the life of Anne Robert Jacques Turgot (1727–1781), a liberal statesman and economist whom Mill greatly admired.

deeply affected me, and I perpetually recurred to them as others do to a favorite poet, when needing to be carried up into the more elevated regions of feeling and thought. I may observe by the way that this book cured me of my sectarian follies. The two or three pages beginning "Il regardait toute secte comme nuisible",[5] and explaining why Turgot always kept himself perfectly distinct from the Encyclopedists,[6] sank deeply into my mind. I left off designating myself and others as Utilitarians, and by the pronoun "we," or any other collective designation. I ceased to *afficher*[7] sectarianism. My real inward sectarianism I did not get rid of till later, and much more gradually....

From Chapter V

A CRISIS IN MY MENTAL HISTORY. ONE STAGE ONWARD.

For some years after this[8] I wrote very little, and nothing regularly, for publication: and great were the advantages which I derived from the intermission. It was of no common importance to me, at this period, to be able to digest and mature my thoughts for my own mind only, without any immediate call for giving them out in print. Had I gone on writing, it would have much disturbed the important transformation in my opinions and character, which took place during those years. The origin of this transformation, or at least the process by which I was prepared for it, can only be explained by turning some distance back.

---

[5] "He considered all sects harmful."

[6] A group of writers, mostly French, rationalistic and materialistic in outlook, who forwarded their views in an *Encyclopédie* (1751–1772). Leading members of the group, also known as the *philosophes*, were Diderot, D'Alembert, Helvétius, and Condorcet.

[7] "To proclaim publicly."

[8] After 1828.

From the winter of 1821, when I first read Bentham, and especially from the commencement of the Westminster Review, I had what might truly be called an object in life; to be a reformer of the world. My conception of my own happiness was entirely identified with this object. The personal sympathies I wished for were those of fellow labourers in this enterprise. I endeavoured to pick up as many flowers as I could by the way; but as a serious and permanent personal satisfaction to rest upon, my whole reliance was placed on this: and I was accustomed to felicitate myself on the certainty of a happy life which I enjoyed, through placing my happiness in something durable and distant, in which some progress might be always making, while it could never be exhausted by complete attainment. This did very well for several years, during which the general improvement going on in the world and the idea of myself as engaged with others in struggling to promote it, seemed enough to fill up an interesting and animated existence. But the time came when I awakened from this as from a dream. It was in the autumn of 1826. I was in a dull state of nerves, such as everybody is occasionally liable to; unsusceptible to enjoyment or pleasurable excitement; one of those moods when what is pleasure at other times, becomes insipid or indifferent; the state, I should think, in which converts to Methodism usually are, when smitten by their first "conviction of sin." In this frame of mind it occurred to me to put the question directly to myself, "Suppose that all your objects in life were realized; that all the changes in institutions and opinions which you are looking forward to, could be completely effected at this very instant: would this be a great joy and happiness to you?" And an irrepressible self-consciousness distinctly answered, "No!" At this my heart sank within me: the whole foundation on which my life was constructed fell down. All my happiness was to have been found in the continual pursuit of this end. The end had ceased to charm, and how could there ever again be any interest in the means? I seemed to have nothing left to live for.

At first I hoped that the cloud would pass away of itself; but it did not. A night's sleep, the sovereign remedy for the smaller vexations of life, had no effect on it. I awoke to a renewed consciousness of the woful fact. I carried it with me into all companies, into all occupations. Hardly anything had power to cause me even a few minutes oblivion of it. For some months the cloud seemed to grow thicker and thicker. The lines in Coleridge's "Dejection"—I was not then acquainted with them—exactly describe my case:

> A grief without a pang, void, dark and drear,
> A drowsy, stifled, unimpassioned grief,
> Which finds no natural outlet or relief
> In word, or sigh, or tear.

In vain I sought relief from my favourite books; those memorials of past nobleness and greatness, from which I had always hitherto drawn strength and animation. I read them now without feeling, or with the accustomed feeling *minus* all its charm; and I became persuaded, that my love of mankind, and of excellence for its own sake, had worn itself out. I sought no comfort by speaking to others of what I felt. If I had loved any one sufficiently to make confiding my griefs a necessity, I should not have been in the condition I was. I felt, too, that mine was not an interesting, or in any way respectable distress. There was nothing in it to attract sympathy. Advice, if I had known where to seek it, would have been most precious. The words of Macbeth to the physician [9] often occurred to my thoughts. But there was no one on whom I could build the faintest hope of such assistance. My father, to whom it would have been natural to me to have recourse in any practical difficulties, was the last person to whom, in such a case as this, I looked for help. Everything convinced me that

[9] Canst thou not minister to a mind diseas'd,
Pluck from the memory a rooted sorrow,
Raze out the written troubles of the brain,
And with some sweet oblivious antidote
Cleanse the stuff'd bosom of that perilous stuff
Which weighs upon the heart?

(*Macbeth*, V. iii. 40–45.)

he had no knowledge of any such mental state as I was suffering from, and that even if he could be made to understand it, he was not the physician who could heal it. My education, which was wholly his work, had been conducted without any regard to the possibility of its ending in this result; and I saw no use in giving him the pain of thinking that his plans had failed, when the failure was probably irremediable, and at all events, beyond the power of *his* remedies. Of other friends, I had at that time none to whom I had any hope of making my condition intelligible. It was however abundantly intelligible to myself; and the more I dwelt upon it, the more hopeless it appeared.

My course of study had led me to believe, that all mental and moral feelings and qualities, whether of a good or of a bad kind, were the results of association; that we love one thing and hate another, take pleasure in one sort of action or contemplation, and pain in another sort, through the clinging of pleasurable or painful ideas to those things, from the effect of education or of experience. As a corollary from this, I had always heard it maintained by my father, and was myself convinced, that the object of education should be to form the strongest possible associations of the salutary class; associations of pleasure with all things beneficial to the great whole, and of pain with all things hurtful to it. This doctrine appeared inexpugnable; but it now seemed to me on retrospect, that my teachers had occupied themselves but superficially with the means of forming and keeping up these salutary associations. They seemed to have trusted altogether to the old familiar instruments, praise and blame, reward and punishment. Now I did not doubt that by these means, begun early and applied unremittingly, intense associations of pain and pleasure, especially of pain, might be created, and might produce desires and aversions capable of lasting undiminished to the end of life. But there must always be something artificial and casual in associations thus produced. The pains and pleasures thus forcibly associated with things, are not connected with them by any natural tie; and it is therefore, I thought, essential to the durability of these associations, that they should have become so intense and inveterate as to be practically indissoluble, before the habitual exercise of the power of analysis had commenced. For I now saw, or thought I saw, what I had always before received with incredulity—that the habit of analysis has a tendency to wear away the feelings: as indeed it has when no other mental habit is cultivated, and the analysing spirit remains without its natural complements and correctives. The very excellence of analysis (I argued) is that it tends to weaken and undermine whatever is the result of prejudice; that it enables us mentally to separate ideas which have only casually clung together: and no associations whatever could ultimately resist this dissolving force, were it not that we owe to analysis our clearest knowledge of the permanent sequences in nature; the real connexions between Things, not dependent on our will and feelings; natural laws, by virtue of which, in many cases, one thing is inseparable from another in fact; which laws, in proportion as they are clearly perceived and imaginatively realized, cause our ideas of things which are always joined together in Nature, to cohere more and more closely in our thoughts. Analytic habits may thus even strengthen the associations between causes and effects, means and ends, but tend altogether to weaken those which are, to speak familiarly, a *mere* matter of feeling. They are therefore (I thought) favourable to prudence and clear-sightedness, but a perpetual worm at the root both of the passions and of the virtues; and above all, fearfully undermine all desires, and all pleasures, which are the effects of association, that is, according to the theory I held, all except the purely physical and organic; of the entire insufficiency of which to make life desirable, no one had a stronger conviction than I had. These were the laws of human nature by which, as it seemed to me, I had been brought to my present state. All those to whom I looked up, were of opinion that the pleasure of sympathy with human beings, and the feelings which made the good of others, and especially of mankind on a large scale, the object of existence, were the greatest and surest sources of happiness. Of the truth of this I was convinced, but to know that a feeling would make me happy if I had it, did not give me the feeling. My education, I thought, had failed to create these feelings in sufficient strength to resist the dissolving influence of analysis, while the whole course of my intellectual cultivation had made precocious and premature analysis the inveterate habit of my mind. I was thus, as I said to myself, left stranded at the commencement of my voyage, with a well equipped ship and a rudder, but no sail; without any real desire for the ends which I had been so carefully fitted out to work for: no delight in virtue or the general good, but also just as little in anything else. The fountains of vanity and ambition seemed to have dried up within me, as completely as those of benevolence. I had had (as I reflected) some gratification of vanity at too early an age: I had obtained some distinction, and felt myself of some importance, before the desire of distinction and of importance had grown into a passion: and little as it was which I had attained, yet having been attained too early, like all pleasures enjoyed too soon, it had made me *blasé* and indifferent to the pursuit. Thus neither selfish nor unselfish pleasures were pleasures to me. And there seemed no power in nature sufficient to begin the formation of my character anew, and create in a mind now irretrievably analytic, fresh associations of pleasure with any of the objects of human desire.

These were the thoughts which mingled with the dry heavy dejection of the melancholy winter of 1826–7. During this time I was not incapable of my usual occupations. I went on with them mechanically, by the mere force of habit. I had been so drilled in a certain sort of mental exercise, that I could still carry it on when all the spirit had gone out of it. I even composed and spoke several speeches at the debating society, how, or with what degree of success I know not. Of four years continual speaking at that society, this is the only year of which I remember next to nothing. Two lines of Coleridge in whom alone of all writers I have found a true description of what I felt, were often in my thoughts, not at this time (for I had never read them), but in a later period of the same mental malady:

> Work without hope draws nectar in a sieve,
> And hope without an object cannot live.[10]

In all probability my case was by no means so peculiar as I fancied it, and I doubt not that many others have passed through a similar state; but the idiosyncrasies of my education had given to the general phenomenon a special character, which made it seem the natural effect of causes that it was hardly possible for time to remove. I frequently asked myself, if I could, or if I was bound to go on living, when life must be passed in this manner. I generally answered to myself, that I did not think I could possibly bear it beyond a year. When, however, not more than half that duration of time had elapsed, a small ray of light broke in upon my gloom. I was reading, accidentally, Marmontel's Mémoires,[11] and came to the passage which relates his father's death, the distressed position of the family, and the sudden inspiration by which he, then a mere boy, felt and made them feel that he would be everything to them—would supply the place of all that they had lost. A vivid conception of the scene and its feelings came over me, and I was moved to tears. From this moment my burthen grew lighter. The oppression of the thought that all feeling was dead within me, was gone. I was no longer hopeless: I was not a stock or a stone. I had still, it seemed, some of the material out of which all worth of character, and all capacity for happiness, are made. Relieved from my ever present sense of irremediable wretchedness, I gradually found that the ordinary incidents of life could again give me some pleasure; that I could again find enjoyment, not intense, but sufficient for cheerfulness, in sunshine and sky, in books, in coversation, in

---

[10] Last two lines of "Work without Hope."

[11] *Mémoires d'un Père* (1804) by the French writer, Jean François Marmontel (1723–1799).

public affairs; and that there was, once more, excitement, though of a moderate kind, in exerting myself for my opinions, and for the public good. Thus the cloud gradually drew off, and I again enjoyed life: and though I had several relapses, some of which lasted many months, I never again was as miserable as I had been.

The experiences of this period had two very marked effects on my opinions and character. In the first place, they led me to adopt a theory of life, very unlike that on which I had before acted, and having much in common with what at that time I certainly had never heard of, the anti-self-consciousness theory of Carlyle.[12] I never, indeed, wavered in the conviction that happiness is the test of all rules of conduct, and the end of life. But I now thought that this end was only to be attained by not making it the direct end. Those only are happy (I thought) who have their minds fixed on some object other than their own happiness; on the happiness of others, on the improvement of mankind, even on some art or pursuit, followed not as a means, but as itself an ideal end. Aiming thus at something else, they find happiness by the way. The enjoyments of life (such was now my theory) are sufficient to make it a pleasant thing, when they are taken *en passant*, without being made a principal object. Once make them so, and they are immediately felt to be insufficient. They will not bear a scrutinizing examination. Ask yourself whether you are happy, and you cease to be so. The only chance is to treat, not happiness, but some end external to it, as the purpose of life. Let your self-consciousness, your scrutiny, your self-interrogation, exhaust themselves on that; and, if otherwise fortunately circumstanced you will inhale happiness with the air you breathe, without dwelling on it or thinking about it, without either forestalling it in imagination, or putting it to flight by fatal questioning. This theory now became the basis of my philosophy of life. And I still hold to it as the best theory for

[12] See the section, "The Everlasting Yea," in *Sartor Resartus* (1833–1834), and the essay "Characteristics" (1831).

all those who have but a moderate degree of sensibility and of capacity for enjoyment, that is, for the great majority of mankind.

The other important change which my opinions at this time underwent, was that I, for the first time, gave its proper place, among the prime necessities of human well-being, to the internal culture of the individual. I ceased to attach almost exclusive importance to the ordering of outward circumstances, and the training of the human being for speculation and for action.

I had now learnt by experience that the passive susceptibilities needed to be cultivated as well as the active capacities, and required to be nourished and enriched as well as guided. I did not, for an instant, lose sight of, or undervalue, that part of the truth which I had seen before; I never turned recreant to intellectual culture, or ceased to consider the power and practice of analysis as an essential condition both of individual and of social improvement. But I thought that it had consequences which required to be corrected, by joining other kinds of cultivation with it. The maintenance of a due balance among the faculties, now seemed to me of primary importance. The cultivation of the feelings became one of the cardinal points in my ethical and philosophical creed. And my thoughts and inclinations turned in an increasing degree towards whatever seemed capable of being instrumental to that object.

I now began to find meaning in the things which I had read or heard about the importance of poetry and art as instruments of human culture. But it was some time longer before I began to know this by personal experience. The only one of the imaginative arts in which I had from childhood taken great pleasure, was music; the best effect of which (and in this it surpasses perhaps every other art) consists in exciting enthusiasm; in winding up to a high pitch those feelings of an elevated kind which are already in the character, but to which this excitement gives a glow and a fervour, which though transitory at its utmost height, is precious for sustaining them at other times. This effect of music I had often experienced; but, like all my pleasurable susceptibilities, it was suspended during the gloomy period. I had sought relief again and again from this quarter, but found none. After the tide had turned, and I was in process of recovery, I had been helped forward by music, but in a much less elevated manner. I at this time first became acquainted with Weber's Oberon,[13] and the extreme pleasure which I drew from its delicious melodies did me good, by showing me a source of pleasure to which I was as susceptible as ever. The good however was much impaired by the thought, that the pleasure of music (as is quite true of such pleasure as this was, that of mere tune) fades with familiarity, and requires either to be revived by intermittence, or fed by continual novelty. And it is very characteristic both of my then state, and of the general tone of my mind at this period of my life, that I was seriously tormented by the thought of the exhaustibility of musical combinations. The octave consists only of five tones and two semi-tones, which can be put together in only a limited number of ways, of which but a small proportion are beautiful: most of these, it seemed to me, must have been already discovered, and there could not be room for a long succession of Mozarts and Webers, to strike out, as these had done, entirely new and surpassingly rich veins of musical beauty. This source of anxiety may perhaps be thought to resemble that of the philosophers of Laputa,[14] who feared lest the sun should be burnt out. It was, however, connected with the best feature in my character, and the only good point to be found in my very unromantic and in no way honourable distress. For though my dejection, honestly looked at, could not be called other than egotistical, produced by the ruin, as I thought, of my fabric of happiness, yet the destiny of mankind in general was ever in my thoughts, and could not be separated from my own. I felt that the flaw in my life, must be a flaw in life itself; that the question was, whether, if the reformers of society and government could succeed in their objects, and every person in

[13] English romantic opera by Carl Maria von Weber (1786–1826), German composer; first produced in 1826.

[14] In *Gulliver's Travels*, Part III.

the community were free and in a state of physical comfort, the pleasures of life, being no longer kept up by struggle and privation, would cease to be pleasures. And I felt that unless I could see my way to some better hope than this for human happiness in general, my dejection must continue; but that if I could see such an outlet, I should then look on the world with pleasure; content as far as I was myself concerned, with any fair share of the general lot.

The state of my thoughts and feelings made the fact of my reading Wordsworth for the first time (in the autumn of 1828) an important event in my life. I took up the collection of his poems from curiosity, with no expectation of mental relief from it, though I had before resorted to poetry with that hope. In the worst period of my depression I had read through the whole of Byron (then new to me) to try whether a poet, whose peculiar department was supposed to be that of the intenser feelings, could rouse any feeling in me. As might be expected, I got no good from this reading, but the reverse. The poet's state of mind was too like my own. His was the lament of a man who had worn out all pleasures, and who seemed to think that life, to all who possess the good things of it, must necessarily be the vapid uninteresting thing which I found it. His Harold and Manfred had the same burthen on them which I had; and I was not in a frame of mind to derive any comfort from the vehement sensual passion of his Giaours, or the sullenness of his Laras.[15] But while Byron was exactly what did not suit my condition, Wordsworth was exactly what did. I had looked into the Excursion two or three years before, and found little in it; and should probably have found as little, had I read it at this time. But the miscellaneous poems, in the two-volume edition of 1815 (to which little of value was added in the latter part of the author's life), proved to be the precise thing for my mental wants at that particular juncture.

In the first place, these poems addressed themselves power-

[15] The gloomy, self-centered heroes of Byron's early poems: *Childe Harold's Pilgrimage* (1812–1818); *Manfred* (1817); *The Giaour* (1813); *Lara* (1814).

fully to one of the strongest of my pleasurable susceptibilities, the love of rural objects and natural scenery; to which I had been indebted not only for much of the pleasure of my life, but quite recently for relief from one of my longest relapses into depression. In this power of rural beauty over me, there was a foundation laid for taking pleasure in Wordsworth's poetry; the more so, as his scenery lies mostly among mountains, which, owing to my early Pyrenean excursion,[16] were my ideal of natural beauty. But Wordsworth would never have had any great effect on me, if he had merely placed before me beautiful pictures of natural scenery. Scott does this still better than Wordsworth, and a very second-rate landscape does it more effectually than any poet. What made Wordsworth's poems a medicine for my state of mind, was that they expressed, not mere outward beauty, but states of feeling, and of thought coloured by feeling, under the excitement of beauty. They seemed to be the very culture of the feelings, which I was in quest of. In them I seemed to draw from a source of inward joy, of sympathetic and imaginative pleasure, which could be shared in by all human beings; which had no connexion with struggle or imperfection, but would be made richer by every improvement in the physical or social condition of mankind. From them I seemed to learn what would be the perennial sources of happiness, when all the greater evils of life shall have been removed. And I felt myself at once better and happier as I came under their influence. There have certainly been, even in our own age, greater poets than Wordsworth; but poetry of deeper and loftier feeling could not have done for me at that time what his did. I needed to be made to feel that there was real, permanent happiness in tranquil contemplation. Wordsworth taught me this, not only without turning away from, but with a greatly increased interest in, the common feelings and common destiny of human beings. And the delight which these poems gave me, proved that with culture of this sort, there was nothing to dread from the most

16 During the year he spent in France (1820–1821), Mill accompanied the Benthams in an excursion to the Pyrenees.

confirmed habit of analysis. At the conclusion of the Poems came the famous Ode, falsely called Platonic, "Intimations of Immortality:" [17] in which, along with more than his usual sweetness of melody and rhythm, and along with the two passages of grand imagery but bad philosophy so often quoted, I found that he too had had similar experience to mine; that he also had felt that the first freshness of youthful enjoyment of life was not lasting; but that he had sought for compensation, and found it, in the way in which he was now teaching me to find it. The result was that I gradually, but completely, emerged from my habitual depression, and was never again subject to it. I long continued to value Wordsworth less according to his intrinsic merits, than by the measure of what he had done for me. Compared with the greatest poets, he may be said to be the poet of unpoetical natures, possessed of quiet and contemplative tastes. But unpoetical natures are precisely those which require poetic cultivation. This cultivation Wordsworth is much more fitted to give, than poets who are intrinsically far more poets than he.

It so fell out that the merits of Wordsworth were the occasion of my first public declaration of my new way of thinking, and separation from those of my habitual companions who had not undergone a similar change. The person with whom at that time I was most in the habit of comparing notes on such subjects was Roebuck,[18] and I induced him to read Wordsworth, in whom he also at first seemed to find much to admire: but I, like most Wordsworthians, threw myself into strong antagonism to Byron, both as a poet and as to his influence on the character. Roebuck, all whose instincts were those of action and struggle, had, on the contrary, a strong relish and great admiration of Byron, whose writings he regarded as the poetry of human life, while Wordsworth's, according to him, was that of flowers and butterflies. We agreed to have the fight out

[17] Wordsworth too said that the ode was not an expression of Platonic philosophy.

[18] John Arthur Roebuck (1801–1879), politician and reformer.

at our Debating Society,[19] where we accordingly discussed for two evenings the comparative merits of Byron and Wordsworth, propounding and illustrating by long recitations our respective theories of poetry: Sterling [20] also in a brilliant speech, putting forward his particular theory. This was the first debate on any weighty subject in which Roebuck and I had been on opposite sides. The schism between us widened from this time more and more, though we continued for some years longer to be companions. In the beginning, our chief divergence related to the cultivation of the feelings.[21] Roebuck was in many respects very different from the vulgar notion of a Benthamite or Utilitarian. He was a lover of poetry and of most of the fine arts. He took great pleasure in music, in dramatic performances, especially in painting, and himself drew and designed landscapes with great facility and beauty. But he never could be made to see that these things have any value as aids in the formation of character. Personally, instead of being, as Benthamites are supposed to be, void of feeling, he had very quick and strong sensibilities. But, like most Englishmen who have feelings, he found his feelings stand very much in his way. He was much more susceptible to the painful sympathies than to the pleasurable, and looking for his happiness elsewhere, he wished that his feelings should be deadened rather than quickened. And, in truth, the English character, and English social circumstances, make it so seldom possible to derive happiness from the exercise of the sympathies, that it is not wonderful if they count for little in an Englishman's scheme of life. In most other countries the paramount importance of the sympathies as a constituent of individual happiness

[19] London Debating Society, organized in 1825 by Mill and some of his friends.

[20] John Sterling (1806–1844), man of letters, clergyman, and friend of Mill, Coleridge, and Carlyle.

[21] There is reason to suppose that the main reason for the break between the men was Roebuck's vocal opposition to Mill's marriage with Harriet Taylor. See Alexander Bain, *John Stuart Mill: A Criticism* (London: Longmans, 1882).

is an axiom, taken for granted rather than needing any formal statement; but most English thinkers almost seem to regard them as necessary evils, required for keeping men's actions benevolent and compassionate. Roebuck was, or appeared to be, this kind of Englishman. He saw little good in any cultivation of the feelings, and none at all in cultivating them through the imagination, which he thought was only cultivating illusions. It was in vain I urged on him that the imaginative emotion which an idea when vividly conceived excites in us, is not an illusion but a fact, as real as any of the other qualities of objects; and far from implying anything erroneous and delusive in our mental apprehension of the object, is quite consistent with the most accurate knowledge and most perfect practical recognition of all its physical and intellectual laws and relations. The intensest feeling of the beauty of a cloud lighted by the setting sun, is no hindrance to my knowing that the cloud is vapour of water, subject to all the laws of vapours in a state of suspension; and I am just as likely to allow for, and act on, these physical laws whenever there is occasion to do so, as if I had been incapable of perceiving any distinction between beauty and ugliness.

While my intimacy with Roebuck diminished, I fell more and more into friendly intercourse with our Coleridgian adversaries in the Society, Frederick Maurice and John Sterling, both subsequently so well known, the former by his writings, the latter through the biographies by Hare [22] and Carlyle. Of these two friends, Maurice was the thinker, Sterling the orator, and impassioned expositor of thoughts which, at this period, were almost entirely formed for him by Maurice. With Maurice I had for some time been acquainted through Eyton Tooke,[23] who had known him at Cambridge, and

---

[22] Frederick Denison Maurice (1805–1872), follower of Coleridge, friend of Mill, originator of the Christian Socialist movement.—Julius Hare (1795–1855), editor of Sterling's *Essays and Tales* and author of a life of Sterling.

[23] Eyton Tooke (1808–1830), an early member of the Utilitarian Society; Mill was deeply affected by his suicide.

though my discussions with him were almost always disputes, I had carried away from them much that helped to build up my new fabric of thought, in the same way as I was deriving much from Coleridge, and from the writings of Goethe and other German authors which I read during those years. I have so deep a respect for Maurice's character and purposes, as well as for his great mental gifts, that it is with some unwillingness I say anything which may seem to place him on a less high eminence than I would gladly be able to accord to him. But I have always thought that there was more intellectual power wasted in Maurice than in any other of my cotemporaries. Few of them certainly have had so much to waste. Great powers of generalization, rare ingenuity and subtlety, and a wide perception of important and unobvious truths, served him not for putting something better into the place of the worthless heap of received opinions on the great subjects of thought, but for proving to his own mind, that the Church of England had known everything from the first, and that all the truths on the ground of which the Church and orthodoxy have been attacked (many of which he saw as clearly as any one) are not only consistent with the 39 articles, but are better understood and expressed in those articles than by any one who rejects them. I have never been able to find any other explanation of this, than by attributing it to that timidity of conscience, combined with original sensitiveness of temperament, which has so often driven highly gifted men into Romanism from the need of a firmer support than they can find in the independent conclusions of their own judgment. Any more vulgar kind of timidity no one who knew Maurice would ever think of imputing to him, even if he had not given public proof of his freedom from it, by his ultimate collision with some of the opinions commonly regarded as orthodox, and by his noble origination of the Christian Socialist movement.[24] The nearest parallel to him, in a moral point of view, is Coleridge, to whom, in merely intellectual power, apart from

[24] Originated by Maurice and Charles Kingsley (1819–1875), it tried to combine Christian and Socialist teachings.

poetical genius, I think him decidedly superior. At this time, however, he might be described as a disciple of Coleridge, and Sterling as a disciple of Coleridge and of him. The modifications which were taking place in my old opinions gave me some points of contact with them; and both Maurice and Sterling were of considerable use to my development. With Sterling I soon became very intimate, and was more attached to him than I have ever been to any other man. He was indeed one of the most loveable of men. His frank, cordial, affectionate and expansive character, a love of truth alike conspicuous in the highest things and the humblest; a generous and ardent nature which threw itself with impetuosity into the opinions it adopted, but was as eager to do justice to the doctrines and the men it was opposed to, as to make war on what it thought their errors; and an equal devotion to the two cardinal points of Liberty and Duty, formed a combination of qualities as attractive to me, as to all others who knew him as well as I did. With his open mind and heart he found no difficulty in joining hands with me across the gulf which as yet divided our opinions. He told me how he and others had looked upon me (from hearsay information), as a "made" or manufactured man, having had a certain impress of opinion stamped on me which I could only reproduce; and what a change took place in his feelings when he found, in the discussion on Wordsworth and Byron, that Wordsworth, and all which that name implies, "belonged" to me as much as to him and his friends. The failure of his health soon scattered all his plans of life, and compelled him to live at a distance from London, so that after the first year or two of our acquaintance we only saw each other at distant intervals. But (as he said himself in one of his letters to Carlyle) when we did meet it was like brothers. Though he was never, in the full sense of the word, a profound thinker, his openness of mind, and the moral courage in which he greatly surpassed Maurice, made him outgrow the dominion which Maurice and Coleridge had once exercised over his intellect; though he retained to the last a great but discriminating admiration of both, and towards Maurice a warm affection. Except in that short and transitory phasis of his life, during which he made the mistake of becoming a clergyman, his mind was ever progressive: and the advance he always seemed to have made when I saw him after an interval, made me apply to him what Goethe said of Schiller, "Er hatte eine furchtliche Fortschreitung." [25] He and I started from intellectual points almost as wide apart as the poles, but the distance between us was always diminishing: if I made steps towards some of his opinions, he, during his short life, was constantly approximating more and more to several of mine: and if he had lived, and had health and vigour to prosecute his ever assiduous self-culture, there is no knowing how much further this spontaneous assimilation might have proceeded.

After 1829 I withdrew from attendance on the Debating Society. I had had enough of speech-making, and was glad to carry on my private studies and meditations without any immediate call for outward assertion of their results. I found the fabric of my old and taught opinions giving way in many fresh places, and I never allowed it to fall to pieces, but was incessantly occupied in weaving it anew. I never, in the course of my transition, was content to remain, for ever so short a time, confused and unsettled. When I had taken in any new idea, I could not rest till I had adjusted its relation to my old opinions, and ascertained exactly how far its effect ought to extend in modifying or superseding them.

The conflicts which I had so often had to sustain in defending the theory of government laid down in Bentham's and my father's writings, and the acquaintance I had obtained with other schools of political thinking, made me aware of many things which that doctrine, professing to be a theory of government in general, ought to have made room for, and did not. But these things, as yet, remained with me rather as corrections to be made in applying the theory to practice, than as defects in the theory. I felt that politics could not be a science of specific experience; and that the accusations against the Benthamic theory of *being* a theory, of proceeding *à priori* by

[25] "He had a tremendous development."

way of general reasoning, instead of Baconian experiment, showed complete ignorance of Bacon's principles, and of the necessary conditions of experimental investigation. At this juncture appeared in the Edinburgh Review, Macaulay's famous attack on my father's Essay on Government.[26] This gave me much to think about. I saw that Macaulay's conception of the logic of politics was erroneous; that he stood up for the empirical made of treating political phenomena, against the philosophical; that even in physical science, his notion of philosophizing might have recognized Kepler, but would have excluded Newton and Laplace.[27] But I could not help feeling, that though the tone was unbecoming (an error for which the writer, at a later period, made the most ample and honourable amends) there was truth in several of his strictures on my father's treatment of the subject; that my father's premises were really too narrow, and included but a small number of the general truths, on which, in politics, the important consequences depend. Identity of interest between the governing body and the community at large, is not, in any practical sense which can be attached to it, the only thing on which good government depends; neither can this identity of interest be secured by the mere conditions of election. I was not at all satisfied with the mode in which my father met the criticisms of Macaulay. He did not, as I thought he ought to have done, justify himself by saying, "I was not writing a scientific treatise on politics—I was writing an argument for parliamentary reform." He treated Macaulay's argument as simply irrational; an attack upon the reasoning faculty; an example of the saying of Hobbes, that when reason is against a man, a man will be against reason. This made me think that there was really some-

---

[26] *Edinburgh Review* (March 1829). James Mill's essay first appeared in 1820.

[27] Johannes Kepler (1571–1630), German astronomer, evolved the laws of planetary motion.—Isaac Newton (1642–1727) derived the law of gravitation from the third of Kepler's laws of planetary motion.—Pierre Simon, Marquis de Laplace (1749–1827), astronomer and mathematician, evolved scientific form of nebular hypothesis.

thing more fundamentally erroneous in my father's conception of philosophical method, as applicable to politics, than I had hitherto supposed there was. But I did not at first see clearly what the error might be. At last it flashed upon me all at once in the course of other studies. In the early part of 1830 I had begun to put on paper the ideas on Logic (chiefly on the distinctions among Terms, and the import of Propositions) which had been suggested and in part worked out in the morning conversations already spoken of. Having secured these thoughts from being lost, I pushed on into the other parts of the subject, to try whether I could do anything further towards clearing up the theory of Logic generally. I grappled at once with the problem of Induction, postponing that of Reasoning, on the ground that it is necessary to obtain premises before we can reason from them. Now, Induction is mainly a process for finding the causes of effects: and in attempting to fathom the mode of tracing causes and effects in physical science, I soon saw that in the more perfect of the sciences, we ascend, by generalization from particulars, to the tendencies of causes considered singly, and then reason downward from those separate tendencies, to the effect of the same causes when combined. I then asked myself, what is the ultimate analysis of this deductive process; the common theory of the syllogism evidently throwing no light upon it. My practice (learnt from Hobbes and my father) being to study abstract principles by means of the best concrete instances I could find, the Composition of Forces, in dynamics, occurred to me as the most complete example of the logical process I was investigating. On examining accordingly, what the mind does when it applies the principle of the Composition of Forces, I found that it performs a simple act of addition. It adds the separate effect of the one force to the separate effect of the other, and puts down the sum of these separate effects as the joint effect. But is this a legitimate process? In dynamics, and in all the mathematical branches of physics, it is; but in some other cases, as in chemistry, it is not; and I then recollected that something not unlike this was pointed out as one of the distinctions between chemical and mechanical phenomena, in the introduction to that favorite of my boyhood, Thomson's System of Chemistry.[28] This distinction at once made my mind clear as to what was perplexing me in respect to the philosophy of politics. I now saw, that a science is either deductive or experimental, according as, in the province it deals with, the effects of causes when conjoined, are or are not the sums of the effects which the same causes produce when separate. It followed that politics must be a deductive science. It thus appeared, that both Macaulay and my father were wrong; the one in assimilating the method of philosophizing in politics to the purely experimental method of chemistry; while the other, though right in adopting a deductive method, had made a wrong selection of one, having taken as the type of deduction, not the appropriate process, that of the deductive branches of natural philosophy, but the inappropriate one of pure geometry, which not being a science of causation at all, does not require or admit of any summing-up of effects. A foundation was thus laid in my thoughts for the principal chapters of what I afterwards published on the Logic of the Moral Sciences; and my new position in respect to my old political creed, now became perfectly definite.

If I am asked what system of political philosophy I substituted for that which, as a philosophy, I had abandoned, I answer, no system: only a conviction that the true system was something much more complex and many sided than I had previously had any idea of, and that its office was to supply, not a set of model institutions, but principles from which the institutions suitable to any given circumstances might be deduced. The influences of European, that is to say, Continental, thought, and especially those of the reaction of the nineteenth century against the eighteenth, were now streaming in upon me. They came from various quarters: from the writings of Coleridge, which I had begun to read with interest even before the change in my opinions; from the Coleridgians with whom I was in personal intercourse; from what I had read

[28] Thomas Thomson (1773–1852), English chemist, published his *System of Chemistry* in 1802.

of Goethe; from Carlyle's early articles in the Edinburgh and Foreign Reviews, though for a long time I saw nothing in these (as my father saw nothing in them to the last) but insane rhapsody. From these sources, and from the acquaintance I kept up with the French literature of the time, I derived, among other ideas which the general turning upside down of the opinions of European thinkers had brought uppermost, these in particular: That the human mind has a certain order of possible progress, in which some things must precede others, an order which governments and public instructors can modify to some, but not to an unlimited extent: That all questions of political institutions are relative, not absolute, and that different stages of human progress not only *will* have, but *ought* to have, different institutions: That government is always either in the hands, or passing into the hands, of whatever is the strongest power in society, and that what this power is, does not depend on institutions, but institutions on it: That any general theory or philosophy of politics supposes a previous theory of human progress, and that this is the same thing with a philosophy of history. These opinions, true in the main, were held in an exaggerated and violent manner by the thinkers with whom I was now most accustomed to compare notes, and who, as usual with a reaction, ignored that half of the truth which the thinkers of the eighteenth century saw. But though, at one period of my progress, I for some time undervalued that great century, I never joined in the reaction against it, but kept as firm hold of one side of the truth as I took of the other. The fight between the nineteenth century and the eighteenth always reminded me of the battle about the shield, one side of which was white and the other black. I marvelled at the blind rage with which the combatants rushed against one another. I applied to them, and to Coleridge himself, many of Coleridge's sayings about half truths; and Goethe's device, "many-sidedness," [29] was one which I would most willingly, at this period, have taken for mine.

The writers by whom, more than by any others, a new

[29] See Mill's essay on Coleridge. One of Goethe's maxims (no. 1337) was "Let us then be many-sided."

mode of political thinking was brought home to me, were those of the St. Simonian school in France.[30] In 1829 and 1830 I became acquainted with some of their writings. They were then only in the earlier stages of their speculations. They had not yet dressed out their philosophy as a religion, nor had they organized their scheme of Socialism. They were just beginning to question the principle of hereditary property. I was by no means prepared to go with them even this length; but I was greatly struck with the connected view which they for the first time presented to me, of the natural order of human progress; and especially with their division of all history into organic periods and critical periods. During the organic periods (they said) mankind accept with firm conviction some positive creed, claiming jurisdiction over all their actions, and containing more or less of truth and adaptation to the needs of humanity. Under its influence they make all the progress compatible with the creed, and finally outgrow it; then a period follows of criticism and negation, in which mankind lose their old convictions without acquiring any new ones, of a general or authoritative character, except the conviction that the old are false. The period of Greek and Roman polytheism, so long as really believed in by instructed Greeks and Romans, was an organic period, succeeded by the critical or sceptical period of the Greek philosophers. Another organic period came in with Christianity. The corresponding critical period began with the Reformation, has lasted ever since, still lasts, and cannot altogether cease until a new organic period has been inaugurated by the triumph of a yet more advanced creed. These ideas, I knew, were not peculiar to the St. Simonians; on the contrary, they were the general property of Europe, or at least of Germany and France, but they had never, to my knowledge, been so completely systematized as by these writers, nor the distinguishing characteristics of a critical period so powerfully set forth; for I was not then acquainted with Fichte's Lectures on

[30] Followers of Claude Henri Saint-Simon (1760–1825), founder of positivism and of French Socialism. Mill was interested primarily in the Saint-Simonian version of history.

"the Characteristics of the Present Age."[31] In Carlyle, indeed, I found bitter denunciations of an "age of unbelief," and of the present age as such, which I, like most people at that time, supposed to be passionate protests in favour of the old modes of belief. But all that was true in these denunciations, I thought that I found more calmly and philosophically stated by the St. Simonians. Among their publications, too, there was one which seemed to me far superior to the rest; in which the general idea was matured into something much more definite and instructive. This was an early work of Auguste Comte,[32] who then called himself, and even announced himself in the title page as, a pupil of Saint-Simon. In this tract M. Comte first put forth the doctrine, which he afterwards so copiously illustrated, of the natural succession of three stages in every department of human knowledge–first, the theological, next the metaphysical, and lastly, the positive stage; and contended, that social science must be subject to the same law; that the feudal and Catholic system was the concluding phasis of the theological state of the social science, Protestantism the commencement and the doctrines of the French Revolution the consummation of the metaphysical, and that its positive state was yet to come. This doctrine harmonized well with my existing notions, to which it seemed to give a scientific shape. I already regarded the methods of physical science as the proper models for political. But the chief benefit which I derived at this time from the trains of thought suggested by the St. Simonians and by Comte, was, that I obtained a clearer conception than ever before of the peculiarities of an era of transition in opinion, and ceased to mistake the moral and intellectual characteristics of such an era, for the normal attributes of humanity. I looked forward, through the present age of loud disputes but generally weak convictions, to a future which

---

[31] Johann Gottlieb Fichte (1762–1814) attacked eighteenth-century skepticism in this work of 1804.

[32] Auguste Comte (1798–1857), chief exponent of the positivist philosophy, in which only positive facts and observable phenomena are recognized to exist.

shall unite the best qualities of the critical with the best qualities of the organic periods; unchecked liberty of thought, unbounded freedom of individual action in all modes not hurtful to others; but also, convictions as to what is right and wrong, useful and pernicious, deeply engraven on the feelings by early education and general unanimity of sentiment, and so firmly grounded in reason and in the true exigencies of life, that they shall not, like all former and present creeds, religious, ethical, and political, require to be periodically thrown off and replaced by others.

M. Comte soon left the St. Simonians, and I lost sight of him and his writings for a number of years. But the St. Simonians I continued to cultivate. I was kept *au courant* of their progress by one of their most enthusiastic disciples, M. Gustave d'Eichthal, who about that time passed a considerable interval in England. I was introduced to their chiefs, Bazard and Enfantin,[33] in 1830; and as long as their public teachings and proselytism continued, I read nearly everything they wrote. Their criticisms on the common doctrines of Liberalism seemed to me full of important truth; and it was partly by their writings that my eyes were opened to the very limited and temporary value of the old political economy, which assumes private property and inheritance as indefeasible facts, and freedom of production and exchange as the *dernier mot*[34] of social improvement. The scheme gradually unfolded by the St. Simonians, under which the labour and capital of society would be managed for the general account of the community, every individual being required to take a share of labour, either as thinker, teacher, artist, or producer, all being classed according to their capacity, and remunerated according to their works, appeared to me a far superior description of So-

---

[33] Gustave d'Eichthal (1804–1886), an enthusiastic Saint-Simonian and lifelong correspondent of Mill.—Saint Amand Bazard (1791–1832).—Barthélemy Prosper Enfantin (1796–1864).

[34] "Last word."

cialism to Owen's.[35] Their aim seemed to me desirable and rational, however their means might be inefficacious; and though I neither believed in the practicability, nor in the beneficial operation of their social machinery, I felt that the proclamation of such an ideal of human society could not but tend to give a beneficial direction to the efforts of others to bring society, as at present constituted, nearer to some ideal standard. I honoured them most of all for what they have been most cried down for—the boldness and freedom from prejudice with which they treated the subject of family, the most important of any, and needing more fundamental alterations than remain to be made in any other great social institution, but on which scarcely any reformer has the courage to touch. In proclaiming the perfect equality of men and women, and an entirely new order of things in regard to their relations with one another, the St. Simonians in common with Owen and Fourier[36] have entitled themselves to the grateful remembrance of future generations.

In giving an account of this period of my life, I have only specified such of my new impressions as appeared to me both at the time and since, to be a kind of turning points, marking a definite progress in my mode of thought. But these few selected points give a very insufficient idea of the quantity of thinking which I carried on respecting a host of subjects during these years of transition. Much of this, it is true, consisted in rediscovering things known to all the world, which I had previously disbelieved, or disregarded. But the rediscovery was to me a discovery, giving me plenary possession of the truths not as traditional platitudes but fresh from their source: and it seldom failed to place them in some new light, by which they were reconciled with, and seemed to confirm while they modified, the truths less generally known which lay in my early

[35] In the socialism of Robert Owen (1771–1858) remuneration would not vary according to the amount of work done; all men would get what they required.

[36] Charles Fourier (1772–1837), an early French communist.

opinions, and in no essential part of which I at any time wavered. All my new thinking only laid the foundation of these more deeply and strongly, while it often removed misapprehension and confusion of ideas which had perverted their effect. For example, during the later returns of my dejection, the doctrine of what is called Philosophical Necessity weighed on my existence like an incubus. I felt as if I was scientifically proved to be the helpless slave of antecedent circumstances; as if my character and that of all others had been formed for us by agencies beyond our control, and was wholly out of our own power. I often said to myself, what a relief it would be if I could disbelieve the doctrine of the formation of character by circumstances; and remembering the wish of Fox[37] respecting the doctrine of resistance to governments, that it might never be forgotten by kings, nor remembered by subjects, I said that it would be a blessing if the doctrine of necessity could be believed by all *quoad*[38] the characters of others, and disbelieved in regard to their own. I pondered painfully on the subject, till gradually I saw light through it. I perceived, that the word Necessity, as a name for the doctrine of Cause and Effect applied to human action, carried with it a misleading association; and that this association was the operative force in the depressing and paralysing influence which I had experienced: I saw that though our character is formed by circumstances, our own desires can do much to shape those circumstances; and that what is really inspiriting and ennobling in the doctrine of freewill, is the conviction that we have real power over the formation of our own character; that our will, by influencing some of our circumstances, can modify our future habits or capabilities of willing. All this was entirely consistent with the doctrine of circumstances, or rather, was that doctrine itself, properly understood. From that time I drew in my own mind, a clear distinction between the doctrine of circumstances, and Fatalism; discarding alto-

[37] Charles James Fox (1749–1806), liberal and humanitarian Whig statesman.

[38] "In regard to."

gether the misleading word Necessity. The theory, which I now for the first time rightly apprehended, ceased altogether to be discouraging, and besides the relief to my spirits, I no longer suffered under the burthen, so heavy to one who aims at being a reformer in opinions, of thinking one doctrine true, and the contrary doctrine morally beneficial. The train of thought which had extricated me from this dilemma, seemed to me, in after years, fitted to render a similar service to others; and it now forms the chapter on Liberty and Necessity in the concluding Book of my "System of Logic."

Again, in politics, though I no longer accepted the doctrine of the Essay on Government as a scientific theory; though I ceased to consider representative democracy as an absolute principle, and regarded it as a question of time, place, and circumstance; though I now looked upon the choice of political institutions as a moral and educational question more than one of material interests, thinking that it ought to be decided mainly by the consideration, what great improvement in life and culture stands next in order for the people concerned, as the condition of their further progress, and what institutions are most likely to promote that; nevertheless, this change in the premises of my political philosophy did not alter my practical political creed as to the requirements of my own time and country. I was as much as ever a radical and democrat, for Europe, and especially for England. I thought the predominance of the aristocratic classes, the noble and the rich, in the English Constitution, an evil worth any struggle to get rid of; not on account of taxes, or any such comparatively small inconvenience, but as the great demoralizing agency in the country. Demoralizing, first, because it made the conduct of the government an example of gross public immorality, through the predominance of private over public interests in the State, and the abuse of the powers of legislation for the advantage of classes. Secondly, and in a still greater degree, because the respect of the multitude always attaching itself principally to that which, in the existing state of society, is the chief passport to power; and under English institutions, riches, hereditary or acquired, being the almost exclusive source of political importance; riches, and the signs of riches, were almost the only things really respected, and the life of the people was mainly devoted to the pursuit of them. I thought, that while the higher and richer classes held the power of government, the instruction and improvement of the mass of the people were contrary to the self-interest of those classes, because tending to render the people more powerful for throwing off the yoke: but if the democracy obtained a large, and perhaps the principal, share in the governing power, it would become the interest of the opulent classes to promote their education, in order to ward off really mischievous errors, and especially those which would lead to unjust violations of property. On these grounds I was not only as ardent as ever for democratic institutions, but earnestly hoped that Owenite, St. Simonian, and all other anti-property doctrines might spread widely among the poorer classes; not that I thought those doctrines true, or desired that they should be acted on; but in order that the higher classes might be made to see that they had more to fear from the poor when uneducated, than when educated.

In this frame of mind the French Revolution of July[39] found me. It roused my utmost enthusiasm, and gave me, as it were, a new existence. I went at once to Paris, was introduced to Lafayette,[40] and laid the groundwork of the intercourse I afterwards kept up with several of the active chiefs of the extreme popular party. After my return I entered warmly, as a writer, into the political discussions of the time; which soon became still more exciting, by the coming in of Lord Grey's ministry, and the proposing of the Reform Bill.[41] For the next few years I wrote copiously in newspapers. It was about this

---

[39] The Revolution of July 1830 deposed Charles X and created the bourgeois monarchy of Louis Philippe.

[40] Marie Joseph Paul Yves Roch Gilbert du Motier, Marquis de Lafayette (1757–1834), French general and statesman, active in the Revolutions of 1789 and 1830.

[41] Lord Grey's Whig ministry lasted from 1830 to 1834. The Reform Bill was passed in 1832.

time that Fonblanque,[42] who had for some time written the political articles in the Examiner, became the proprietor and editor of the paper. It is not forgotten with what verve and talent, as well as fine wit, he carried it on, during the whole period of Lord Grey's ministry, and what importance it assumed as the principal representative, in the newspaper press, of radical opinions. The distinguishing character of the paper was given to it entirely by his own articles, which formed at least three fourths of all the original writing contained in it; but of the remaining fourth I contributed during those years a much larger share than any one else. I wrote nearly all the articles on French subjects, including a weekly summary of French politics, often extending to considerable length; together with many leading articles on general politics, commercial and financial legislation, and any miscellaneous subjects in which I felt interested, and which were suitable to the paper, including occasional reviews of books. Mere newspaper articles on the occurrences or questions of the moment, gave no opportunity for the development of any general mode of thought; but I attempted, in the beginning of 1831, to embody in a series of articles, headed "The Spirit of the Age," some of my new opinions, and especially to point out in the character of the present age, the anomalies and evils characteristic of the transition from a system of opinions which had worn out, to another only in process of being formed. These articles were, I fancy, lumbering in style, and not lively or striking enough to be at any time acceptable to newspaper readers; but had they been far more attractive, still, at that particular moment, when great political changes were impending, and engrossing all minds, these discussions were ill timed, and missed fire altogether. The only effect which I know to have been produced by them, was that Carlyle, then living in a secluded part of Scotland, read them in his solitude, and saying to himself (as he afterwards told me) "here is a new Mystic," enquired on coming to London that autumn respecting their authorship; an

42 Albany Fonblanque (1793–1872), radical journalist, editor of the *Examiner*, 1830–1847.

enquiry which was the immediate cause of our becoming personally acquainted.

I have already mentioned Carlyle's earlier writings as one of the channels through which I received the influences which enlarged my early narrow creed; but I do not think that those writings, by themselves, would ever have had any effect on my opinions. What truths they contained, though of the very kind which I was already receiving from other quarters, were presented in a form and vesture less suited than any other to give them access to a mind trained as mine had been. They seemed a haze of poetry and German metaphysics, in which almost the only clear thing was a strong animosity to most of the opinions which were the basis of my mode of thought; religious scepticism, utilitarianism, the doctrine of circumstances, and the attaching any importance to democracy, logic, or political economy. Instead of my having been taught anything, in the first instance, by Carlyle, it was only in proportion as I came to see the same truths through media more suited to my mental constitution, that I recognized them in his writings. Then, indeed, the wonderful power with which he put them forth made a deep impression upon me, and I was during a long period one of his most fervent admirers; but the good his writings did me, was not as philosophy to instruct, but as poetry to animate. Even at the time when our acquaintance commenced, I was not sufficiently advanced in my new modes of thought, to appreciate him fully; a proof of which is, that on his showing me the manuscript of Sartor Resartus, his best and greatest work, which he had just then finished, I made little of it; though when it came out about two years afterwards in Fraser's Magazine, I read it with enthusiastic admiration and the keenest delight. I did not seek and cultivate Carlyle less on account of the fundamental differences in our philosophy. He soon found out that I was not "another mystic" and when for the sake of my own integrity I wrote to him a distinct profession of all those of my opinions which I knew he most disliked, he replied that the chief difference between us was that I "was as yet consciously nothing of a mystic." I do not know at what period he gave up the expectation that I was destined to become one; but though both his and my opinions underwent in subsequent years considerable changes, we never approached much nearer to each other's modes of thought than we were in the first years of our acquaintance. I did not, however, deem myself a competent judge of Carlyle. I felt that he was a poet, and that I was not; and that as such, he not only saw many things long before me, which I could only when they were pointed out to me, hobble after and prove, but that it was highly probable he could see many things which were not visible to me even after they were pointed out. I knew that I could not see round him, and could never be certain that I saw over him; and I never presumed to judge him with any definiteness, until he was interpreted to me by one greatly the superior of us both—who was more a poet than he, and more a thinker than I—whose own mind and nature included his, and infinitely more.[43]

---

[43] Harriet Taylor.

Selected Letters

1831–1869

Mill's letters show that as he grew older he gave less and less time to subjects not immediately connected with politics. After his disenchantment with orthodox Benthamism, he always spoke respectfully of literature and of its role in the education and culture of the individual, but he seems to have had periods of doubt, beginning in the fifties, as to the relevance of art to politics.

In the diary that Mill kept from January 8 to April 15, 1854, the question of the role of art in modern life is raised many times. In his entry for January 27, Mill writes that it may be advisable to suspend verse-writing altogether for a time because "the regeneration of the world in its present stage is a matter of business, and it would be as rational to keep accounts or write invoices in verse as to attempt to do the work of human improvement in it." Two days later he says that in his time music is the only one of the arts that flourishes, because it is the least intellectual; the more intellectual arts decline because "in this age the people of intellect have other things to do."

The question of the proper relation between art and social problems is often discussed in Mill's letters. In one of October 1840 to his friend John Sterling, Mill writes:

What you say about the absence of a disinterested & heroic pursuit of Art as the greatest want of England at present, has often

---

From *The Earlier Letters of John Stuart Mill: 1812–1848*, ed. Francis E. Mineka (Toronto: University of Toronto Press, 1963). Letters from this edition are reprinted by permission of University of Toronto Press and Professor Francis E. Mineka.

John Stuart Mill and Harriet Taylor: Their Friendship and Subsequent Marriage, ed. F. A. Hayek (Chicago: University of Chicago Press, 1951). Letters from this volume are reprinted by permission of The University of Chicago Press.

The Letters of John Stuart Mill, ed. Hugh S. R. Elliot (London: Longmans, Green and Co., 1910).

struck me, but I suspect it will not be otherwise until our social struggles are over. Art needs earnest but quiet times—in ours I am afraid Art itself to be powerful must be polemical—Carlylean not Goethian. . . .

Mill respected the classical quality of disinterestedness in art which Arnold was later to prescribe, but he considered the demands of modern life to be dealt with in art more important than the requirements of formal perfection in works of art. He habitually praised the drama and poetry of Greece (see the letter of March 12, 1841) for their formal correctness and excellence of style, and admitted them to be superior as works of art to modern works, which were more experimental psychologically; yet he concluded that the latter were more relevant and necessary.

Mill believed that the period through which he was living—a period of transition, of experimentation, and of unsettled beliefs—could not be satisfactorily dealt with unless the classical requirements for poetry were suspended. The best poets of the age being apparently unable to suspend them, Mill looked outside poetry for solutions to social problems. But he remained aware both of what men lost by transferring their interests away from poetry, and of the inevitability of poetry's re-ascendance. In a letter to his friend R. B. Fox, dated May 6, 1841, Mill recognized the forces which in his age made it almost impossible for poetry to deal with the great problems that beset a society trying to bring order out of disorder; but he warned, from what basis of personal experience all readers of the *Autobiography* know, that the achievement of social and political reform would not necessarily bring with it the perfection of the individual soul.

To John Sterling

From the 20th of October to the 22.
India House. 1831.

DEAR STERLING

. . . I have done nothing in this letter but talk to you about the world in general and about myself. I must now talk to you about other people, and particularly about several new acquaintances of mine that I had not made or had only just begun to make when you left this white world. First of all, I went this summer to the Lakes,[1] where I saw much splendid scenery, and also saw a great deal both of Wordsworth and Southey; and I must tell you what I think of them both. In the case of Wordsworth, I was particularly struck by several things. One was, the extensive range of his thoughts and the largeness & expansiveness of his feelings. This does not appear in his writings, especially his poetry, where the contemplative part of his mind is the only part of it that appears: & one would be tempted to infer from the peculiar character of his poetry, that real life & the active pursuits of men (except of farmers & other country people) did not interest him. The fact however is that these very subjects occupy the greater part of his thoughts, & he talks on no subject more instructively than on states of society & forms of government. Those who best know him, seem to be most impressed with the catholic character of his ability. I have been told that Lockhart [2] has said of him that he would have been an admirable country attorney. Now a man who could have been either Wordsworth or a country attorney, could certainly have been anything else which circumstances had led him to desire to be. The next thing that struck me was the extreme comprehensiveness and philosophic spirit which is in him. By these expressions I mean the direct antithesis of what the Germans most expressively call onesidedness. Wordsworth seems always to know the pros and the cons of every question; & when you think he strikes the balance wrong, it is only because you think he estimates erroneously some matter of fact. Hence all my differences with him, or with any other philosophic Tory, would be differences of matter-of-fact or detail, while my differences

[1] Region of mountains and lakes in Cumberland, Westmorland, and Lancashire, England.

[2] John Gibson Lockhart (1794–1854), Scottish lawyer and literary critic.

with the radicals & utilitarians are differences of principle: for *these see* generally only one side of the subject, & in order to convince them, you must put some entirely new idea into their heads, whereas Wordsworth has all the ideas there already, & you have only to discuss with him concerning the "how much," the more or less of weight which is to be attached to a certain cause or effect, as compared with others: thus the difference with him turns upon a question of varying or fluctuating quantities, where what is *plus* in one age or country is *minus* in another & the whole question is one of observation & testimony & of the value of particular articles of evidence. I need hardly say to you that if one's own conclusions & his were at variance on every question which a minister or a Parliament could to-morrow be called upon to solve, his is nevertheless the mind with which one would be really in communion: our principles would be the same, and we should be like two travellers pursuing the same course on the opposite banks of a river.—Then when you get Wordsworth on the subjects which are peculiarly his, such as the theory of his own art—if it be proper to call poetry an art, (that is, if art is to be defined the expression or embodying in words or forms, of the highest & most refined parts of nature) no one can converse with him without feeling that he has advanced that great subject beyond any other man, being probably the first person who ever combined, with such eminent success in the practice of the art, such high powers of generalization & habits of meditation on its principles. Besides all this, he seems to me the best talker I ever heard (& I have heard several first-rate ones); & there is a benignity & kindliness about his whole demeanour which confirms what his poetry would lead one to expect, along with a perfect simplicity of character which is delightful in any one, but most of all in a person of first-rate intellect. You see I am somewhat enthusiastic on the subject of Wordsworth, having found him still more admirable & delightful a person on a nearer view than I had figured to myself from his writings; which is so seldom the case that it is impossible to see it without having one's faith in man greatly increased & being made greatly happier in consequence.

. . . .

Another acquaintance which I have recently made is that of Mr. Carlyle, whom I believe you are also acquainted with. I have long had a very keen relish for his articles in the Edinburgh & Foreign Reviews, which I formerly thought to be such consummate nonsense; and I think he improves upon a nearer acquaintance. He does not seem to me so entirely the reflexion or shadow of the great German writers as I was inclined to consider him; although undoubtedly his mind has derived from their inspiration whatever breath of life is in it. He seems to me as a man who has had his eyes unsealed, and who now looks round him & sees the aspects of things with his own eyes, but by the light supplied by others; not the pure light of day, but another light compounded of the same simple rays but in different proportions. He has by far the largest & widest liberality & tolerance (not in the sense which Coleridge justly disavows,[3] but in the good sense) that I have met with in any one; & he differs from most men who see as much as he does into the defects of the age, by a circumstance greatly to his advantage in my estimation, that he looks for a safe landing *before* and not *behind:* he sees that if we could replace things as they once were, we should only retard the final issue, as we should in all human probability go on just as we then did, & arrive again at the very place where we now stand. Carlyle intends staying in town all the winter: he has brought his wife to town (whom I have not seen enough of yet to be able to judge of her at all): his object was to treat with booksellers about a work which he wishes to publish,[4] but he has given up this for the present, finding that no bookseller will publish anything but a political pamphlet in the present state of excitement. In fact literature is suspended; men neither read nor write. Accordingly Carlyle means to employ his stay here in

[3] See *Aids to Reflection* (London, 1825), pp. 101–103.
[4] *Sartor Resartus.*

improving his knowledge of what is going on in the world, at least in this part of it, I mean in that part of the world of ideas and feelings which corresponds to London. He is a great hunter-out of acquaintances; he hunted me out, or rather hunted out the author of certain papers in the Examiner[5] (the first, as he said, which he had ever seen in a newspaper, hinting that the age was not the best of all possible ages): & his acquaintance is the only substantial good I have yet derived from writing those papers, & a much greater one than I expected when I wrote them. . . .

Yours faithfully
J. S. MILL

To Thomas Carlyle

London, 17th July 1832

MY DEAR FRIEND

. . . I have read your little paper on Göthe in Bulwer's Magazine.[6] There was little in it which I had not already heard from your lips, otherwise there are passages which would if they had been entirely new to me, have excited me to much thought, and may therefore do that service to any other mind which is prepared for them. I do not myself, as yet, sufficiently know Göthe, to feel certain that he is the great High Priest and Pontiff you describe him; I know him as yet only as one of the wisest men, and men of greatest genius, whom the world has yet produced; but if *he* be not all that you say he is, certainly no other man has arisen in our times, who can even for a moment be suspected of being so. In him alone, of all the celebrated men of this and the last age, does a more familiar

[5] The series of essays called "The Spirit of the Age."
[6] "Death of Goethe," *New Monthly Magazine* (June 1832).

knowledge, and the growth of our own faculties, discover more and more to be admired and less and less to be rejected or even doubted of. Who shall succeed him? or when shall he find even an *unworthy* successor. There is need that the "march of mind" should raise up new spiritual notabilities; for it seems as though all the old ones with one accord were departing out of the world together. In a few days or weeks the world has lost the three greatest men in it, in their several departments; Göthe, Bentham, and Cuvier [7]; & during the same period what a mortality among those second-rate great men, who are generally in their own time much more celebrated than the first, because they take pains to be so; such men as Casimir Périer, or Mackintosh, or Sir William Grant, or General Lamarque, or the last of Scotch judges, John Clerk of Eldin, or even (to descend low indeed) Charles Butler.[8] And here is Sir Walter Scott about to follow.[9] I sometimes think that instead of mountains and valleys, the domain of Intellect is about to become a dead flat, nothing greatly above the general level, nothing very far below it. It is curious that this particular time, in which there are fewer great intellects above ground and in their vigour, than can be remembered for many ages back, should be the precise time at which every body is cackling about the progress of intelligence and the spread of knowledge. I do believe that intelligence and knowledge are less valued just now, except for purposes of money-making, than at any other period since the Norman Conquest, or possibly since the invasion of the Romans. I mean, in our own country. But even in Germany, the great men seem to have

[7] Goethe had died on March 22; Jeremy Bentham on June 6; and Georges Cuvier (b. 1769), French zoologist and geologist, on May 13.

[8] Casimir Périer (b. 1777), French banker and statesman.–Sir James Mackintosh (b. 1765), philosopher and historian.–Sir William Grant (b. 1752), advocate of law reform.–Maximilien Lamarque (b. 1770), French general and orator.–John Clerk, Lord Eldin (b. 1757).–Charles Butler (b. 1750), lawyer and writer.

[9] Scott died on September 21, 1832.

died out, though much of their spirit remains after them, and is, we will hope, permanently fixed in the national character.

. . . .

I am about to make a short ramble in the country just now, after which I shall return to work, and I hope with more solid and valuable results than I have hitherto done: that so I may produce something worthy of the title you give me, and in which I rejoice, that of one of your scholars. You also call me one of your teachers; but if I am this, it is as yet only in the sense in which a schoolmaster might speak of his teachers, meaning those who teach under him. I certainly could not now write, and perhaps shall never be able to write, any thing from which any person can derive so much edification as I, and several others, have derived in particular from your paper on Johnson.[10] My vocation, as far as I yet see, lies in a humbler sphere; I am rather fitted to be a logical expounder than an artist. You I look upon as an artist, and perhaps the only genuine one now living in this country: the highest destiny of all, lies in that direction; for it is the artist alone in whose hands Truth becomes impressive, and a living principle of action. Yet it is something not inconsiderable (in an age in which the understanding is more cultivated and developed than any of the other faculties, & is the only faculty which men do not habitually distrust) if one could address them through the understanding, & ostensibly with little besides mere logical apparatus, yet in a spirit higher than was ever inspired by mere logic, and in such sort that their understandings shall at least have to be *reconciled* to those truths, which even then will not be *felt* until they shall have been breathed upon by the breath of the artist. For, as far as I have observed, the majority even of those who are capable of receiving Truth into their minds, must have the logical side of it turned *first* towards them; then it must be quite turned round before them, that they may see

[10] The paper appeared in two parts: "Biography," *Fraser's Magazine,* V (April 1832), 253–260; and "Boswell's Life of Johnson," *Fraser's Magazine,* V (May 1832), 359–413.

it to be the same Truth in its poetic that it is in its metaphysical aspect. Now this is what I seem to myself qualified for, if for any thing, or at least capable of qualifying myself for; and it is thus that I may be, and therefore ought to be, not useless as an auxiliary even to you, though I am sensible that I can never give back to you the value of what I receive from you. . . .

Yours ever faithfully,

J. S. MILL.

To Thomas Carlyle

India House 11th & 12th April 1833

MY DEAR CARLYLE

I write to you again a letter which I could wish were better worth having—*really* an apology for a letter: Your last, which you *called* so, deserved a better name. I would write, if it were only to thank you for having a better opinion of me than I have of myself. It is useless discussing which is right; time will disclose that; though I do not think that my nature is one of the many things into which you see "some ten years farther" than I do. At all events I will not if I can help it give way to gloom and morbid despondency, of which I have had a large share in my short life, and to which I have been indebted for all the most valuable of such insight as I have into the most important matters, neither will this return of it be without similar fruits, as I hope and almost believe; nevertheless I will and must, though it leaves me little enough of energy, master it, or it will surely master me. Whenever it has come to me it has always lasted many months, and has gone off in most cases very gradually.

. . . .

You will have received long before this time by Fraser, two tracts of mine, of very different kinds, a political or rather ethico-political one on Church & Corporation Property,[11] and the one I told you of, long ago, in Fox's periodical, on Poetry and Art.[12] That last you promised me a careful examination and criticism of: I need it much; for I have a growing feeling that I have not got quite into the heart of that mystery, and I want you to shew me how. If you do not teach me you will do what is better, put me in the way of finding out. But I begin to see a not very far distant boundary to all I am qualified to accomplish in *this* particular line of speculation. . . .

Yours ever faithfully
J. S. Mill

To Thomas Carlyle

[London,] 5th July 1833.

My dear Carlyle

. . . This brings to my mind that I have never explained what I meant when writing once before in this strain I called you a Poet and Artist. I conceive that most of the highest truths, are, to persons endowed by nature in certain ways which I think I could state, intuitive; that is, they need neither explanation nor proof, but if not known before, are assented to as soon as stated. Now it appears to me that the poet or artist is conversant chiefly with *such* truths and that his office in respect to truth is to declare *them*, and to make them *impressive*. This, however, supposes that the reader, hearer, or spectator is a person of the kind to whom those truths *are* intuitive. Such will of course receive them at once, and will lay them to heart in proportion to the impressiveness with which the artist delivers and embodies them. But the other and more numerous

---

11 "Corporation and Church Property," *Jurist*, IV (February 1833), 1–26.

12 "What is Poetry?" *Monthly Repository*, VII (January 1833), 60–70.

kind of people will consider them as nothing but dreaming or madness: and the more so, certainly, the more powerful the artist, *as* an artist: because the means which are good for rendering the truth impressive to those who know it, are not the same and are often absolutely incompatible with those which render it intelligible to those who know it not. Now this last I think is the proper office of the logician or I might say the metaphysician, in truth he must be both. The same person may be poet and logician, but he cannot be both in the same composition: and as heroes have been frustrated of glory "*carent quia vate sacro*,"[13] so I think the *vates*[14] himself has often been misunderstood and successfully cried down for want of a Logician in Ordinary, to supply a logical commentary on his intuitive truths. The artist's is the highest part, for by him alone is real *knowledge* of such truths conveyed: but it is possible to convince him who never could *know* the intuitive truths, that they are not inconsistent with anything he *does* know; that they are even very *probable*, and that he may have faith in them when higher natures than his own affirm that they are truths. He may then build on them and act on them, or at least act nothing contradictory to them. Now this humbler part is, I think, that which is most suitable to my faculties, as a man of speculation. I am not in the least a poet, in any sense; but I can do homage to poetry. I can to a very considerable extent feel it and understand it, and can make others who are my inferiors understand it in proportion to the measure of their capacity. I believe that such a person is more wanted than even the poet himself; that there are more persons living who approximate to the latter character than to the former. I do not think myself at all fit for the one; I do for the other; your walk I conceive to be the higher. Now one thing not useless to do would be to exemplify this difference by enlarging in my logical fashion upon the difference itself: to make those who are not poets, understand that poetry is higher than Logic, and that the union of the two is Philosophy—

[13] "Because they lack the inspired poet's aid."
[14] "Prophet," i.e., poet.

I shall write out my thoughts more at length somewhere, and some*when*, probably soon. Yours faithfully,

J. S. Mill

To Thomas Carlyle

India House, 2nd August 1833.

My dear Carlyle

. . . Of logic, as the theory of the processes of intellect, I think not wholly as you, yet nearly: he who has legs can walk without knowledge of anatomy, yet you will allow that such knowledge may be made substantially *available* for the cure of *lameness*. By logic however I meant the antithesis of Poetry or Art: in which distinction I am learning to perceive a twofold contrast: the *literal* as opposed to the *symbolical*, and *reasoning* as opposed to *intuition*. Not the *theory* of reasoning but the *practice*. In reasoning I include all processes of thought which are *processes* at all, that is, which proceed by a series of steps or links. What I would say is that my vocation is, I think, chiefly for this last; a more extended & higher one than for any branch of mere "Philosophy of Mind" though far inferior to that of the artist.—We shall talk doubtless of these things, and also of many others, not excepting the one you mention, *Paris* —My notion of it is chiefly taken from its recent literature, which *is* exactly what Goethe called it, the literature of Despair—die Litteratur der Verzweiflung. You will not wonder at that—nor do I. . . . Yours faithfully

J. S. Mill

To Thomas Carlyle

Kensington
2d March 1834

My dear Carlyle

. . . If I have any *vocation* I think it is exactly this, to translate the mysticism of others into the language of Argument. Have not all things two aspects, an Artistic and a Scientific; to the former of which the language of mysticism is the most appropriate, to the latter that of Logic? The mechanical people, whether theorists or men of the world, find the former unintelligible, & despise it. Through the latter one has a chance of forcing them to respect even what they cannot understand—and that once done, they may be made to *believe* what to many of them must always be in the utmost extent of the term "things unseen." This is the service I should not despair of assisting to render, & I think it is even more needed now than works of art, because it is their most useful precursor, & one might, almost say, in these days their necessary condition. . . .

Yours faithfully
J. S. Mill

To John Pringle Nichol[15]

India House,
15th April, 1834.

My dear Sir,

. . . Few persons have exercised more influence over my thoughts and character than Coleridge has; not much by per-

[15] John Pringle Nichol (1804–1859), astronomer interested in political economy.

sonal knowledge of him, though I have seen and conversed with him several times, but by his works, and by the fact that several persons with whom I have been very intimate were completely trained in his school. Through them, too, I have had opportunities of reading various unpublished manuscripts of his; and, on the whole, I can trace through what I know of his works, pieced together by what I have otherwise learned of his opinions, a most distinct thread of connection. I consider him the most systematic thinker of our time, without excepting even Bentham, whose edifice is as well bound together, but is constructed on so much simpler a plan, and covers so much less ground. On the whole, there is more food for thought—and the best kind of thought—in Coleridge than in all other contemporary writers; and it is in many respects a great good that almost all the most accomplished and zealous of the rising defenders of the Church of England are pupils of his. They are mischievous only in this, that they will be effectual in keeping up, for a time, what they will not be effectual in shaping to their ideal of what it ought to be. . . .

Yours ever faithfully,
J. S. MILL

To John Pringle Nichol

India House,
30th August, 1834.

MY DEAR SIR,

. . . Those scraps on Poetry in the *Repository* [16] I believe to be true as far as they go, but that is not far. There is much more ready to be written in the Review on that matter. I am much obliged to you for the little paper you sent me. I do not see any traces of the thoughtlessness or want of information you

16 "What is Poetry?" and "The Two Kinds of Poetry."

speak of, nor of presumption, unless you allude to the sarcastic sentence on Bentham. I think I agree in your view of the character of Hamlet, though you appear to go farther or to have gone farther at that time with the Coleridgian and German metaphysics than I do. But it is a great pleasure to meet you as I do in all regions of speculation. I believe, contrary to the vulgar opinion, that there never was a first-rate mind which was not universal, I mean in its studies, reflections, and feelings, although almost everyone must limit himself to a comparatively narrow sphere in his actual contributions to science, or art, or the business of life, for want of time to acquire the requisite practical skill in many different lines of activity. . . .

Yours ever faithfully,
J. S. MILL

To Thomas Carlyle

I.H.
Wednesday
[July 20(?), 1836]

MY DEAR CARLYLE My annotations,[17] & proposed alterations in phraseology, amount as you will see, to but little; less than I expected—& you will probably think most of them trifling. My object has been to remove, when it can be done without sacrifice, anything *merely* quaint in the mode of expression—but I have very often not ventured to touch it for fear of spoiling something which I could not replace. The only general remark I have to make on the stile is that I think it would often *tell* better on the reader if what is said in an abrupt, exclamatory, & interjectional manner were said in the ordinary grammatical mode of nominative & verb—but on that as on everything else

[17] The manuscript referred to is Carlyle's article on Mirabeau, published in the *London and Westminster Review* (January 1837).

I ask nothing but that you will deal with it as you like, disregarding all my observations if you do not think them just—& in any case that you will not make the thing an annoyance to you. It is quite good enough & too good for us as it is.

Ever faithfully yours
J. S. MILL

To Edward Lytton Bulwer[18]

India House
23d November
1836

MY DEAR SIR

. . . I have, since my return, read your article on Sir Thomas Browne[19] with an admiration I have seldom felt for any English writings on such subjects—I did not know, at the time, that it was yours, & could not conceive what new accession had come to the Edinburgh Review. I first thought it might possibly be Macaulay's, but as I read on I felt it to be far too good for him—it has much of the same brilliancy, but not his affected and antithetical stile, & above all a perception of truth, which he never seems to have, & a genuine love of the True & the Beautiful, the absence of which in him, is the reason why among his thousands of clever things & brilliant things there are so few *true* things—& hardly one which is the *whole* truth, & *nothing* but the truth. I could not help saying to myself, who would look for these qualities in the Edinburgh Review? how the readers of that review must be puzzled & bewildered by a writer who actually takes decided views, who is positively in earnest, & is capable of downright admiration & even enthusiasm! I am sure your writing must be lost upon them; they are not people who can recognise or care about truth;

18 Edward Lytton Bulwer (1803–1873), novelist and playwright.
19 Sir Thomas Browne (1605–1682), prose stylist and physician.

your beautiful things will be to them merely clever things & amusing things *comme tant d'autres.*[20] Among us you would at least find both writers and readers who are in earnest. I grant that you, & such writing as yours, would be nearly as much out of place in our review *as it has been,* as in the Edinburgh: but not, as I hope it will hereafter be. As good may be drawn out of evil—the event which has deprived the world of the man of greatest philosophical genius it possessed[21] & the review (if such little interests may be spoken of by the side of great ones) of its most powerful writer, & the only one to whose opinions the editors were obliged to defer—that same event has made it far easier to do that, in the hope of which alone I allowed myself to become connected with the review—namely to soften the harder & sterner features of its radicalism and utilitarianism, both which in the form in which they originally appeared in the Westminster, were part of the inheritance of the 18th century. The Review ought to represent not radicalism but neoradicalism, a radicalism which is not democracy, not a bigotted adherence to any forms of government or to one kind of institutions, & which is only to be called radicalism inasmuch as it does not palter nor compromise with evils but cuts at their roots—& a utilitarianism which takes into account the whole of human nature not the ratiocinative faculty only—the utilitarianism which never makes any peculiar figure as such, nor would ever constitute its followers a sect or school—which fraternizes with all who hold the same *axiomata media*[22] (as Bacon has it) whether their first principle is the same or not—& which holds in the highest reverence all which the vulgar notion of utilitarians represents them to despise—which holds Feeling at least as valuable as Thought, & Poetry not only on a par with, but the necessary condition of, any true & comprehensive Philosophy.

Ever yours faithfully,
J. S. MILL

---

[20] "Like so many others."
[21] James Mill.
[22] Middle (intermediate) axioms.

To Edward Lytton Bulwer

I.H.
Wednesday
[May or June (?), 1837]

My dear Sir

I have read your article [23] with great eagerness and delight—it is such as I expected from you & if we could have one such article in every number I should have no misgivings respecting our critical reputation.

I have hardly found a sentence in the article which has not my heartiest concurrence except perhaps some part of what you say of Shelley, & *there* I am not sure that there is any difference—for all that you say to his disparagement, I allow to be true though not I think the whole truth—it seems to me, that *much*, though not *most* of Shelley's poetry is full of the truest passion, & it seems to me hardly fair to put Shelley's poetry in the same *genus* as Gray when the imagery of the one however redundant & occasionally farfetched is always *true* to nature, that of the other as you say yourself drawn from books, & false—the one the exuberant outpouring of a seething fancy, the other elaborately studied & artificial. . . .

Ever yours,
J. S. Mill

[23] "The Works of Thomas Gray," *London and Westminster Review* (January 1837).

To John Sterling

I.H.
1st Oct. 1840

My dear Sterling

. . . What you say about the absence of a disinterested & heroic pursuit of Art as the greatest want of England at present, has often struck me, but I suspect it will not be otherwise until our social struggles are over. Art needs earnest but quiet times —in ours I am afraid Art itself to be powerful must be polemical—Carlylean not Goethian—but "I speak as to the wise—judge ye what I say."—

Ever yours,
J. S. Mill

To George Henry Lewes[24]

I.H.
Thursday
[probably late 1840]

My dear Sir

I lost no time in setting about your paper on Shelley. It abounds in true & important things & yet (for I know you want me to tell you exactly the impression it has made upon me) there is something about it which satisfies me less than is usually the case with your writings. It is easier however to say this, than to tell exactly what that *something* is, or to point out

24 George Henry Lewes (1817–1878), literary critic, scientist, husband of George Eliot from 1854. The paper on Shelley to which Mill refers was published in *Westminster Review* (April 1841).

how the article could have been or could now be improved. After thinking a good deal about it I can get no nearer than this—that you do not seem to me to have laid down for yourself with sufficient definiteness, what precise impression you wished to produce, & upon what class of readers. It was particularly needful to have a distinct view of this sort when writing on a subject on which there are so many rocks & shoals to be kept clear of. For example I think you should have begun by determining whether you were writing for those who required a *vindication* of Shelley or for those who wanted a *criticism* of his poems or for those who wanted a biographic Carlylian *analysis* of him as a *man*. I doubt if it is possible to combine all these things, but I am sure at all events that the unity necessary in an essay of any kind as a work of art requires at least that one of these should be the predominant purpose & the others only incidental to it. If I can venture an opinion on so difficult & delicate a matter, I would say that the idea of a *vindication* should be abandoned. Shelley can only be usefully vindicated from a point of view nearer that occupied by those to whom a vindication of him is still needed. I have seen very useful and effective vindications of him by religious persons, & in a religious tone: but *we*, I think, should leave that to others, & should take for granted, boldly, all those premisses respecting freedom of thought & the morality of acting on one's own *credo*, which to anyone who admits them, carry Shelley's vindication with them. By descending into that other arena I think we only spoil what is already going on much better than anything we can do in that way can possibly mend.

. . . .

You are certainly a conjurer, in finding out my old obscure articles. The only valuable thing in these two [25] is I think the distinction between poetry & oratory. The "Genius" [26] paper is no favorite with me, especially in its boyish stile. It was written in the height of my Carlylism, a vice of style which I

[25] "What is Poetry?" and "The Two Kinds of Poetry."

[26] "On Genius"; see above, p. 30.

have since carefully striven to correct & as I think you should do—there is too much of it in the Shelley. I think Carlyle's costume should be left to Carlyle whom alone it becomes & in whom it would soon become unpleasant if it were made common—& I have seen as you must have done, grievous symptoms of its being taken up by the lowest of the low.

As to my Logic, it has all to be rewritten yet.

ever yours,
J. S. Mill

come soon.

To George Henry Lewes

I.H.
Wed^y.
[Feb.?, 1841]

My dear Sir,

. . . You have not . . . yet convinced me that the line between poetry, & passionate writing of any kind, is best drawn where metre ends & prose begins. The distinction between the artistic expression of feeling for feeling's sake & the artistic expression of feeling for the sake of compassing an end, or as I have phrased it between poetry & eloquence, appears to me to run through all art; & I am averse to saying that nothing is poetry which is not in *words*, as well as to saying that all passionate writing in verse is poetry. At the same time I allow that there is a natural, not an arbitrary relation between metre & what I call poetry. This is one of the truths I had not arrived at when I wrote those papers in the Repository [27] but what afterwards occurred to me on the matter I put (in a very condensed form) into the concluding part of an article in the L. & W. on Alfred de Vigny.[28] I wish you would look at that same when

27 See above, note 25.

28 "Poems and Romances of Alfred de Vigny," *London and Westminster Review* (April 1838); see above, p. 184.

you have time, (I will shew it to you) & tell me whether what I have said there exhausts the meaning of what you say about the *organic* character of metre, or whether there is still something further which I have to take into my theory. . . .

ever yours
J. S. MILL

To George Henry Lewes

18 Kensington Square
1st March 1841

MY DEAR LEWES

I suspect the difference between us is a difference of classification chiefly. I accept all your inferences from my definition & am willing to stand by them. I do *not* think that epos *quâ* epos,[29] that is, quâ narrative, is poetry, nor that the drama *quâ* drama is so. I think Homer & Aeschylus poets only by virtue of that in them which might as well be lyrical. At the same time you have just as much right to use the word Poetry in a different extension & as synonymous with "Art by the instrument of words" as music is Art by the instrument of rhythmic sounds, & painting, Art by the instrument of colours on canvas. Taking Poetry in this sense I admit that metre is of the essence of it or at least necessary to the higher kinds of it. In that case I claim the privilege of drawing within this large circle a smaller inner circle which shall represent poetry κατ' ἐξοχήν [30] or poet's poetry as opposed to everybody's poetry & of that I think mine the right definition. But "I speak as to the wise, judge ye what I say."

I return your Ms. with a good deal of pencil scratching at the back, for I have been, & intended to be, *hyper*critical. I

---

29 "Epic as epic."
30 "Par excellence."

have *studied* to find fault insomuch that you are to assume that I like & admire whatever I have not directly or by obvious implication objected to.

Your notion of the essentially religious nature of poetry seems to me to need a world of explanation. I think it will give entirely false ideas to English readers, & is only true in *any* degree if we, *more Germanico*,[31] call every idea a religious idea which either grows out of or leads to, feelings of infinity & mysteriousness. If we do this, then religious ideas are the *most* poetical of all, an inmost circle within my inner circle; but surely not the *only* poetical, especially if your other definition of poetry be right. . . .

J. S. Mill

To Robert Barclay Fox[32]

India House
12th March
1841

My dear Friend

. . . Have you ever read any of the great Athenian Dramatists? I had read but little of them before now & that little at long intervals so that I had no very just & nothing like a complete impression of them—yet nothing upon earth can be more interesting than to form to oneself a correct & living picture of the sentiments, the mode of taking life & of viewing it, of that most accomplished people. To me that is the chief interest of Greek poetic literature, for to suppose that any modern mind can be satisfied with it as a literature or that it can, in an equal degree with much inferior modern works of art (provided these be really genuine emanations from sincere minds), sat-

[31] "In the German fashion."

[32] Robert Barclay Fox (1817–1855), member of a prominent Quaker family, carried on a long correspondence with Mill.

isfy the requiremen[ts] of the more deeply feeling, more introspective, & (above even that) more genial character which Christianity & chivalry & many things in addition to these have impressed upon the nations of Europe, it is if I may judge from myself quite out of the question. Still, we have immeasurably much to win back as well as many hitherto undreamed of conquests to make & the twentieth & thirtieth centuries may be indebted for something to the third century before Christ as well as to the three immediately after him—

Here is a long letter full of nothing but the next shall be better. With kindest regards to your delightful circle—

yours ever,
J. S. Mill.

To George Henry Lewes

I.H.
24 April 1841

My dear Lewes

. . . You have come a little way to meet me, I see, & I believe I have come about as far, meanwhile, to meet you. As one hint among many towards a definition of poetry that has occurred to me, what do you think of this—"feeling expressing itself in the forms of thought." (That serves for *written* poetry, grammatical language being the form of *thought* not feeling) & it denotes that oh! & ah! are not poetry though Körner's[33] battle songs are. Then for the poetry of painting, sculpture &c. we have "feeling expressing itself in symbols" a definition which though often given for *all* poetry really serves very ill for the poetry of written or spoken language. . . .

Ever yours
J.S.M.

Vive, vale, et *scribe*.[34]

[33] Karl Theodor Körner (1791–1813), patriotic German poet.
[34] "Live, prosper, and *write*."

To Robert Barclay Fox

India House
6th May 1841

My dear Friend—I will be more prompt this time in contributing my part towards keeping the thread of our correspondence unbroken.

I am glad that you do not write *only* poetry—for in these days one composes in verse (I don't mean *I* do for I don't write verses at all) for oneself rather than for the public—as is generally the case in an age chiefly characterized by earnest practical endeavour. There is a deep rooted tendency almost everywhere, but above all in this England of ours, to fancy that what is written in verse is not meant in earnest, nor should be understood as serious at all (for really the common talk about being *moral* & so forth means only that poetry is to treat with respect whatever people are used to profess respect for, & amounts to no more than a parallel precept not to play at any indecent or irreverent *games*). Prose is after all the language of *business*, & therefore is the language to do good by in an age when men's minds are forcibly drawn to external effort—when they feel called to what my friends the St Simonians not blasphemously call "continuing the work of Creation" i.e. cooperating as instruments of Providence in bringing order out of disorder. True, this is only a part of the mission of mankind & the time will come again when its due rank will be assigned to Contemplation, & the calm culture of reverence and love. Then Poetry will resume her equality with prose, an equality like every healthy equality, resolvable into reciprocal superiority. But that time is not yet, & the crowning glory of Wordsworth is that he has borne witness to it & kept alive its traditions in an age which but for him would have lost sight of it entirely & even poetical minds would with us have gone off into the heresy of the poetical critics of the present day in

France who hold that poetry is above all & preeminently a *social* thing. . . .

J. S. MILL.

To George Henry Lewes

I.H.
Wed^y
[Aug., 1841]

MY DEAR LEWES,

. . . I think you should dwell much more, & in a more explanatory manner on the *idée mêre* [sic] of Nisard & of the article,[35] the necessity of considering literature not as a thing per se, but as an emanation of the civilization of the period. The idea is one which it is of great importance to impress upon people. . . .

ever yours
J.S.M.

To John Sterling

I.H.
Saturday
[November 1842]

MY DEAR STERLING

. . . I have been reading your review of Tennyson[36] for the second time, after an interval of several weeks. I have found

[35] "Basic idea" of Désiré Nisard (1806–1888), literary historian and critic, and of the article upon which Lewes was working. Mineka suggests it may have become "The State of Criticism in France," published in the *British and Foreign Review* (December 1844).

[36] "Poems by Alfred Tennyson," *Quarterly Review,* LXX (September 1842), 385–416.

more difference than I expected in our judgments of particular poems, & I will not pretend that I think yours the more likely to be right,[37] for I have faith in my own *feelings* of Art, but I have read & reflected so little on the subject compared with you, that I have no doubt you could give many more reasons for your opinions than I should be fully competent to appreciate. Still, I think I could justify my own feelings on grounds of my own, if I took time enough to meditate—but I doubt its being worth while—the thing is not in my *fach*.[38]

The preliminary remarks are very delightful reading, & I think they do as much as can be done to render this age, what Carlyle says no age is, romantic to itself. But I think Tennyson, having taken up the same theory, has miserably misunderstood it. Because mechanical things may generate grand results he thinks that there is grandeur in the naked statement of their most mechanical details. Ebenezer Elliott has written a most fiery ode on the Press,[39] which is a mechanical thing like a railroad, but the mechanicality is kept studiously out of sight. Tennyson obtrudes it.

ever yours
J. S. MILL

---

[37] In a penciled marginal comment in his copy of Sterling's review (as reprinted in *Essays and Tales*, 1848), Mill wrote: "Nearly everything in Tennyson which he praises appears to me poor, & nearly everything which he dispraises, fine."

[38] "Department."

[39] "The Press: Written for the Printers of Sheffield on the Passing of the Reform Bill," in *The Splendid Village . . . and Other Poems* (1833–1835).

To John Sterling

I.H.
Wed^{y}
[Nov. 1842]

MY DEAR STERLING,

I am very glad indeed to hear that you are writing the sort of paper you mention. As to Tennyson, you were right in getting so much praise of him into the Quarterly by no greater sacrifice than leaving some of the best of the earlier poems unmentioned. I do not differ from your principle that the highest forms of poetry cannot be built upon obsolete beliefs—although what you say of the Ancient Mariner & Christabel seems to me true of the Lady of Shalott, and the objection does not seem to me to lie strongly against the Lotos eaters or OEnone.[40] But neither is the idyl one of the *highest* forms of poetry—neither Spenser, Tasso, nor Ovid[41] could have been what they were by means of *that*. And greatly as I admire Michael & its compeers, that is not the crowning glory of Wordsworth. And how poor surely is Dora compared with some dozen of Wordsworth's poems of that kind.

My remark on mechanical details does not apply to Burleigh, which seems to me Tennyson's best in that stile—not much, if at all, to the Gardener's Daughter, a good deal to Dora which I do not like—a little to some parts of Locksley Hall: but in a most intense degree to such things as Audley Court, Walking to the Mail, the introduction to Morte d'Arthur; & the *type* of what I object to is the three lines of introduction to Godiva, which he has stuck in, as it were in

40 The first two poems mentioned are by Coleridge, the last three by Tennyson.

41 Edmund Spenser (*ca.* 1552–1599), English poet.—Torquato Tasso (1544–1595), Italian epic poet.—Publius Ovidius Naso (43 B.C.–A.D. 18), Latin poet.

defiance. But, mind, I do not give my opinion as worth anything, to you especially—& my feeling is only to be reckoned as that of one person, competent in so far as capable of almost any degree of *exalté* feeling from poetry.

Have you seen Macaulay's old-Roman ballads? [42] If you have not, do not judge of them from extracts, which give you the best passages without the previous preparation. They are in every way better, & nearer to what one might fancy Campbell [43] would have made them, than I thought Macaulay capable of. He has it not in him to be a great poet; there is no real genius in the thing, no revelation from the depths either of thought or feeling—but that being allowed for, there is real *verve*, & much more of the simplicity of ballad poetry than one would at all expect. The latter part of the Battle of the Lake Regillus, & the whole of Virginia,[44] seem to me admirable.—

Yours ever,
J. S. Mill

To George Henry Lewes

I.H.
Friday
[Nov. (25?) 1842]

My dear Lewes,

I return Sand's [45] letter which it was very pleasant to have an opportunity of reading. I have no right or claim to send any message to her but I should be very willing she should know that there [are] other warm admirers of her writings & of

---

[42] *Lays of Ancient Rome* (1842).
[43] Thomas Campbell (1777–1844), Scottish narrative and lyric poet.
[44] Sections of Macaulay's poem.
[45] George Sand.

herself even in this canting land—among whom I am neither the only nor the best.

I think your article on Göthe [46] decidedly your highest flight, as yet. Without being the *dernièr* [sic] *mot* on such a man, it recommends itself to my knowledge of him as *truer* than any other writing on the subject which I have met with. There are also some striking thoughts in it & although there is considerable Carlylism in the opening pages, & something of the tranchant [47] manner which makes people call you by various uncomplimentary names indicative of self-conceit, both these defects disappear as you go on. . . .

Yours (in the dual number)
J. S. MILL

To Harriet Taylor

[London]
Saturday
27 Jan^y [1849]

. . . I am reading Macaulay's book: [48] it is in some respects better than I expected & in none worse. I think the best character that can be given of it is that it is a man without genius, who has observed what people of genius do when they write history, & tries his very best to do the same—without the amount of painful effort, & affectation, which you might expect & which I did expect from such an attempt & such a man. I have no doubt like all his writings it will be & continue popular—it is exactly au niveau [49] of the ideal of shallow peo-

[46] "Character and Works of Goethe," *British and Foreign Review,* XIV (March 1843), 78–135.

[47] I.e., "trenchant."

[48] The first two volumes of Macaulay's *History of England* had appeared in December 1848.

[49] "At the level."

ple with a touch of the new ideas—& it is not sufficiently bad to induce anybody who knows better to take pains to lower people's estimation of it. I perceive no very bad tendency in it as yet, except that it in some degree ministers to English conceits. . . .

To Harriet Taylor

[London]
17 March (?) 1849

. . . I was wrong in expressing myself in that way about the Athenians,[50] because without due explanation it would not be rightly understood. I am always apt to get enthusiastic about those who do great things for progress & are immensely ahead of everybody else in their age—especially when like the Athenians it has been the fashion to run them down for what was best in them—& I am not always sufficiently careful to explain that the praise is *relative* to the then state & not the *now* state of knowledge & what ought to be improved feeling. I *do* think, however, even without these allowances, that an average Athenian was a far finer specimen of humanity on the whole than an average Englishman—but then unless one says how low one estimates the latter, one gives a false notion of one's estimate of the former. . . .

[50] According to F. A. Hayek, Mill refers to the concluding passage of his review of Volumes V and VI of George Grote's *History of Greece* in the *Spectator* (March 3 and 10, 1849): "If there was any means by which Grecian independence and liberty could have been made a permanent thing it would have been by the prolongation for some generations more of the organization of the larger half of Greece under the supremacy of Athens; a supremacy imposed, indeed, and upheld by force—but the mildest, the most civilizing, and, in its permanent influence on the destinies of human kind, the most brilliant and valuable, of all the usurped powers known to history."

To the Reverend H. W. Carr, of South Shields

[London]
7th January 1852

Sir,—Want of time has prevented me from returning an earlier answer to your letter of 31st December. The question you ask me is one of the most difficult which any one can put either to others or to himself, namely, how to teach social science to the uneducated, when those who are called the educated have not learnt it; and nearly all the teaching given from authority is opposed to genuine morality.

What the poor as well as the rich require is not to be indoctrinated, is not to be taught other people's opinions, but to be induced and enabled to think for themselves. It is not physical science that will do this, even if they could learn it much more thoroughly than they are able to do. After reading, writing, and arithmetic (the last a most important discipline in habits of accuracy and precision, in which they are extremely deficient), the desirable thing for them seems to be the most miscellaneous information, and the most varied exercise of their faculties. They cannot read too much. Quantity is of more importance than quality, especially all reading which relates to human life and the ways of mankind; geography, voyages and travels, manners and customs, and romances, which must tend to awaken their imagination and give them some of the meaning of self-devotion and heroism, in short, to unbrutalise them. By such reading they would become, to a certain extent, cultivated beings, which they would not become by following out, even to the greatest length, physical science. . . .

To Harriet Taylor

Naples, 17 February [1855]

. . . I have been reading here, for want of another book, Macaulay's Essays.[51] He is quite a strange specimen of a man of abilities who has not even one of the ideas or impressions characteristic of this century & which will be identified with it by history—except, strangely enough, in mere literature. In poetry he belongs to the new school, & the best passage I have met with in the book is one of wonderful (for him) admiring appreciation of Shelley. But in politics, ethics, philosophy, even history, of which he knows superficially very much—he has not a single thought of either German or French origin, & that is saying enough. He is what all cockneys are, an intellectual dwarf—rounded off & stunted, full grown broad & short, without a germ of principle of further growth in his whole being. Nevertheless I think he feels rightly (what little he does feel, as my father would say) & I feel in more charity with him than I have sometimes done, & I do so the more, since Lucas[52] told me that he has heart disease, & is told by his physician that whenever he speaks in the H. of Commons, it is at the hazard of falling dead.

To Harriet Taylor

Palermo, 24 February [1855]

. . . These travels of Goethe[53] give me a number of curious feelings. I had no idea that he was so young[54] & unformed on

[51] *Critical and Historical Essays* (1843).

[52] Frederic Lucas (1812–1855), barrister and Catholic convert whom Mill accidentally encountered in Rome on his journey.

[53] *Italienische Reise* (*Italian Journey*, 1816–1817).

[54] Goethe began his Italian journey in 1787 when he was thirty-seven.

matters of art when he went to Italy. But what strikes me most in this & in him is the grand effort of his life to make himself a Greek. He laboured at it with all his might, & seemed to have a chance of succeeding—all his standards of taste & judgement were Greek—his idol was symmetry: anything either in outward objects or in characters which was great & incomplete (*exorbitant* as Balzac says of a visage d'artiste [55]) gave him a cold shudder—he had a sort of contemptuous dislike for the northern church architecture, but I was amused (& amazed too) at his most characteristic touch—that even Greek, when it is the Greek of Palmyra,[56] is on too gigantic a scale for him: he must have something little & perfect, & is delighted that a Greek temple he saw at Assisi was of that & not the other *monstrous* kind. He judged human character in exactly the same way. With all this he never could succeed in putting symmetry into any of his own writings, except very short ones—shewing the utter impossibility for a modern with all the good will in the world, to tightlace himself into the dimensions of an ancient. Every modern thinker has so much wider a horizon, & there is so much deeper a soil accumulated on the surface of human nature by the ploughings it has undergone & the growths it has produced of which soil every writer or artist of any talent turns up more or less even in spite of himself—in short the moderns have vastly more material to reduce to order than the ancients dreamt of & the secret of harmonizing it all has not yet been discovered—it is too soon by a century or two to attempt either symmetrical productions in art or symmetrical characters. We all need to be blacksmiths or ballet dancers with good stout arms or legs, useful to do what we have got to do, and useful to fight with at times—we cannot be Apollos and Venuses just yet. . . .

55 "An artist's face."

56 Palmyra's ruins include the great temple of Bel, colonnaded streets, and triumphal arches.

To Harriet Taylor

Syracuse, 21 March [1855]

. . . I do not think there is any town, not even Athens, which I have so much feeling about as Syracuse:[57] it is the only ancient town of which I have studied, & know & understand, the locality: so nothing was new or dark to me. I cannot look at that greater harbour which my window in the Albergo del Sole looks directly upon, without thinking of the many despairing looks which were cast upon the shores all round (as familiar to me as if I had known them all my life) by the armament of Nicias & Demosthenes.[58] That event decided the fate of the world, most calamitously. If the Athenians had succeeded they would have added to their maritime supremacy all the Greek cities of Sicily & Italy, Greece must soon have become subordinate to them & the empire they formed in the only way which could have united all Greece, might have been too strong for the Romans and Carthaginians. Even if they had failed & got away safe, Athens could never have been subdued by the Peloponesians but would have remained powerful enough to prevent Macedonia from emerging from obscurity, or at all events to be a sufficient check on Phillip & Alexander.[59] Perhaps the world would have been now a thou-

---

[57] A port on the Ionian sea, Syracuse was founded by Greeks in 743 B.C. In 413 B.C. Syracuse defeated a great Athenian force sent against it.

[58] Nicias (d. 413 B.C.), Athenian statesman, was a commander of the Athenian expedition. Demosthenes (d. 413 B.C.), Athenian general, commanded the armament sent to reinforce Nicias at Syracuse.

[59] Athens never recovered from the disastrous losses of the Syracuse expedition, and in 404 B.C. she was conquered by Sparta, under the leadership of Lysander. Macedonia, an ancient country of the Balkan peninsula, became the master state of Greece under the military and political leadership of Philip II, who achieved his great victory at Chaeronea in 338 B.C. Philip's son, Alexander the Great, carried the victory to the limits of the known world.

sand years further advanced if freedom had thus been kept standing in the only place where it ever was or could then be powerful. I thought & felt this as I approached the town till I could have cried with regret & sympathy. . . .

To Alexander Bain [60]

St. Véran, 6th August 1859

DEAR BAIN,

. . . The "Liberty" has produced an effect on you which it was never intended to produce, if it has made you think that we ought not to attempt to convert the world. I meant nothing of the kind, and hold that we ought to convert all we can. We must be satisfied with keeping alive the sacred fire in a few minds when we are unable to do more—but the notion of an intellectual aristocracy of *lumières* [61] while the rest of the world remains in darkness fulfils none of my aspirations—and the effort I aim at by the book is, on the contrary, to make the many more accessible to all truth by making them more open-minded. . . .

To C. A. Cummings, of Boston

Blackheath Park, 23rd February 1863

DEAR SIR,

. . . I do not, as you seem to think, take a gloomy view of human prospects. Few persons look forward to the future

[60] Alexander Bain (1818–1903), Scottish philosopher and psychologist, biographer of James and J. S. Mill.

[61] "Lights," i.e., enlightened ones.

career of humanity with more brilliant hopes than I do. I see, however, many perils ahead, which unless successfully avoided would blast these prospects, and I am more specially in a position to give warning of them, since, being in strong sympathy with the general tendencies of which we are all feeling the effects, I am more likely to be listened to than those who may be suspected of disliking them. You think from American experience that I have overrated the magnitude of some of the dangers. I am, perhaps, of all Englishmen, the one who would most rejoice at finding that I had done so, and who most warmly welcomes every indication which favours such a conclusion. But whatever may be their amount, the dangers are real, and unless constantly kept in view, will tend to increase; and neither human nature nor experience justify the belief that mankind will be sufficiently on their guard against evils arising from their own shortcomings shared by those around them. In order that political principles, requiring the occasional sacrifice of immediate inclinations, should be habitually present to the minds of a whole people, it is generally indispensable that these principles should be embodied in institutions. I think it therefore essential that the principle that superior education is entitled to superior political might, should be in some way constitutionally recognised. I suggested plural voting as a mode of doing this: [62] if there be any better mode I am ready to transfer my advocacy to that. . . .

To Lord Amberley [63]

Blackheath Park, 9th April 1869

Dear Lord Amberley,—It gave me great pleasure to hear from you, and to find my anticipation confirmed, that you

[62] See *Thoughts on Parliamentary Reform* (1859).

[63] John Russell, Viscount Amberley (1842–1876), eldest son of Lord John Russell, the statesman; friend of Mill, father of Bertrand Russell.

would enjoy your liberation from trammels as much as I do myself. There certainly is no blessing in human life comparable to liberty, for those at least who, having any good use to put it to, can indulge themselves in it with a good conscience. I envy you the pleasure of having got to a Latin classic. I hope to be able to give myself the same satisfaction by-and-by. I have not read a Greek or Latin book for at least half-a-dozen years with the exception of Plato, whom I read right through preparatory to reviewing Mr. Grote's account of him.[64] Cicero's philosophical writings[65] are very pleasant reading, and of considerable value historically, as our principal authority for much of the speculations of the Greek philosophical sects, and a brilliant specimen of the feelings of the best sort of accomplished and literary Romans towards the close of the Republic; but as philosophy they are not worth much, and I like his orations and letters better. It is true I am much interested in everything that relates to that great turning-point of history, the going out of what was left of liberty in the ancient world, and that calm after the storm, that tragical pause at the beginning of the downhill rush, which is called the Augustan Age[66]—so solemn in its literary monuments, so deformed by the presence of Augustus in it. No historian has treated that cunning, base, and cruel adventurer as he deserved except Arnold in the "Encyclopædia Metropolitana" and Ampère in "L'Empire Romain à Rome," merely because Virgil and Horace flattered him.[67]

---

[64] Mill reviewed George Grote's *Plato and other Companions of Sokrates* in the *Edinburgh Review* (April 1866).

[65] Marcus Tullius Cicero (106–43 B.C.), Roman orator, politician, philosopher. His philosophical writings include *On Ends* and *On the Nature of the Gods.*

[66] Out of the anarchy following Caesar's murder in 44 B.C. his adopted son Augustus (63 B.C.–A.D. 14), after defeating Anthony at Actium (31 B.C.), came to power and established the Roman Empire; architecture and literature flourished under his rule.

[67] Thomas Arnold (1795–1842), English educator, headmaster at Rugby, historian of Rome.—Jean-Jacques-Antoine Ampère (1800–1864), man of letters and historian.—Virgil (70–19 B.C.) and Horace (65–8 B.C.) were both Roman poets patronized by Augustus.

To a correspondent who asked Mill's advice as to whether he should desert his mercantile pursuits for a literary career

AVIGNON, *24th October* 1869

DEAR SIR,—I have received your letter dated the 18th inst.[68] I need hardly say that I sympathise in your preference of literary to mercantile occupation; but all experience proves that of these two, considered as professions, the latter alone is to be depended on as a means of subsistence, and that the former can only be prudently taken up by persons who are already in independent circumstances. It is a rare good fortune if an author can support himself by his pen, unless as an editor or sub-editor of a newspaper or other periodical; and I suppose there is not in our day a single instance in which it has been done by poetry of any kind. All my experience of life confirms the advice which Coleridge, in his "Biographia Literaria," gives to writers even of the greatest genius—to let, if possible, their regular business, on which they rely for support, be something foreign to their favourite pursuits, reserving these as the consolation of their leisure hours. In that case, success, and the favourable estimation of others, are not a matter of necessity to them; if they produce anything worthy of being remembered, they can wait for it to be appreciated, or can be content with the pleasure of the occupation itself. My own conviction is that to be independent of immediate success is almost an absolute condition of being able to do anything that greatly deserves to succeed. Many of the meritorious literary men would feel themselves saved from lifelong disappointment if they could exchange their position for one of assured though moderate income in the vocation which you are so desirous of quitting for theirs.

68 Instant (the present month).

To James M. Barnard, of Boston

Avignon, 28th October 1869

Dear Sir,

. . . The multiplication of casts of the finest works of ancient sculpture is very useful as one among many means of educating the public eye. Both in art and in nature a certain degree of familiarity is necessary not merely to the intellectual appreciation, but to the enjoyment of the higher kinds of beauty. Every one who takes pleasure in a simple tune has the capacity of fully enjoying Weber [69] and Beethoven, but very often he derives little or no pleasure from a first hearing of them. It is a great mistake to think that children are not benefited by living and growing up among models of beauty. They are, on the contrary, more benefited than any one else, though not, at the time, conscious of the benefit. I can trace a great influence in my own development to the accident of having passed several years of my boyhood in one of the few old abbeys which are still inhabited,[70] instead of a mean and graceless modern house, and having at the same time and place been familiar with tapestries from Raphael's cartoons, which peopled my imagination with graceful and dignified forms of human beings. There is a great want of this training of the perceptions and taste in our modern societies; but it is not by any one help or stimulus that the want can be supplied. The great desideratum in America–and though not quite in an equal degree, I may say in England too–is the improvement of the higher education. America surpasses all countries in the amount of mental cultivation which she has been able to make universal; but a high average level is not everything. There are wanted, I do not say a class, but a great number of persons of the highest degree of cultivation which the accumulated acquisitions of

[69] Carl Maria von Weber.
[70] Ford Abbey.

the human race make it possible to give them. From such persons, in a community that knows no distinction of ranks, civilisation would rain down its influences on the remainder of society, and the higher faculties, having been highly cultivated in the more advanced part of the public, would give forth products and create an atmosphere that would produce a high average of the same faculties in a people so well prepared in point of general intelligence as the people of the United States.

Diary

The following are entries from the diary which Mill kept from January 8 to April 15, 1854.

January 11.

Those who think themselves called upon, in the name of truth, to make war against illusions, do not perceive the distinction between an illusion and a delusion. A delusion is an erroneous opinion—it is believing a thing which is not. An illusion, on the contrary, is an affair solely of feeling, and may exist completely severed from delusion. It consists in extracting from a conception known not to be true, but which is better than the truth, the same benefit to the feelings which would be derived from it if it were a reality.

January 13.

The inferiority of the present age is perhaps the consequence of its superiority. Scarcely any one, in the more educated classes, seems to have any opinions, or to place any real faith in those which he professes to have. At the same time, if we compare the writings of any former period with those of the present, the superiority of these is unspeakable. We are astonished at the superficiality of the older writers; the little depths to which they sounded any question; the small portions of the considerations requiring to be looked at, which those writers appear to have seen. It requires in these times much more intellect to marshal so much greater a stock of ideas and observations. This has not yet been done, or has been done only by very few: and hence the multitude of thoughts only breeds increase of uncertainty. Those who should be the guides of the rest, see too many sides to every question. They hear so much said, or find that so much can be said, about everything, that they feel no assurance of the truth of anything. But where there are no strong opinions there are (unless, perhaps, in private matters) no strong feelings, nor strong characters.

JANUARY 15.

It seems to me that there is no progress, and no reason to expect progress, in talents or strength of mind; of which there is as much, often more, in an ignorant than in a cultivated age. But there is great progress, and great reason to expect progress, in feelings and opinions. If it is asked whether there is progress in intellect, the answer will be found in the two preceding statements taken together.

JANUARY 21.

It is long since there has been an age of which it could be said, as truly as of this, that nearly all the writers, even the good ones, were but commentators: expanders and appliers of ideas borrowed from others. Among those of the present time I can think only of two (now that Carlyle has written himself out, and become a mere commentator on himself) who seem to draw what they say from a source within themselves: and to the practical doctrines and tendencies of both these, there are the gravest objections. Comte,[71] on the Continent; in England (ourselves excepted) I can think only of Ruskin.[72]

JANUARY 22.

In this age a far better ideal of human society can be formed, and by some persons both here and in France has been formed, than at any former time. But to discern the road to it—the series of transitions by which it must be reached, and

---

[71] Auguste Comte (1798–1857), French philosopher, apostle of positivism.

[72] Ruskin had an intense dislike for Mill and attacked him on many occasions for his views on liberty and on economics.

what can be done, either under existing institutions or by a wise modification of them, to bring it nearer—is a problem no nearer being resolved than formerly. The only means of which the efficacy and the necessity are evident, is universal Education: and who will educate the educators?

JANUARY 23.

There is no doctrine really worth labouring at, either to construct or to inculcate, except the Philosophy of Life. A Philosophy of Life, in harmony with the noblest feelings and cleared of superstition, is the great want of these times. There has always been talent enough in the world when there was earnestness enough, and always earnestness enough when there were strong convictions. There seems to be so little talent now, only because there is universal uncertainty about the great questions, and the field for talent is narrowed to things of subaltern interest. Ages of belief, as Goethe says, have been the only ages in which great things have been done. Ages of belief have hitherto always been religious ages: but Goethe did not mean, that they must necessarily be so in future. Religion, of one sort or another, has been at once the spring and the regulator of energetic action, chiefly because religion has hitherto supplied the only Philosophy of Life, or the only one which differed from a mere theory of self-indulgence. Let it be generally known what life is and might be, and how to make it what it might be, and there will be as much enthusiasm and as much energy as there has ever been.

JANUARY 27.

Is composition in verse, as one is often prompted in these days to think, a worn-out thing, which has died a natural death, never to be revived? Only if Art, in every one of its other branches, is also destined to be extinguished. Verse is Art applied to the language of words; it is speech made musical; the most flexible and precise expression of thoughts and feelings, thrown into beautiful poems. Verse, therefore, I take to be eternal; but it ought, as well as every other attempt at public Art, to be suspended at the present time. In a militant age, when those who have thoughts and feelings to impress on the world have a great deal of hard work to do, and very little time to do it in, and those who are to be impressed need to be told in the most direct and plainest way possible what those who address them are driving at—otherwise they will not listen—it is foppery to waste time in studying beauty of form in the conveyance of a meaning. The shortest and straightest way is the best. The regeneration of the world in its present stage is a matter of business, and it would be as rational to keep accounts or write invoices in verse as to attempt to do the work of human improvement in it.

JANUARY 29.

That the mind of this age, in spite of its prosaic tendencies, is quite capable of and gifted for Art is proved by its achievements in music, in which it has excelled all previous times. Why, then, does it fail in all the other so-called fine arts? Because music, which excites intenser emotions than any other art, does so by going direct to the fountains of feeling, without passing through thought. It thus can be carried to any degree of perfection without intellect, or at least with only as much as is needed for mastering the technicalities of that as of any other pursuit. This is not true of any other of the arts; greatness in any of them absolutely requires intellect, and in this age the people of intellect have other things to do. In the ages of great architects, painters, or sculptors, these were among the men of greatest capacity whom the time produced; Leonardo was a great mathematician and discoverer in the sciences: Rubens was an ambassador; Michael Angelo was everything—poet, diplomatist, military engineer, as well as architect, sculptor, and painter; *all* were from their lives and circumstances obliged to be men of great practical address and ability, as may be seen from the life of such a man as Benvenuto

Cellini.[73] No such men now undertake the artist career, even in the countries in which the so-called arts are still honoured.

FEBRUARY 6.

Almost everything Carlyle says of Goethe appears to me to be mistake and misapprehension. But perhaps the greatest mistake of all is to imagine, as Carlyle does, that Goethe is the typical modern man; that he has shown to the modern world what it should be, and furnished the example by which modern life and the modern mind tend henceforth to shape themselves. To me it seems that nothing can be so alien and (to coin a word) antipathetic to the modern mind as Goethe's ideal of life. He wished life itself, and the nature of every cultivated individual in it, to be rounded off and made symmetrical like a Greek temple or a Greek drama. It is only small things, or at least things uncomplex and composed of few parts, that admit of being brought into that harmonious proportion. As well might he attempt to cut down Shakespeare or a Gothic cathedral to the Greek model, as to give a rounded completeness to any considerable modern life. Not symmetry, but bold, free expansion in all directions is demanded by the needs of modern life and the instincts of the modern mind. Great and strong and varied faculties are more wanted than faculties well proportioned to one another; a Hercules or a Briareus more than an Apollo.[74] Nay, at bottom are your well-balanced minds *ever* much wanted for any purpose but to hold and

[73] Benvenuto Cellini (1500–1571), Italian sculptor, metalworker, and author, was often involved in political-military affairs, defending the pope during the 1527 attack on Rome by the constable of Bourbon, and organizing the defenses of Florence against attack by Siena.

[74] Hercules, the most popular hero of Greek and Roman legends, was famed for his great strength and courage; Briareus, in Greek religion, was a hundred-handed monster who warred against the gods. Apollo, far from being identified with a single, special quality, was in Greek religion the Olympian god of light, music, poetry, pastoral pursuits, and prophecy.

occasionally turn the balance between the others? Even the Greeks did and could not make their practical lives symmetrical as they made their art; and the ideal of their philosophers, so far from being an ideal of equal and harmonious development, was generally one of severe compression and repression of the larger portion of human nature. In the greater huddle of multifarious elements which compose modern life, symmetry and mental grace are still less possible, and a strong hand to draw one thing towards us and push another away from us is the one thing mainly needful. All this is distinctly or obscurely felt by all who are entitled to any voice on such questions; and accordingly Goethe never influenced practical life at all, unless indeed by making scepticism illustrious; and his influence of any kind even in Germany seems to be now entirely gone.

February 10.

The clergy, who in all the countries of modern Europe (except France and Germany in very recent times) have had education in their hands, and in England have it still as much as ever, have contrived to make discreditable all the branches of knowledge which they taught or pretended to teach. Thanks to them, Greek and Latin are commonly reckoned useless or worse, because they have taught them *minus* almost everything in them which is useful. Cambridge has brought discredit even upon mathematics, making it appear in practice to be a thing which narrows the mind, as it does whenever it is not taught with an express purpose of forming the intellect through it to things beyond it.

February 11.

It would certainly be unfair to measure the worth of any age by that of its popular objects of literary or artistic admiration. Otherwise one might say the present age will be known and estimated by posterity as the age which thought Macaulay a great writer.

FEBRUARY 12.

I suppose all things which are fundamentally true must, on the whole, produce by their promulgation (at least in the end) more good than harm; otherwise one would be apt to regret greatly the things which have been written in late times, as by Carlyle,[75] in exaltation of the literary character, meaning thereby the office or function of literature—that it is the new priesthood, and so on. The consequence of the vulgarisation of these notions has been to make that very feeble and poor minded set of people, taken generally, the writers of this country, so conceited of their function and of themselves, however unworthy of it, and has at the same time made fine people think so much more of them, and admit them so much more easily to a distant participation of finery, under a polite show of equality of which they are invariably the dupes, that it has at once inflated their vanity and lowered their ambition. They aim at a sort of under-finery instead of aiming at things above finery. They would like to be indeed a priesthood, an aristocracy of scribblers, dividing social importance with the other aristocracies, or rather receiving it from them and basking in their beams. Why must it continue to be true of all professions and classes: "Starve them that they may work. Refuse them honour that they may be honest!"

APRIL 11.

The Germans and Carlyle have perverted both thought and phraseology when they made Artist the term for expressing the highest order of moral and intellectual greatness. The older idea is the truer—that Art, in relation to Truth, is but a language. Philosophy is the proper name for that exercise of the intellect which enucleates the truth to be expressed. The Artist is not the Seer; not he who can detect truth, but he who can clothe a given truth in the most expressive and impressive symbols.

[75] See "The Hero as Man of Letters" in *On Heroes, Hero-Worship, and the Heroic in History* (1841).

APRIL 13.

In how many respects it is a changed world within the last half-dozen years. Free trade instead of restriction–cheap gold and cheapening, instead of dear and growing dearer–despotism (in France) instead of liberty–under-population instead of over-population–war instead of peace. Still, there is no real change in education, therefore all the other changes are superficial merely. It is still the same world. A slight change in education would make the world totally different.

APPENDIX

Wordsworth and Byron

1829

In the *Autobiography*, Mill wrote that "the merits of Wordsworth were the occasion of my first public declaration of my new way of thinking, and separation from those of my habitual companions who had not undergone a similar change." This declaration of independence from orthodox Benthamism took the form of a speech given at the London Debating Society in February 1829, during a debate on the relative merits of Byron and Wordsworth. On the first of the two nights of the debate, John Arthur Roebuck, a Benthamite law student who was later to gain fame as a politician, espoused the cause of Byron at the expense of Wordsworth; on the second evening Mill came to the defense of the poet whose work had been instrumental in restoring his capacity to feel.

The speech is a major document in the history of nineteenth-century sensibility because it is the first of many tributes which were to be paid to that quality which Matthew Arnold, in his poem "Memorial Verses" (1850), called "Wordsworth's healing power." It has about it too the unique immediacy of an apologia for apostasy addressed by Mill to the masters he had denied. But its intrinsic value as a critical essay rests in its definition of those qualities in Wordsworth's poems (and Mill usually chooses poems that anthologists now agree in calling Wordsworth's best) which had enabled Mill, and can enable us, to appreciate the value of quiet contemplation and to understand "that happiness may co-exist with being stationary."

Although Mill wrote out much of the speech, a substantial portion exists merely in the form of notes. In the present edition the speech notes have been altered as little as possible; where editorial interpolations seemed essential to coherence they have been added in brackets. In a few instances notes are included, in parentheses, which Mill seems to have written to himself sometime between drafting the speech and delivering it, and which cannot logically be fitted into the already existing sentences.

In order to spare the reader the irritation of a great many footnotes attributing poems to one or the other of the two poets discussed, all the poems by Byron and Wordsworth mentioned by Mill in the course of the speech are listed here. Byron: *The Giaour; Parisina; Marino Faliero; The Prisoner of Chillon; Childe Harold's Pilgrimage; Lara; Cain; Manfred; Don Juan.* Wordsworth: "I Wandered Lonely as a Cloud"; "Alice Fell"; "Yew Trees"; "Nutting"; "Resolution and Independence"; "Intimations of Immortality"; "The Morning Exercise"; "The Kitten and Falling Leaves"; "The Mad Mother"; "The Reverie of Poor Susan"; "The Female Vagrant"; "Complaint of an Indian Woman"; "The Last of the Flock"; "The Sailor's Mother"; "Adam of Tilsbury Vale"; "The Miller and Two Dames"; "To a Highland Girl"; *The Excursion; The Recluse;* "Ode to Duty"; "Lines Composed a Few Miles above Tintern Abbey"; "Lines Left upon a Seat in a Yew-Tree"; Sonnets on "Scandal" ("Personal Talk"); "The Solitary Reaper"; "Laodamia"; "The Fountain"; "Michael"; "Character of the Happy Warrior"; "Andrew Jones"; "Peter Bell"; "The Two Thieves."

Remark on the manner in which the debate has been conducted.

Begin by remarks on the manner in which the debate has been conducted, and by reprehending any attempt to turn Wordsworth into ridicule: (one of the tenets which it would be well for him to learn from the very poet whom he despises is to be less ready with his feelings of contempt) saying to the person who attempts it,

1. Whether he imagines that the tone of mind which is constantly on the search for the ridiculous and which is contemplating other human beings and their works takes delight in picking out whatever is capable of being food for scorn, is the proper tone for weighing great poets.

I must say that in a question between two poets there is some presumption in favor of that poet whose advocates in laying his pretensions before me, endeavour to bring my mind into a state more capable of appreciating and feeling fine poetry—into a state, in that, a little more like that state to which poetry addresses itself.

In Roebuck's speech last evening I found very much to

admire. I admired all that part of it in which he addressed himself to the highest minds in the Society and to the highest part of those minds, but I cannot admire that part which he must have been conscious would produce a greater effect on any mind, in proportion as that mind was farther removed from the highest state.

I am perfectly willing to refer all my ideas on this subject to the verdict of those among my audience, and no doubt there are many[,] who are my equals or my superiors in intellectual and moral cultivation. But I cannot consent [to make] those the judges of it whom I consider as my inferiors in both—My honorable friend must be aware that that contemptuous laugh with which some passages which he recited from Wordsworth were received could only proceed from that portion of the Society whose suffrages a mind like his would least desire to receive [and] that most of them probably were habitually and all of them at that moment quite as incapable of comprehending the real beauties of Byron, as of Wordsworth and that many passages from those parts of Wordsworth which he has the sense, taste, feeling and virtue to admire, would have been received with the very same laugh if they had been recited in the same manner.

Show how he disguised the real beauties of the poem of the Daffodils.[1] Also what Wordsworth meant by it. As to the other poems, show that Wordsworth writes everything in verse if it is fit to be written at all. Wonderful if he did not write some things which would be better in prose—but nothing ridiculous in it. They might have chosen some more apparently ridiculous. Alice Fell—Compare it with Parisina.

With respect to myself have one request to make. I shall say a great deal which many of them will think absurd, and which very possibly is absurd. When they are inclined to condemn me for any errors I may commit, ask them to consider in what a very imperfect state the science of criticism is—almost may be said to have commenced in this country with Wordsworth's prefaces. Beg them to apply the rule I apply.

Persons who are not entitled to give an opinion on the ques-

1 "I Wandered Lonely as a Cloud."

tion—viz. those who regard poetry as a mere elegant amusement, which is to give them a momentary pleasure, but to leave no permanent impression. Show, that Poetry is an important branch of education. Education is 1. the education of the intellect. 2. that of the feelings. Folly of supposing that the first suffices without the last. Of the last, so far as influenced by literature, the great instrument is poetry. Why therefore if the end of poetry be so, should not he be considered the greatest poet who has best fulfilled this end? Not unreasonable to suppose that far from philosophy and poetry being unconnected, he ought to be called the greatest poet who is the greatest master of that branch of philosophy, which respects the education of the feelings, and has practised it most.

But waive this as being too little consonant to ordinary ideas and because the side I mean to espouse can be sufficiently vindicated without it. This the more necessary because at any rate I must call upon the Society to adopt what to many of them is a new mode of judging of the merits of a poet. In most persons criticism is not an affair of thought but of mere feeling: They read a writer and the one who moves them most they pronounce the greatest poet. Therefore as it is in the nature of different men to be affected with any given emotion by different things, men scarcely ever agree in their criticisms, and men generally despise all poetry but that which is written for and addressed precisely to them. No doubt the immediate purpose of all poetry is to move: and no doubt also, that the merit of a poet, his subject being given, is in proportion to the degree in which his means are well chosen for that end. What I desire is, that men would not take their emotion in the gross, and ascribe it to the poet, but would so far analyse it as to endeavour to find out for how much of it they are indebted to his genius, and how much to the previous state of their own minds. It is only thus that beauties, which depend upon the casual and transitory associations of a particular nation or a particular age, would be distinguished from those which derive their power to please, from the original constitution of human nature itself. Persons habituated to this exercise, would hesitate to treat as puerile and absurd what other persons of mind equally cultivated with themselves admire, until they had first considered whether it was not possible that there might be some deficiency in their own minds which prevented them from being affected by poetry of a particular kind and on the other hand, if on a close examination of that poetry which they most admired, they found that a great part of the effect it produced upon them was the effect of a not very enviable or creditable state of mind in themselves, they would perhaps find some reason for suspecting, that the very cause which made them so admire, must make them incapable of feeling and appreciating the highest kind of poetry: for the highest kind of poetry is that which is adapted to the highest state of mind: as a man of knowledge is superior to an ignorant one, a man of strong social affections to a malevolent one, a gentle and modest to a proud and scornful man, a man of regulated to a man of uncontrollable passions, a man of a joyful to one of a melancholy disposition, in the same proportion the poetry which delights the one is of a superior kind to that which is adapted to excite the emotions of the other.

By this test the superiority of Wordsworth obvious—but not fair to try by this test because not the usual sense of the words *great poet* which refer to the *degree* of power solely as the test of greatness without thinking of the *kind*. But Byron had advantages which make him appear to have more power than he *has*. 1. the prestige of a story—illustrate the immense effect of this—how it upheld Scott's poems—upholds bad novels—believe the number of Byron's admirers swelled immensely by those who think only of the story. 2. next, the interest turns upon the more intense feelings—with which we more readily sympathize than with the calmer: and among these chiefly upon love—almost the only passion, not of the selfish kind, which the present arrangements of society allow to attain its natural growth. Proof of the effect of this—the poems from Giaour to Parisina most admired[,] from Marino Faliero downwards scarcely read. Wordsworth nearly precludes himself from these.

Criticize Roebuck's *method*.

Now the test. Not to fetter myself by any arbitrary narrowing of the word poetry I shall make it include all it ever includes. They may be judged by the mode in which, 1. they describe objects. 2. feelings. 3. the felicitous expression of thoughts. This [is] poetry, provided the thoughts are of a nature to excite emotions, or are made to do so by the manner in which they are expressed.

1. Describing objects. Here observe that describing objects is not poetry except insofar as they are presented in some light or viewed in some manner which makes them excite different emotions from what a naked delineation would. Example—leaps the live thunder—and the stockdove broods.[2]

Immense superiority of Wordsworth. Extreme rarity of accurate description of nature. Pope's false imagery contrasted with Coleridge—The amber clouds and Wordsworth's orange sky. Immense number of such passages in Wordsworth. His descriptions of yewtrees—of nutting.[3] Read the first two stanzas of his Resolution and Independence, and the three beginning "as a huge stone"[4] giving the reason for omitting the others, and the reason why not quot[ing] the Intimations of Immortality. In Byron nothing of this sort worth remembering, scarcely one new image drawn from external nature, and his descriptions vague and unimpressive. Nearest approach in the Prisoner of Chillon but a reminiscence of Christabel. Then an entire *genus* of Wordsworth not known to Byron—that which adorns and renders interesting ordinary objects. The Morning Exercise. The Kitten and Falling Leaves—etc. which entitle him to rank next to Milton—Nothing of this sort in Byron and why.

2. Describing feelings. It is here that Byron will be supposed the superior; and here I must allow that he comes nearer to Wordsworth than in any thing else.

---

[2] The second example is from line 5 of Wordsworth's "Resolution and Independence."

[3] See the poems entitled "Yew-Trees" and "Nutting."

[4] Stanzas IX–XI.

There are certain feelings which they both have aimed at describing, and others which may be considered peculiar to each.

What they have both described, are [5] those feelings which are produced in ordinary persons, by causes which in the ordinary course of events, many persons are exposed to, not perhaps in the same degree, but in a sufficient degree to know perfectly what the feelings are, and to be able to recognize a just description of them. In this *genre,* both poets are so admirable, that it is difficult to pronounce which has displayed greatest power. The Prisoner of Chillon is certainly equal to the finest poem of the kind in the language: but Wordsworth has produced twenty poems, each for its length quite equal to it. Difference illustrated by Scott and Coleridge in their descriptions of nature. Wordsworth's pathetic poems each comprise some very deep and delicate touch of nature. Byron's touches separately of less value, but many of them very skilfully put together producing a whole at once consistent and true. Difficult to state which the greatest merit. The Mad Mother–The Female Vagrant–Complaint of an Indian Woman–The Last of the Flock–The Sailor's Mother/a very good instance/ The Reverie of Poor Susan–and Adam of Tilsbury Vale.–But Wordsworth has a much wider range–Byron paints merely painful feelings–Wordsworth in addition to this presents a greater number of delightful pictures of tranquil enjoyment than any poet perhaps who ever wrote. Read what he can make of so little a subject as the "Miller and two Dames" [:] the people listening to a musician in the street –but above all the Highland Girl, the Solitary Reaper etc. Byron only tumultuous pleasures–which can only be described in frenzy and have been so often.

Now as to the feelings peculiar to Byron. And here I must enter a little into what may be called the metaphysics of criticism.

Must be granted that those feelings which we describe from

[5] Here Mill has crossed out "feelings of mental suffering arising from external circumstances and from these mental affections."

observation only, must necessarily be described superficially. There is no depth, no intensity, no force, in our descriptions of feelings unless we have ourselves experienced the feelings we describe. But yet, to readers who have never experienced the feelings, a superficial description may appear sufficient: and an attempt at a profound one, but thoroughly false, may be taken for true and profound both. This is the secret of their admiring bad poetry and bad acting.

Three kinds of feelings which Byron—(Wordsworth could [be] a very acute *observer* of character)—has described: tumultuous passion, of love or hatred, as in the Giaour etc. Scorn of mankind and dissatisfaction with all human enjoyment, as in Childe Harold, Lara, Cain, and Don Juan and in his dramas; all the passions and feelings of minds of a high order. The second set of feelings only I imagine him to have experienced, and therefore they are the only ones that he has shown much power in delineating.

From what we know of Byron's life we have no reason to suppose that he was ever in the Giaour state—we know he was in the Childe Harold [state] very early. I believe the Giaour pictures are entirely from imagination. Whether they are true or not I say candidly I do not know [and am] persuaded none of the Society do. In the South there may be such persons—none here. No man in the Society will pretend he ever was in the Giaour state—else he would have come to the same end as the Giaour.[6] Burns' love poems represent the passion better as it is in this country. But I am sure it is very easy to paint all this from mere imagination—Easy to paint men of *one idea.* You leave out all other ideas and then you have only to exaggerate—which you may easily do—for we have all experiences enough of the same feelings to have some notion of what they are, and we have only to magnify them.

Next as to the personages in his dramas. Dramatic poetry the easiest of all and almost the only one in which men can be true to nature from mere observation—People are made to show their feelings by what they speak. Now all who have ever

[6] The Giaour dies in the refuge of a monastery.

experienced deep feelings of any kind, know that the least and most insignificant part, the part nearest the surface, is all which shows itself in talk—at the same time this part is that which most obviously appears to the observer.

There remains then, as the only feeling which Byron has painted with any depth, the feeling of dissatisfaction with life and all which is in it: which feeling he has painted in a great variety of forms—in one form and that a very weak and commonplace and uninteresting one in Childe Harold and Don Juan—that is obviously the form in which it existed in himself: the same feeling is delineated in three other different shapes and in all these instances very powerfully, in Lara, Manfred, and Cain, in each of which he seems to have exceedingly skilfully fixed and embodied in a permanent character, feelings which had passed through his own mind at certain times, but did not permanently exist in him, and it is upon these three works, in my opinion, that his claim must rest to the honor of having done what a poet cannot I think be called great unless he does, viz. to have enlarged our knowledge of human nature. And those only who are or have been in this unhappy state of mind can thoroughly sympathize in or understand these poems.

We next see what are the feelings which Wordsworth has described and Byron not.

Certain in the first place, that whatever he has described: he has felt. No poet in whom you have the same certainty. Every poem of Wordsworth almost, except his great one, was written on the occasion of some thing or other which affected his feelings at the time and gave him a desire to fix and recall these feelings by putting them into verse. Now he is a remarkable man and his feelings consequently of a remarkable kind: and people who only read one poem only having a single case of the feeling presented to them, cannot sympathize in it and think it mere affectation. But this is a disadvantage which every poet who has feelings that are not common ones, must labour under, viz. the necessity of in some measure educating his reader's mind to make him susceptible of these feelings. For this reason no one can appreciate him who does not read his writing consecutively.

Objection to Wordsworth that he represents feelings as excited by objects which are not in themselves capable of exciting such feelings (finds human sympathies so when every object speaks to him of man and of his duties.) That they do not excite such feelings in all persons and in very few in the same degree is true. I cannot say they always excite the same feelings in me. But he who should pronounce them unreal or unnatural on this account would prove himself to have a very contracted knowledge of the powers of the human mind. Wordsworth is a man of extremely meditative habits: and the habitual subjects of his meditations are two: 1. natural objects. 2. the feelings and duties of man: show how by meditating on these two subjects and constantly as a poet illustrating the one by the other each becomes capable of exciting the other. If people tell me then of his exaggeration and mystification of this, his talking of holding communion with the great forms of nature, his finding a grandeur in the beatings of the heart and so forth, I allow that this is nonsense but the introduction of this into the present question is charging Wordsworth the poet with the faults of Wordsworth the metaphysician. Show the difference between describing feelings and being able to analyse them—the tendency of a man who by a long indulgence of particular trains of association, has connected certain feelings with things which excite no such feelings in other men, if he then attempts to explain is very likely to go into mysticism—to think that there is a natural connexion between those objects and those feelings, and as he knows there is not in the objects as they appear to the world any thing to excite such feelings, he looks *beyond* them and conceives something spiritual and ideal in them which the mind's eye only can see—witness the mysticism of devotion—communion with God etc.

What is bad then in Wordsworth's account of his own peculiar feelings is not where he describes them, nor where he gives the history of them, but where he philosophizes over them and endeavours to account for them as in certain parts of the Excursion, and some of the published passages of the Recluse. He must be considered as having enlarged our knowledge of human nature by having described to us most powerfully and movingly a state of feeling which very few if any of us previously knew to exist. You may tell me that on my own showing, as these feelings can only exist in the mind of a person of very peculiar habits, scarcely in any but a poet–it is of very little importance and the knowledge of it conduces very little to human happiness. I allow that there is much of it which can hardly exist in the many, but there is much that can. I have learned from Wordsworth that it is possible by dwelling on certain ideas [and by] a proper regulation of the associations to keep up a constant freshness in the emotions which objects excite and which else they would cease to excite as we grow older–to connect cheerful and joyous states of mind with almost every object, to make everything speak to us of our own enjoyments or those of other sentient beings, and to multiply ourselves as it were in the enjoyments of other creatures: to make the good parts of human nature afford us more pleasure than the bad parts afford us pain–and to rid ourselves entirely of all feelings of hatred or scorn for our fellow creatures. Immense importance of this state of mind–difficulty of painting it because no prototype–my own changes since I thought life a perpetual struggle [;] how much more there is to aim at when we see that happiness may coexist with being stationary and does not require us to keep moving. This state of feeling to be looked to as an end, but I fear in the present state of society something stronger is required. Quote Wordsworth's Ode to Duty.

This not the only state of feeling that Wordsworth has painted better than anyone else. He has painted all the successive states of his own mind. 1. the mere animal delights received from the beauties of nature. 2. the decay of those feelings, and their being replaced by others which have been described. Quote from his Tintern Abbey and his Intimations of Immortality. He has also painted many other feelings, but this will come better under the third head—because it is the peculiarity of Wordsworth that his feelings are excited by thoughts more than those of poets usually are—which is a test of the highest state of a mind. III. Felicitous expression of thoughts which either are in themselves or are made by the expression, capable of exciting emotions.

What valuable thoughts are there in Byron? All *negative* and therefore will cease to be valuable. Wordsworth's thoughts comprise a better and a more comprehensive morality than all other poets together—and alone of all poets he seems to be able to make moralizing interesting. Other moralists merely tell you what not to be: to avoid certain acts—or certain dispositions, and by way of directions as to what you are to *be* they tell you something vague, to turn your heart to God and so on. Wordsworth illustrates all the most important features of the happiest and most virtuous character and unfolds most recondite truths in morals and mental philosophy—while the poems in which he does this are by far the most delightful as mere poems that he ever wrote.

1. A philosopher's scorn of scorn. The lines under a yew tree—and the series of sonnets on *scandal.*

2. The propriety of diffusing and not concentrating our sympathies—Laodamia.

3. The influence of certain acts in producing habits of benevolence and virtue—The Cumberland Beggar.

4. The poem beginning "We talked with open heart and tongue" [7] also Michael.

5. A Poet's Epitaph. The Happy Warrior and Ode to Duty.

Under the head of common feelings defend Wordsworth from the charge of painting only the emotions of rustics with whom we cannot sympathize.

Answer. He has painted *men*—abstracting from their education. Uncultivated—yes—but not *morally* only *intellectually* and not even intellectually, for they have no prejudices or vulgarities of thought and those other things which disgust us

[7] "The Fountain."

in uncultivated men. You may say rustics are not such—but they *may be*, and his object was to show that. By choosing a virtuous character from a village, you do not imply that there are no vicious ones. He has painted vicious rustics. Most powerfully in Peter Bell—also in Andrew Jones, The Two Thieves and sundry others. (Not deceived by it let them read Crabbe [8] as an antidote.)

Under the head of Wordsworth's feelings

That Wordsworth tends to make men quietists, to make them *bear*. This only a just charge, if men were to read nothing but Wordsworth. Allow that at present great struggles are necessary and that men who were nourished only with his poetry would be unnerved for such struggles. What then? Is a poet bound to do everything? Allow that the habit of bearing those evils, which can be avoided, is a bad habit. But because there are some things which ought not to be borne, does it follow that there is no use even now, in learning to bear many evils even now which must be borne. Hope the time will come when no evils but those arising from the necessary constitution of man and of external nature.

[8] George Crabbe (1754–1832), English poet of village life who wrote of the sordid existence of the very poor.

The Library of Literature

CRANE, STEPHEN, *The Red Badge of Courage,* ed. Frederick C. Crews, 6

DICKENS, CHARLES, *Great Expectations,* ed. Louis Crompton, 2

HAWTHORNE, NATHANIEL, *The Scarlet Letter,* ed. Larzer Ziff, 1

MELVILLE, HERMAN, *Moby Dick,* ed. Charles Feidelson, 5

One Hundred Middle English Lyrics, ed. Robert D. Stevick, 7

SWIFT, JONATHAN, *Gulliver's Travels,* ed. Martin Price, 3

TWAIN, MARK, *The Adventures of Huckleberry Finn,* ed. Leo Marx, 4

First Introduction to the
Critique of Judgment
Foundations of the
Metaphysics of Morals
The Metaphysical Elements of
Justice, Part I of
Metaphysik der Sitten
The Metaphysical Principles
of Virtue, Part II of
Metaphysik der Sitten
On History
Perpetual Peace
Prolegomena to Any Future
Metaphysics
LEIBNIZ, G., Monadology and
Other Philosophical
Essays
LUCIAN, Selected Works
LUCRETIUS, On Nature
MACHIAVELLI, N., The Art of War
MILL, J. S., Autobiography
On Liberty
On the Logic of the Moral
Sciences
Utilitarianism
MOLIÈRE, Tartuffe
PAINE, T., The Age of Reason
PICO DELLA MIRANDOLA, On the
Dignity of Man, On
Being and the One, *and*
Heptaplus

Plato's Cosmology
Plato's Theory of
Knowledge
HACKFORTH, R., Plato's
Examination of
Pleasure
Plato's Phaedo
Plato's Phaedrus
POPE, A., An Essay on Man
PLAUTUS, The Menaechmi
QUINTILIAN, On the Early
Education of the
Citizen-Orator
REYNOLDS, J., Discourses on Art
Roman Drama, Copley and Hadas,
trans.
RUSSELL, B., Philosophy of Science
Sappho, The Poems of
SCHLEGEL, J., On Imitation and
Other Essays
SCHOPENHAUER, A., On the Basis
of Morality
SHELLEY, P., A Defence of Poetry
Song of Roland, Terry, trans.
TERENCE, The Woman of Andros
VERGIL, Aeneid
VICO, G. B., On the Study Methods
of Our Time
XENOPHON, Recollections of
Socrates *and* Socrates'
Defense Before the Jury